IMMIGRANT LIFE IN
NEW YORK CITY
1825-1863

IMMIGRANT LIFE IN
NEW YORK CITY
1825-1863

Robert Ernst

IRA J. FRIEDMAN, INC.
Port Washington, N. Y.

IMMIGRANT LIFE IN NEW YORK CITY 1825-1863

Copyright 1949 by Robert Ernst
Reissued in 1965 by Ira J. Friedman, Inc.
by arrangement with the author

Manufactured in the United States of America

Library of Congress Catalog Card No: 64-8789

EMPIRE STATE HISTORICAL PUBLICATIONS XXXVII

To
HARRY JAMES CARMAN
Dean of Columbia College
Teacher and Friend

PREFACE

THE OPENING of the Erie Canal symbolized a new era in American history. When in 1825 Governor Clinton celebrated the "marriage of the waters" by pouring Lake Erie water into the Atlantic Ocean, the labors of thousands of immigrants were brought to fruition. The new waterway fostered the material growth of the Empire State and, by affording an excellent route to the interior of the country, transformed New York City into the greatest immigrant port in the world.

As used in this book, the term "immigrant" refers to persons of foreign birth, most of whom may be presumed to have taken up permanent residence in the United States. The vast majority of immigrants in New York City were born in Europe, and for this reason I have spun my story around them; but I have not neglected the newcomers from British North America and Latin America and the tiny nucleus of Asiatics which became the basis of Chinatown in later years.

Before the Civil War, New York City was synonymous with Manhattan Island. Artificial boundaries, however, did not prevent the spread of population to Brooklyn, Williamsburg, Hoboken, Jersey City, and other adjacent communities. Limitations of time and expense made it necessary to confine this study to Manhattan, but I am convinced that an examination of census reports for the towns and villages in the metropolitan area would yield results similar to mine.

In the first two chapters I have presented the prologue and the scenery for the human drama of the remaining chapters. These introductory chapters are necessarily condensed; they are based largely upon standard secondary works, including local and specialized histories. The ensuing chapters make extensive use of varied source materials, and Chapters VI, VII, and VIII, on the immigrants' occupational status, are based mainly upon manuscript and printed census reports. Although the titles of these three chapters leave something to be desired, I have rejected other possible titles as even less adequately descriptive of their contents. The professions receive relatively cursory treatment in Chapter VIII because of the small number of immigrant professional people, but developments in journalism, art, and the theater are sketched elsewhere. In the final chapter, the discussion of intermarriage is necessarily brief, owing to the unfortunate lack of statistical data.

My use of the year 1863, the period of the draft riots, as a terminal point represents an attempt to avoid the customary and unsatisfactory dates of 1860 or 1865. The riots of 1863 were of greater significance as a landmark in the social and economic history of the city, for they were an expression of working-class discontent. Since most of the city's workers and tradespeople were immigrants, opposition to the enforcement of the Conscription Act was symbolic of the identification of the newcomers with the underprivileged groups in society.

Of the many generous people who helped me to write this book, only a few can be mentioned by name. First and foremost is Harry J. Carman, Dean of Columbia College, who sponsored this work and whose inspiring personality and gentle encouragement guided it to completion. Professors John A. Krout, Carter Goodrich, Dwight C. Miner, and G. S. Delatour, of Columbia University, read the manuscript and offered helpful advice, as did Professor Merle Curti, of the University of Wisconsin, whose criticism was particularly enlightening. Dr. Carl Wittke, Dean of the Graduate School of Western Reserve University, Dr. Oscar Handlin, of Harvard University, and Professor Richard J. Purcell, of the Catholic University of America, answered puzzling questions and made friendly suggestions. In classifying the occupations listed in the manuscript schedules of the New York State Census of 1855, I was enthusiastically aided by Professor Paul F. Brissenden, of the Columbia University School of Business. At the New York Public Library, Louis H. Fox, Director of the Newspaper Division, was most cooperative at all times, while in the Manuscripts Division, Robert Hill, W. R. Leech, and Edward B. Morrison were helpful in many ways, as was Rebecca Rankin, of the Municipal Reference Branch. I am also indebted to John T. Washbourne, formerly of the New York Historical Society, and to Edna L. Jacobsen, head of the Manuscripts and History Section of the New York State Library at Albany.

Material in the possession of the American Irish Historical Society was kindly placed at my disposal by J. F. Cahill, the society's Executive Secretary. For permission to use the annual reports of the German Society of the City of New York, I am grateful to Friedrich Bossert, Treasurer of the society. Through the courtesy of Boris Nicolaevsky, of the American Labor Archive, I was enabled to use original documents of the radical German labor movement in New York City.

The Reverend Charles F. Graf, minister of St. John's in the Village, allowed me to use an old register in the possession of his church, and the

Reverend L. Humphrey Walz, minister of the Second Presbyterian Church, did me a similar favor. The Very Reverend Victor F. O'Daniel permitted me to examine the remarkably complete file of the *Freeman's Journal* at the Dominican College of the Immaculate Conception, Washington, D.C.

At the National Archives, Drs. Neil Franklin, Westel Willoughby, and Almon P. Wright supplied me with important documents, as did Dr. St. George L. Sioussat and Edith Lenel, of the Manuscripts Division, and H. S. Parsons, of the Newspaper and Periodicals Division of the Library of Congress.

For all kinds of nonstatistical information I relied heavily upon newspapers. In the translation of items in the Italian and Spanish language press, Giovanna Petruzzelli and the late Cosme Orraca were of great assistance. Ferdinand Schultz gave me some notes on the Germans, and Albert Ulmann supplied me with "local color" in his reminiscences of old New York. For help in searching the manuscript census schedules I thank Howard M. Trueblood, Jr. Finally, no acknowledgment ever can repay my parents, Arthur O. and Florence P. Ernst, for their sympathy and patience, their endurance of many impositions, and, incidentally, for the stylistic changes which they suggested. I thank these people and many others, but I accept responsibility for errors or misinterpretations.

R. E.

Dobbs Ferry, N.Y.
November 1, 1948

CONTENTS

I. THE LURE OF AMERICA   1

II. THE EMPIRE CITY   12

III. THE IMMIGRANT ARRIVES   25

IV. THE IMMIGRANT SETTLES   37

V. TENEMENT LIFE   48

VI. GAINING A FOOTHOLD: UNSKILLED LABOR   61

VII. GAINING A FOOTHOLD: INDUSTRY   73

VIII. GAINING A FOOTHOLD: TRADE, BUSINESS, AND THE PROFESSIONS   84

IX. IMMIGRANT AND NATIVE WORKERS   99

X. THE GERMAN WORKERS ORGANIZE   112

XI. CONSCIOUSNESS OF KIND   122

XII. CHURCH, SCHOOL, AND CULTURAL ATTAINMENT   135

XIII. THE VOICE OF THE PEOPLE   150

XIV. THE FOREIGN VOTE   162

XV. THE MAKING OF AMERICANS   172

APPENDICES

   I. NOTE ON CENSUS STATISTICS   185

  II. IMMIGRATION   187

 III. POPULATION   191

 IV. HEALTH   200

  V. PAUPERISM   201

 VI. CRIME   202

VII. OCCUPATIONS   206

VIII. IMMIGRANT LAND OWNERS IN TWO SELECTED WARDS   222

 IX. NATIVE AND NATURALIZED VOTERS AND ALIENS, 1855   223

NOTES   225

BIBLIOGRAPHY   297

INDEX   321

MAPS

LIMITS OF THE BUILT-UP AREA OF MANHATTAN, 1808–1862   21

WARD DIVISIONS OF LOWER MANHATTAN, 1855, SHOWING GEO-
GRAPHICAL DISTRIBUTION OF IRISH AND GERMAN POPULATIONS   43

TABLES

1. THE BUILDING TRADES   74
2. THE CLOTHING INDUSTRY   76
3. SHOEMAKERS   78
4. PEDDLERS   85
5. MERCHANTS   95
6. POLICEMEN   164
7. COMPARISON OF IMMIGRATION AND CITY POPULATION GROWTH, 1820–1860, BY DECADES   187
8. COMPARISON OF IMMIGRANTS FROM GREAT BRITAIN WITH IMMIGRANTS FROM GERMANY, 1820–1855   187
9. IMMIGRANTS DISEMBARKING AT THE PORT OF NEW YORK FROM MAY 5, 1847, TO DECEMBER 31, 1860, SHOWING NUMBERS AND NATIVITIES OF THOSE FOR WHOM COMMUTATION AND HOSPITAL MONEYS WERE PAID OR BONDS EXECUTED   188
10. AVOWED DESTINATION OF IMMIGRANTS LANDED AT CASTLE GARDEN FROM ITS OPENING AS A LANDING DEPOT, AUGUST 1, 1855, TO DECEMBER 31, 1860   189
11. AVOWED DESTINATION OF GERMAN IMMIGRANTS LANDED AT THE PORT OF NEW YORK IN 1855   190
12. POPULATION GROWTH ON MANHATTAN ISLAND, 1790–1865   191
13. POPULATION OF NEW YORK CITY BY WARDS, 1845   192
14. COMPARISON OF NATIVE AND IMMIGRANT POPULATION, 1855   193
15. FOREIGN-BORN POPULATION OF NEW YORK CITY BY WARDS, 1855   194
16. TENEMENT HOUSES AND CELLARS AND THEIR POPULATION IN NEW YORK CITY AT THE CLOSE OF THE YEAR 1864   197
17. NATIVITY OF THE POPULATION OF NEW YORK CITY, 1860   198
18. ADMISSIONS TO BELLEVUE HOSPITAL FOR ALL CAUSES, 1846–1858   200

19. Admissions to the Lunatic Asylum, 1849–1858   200

20. Admissions to the Alms House, May 8, 1849–December 31, 1858   201

21. New York City Prison Commitments, 1850–1858   202

22. Prison Commitments of Immigrants, 1858   203

23. Convictions in New York City Courts of Special Sessions, 1859   204

24. Ages at Which Crimes Were Most Frequently Committed, 1850   204

25. Juvenile Delinquency: Nativity of Parents of Children Admitted to the House of Refuge (of the Society for the Reformation of Juvenile Delinquents), 1834–1866   205

26. Number and Percentage of Gainfully Employed Immigrants of Each Nationality, 1855   213

27. Occupations of Gainfully Employed Immigrants, by Nationality, 1855   214

28. Occupational Grouping of Immigrant Workers, 1855   218

29. Immigrant Laborers, by Nativity, 1855   219

30. Immigrant Domestic Servants, by Nativity, 1855   219

31. Relative Status of First and Second Generations, Sixth Ward, 1855   220

32. Relative Status of First and Second Generations, Tenth Ward, 1855   221

33. Gainfully Employed Immigrant Land Owners in the Sixth Ward (Chief "Irish" Ward), by Nativity, 1855   222

34. Gainfully Employed Immigrant Land Owners in the Tenth Ward, by Nativity, 1855   222

35. Native and Naturalized Voters and Aliens, 1855   223

IMMIGRANT LIFE IN
NEW YORK CITY
1825-1863

I

THE LURE OF AMERICA

THE MOST PHENOMENAL MIGRATION of modern times began after the Napoleonic Wars—a tremendous movement of peoples which expanded for a full century. One phase of this movement was the ever increasing flow of European migrants to the Americas. Before the Civil War immigrants to the United States came almost entirely from western and central Europe: Irish, English, Scotch, Welsh, the German-speaking peoples, the French, Scandinavians, and Netherlanders. Jews from all over Europe, but chiefly from Germany and Poland, found a new home in America, and by the mid-fifties a trickle of Italians prepared the way for the flood after 1880.[1] Between 1815 and 1865 some five million persons forsook the soil of Europe.

Of those who put their faith in the United States, the huge majority were Irish and Germans, not because of national characteristics, but because they were the most numerous of those who experienced the profound economic and social changes in the first half of the nineteenth century. Many left voluntarily when they saw little hope of altering their depressed legal or political status; others who tried to change this condition found it necessary to flee as exiles. Some, like the Jews, left because of restrictions upon their religion. Some were adventurers seeking the excitement of novelty, travel, or California gold, but most abandoned their homes as the direct result of economic hardship.

The emigrant of the 1820's was truly a pioneer. He could not be sure of his prospects of success in America. Although the United States was on the threshold of great physical development, there was as yet no organized method of recruiting the European farmers and workers who made possible this development in later years. Those immigrants who braved the trip before the late forties worked out such an arrangement and smoothed the path of those to come. The newcomer of the fifties, therefore, came to America knowing that a network of immigrant aid societies and labor contractors would hire him, distribute him, train him, and, above all, give him opportunities to better himself.[2]

After the completion of the Erie Canal in 1825, Europeans began to realize America's need of labor for its public works and industrial plants. Ship captains brought news of glowing chances of advancement in the building of canals and turnpikes, and later, of railroads. Contractors sent their agents to Europe to recruit cheap labor. Several states set up immigration commissions to paint in rosy hues the panorama of Wisconsin, Minnesota, or Nebraska. Earlier immigrants themselves wrote of good times in America to relatives and friends in their former homes. Finally, hard times in the Old World induced the peasant and the artisan to lend a willing ear to the call of the New.

In Europe large-scale factory enterprises were gradually displacing handicraft production. This was apparent first in England, where mechanical inventions transformed into large factories the traditional small, individually operated textile industries. The artisans who were thus displaced became the factory proletariat in a marked country-to-city movement. Strange as it may appear, it was not these urban workers who emigrated, but rather the remaining independent craftsmen whose standards were steadily lowered by factory competition.[3] However, even after the removal of legal restrictions on emigration, few had the means or even the will to forsake their native England.

Wales was affected early by industrial change. In response to the demands of the railroad builders, Welsh farmers turned to the mining of coal and iron. The Welshman had a traditional fear of being landless, so instead of entirely forsaking his farm, he became part farmer, part miner.[4] This dual occupation spelled doom when railroad building halted during the depression years after 1837, and the rural parishes were forced to care for the unemployed of the coal and iron trades. To make matters worse, the progressively poor harvests of 1840 and 1841 led many to join the communities already established by fellow Welshmen in central New York and Ohio, or to seek the mining regions of Pennsylvania.[5]

From England, Scotland, and Wales, the industrial changes spread to the Continent, first to France and Belgium, and later to Germany, setting artisans adrift all over western Europe. The exodus of craftsmen from Germany was greater than from England or France. Since Germany consumed English machine-made textiles, her spinners and hand-loom weavers could not find adequate employment in the towns. This was particularly true in the linen districts of Hanover, in the western provinces of Prussia, and in Silesia. Without government supervision of the transition to machine production, as in Belgium, the spinners of western Germany worked harder and longer by old methods, and fierce competition lowered the quality of their yarn.[6] Manufacturers naturally preferred to use the better English yarns, and as machine looms were introduced in Germany, the household weavers also were driven to the wall.[7] When in the late thirties and early forties the linen industry of western Germany reached a crisis, whole families of spinners and weavers sold their land and emigrated on the proceeds. In Silesia, where the textile workers were poorer and less independent, only the more prosperous were able to leave the country, while the majority became a landless proletariat reduced to living on charity until cotton factories and railroads gradually absorbed them.[8]

Coextensive with this industrial revolution was the expansion of urban markets and the introduction of new agricultural techniques. A growing population needed larger supplies of wheat, barley, and oats, and since these could be produced more profitably on large farms, the time-honored method of communal farming was transformed into large-scale capitalist agriculture. In England the process was stimulated by the enclosure acts which broke up the open fields. Farmers who could display no legal title to their land were ejected, while those who remained on the land competed at a disadvantage with the new scientific agriculture.[9] Many who lost their farms sought employment in the towns, and some scraped together enough money to pay their passage across the sea.[10]

In Scotland, the steady conversion of farm land into pasturage in the late 1820's accentuated the depopulation which had been so marked after the breakup of the clans in the eighteenth century. England's cities needed meat, and the steamboat made it possible to bring livestock over long distances without loss of weight. Seeing a profitable future in the raising of cattle and sheep, landlords replaced farmers with shepherds, and the highland countryside ceased to be a land of wheat and oats.[11] Irish immigrants, whose standard of living was far below that of the Scotch farm hands, met the need for seasonal labor. The more prosperous of the dispossessed Scotsmen took passage for North America, but the majority went to the manufacturing or commercial towns, or tried to remain independent by farming marginal soil in the lowlands or by becoming fishermen.[12]

Unlike Scotland, the Continent of Europe saw a rapid increase in population. In Scandinavia the partitioning of land among heirs had made farms so small that further division was economically impossible. An outmoded system of agriculture could not support the fast-growing population, and the spread of enclosures further limited the opportunities of the peasantry.[13] Thousands of Swedish and Norwegian *Bønder* were faced with the choice of emigrating or of falling to the status of agricultural laborers. The more ambitious took passage for America. Of these, many were family heads in good circumstances who saw in

America's cheap lands the assurance of a bright future for their children.[14]

In southwest Germany, as in Scandinavia, the custom of dividing the already small holdings among the children of each generation contributed greatly to recurring agricultural crises in the nineteenth century.[15] The expansion of the market for food created a tendency toward higher prices and higher rents, making the small farms of Bavaria, Württemberg, Baden, and the Rhineland comparatively unprofitable. Some of the peasants were reduced to the almost exclusive cultivation of the potato, but wealthier ones joined in the effort to apply large-scale techniques to agriculture. In the years before 1845 many German farmers borrowed money to make extensive improvements, but the years of depression and crop failures which followed witnessed foreclosures and forced sales. If the farmer avoided such a calamity, he sold his land at any price and, not entirely without capital, set out for America.[16] Local floods and crop failures heightened the discontent of the peasants, and with few factory towns to give them immediate employment, many of the poorer farmers had no choice but to emigrate.[17]

In the 1850's fully 90 per cent of the emigration from the Continent of Europe originated in the German states.[18] To the stream of south German emigrants was added an ever faster flow from northern Germany, as the dark clouds of depression hung over the grain-exporting regions from Hanover to Pomerania. Unlike the farmer of southwestern Germany, the northern peasant was an economic vassal of his landlord; he owned no land and therefore had none to sell, and he had few personal possessions. As landlords sought to reduce expenses, they got rid of this surplus labor and encouraged emigration.[19]

Elsewhere on the Continent agricultural conditions were less conducive to emigration. Denmark witnessed no rural upheaval, and the departures from this country had a religious rather than an economic basis.[20] In France agricultural difficulties were generally less severe than in Germany or Scandinavia. Financial and labor dues had been swept away by the French Revolution, and crops on the many small independent farms were diversified according to the nature of the terrain and the needs of the locality.[21] In some regions, however, French farmers were not so fortunate. From the left bank of the Rhine to the Vosges Mountains, economic life was similar to that across the river: vineyards, small holdings, and mountain industries. Despite their highly developed agriculture, these Frenchmen had no more control over agricultural crises than their German neighbors. To the southeast, small farms and highland pastures were tended by people who migrated seasonally to more favored areas, while in the central highlands of France and in the Pyrenees marginal lands offered a similarly precarious existence.[22] In Italy scantily paid agricultural laborers competed for employment or to obtain leases of land, and it was not until the decade of the fifties that the vanguard of impoverished Italians found its way to the United States.[23]

Belgian agriculture was characterized by small farms, many of which were merely isolated plots dedicated to spinning, weaving, nail making, and gunsmithing. For the textile artisans machine competition was a constant worry, while subdivision of the land led to the cultivation of the potato as the staple crop.[24] In the Netherlands, on the other hand, small but scientifically cultivated holdings and well-developed cattle industries contributed to a balanced agriculture which tended to prevent such violent crises as shook Germany and Ireland.[25]

Without doubt, the suffering in Ireland in the nineteenth century was unmatched anywhere on the Continent. Since the days of Oliver Cromwell, a landlord class of foreign birth and religion dominated the country. Under the policy of surrender and regrant of land, the communal basis of ownership had long since been destroyed, and the bulk of Irish farmers had become mere rent-paying tenants. With his tiny plot and uncertain tenure, the Irish tenant lived a precarious life. When his lease expired he received no preference over a higher bidder. Not only did this system discourage permanent improvements on the land, but the land itself rose far above its true value as farmers competed for it.[26] Peasants lucky enough to remain on the land therefore concentrated on rent-paying crops. While grain and cattle were raised for the market, the potato met the need for food. Even more unfortunate were the cottiers, or landless farm laborers, comprising the vast majority of the Irish population. Living in abject poverty, the cottier subsisted upon his small potato patch, for the use of which he labored for the landlord or sold his pig.[27]

As population grew and competition for land became more intense, Irish agriculture degenerated. Subdivision and subletting of land reduced the size of farms, so that by 1841 no less than 563,153 of the 691,-114 holdings consisted of less than fifteen acres.[28] Throughout the eighteenth and early nineteenth centuries a growing number of Irish cottiers migrated seasonally to England and Scotland as agricultural laborers. As the enclosure movement drew Irish day laborers to the country, the growing demand for industrial workers induced many to settle in English and Scottish towns.[29] Later, as steam navigation brought them swiftly and cheaply across the Irish Sea and a spreading railway network provided jobs, the migration brought thousands of laborers who remained in England. By 1841 fully 419,256 Irish-born persons were living permanently in England and Scotland.[30]

This movement across the Irish Sea brought no relief to those remaining in Ireland, where distress was chronic and local crop failures brought disaster from time to time. To make matters worse, landlords no longer found it profitable to keep their tenants. The fall of grain prices after the Napoleonic wars made it difficult to collect rents, and pasturage now offered better prospect of profits, so landlords began to evict tenants.[31] Until the Irish Poor Law of 1838, evictions were relatively few, the gentry fearing the growth of a desperate landless class which menaced life and property. Nevertheless, an increasing number of farmers voluntarily gave up their holdings. Having tasted independence, they preferred to find "a permanency in another country" than risk "an uncertain elevation from poverty at home."[32] Until 1835 most of those leaving for America hailed from the north of Ireland and included displaced artisans of Ulster and many female domestic servants.[33] Thereafter, the poorer peasants began to emigrate from southern and western Ireland.[34] It was not until the passage of the Irish Poor Law, however, that the landlords took a general interest in stimulating the exodus.

By the 1820's English poor rates had reached unprecedented heights. The English rate-payers blamed the Irish paupers in England and demanded a poor law for Ireland. Parliament responded in 1838 with an act taxing the Irish landlords so highly that they showed a sudden zeal to promote emigration.[35] The new law integrated emigration with evictions by setting up workhouses for the dispossessed, and since the same act provided for assisted emigration, the workhouse became the intermediate step between eviction and departure from Ireland.[36] Henceforth eviction evolved into a settled policy, stimulated in 1846 by the repeal of the Corn Laws, which long had given Ireland a protected position in the English market.[37]

At this time of crisis in Irish agriculture, disaster struck at the very basis of Ireland's economy. The potato rot, which first appeared in 1845, resulted in five gruesome years of misery and starvation in the Emerald Isle. Famine, which favors no man, affected all classes of the population. Peasants, unable to pay their rent, were ruthlessly driven from their holdings to the poorhouses, which they filled beyond capacity. Thousands, driven by poverty and despair, flocked to the seaports. Aided by subsidies from landlords, who were often glad to be rid of them, great masses of the hopelessly poor boarded emigrant ships and fled their native land.[38]

While aid to persons unable to pay their way across the ocean affected but a small proportion of the total, "assisted" emigration of one sort or another took place throughout the century. One type of aid was that furnished by the landlords, the private subsidies of the Irish gentry being paralleled by similar payments in northern Germany.[39] Prospective emigrants were also helped by individual philanthropists, such as the Kentish gentleman who sent off the poor "by waggon loads to the United States."[40] Vere Foster, one of the most notable of the good Samaritans, paid the passage to America of some fifteen thousand Irish women.[41] Charitable institutions and religious organizations, notably the Society of Friends, aided others to depart; and as early as the 1840's English trade unions were advancing funds for emigration.[42] Public subscriptions sometimes served to stimulate departures. During hard times in 1841–1843 a national subscription enabled many skilled artisans of the Paisley district in Scotland to leave for America.[43]

More widespread was the public aid granted by parishes, towns, and communities. During the first quarter of the century European governments looked with disfavor upon the departure of their nationals, and in many countries regulations existed to prevent it.[44] However, in the thirties and forties, the accumulated distress of much of the European population, with the attendant possibility of social disorders, forced a change of official attitude.[45] Early schemes of public assistance aimed at directing the stream of emigrants either toward colonies or areas where it was hoped colonies would be established. English parishes, seeing that the emigration of surplus laborers brought about a decline in the poor rates, took advantage of a parliamentary act in 1834 authorizing the use of local funds for assisted emigration to the British colonies.[46] In the same year, and until 1878, Parliament annually voted sums varying in amount up to £25,000 to promote the removal of the indigent.[47] In Germany, local communities were also encouraged by government subsidies. Most of the states along the upper Rhine made small appropriations, Baden developing a co-ordinated system of state, local, and individual aid.[48] Probably because of American protests, a relatively small number of paupers thus emigrated from Germany.[49]

While crop failures, changes in methods of agriculture, and the demands of a spreading factory civilization uprooted countless farmers and artisans, local religious or political conditions drove others to seek new homes. Among the religious malcontents were the followers of

Martin Stephan, a religious mystic of Dresden. After arousing the suspicions of the civil and religious authorities, Stephan and his followers departed for America in 1838. More oppressed and numerically more important than the Stephanist group were the "Old Lutherans" of Prussia. Frederick William III, seeking to compromise the differences between the Lutheran and German Reformed churches, created a United Evangelical Church based on a new prayer book. Despite dire threats, the most orthodox of the Lutherans refused to conform; and they abandoned the restrictive atmosphere of Pomerania, Posen, Magdeburg, and Berlin for the religious freedom of the United States.[50]

Another religious group which left Germany in ever larger numbers consisted of Jews, particularly of the southern German states. Their religious zeal was probably secondary to their desire to seek refuge from anti-Semitic restrictions. Following an edict of 1813, Bavaria limited by a license system the number of Jews in the professions and in such businesses as innkeeping.[51] Württemberg adopted in 1828 a law prohibiting the sale or exchange of property by Jews unless it had been occupied or farmed by the owner for at least three years. The resulting exodus of Jewish tradespeople and professionals was later augmented by industrial depression, affecting Jew and Gentile alike.

Switzerland, the Netherlands, and the Scandinavian countries likewise contained religious communities which chafed under restrictions. Swiss Methodists and Baptists were not happy in an austere Calvinist society and left it either individually or in small groups.[52] Religious dissension in the Netherlands, coupled with unemployment and high taxes, sent Dutch separatists to America.[53] In Norway the departure of the famous "sloop party" in 1825 reflected religious discontent.[54] Quaker communities in southwestern Norway stimulated the emigration fever, while no less influential were the Haugeans, followers of Hans Nielson Hauge, a martyred pietist.[55]

Pietism also appeared in Sweden, where the state church vigorously combated nonconformity. Protesting against the rationalism of the Lutheran Church, religious dissenters turned to a powerful pietistic religion founded by the peasant and lay preacher Eric Janson. The persecuted Jansonites migrated in groups to America and were soon followed by members of other persecuted sects in what became a veritable religious exodus from 1846 to 1854.[56] During the fifties the emigrants included Baptists and Mormons converted by active missionaries, and in the sixties they were joined by the Methodists, who likewise looked to America as their new home.[57] It was in Denmark that the Mormons were especially successful. Danish emigration was the direct result of their tireless missionary work, the first Mormon party setting forth in 1852.[58]

More violent than religious unrest was the political discontent during the decades following the Vienna settlement of 1815. Occasioned by the uprising at Paris in July, 1830, the revolutionary spirit spread like wildfire to the Low Countries, Germany, Poland, and several of the Italian states. Erecting barricades in the streets of Brussels, the Belgians soon won their political independence. German students formed secret societies and held demonstrations for political liberty, and peasants in many communities refused to pay taxes. For their recalcitrance these Germans paid a high price, as the authorities took stern and vengeful suppressive measures.[59] Many of the young revolutionary enthusiasts recanted, and others, seeing the cause deserted, lost hope of ultimate success and fled to Switzerland. There they were joined by Poles who fled after their own revolt had been crushed by Nicholas I of Russia. In time these refugees dispersed to France, England, and the United States, and they were joined later by Italians, Hungarians, and others. However, political exiles were few as compared with the far greater number who came to America to escape the economic burdens occasioned by the unsuccessful rebellions: the collapse of internal trade on the Continent, and heavier taxation necessitated by enlarged police and military forces.[60]

Although the large majority of Germans reaching American shores in the middle of the century were motivated by economic reasons, political revolutions sent a few thousand well-educated and vocal professional men, mostly Germans, to the United States. The German outbreaks of 1848 and 1849 placed the authorities in a dilemma. To detain thousands of political prisoners was an expense; to free them entailed loss of prestige and the probability of future revolts. Baden sought a way out by offering to send the rank and file at its own expense to America. Only a dozen or more accepted, the rest preferring jail and martyrdom.[61] Thousands who found asylum in Switzerland also hesitated to emigrate. Some quietly returned to Germany; some went to London, traditionally an asylum and center of intrigue for exiles; others, such as Hecker, Kinkel, and Schurz, accepted invitations to come to the United States. Of these, several were military men, like Franz Sigel, who later served in the Union Army.

While the "forty-eighters" were militant republicans, others of a more humble nature saw in the United States a haven to which they could flee from enforced service in European armies. It is impossible to determine the extent of the desire to avoid military service as a reason for emigration in this period. Some young men were undoubtedly influenced by it. During the Crimean War the German states kept an unusually watchful eye upon able-bodied men of military age; that many Germans escaped across the border is attested by long newspaper lists of those failing to register for military duty.[62] It was not until the latter part of the century, however, that many prospective draftees sought a new life in America.

Whatever may have been the all-powerful motive for leaving his native land, the emigrant was strongly influenced by news about America. In the thirties and forties literate persons contemplating emigration sought data on the New World by poring over gazetteers and geographies, studying the abundant emigrant guidebooks, and reading the accounts of travelers.[63] They read newspapers in the taverns, consulted their ministers or parish priests, and organized clubs. Village reading clubs were numerous, especially in Germany, where history and travel books were thoroughly discussed under the supervision of the local minister amid the *Gemütlichkeit* afforded by beer and tobacco. Among the Jews, many such societies learned of Jewish liberties in faraway lands. All of these clubs were socially and intellectually profitable, and some were conducted with a direct view to emigration.[64]

The aroused interest in America was carefully fostered by individuals and concerns seeking to profit from the emigrant trade. Shipping companies and their ubiquitous agents not only advertised in the newspapers but actively propagandized in remote hamlets until the flood of emigrants at the seaports was greater than they could handle. Their activities were tacitly supported by innkeepers, land speculators, labor contractors, and immigration agents from undeveloped regions of America.[65] Emphasizing the economic advantages, the accessibility, and the scenic beauty of Michigan or Wisconsin, posters and handbills advised the newcomers to seek particular areas in the United States.

More powerful a magnet than all the printed matter was the personal letter. Every word of some relative or friend in the United States was weighed, and a single letter often had more influence than a score of pamphlets, newspapers, and books.[66] An unfavorable personal report was more likely to prevent emigration than all the official propaganda directed to the same end.[67] A favorable report had the opposite effect. Whole families knew that Patrick, or Johannes, or Louis would have no motive for deception. When a son wrote home that he was making good in America and urged his dear ones to join him, his words carried the force of authority, especially when accompanied by a remittance or prepaid passage across the Atlantic. In some cases a member of a family was financed in a pioneer trip to the United States. When in a few years he returned to his native village or city, he was visible proof of the wonderful opportunities awaiting the industrious.[68]

Not all of those who returned had prospered, for the ebb and flow of the immigrant tide was perceptibly governed by industrial or agricultural conditions in America. In years of depression and unemployment, the face of the returned emigrant bespoke nothing but stark disillusionment as he warned his family and friends against leaving.[69] After the Panic of 1837, for example, immigration to the United States was cut in half. The effect of hard times was all the more marked, since the accretion of foreign labor in flush years had glutted the market and resulted in widespread misery. Yet the lean years were few and the prosperous years many. Wages were high in the United States, even for the heaviest labor; domestic service attracted the women of all nationalities; and land was available for farmers with ready cash. The average peasant from northern Europe could easily become a mason, bricklayer, or carpenter, and perhaps ultimately buy himself a farm, while the wealthier farmer could buy in America a tract of land several times as large as the one he owned in Europe. Thus it was that proportionally few persons returned to die in the land of their birth, while hundreds of thousands became American citizens and achieved a comfortable living.

The chance to improve one's economic and social status was the brightest beacon on American shores, but there were others. In the United States a person was free to worship in his own way. He was free to agitate for Irish, German, Polish, or Italian republicanism without fear of being thrown into prison. His private affairs were free from official scrutiny. He bore no heavy burden of taxation. Except during the Civil War he was not required to serve in the army. He was in a land where all citizens were equal before the law, where the esteem traditionally accorded the upper classes of Europe was replaced by the American respect for the self-made man.[70]

II

THE EMPIRE CITY

As FAMILIES OR FRIENDS WAVED a last farewell, the emigrants started the first lap of their journey to the New World. For Continental Europeans, Le Havre, first, and later, Bremen were the principal ports of embarkation.[1] The Germans went in both directions, those from the south taking the stage to Strasbourg, where they climbed into cotton wagons returning from the Alsace factories to Paris; from the French capital, German, French, and Swiss emigrants were borne in steamboats down the Seine to Le Havre. Those leaving central and northern Germany boarded boats on the Weser and the Elbe, which took them to Bremen and Hamburg. Scandinavians made their way to Hamburg or to Liverpool, where they awaited passage across the ocean.[2] By far the largest number of Irish, English, Scotch, and Welsh descended upon Liverpool, which was unrivaled as an embarkation port. The presence of hundreds of ships every year in this great commercial city afforded opportunities for cheap passage to America.[3] An easy crossing by steamer from Cork and Dublin brought many Irish to Liverpool, and the Irish exodus of the fifties completely overtaxed the service.[4] From 1832 on, the British authorities considered nine tenths of the Liverpool emigrants to be Irish.[5] Sometimes, however, the Irish left directly from Cork and Galway, the Scotch from Greenock and Glasgow, and the English, together with many Germans, from London.[6]

Emigrants usually found it necessary to remain for some time in the seaports. Since most of them crossed the ocean in sailing ships, their departures depended upon the weather, and although sometimes the travelers barely had time to climb aboard, the majority tarried from a week to a month before leaving. During this enforced delay, the stranger was besieged with tavern keepers, ship brokers, and land agents, whom he regarded as villains fleecing the innocent. The waterfront inns, boardinghouses, and liquor shops carried on a flourishing business among the strangers looking for cheap lodgings. Although honest merchants and brokers attempted to insure clean and reasonable housing, some unscrupulous innkeepers charged what the traffic would bear, while others kept disorderly or insanitary premises.[7] Some of the transportation agents who circulated among the emigrants recruiting their cargo were swindlers who misdirected the passengers or overcharged them for tickets to inland cities in the United States which proved worthless upon presentation in America.[8] In general, however, the agents performed a useful and, indeed, indispensable function as middlemen between shipowners and prospective passengers. On the Continent the scramble for passengers first took place at the ports, but as competition increased ship brokers journeyed inland to meet the advancing emigrants; later they opened local offices in the interior of Germany and Switzerland. The Liverpool agents, on the other hand, encountered the distrusting Irish, who usually refused to pay their passage until they saw the ship in the harbor or until passenger rates "broke" at the last minute.[9]

Having secured their passage, the emigrants busied themselves with final preparations for the voyage. They bought specialized equipment which included provision boxes which would withstand the gnawing of rats; cooking and eating utensils; and hooks and nails to be driven into the ship walls for suspending cheeses, meats, fish, and clothing. These supplies were readily found at the "Emigrant Provision Stores" near the wharves. At the same time, to avoid loss, breakage, and expense, the emigrants disposed of their family heirlooms.[10] At last the sailing was announced, and the passengers embarked.

Although ships designed especially for the emigrant traffic appeared before the middle of the century, the majority of emigrant ships were freighters rarely over three or four hundred tons in size. Some carried cotton, tobacco, and timber from America and returned in ballast, and some were antiquated liners and East Indiamen. For the privilege of herding emigrants into the steerage, agents paid a fixed rate to shipowners, and neither owner nor agent showed much concern about overloading a ship with human cargo. The steerage deck was usually four to six feet high and contained hard wooden berths arranged in two layers and filling most of the floor space, while the lower part of the hold contained heavy baggage and chests, water, and cordwood. Since the only entrance to the steerage was by ladder from a hole in the deck of the hatchway, there was almost no ventilation. Fresh air was admitted only through the hatches, which were shut in rough weather when air was most needed.[11]

The sea voyage was fraught with the perils of hunger, disease, and death. If the horrors of the passage were exaggerated in the many contemporary accounts, tales of unhealthy conditions, of neglect, and of brutal treatment of immigrants were substantiated. In the filth stirred up by every storm, disease broke out among the passengers, hundreds being seriously weakened or dying of "ship fever" (typhus), cholera, smallpox, and dysentery. Added to these illnesses and the usual discomforts of overcrowding and lack of sanitary conveniences were the contamination or exhaustion of food and water supplies, the frequent brawls which occurred aboard ship, the molestation of women—for the sexes were not separated—the sometimes tyrannous conduct of the captains, and fear of the ever present possibility of shipwreck. After a voyage of about two months under any or all of these conditions, hundreds of sick or disabled passengers—sometimes entire boatloads—might be thrust upon the overburdened port facilities of American seaboard cities, especially New York.[12]

The approaching foreigner was glad to see New York as it loomed in the distance. It meant to him at least the end of his miserable voyage across the Atlantic. For some immigrants the city was a mere way station on the long trip westward; for others it was at once the end of the journey and the beginning of new opportunity.

Long a center of trade, New York City had maintained since 1797 an indecisive commercial lead over her chief rivals, Boston, Philadelphia, and Baltimore. Not until after the War of 1812, however, did New York rise to undisputed leadership. The British policy of dumping at New York an avalanche of cloth, hardware, and other goods gave the city an initial advantage by flooding the market with cheap articles which were sacrificed at auction and attracted buyers from afar.[13] A further encouragement to imports was the establishment of a scheduled shipping service between New York and Liverpool. In 1818 the first packets of this pioneer venture had pulled anchor, laying the basis for the reputation of the famous Black Ball Line.[14] Shippers were attracted, not only by this regular service, but also by the encouragement which New York gave to the coastwise steamboat trade with New England and New Jersey. Moreover, the South drew most of its imports by way of New York, whither Southern staples, particularly cotton, were routed as return cargoes.[15] Thus, even before the completion of the Erie Canal, the Empire City had won distinction as a "commercial emporium."[16]

The opening of the Erie Canal in 1825 added a flourishing Western trade to the business of New York, now the dominant Eastern seaport of the United States. Strategic location, the initiative of the mercantile community, and the digging of De Witt Clinton's "big ditch" had wrought a miracle for New York City. From the Great Lakes region and beyond, forest and farm products flowed eastward to Albany and thence down the Hudson for 150 miles to the large and well-protected harbor of New York. In the late twenties, between five and seven hundred merchant vessels and fifty steamboats operated in busy seasons, and an average of fourteen hundred ships arrived every year from foreign ports, while nearly three times as many brought their cargoes from American coastal cities.[17] After 1830 the annual value of New York's exports never dropped below $20,000,000, and imports never below $50,000,000.[18]

The development of railroads in the forties and fifties enabled New York to retain its commercial primacy. Joining Buffalo with Albany and Troy in 1853, the New York Central made connections with railroads from New York and Boston and with the Hudson River steamboats.[19] From New York City the Hudson River Railroad reached northward and, on the last day of 1849, opened its train service to Poughkeepsie.[20] These roads successfully competed with the Erie, the Pennsylvania, and the Baltimore and Ohio for the inland freight and passenger traffic of the Middle Atlantic states. Owing to this development of inland transportation, New York rapidly increased in wealth, and by mid-century the Empire City was the financial center of the Western Hemisphere. Banks and insurance companies multiplied. Wall Street became a synonym for the moneyed class. Real and personal estate rose in value from about $70,000,000 in 1820 to $320,000,000 in 1850, and fortunes were amassed from heightened property values.[21] From the seed of commerce New York was growing up.

Since colonial times, New York's aristocracy had been merchants. Unlike Boston's socially prominent commercial families, who had established themselves in pre-Revolutionary days, men of far more varied background came to dominate New York's commercial scene. Strangely enough, the old Dutch families played a relatively minor role, many being content with their income from lands which appreciated as the population of Manhattan swept northward. Before 1820 the real strength of the New York merchant princes had been in the old Knickerbocker society, with its British and Huguenot elements, and a growing number of foreign newcomers, led by John Jacob Astor, the fur king, and the Scotsmen Archibald Gracie and Robert Lenox. When success crowned the work of such men, New York beckoned to outsiders, many of whom were partners, relatives, or employees of established firms in Great Britain and the Continent of Europe. Although hundreds of these agents returned to their homes after residing in New York, many settled there permanently, and some became American citizens. These Europeans were easily outnumbered, however, by the swarms of Americans, nearly all from New England, who descended upon New York.

Gaining a firm foothold in the twenties, these New Englanders dominated the city's importing and exporting. They built and commanded most of the ships and amassed riches as merchants and shipowners. Most of them were from near-by Connecticut, but others came

from Rhode Island and southern Massachusetts, particularly New Bedford, Nantucket, and Cape Cod. Some were expanding their shipping
enterprises by moving them to prosperous New York, some were creating
branches of New England concerns, others were sea captains who decided to go into business in the big city or adventurous youths who had
reached New York and worked their way to prominence.[22]

Thus it came about that New England firms were among the leading
New York shipping houses for four decades. The Grinnells from New
Bedford were among the greatest; so were the Griswolds from Old Lyme
and the Lows from Salem, both engaged in the China trade. So were the
Howlands from Norwich who headed a large commission house, and
Anson Phelps and Elisha Peck, who imported metals and exported
cotton, laying the foundation for Phelps Dodge and Company.[23]

Together with the old New York families, these merchants composed
the social aristocracy. Their addiction to good living in a sumptuous
society rivaled their devotion to the almighty dollar. One of the leaders
of the social elite was Philip Hone, mayor of the city in 1825–1826,
who preserved in his diary the atmosphere of dinner and theater
parties.[24] There were, however, many lesser merchants who lived
unostentatiously and a few reformers who frowned upon frivolous living
and devoted their lives to human betterment. Among the latter were
the prosperous silk jobbers, Arthur and Lewis Tappan, who had
migrated from Northampton, Massachusetts. The Tappan brothers
were active in the Bible society, the peace society, mission boards, and
in other religious and idealistic causes. Above all, they were vigorous
abolitionists. Because of close commercial ties with the South, few
of the New York merchants were willing to uphold the viewpoint of the
Tappans.

While not extremists like the Tappans, many of the merchants supported charitable and philanthropic enterprises. Some were remarkably
public spirited. Robert Minturn, later one of the commissioners of
emigration, was instrumental in the founding of the Association for
Improving the Condition of the Poor. Captain Charles Marshall helped
to improve the condition of sailors in port, while Anson Phelps and
many others gave generously to religious and missionary agencies.[25] Perhaps the majority of well-to-do families were indifferent to the problems
of the poor, but those who gave to charity did so from religious or
humanitarian impulses rather than from any general philosophy of
social progress. As the poor became identified with the hordes of newly
arrived immigrants, indifference often took the form of hostility.[26] For
some New Yorkers aid to the poor was but a means of self-protection

from occasional lawless mobs, street gangs of undernourished children, and the violence of hoodlums at election time.

A similar indifference or even hostility to the masses made its appearance in industry. In 1825, the artisan who had his own building and his own tools was economically independent, and between master and journeyman there was personal contact and mutual respect. Likewise, there was an intimate relation between the artisan and his customers, who represented a local and a limited market.[27] This relationship changed in the next quarter-century. Although domestic and handicraft production persisted, more and more persons sold their labor to factory owners, and relatively large manufacturing plants hired cheap immigrant labor. The workers, especially in mechanized industries like textiles, had little or no ownership in plant or equipment and merely worked at a dull routine for long hours at low wages.[28]

Under these circumstances it was no wonder that new class alignments of capitalists and workers developed and hardened in the second quarter of the nineteenth century. While the worker was depressed by conditions beyond his control, a rising industrialist class began to challenge the leadership of the old landed and commercial aristocracy. Originally, these manufacturers were from all walks of life: thrifty farmers, skilled craftsmen, retired sea captains or their sons—some of them native-born, some immigrants.[29] The innate ability, training, contacts, and good luck of some had brought financial success. Now they were knocking at the doors of political power and social prestige so long guarded by their commercial brethren. With few exceptions, however, the reigning social set remained exclusive.

If the manufacturers could not be social leaders at once, at least they could live comfortably and respectably on the profits of industry. Shipbuilding, sugar refining, metalworking, and the making of furniture and musical instruments were the city's big industries in the late twenties. While metalworking and cabinetmaking were primarily handicraft industries in the hands of skilled artisans, the manufacture of musical instruments was semicapitalistic, and shipbuilding and sugar refining were the leading large-scale producers. In fact, New York offered the interesting contrast of a few large industries producing much and many small ones producing little.[30]

Nowhere was the factory system more evident than in the expanding clothing industry of the Empire City. By 1830 some of the city's many establishments were employing from three to five hundred "operatives," mainly women. Custom-made clothes were the rule, but ready-made clothing was appearing, first as "slop clothing" for seamen and later in response to the demand of the growing middle class for cheap yet dignified clothes.[31] New York became the center of the ready-made clothing industry and offered an immense field of employment, not only to women, but to immigrants, first Irish, then German and Jewish. Hanford & Brother, reputed to be the most extensive clothing manufacturers in the United States, employed in 1854 over two thousand workers, the males being mainly Irish and Germans.[32] After the cloth was received at the store, it was cut, trimmed, and then given out to be sewed and finished. A contractor might take the cloth in bulk and set up his own factory, or the work might be handed out to individual tailors who worked at home with their wives and children.[33] Trousers, waistcoats, and cloaks were made mostly by women, particularly after the invention of the sewing machine in 1846. Although machines were owned by a few tailoresses, the majority of the women rented them from the contractors.[34] Mechanization permitted the industry to meet the enormous demand for clothing. From 1841 to 1853 the value of clothing sold wholesale in New York City jumped from $2,500,000 to $20,-000,000.[35]

Mass production, with its low pay and tedious work under harmful conditions, contributed to the artisan's keenly felt loss of status. Reflecting the acute discontent and the demand for social reform, short-lived labor parties led by reformers sprang up in the Eastern cities. In New York the Working Men's party, organized in 1829, grew out of protests against attempts to lengthen the ten-hour day, out of the demand for an effective lien law for laborers on buildings, and the opposition to imprisonment for debt.[36] Deprived of adequate educational opportunities for themselves and their children, the workingmen sought universal education as a basic reform. "Next to life and liberty," the "Workies" resolved, "we consider education the greatest blessing bestowed on mankind." [37] During the thirties the wage earners launched another crusade, this time against the power of banks and monopolies and against the use of paper money, which depreciated in value and, in effect, lowered their wages.[38]

While the labor movements of the pre-Civil War period were inextricably bound with demands for humanitarian reforms, agrarianism, association, and other utopias, the forties and fifties witnessed intense struggles between capital and labor. When machines were introduced for operation by ill-trained or unskilled workers, when employers imported foreign labor to depress wages, when the cost of living rose, craftsmen and laborers organized and demanded immediate redress. Encouraged by immigrants strongly imbued with the class consciousness of the revolutionary years in Europe, labor unions staged frequent—if often abortive—strikes for higher wages and shorter hours.

It was natural for the "substantial" and "respectable" folk of New York to voice their opposition to what they regarded as dangerous trends. Whenever the workingmen's agitation involved changing the accepted standards of business conduct it was branded as criminal and of foreign origin. As early as 1830, the merchant John Pintard complained to his daughter of,

the Working people & Fanny right [sic] men arrayed to level all distinctions [,] to equalize property, abrogate marriages, release children from parental restraint, to feed clothe & educate them at the public expense, & to have no taxes, & there are fools enough among the ignorant to be gulled by these extravagant notions. One w^d suppose it hardly possible in a country enjoying so many civil & religious blessings that persons sh^d be found to hatch & promulge [sic] such chimæras or that others sh^d believe them. It is owing to the debased English migration that such abominable stuff is circulated thro' presses devoted to decry Christianity & loosen the bonds of Society & government.[89]

Some three decades later, following the abortive labor demonstrations of 1858, the Association for Improving the Condition of the Poor deplored the "dangerous and untenable theories in respect to the rights of labor . . . that were promulgated by the leaders." In America there might be differences in wealth and social position, but there was no inequality of rights, and nobody had the right to demand work and wages from another.

The doctrine so pertinaciously urged, that a man has a right to work and wages from the government, or from any one, whether his services are needed or not, originated in those countries where the subject held land of a superior, to whom he owed subjection as a bondsman and became a vassal or slave under the absolute control of his master. . . . Such is the doctrine of the monarchies, aristocracies, and feudatory systems of the Old World, whose perpetuity depends upon the successful degradation of their subjects. . . . The theories in question are mainly urged by our foreign-born citizens, who would introduce here the wrongs and oppressions of their native land, from which they have come hither to escape.[40]

Such class antagonisms were enhanced, not only by the decline of the aristocracy in New York's politics and the development of Tammany Hall as a well-oiled political machine, but also by the inevitable expansion of business in crowded lower Manhattan. Throughout the pre-Civil War period commerce extended northward, the fashionable stores moved up Broadway, and the pulsating business district crept into the wealthy uptown residential areas. Well-to-do New Yorkers moved farther north and left their substantial homes to be occupied by the less fortunate persons who worked in the neighborhood. To save expense, four, five, or six poor families crowded together in these abandoned one-family houses, creating new slum areas along the West Side as far as Greenwich Village and on the East Side into the Fourth Ward, with its fine old mansions.[41] Into these neglected parts of town poured waves of immigrants before 1850, enriching the "mercenary landlords who only contrive in what manner they can stow the greatest number of human beings in the smallest space." [42]

Manhattan's 166,000 inhabitants in 1825 increased in twenty years to 371,000 and, during the period of largest immigration, expanded phenomenally to nearly 630,000 in 1855.[43] By the outbreak of the Civil War there were over 805,000 residents of Manhattan and well over a million in the metropolitan area.[44] While the narrowness of the island constricted its population, the proximity of the Brooklyn and Williamsburg settlements across the East River and Jersey City and Hoboken across the Hudson permitted many New Yorkers to live in outlying areas.

New York was in many ways physically unsuited to this growing population. Once serving the needs of a quiet seaport town, many of the city's dwellings became outmoded firetraps. Some were converted into tenements, others into factories and stores, their wooden walls and shingle roofs creating unprecedented fire hazards. The frenzy to build new mansions and business structures of brick, stone, and white marble was solid proof of the haunting fear of fires which so often ravaged the city's frame buildings.[45] The great fire of 1835 destroyed some thirteen acres of old buildings centering around Hanover Square, William, Pearl, Water, and Front streets; ten years later a fire broke out in the vicinity of Wall Street and laid waste the entire district between Broadway and the eastern side of Broad Street.[46] It was no wonder that John Jacob Astor, the richest landowner in the city, insisted that all property pledged to him should be adequately insured against fire by the mortgagors.[47] Fire protection remained rudimentary, with picturesque volunteer firemen unable to cope with the problems posed by the city's growth. It was not until 1865 that professional firemen were introduced.[48]

If fire fighting lagged behind the needs of the thriving metropolis, so did other services and facilities. Travelers stopping in the town in the 1830's noticed the inadequate water supply.[49] Even after the gala Fourth of July celebration of 1842, when the water of the Croton aqueduct was

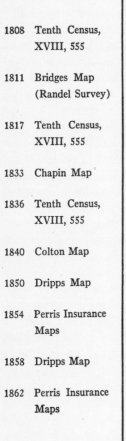

1808　Tenth Census,
　　　 XVIII, 555

1811　Bridges Map
　　　 (Randel Survey)

1817　Tenth Census,
　　　 XVIII, 555

1833　Chapin Map

1836　Tenth Census,
　　　 XVIII, 555

1840　Colton Map

1850　Dripps Map

1854　Perris Insurance
　　　 Maps

1858　Dripps Map

1862　Perris Insurance
　　　 Maps

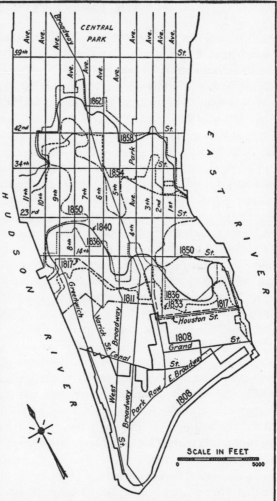

LIMITS OF THE BUILT-UP AREA OF MANHATTAN, 1808–1862

These lines are interpretations of data given in the sources cited above and may be incorrect in detail but are sufficiently accurate for the present purpose.

Between 1833–1862, the city streets below each line were solidly built up of two-, three-, and four-story buildings. Few structures were as tall as six stories. North of each line were a few groups of undetached buildings, but most were single houses with gardens, occasional cultivated fields, pastures, and bits of woodland. Toward mid-century, immigrants' shanties dotted upper Manhattan.

This map, with a fuller explanation, originally appeared in T. Adams *et al., Population, Land Values and Government . . . (Regional Survey of New York and Its Environs* [New York, 1929], II, 53). It is used with the permission of the Russell Sage Foundation.

21

emptied into the city reservoir, few persons used the Croton water in their homes.[50] Less spectacular was the gradual extension of gas lighting in the city streets. When gas was introduced in the twenties, many streets were still dimly lit at intervals of 150 feet by ancient oil lamps which remained dark when the moon was bright.[51] Gradually, however, the number of gaslit thoroughfares increased, the New York Gas Light Company supplying the lower part of the island and the Manhattan Gas Light Company the area above Canal and Grand streets.[52]

The means of protecting life and property in New York were notoriously ineffective. Until the middle of the forties, the city had no system of paid professional policemen. Prior to the Municipal Police Act of 1844, New York's police force consisted of two constables elected annually in each ward, of a small body of men appointed by the mayor— the mayor's marshals—and of a "watch" composed of citizens who patrolled the streets at night. During the daytime, the constables served summonses and made arrests when a judge ordered them to do so, and at night the watchmen were expected to detain offenders and assist one another in case of riot or disorder.[53] The act of 1844 abolished the watch and established a day-and-night police.[54] Under the new system, complaints continued to run far ahead of arrests, and the lawlessness of New York, climaxed by the Astor Place riot of 1849 gave the city a well-earned notoriety. Owing partly to the inefficiency of the municipal police, but largely for political reasons, the state created in 1857 a Metropolitan Police for the New York area. Mayor Fernando Wood defied the authority of the state, and for a brief and tense moment a pitched battle ensued between two rival police forces, the Metropolitans emerging the victors.[55]

As the population sprawled up Manhattan, public health became a serious problem. Although pigs no longer roamed the streets, the age-old urban difficulty of garbage and rubbish disposal was intensified by the accumulation of filth in back yards, alleys, and narrow, unpaved streets. As late as 1859 more than two thirds of the city was unsewered.[56] Families living in tenements suffered grievously from typhoid, typhus, and other common diseases of the slums.[57] When epidemics struck New York, the poor, who were unable to leave town, were the chief victims. Yellow fever hit the city five times between 1795 and 1822, and in 1832 the Asiatic cholera, sweeping into the city from Europe and Canada, caused fearful loss of life and created consternation when it reappeared in 1834, 1849, and again in 1855.[58] To meet such visitations, the city's public health system was hopelessly feeble. The posts of the health wardens were among the poorest in the gift of the Common Council and were rarely sought by competent or educated persons. Being nonprofessional men, the wardens were often wholly unfit for their urgent duties, and a competent doctor accused them of fearing even to approach the sick in times of epidemic or contagious diseases.[59]

Such were the conditions of life in the Empire City; this was the New York to which the immigrant came. In 1830 only 18,000 of the city's 200,000 inhabitants were unnaturalized foreigners, the majority of native residents tracing their family trees to roots in the United Kingdom or the Netherlands. The city's "first families" had made room for enterprising New Englanders and for thrifty merchants from the British Isles. Less prominent socially but more instrumental in New York's growth was the mass of artisans, small businessmen, and wage earners, their numbers augmented by immigrants.[60] The great famine of 1816 and 1817 had driven several thousands across the ocean, and as New York State entered the canal-building era thousands of foreign laborers arrived.[61] Irish laborers were imported, at least indirectly, by contractors who advertised in the Irish and Catholic newspapers and by labor recruiters in Ireland; this immigrant brawn likewise made possible the laying of railroad lines and the construction of other public works.[62] During the twenties and thirties, fully three fourths of the immigrants were from Great Britain, with one third to one half of these from Ireland. Many of these early Irish were Presbyterian Protestant farmers and skilled workingmen from Ulster and Dublin and from the Protestant colonies in the south and west.[63] By 1840 the Catholic Irish comprised a majority of the total British emigration. Beginning in the thirties, the Germans came in large numbers as a result of economic hardships and the failure of the revolutionary movements of 1830–1833.[64] During the latter forties and early fifties immigration reached new heights as the potato famine struck at Ireland and agricultural changes cut off the livelihood of thousands of German farm families.[65] In addition, individuals from almost all the European nations and from South and Central America continued to arrive at the metropolis, some on business or on their way to the interior of the United States, a few as political exiles, others as permanent settlers.

These newcomers were easily recognized by their strange customs and languages. As early as 1835, Francis Lieber heard in New York a babel of tongues: "English, German, French, and Spanish, which, with the addition of Italian, you may hear almost any day, in Broadway, at the hours when it is most frequented."[66] In mid-century, another observer called attention to the "free negroes, or as they are called people of color . . . Germans and Dutch . . . Irish . . . French, Danes,

Swiss, Welsh, English, Scotch, Italians, Turks, Chinese, Swedes, Russians, Norwegians, Poles, Hungarians, Spaniards, Sicilians, Africans, and, in short, a few of all the nations upon the earth." [67] Thus did the city acquire a cosmopolitan look—a look which New York has never lost.

III

THE IMMIGRANT ARRIVES

WITH TEARS OF JOY and thanks to the Lord for his safe arrival, the immigrant viewed America for the first time. Sailing past the Narrows, he pressed against the ship's rail and scanned the vast harbor of New York, surrounded by inviting rural landscapes dotted here and there with quiet cottages. In the distance lay the city itself, its church spires bidding welcome, but disguising a soulless impersonality which paradoxically emphasized a foreigner's sense of strangeness yet absorbed him like one more grain of sand on a storm-tossed beach.

The southern part of Manhattan was the usual landing place for immigrants, some vessels finding their berths in the Hudson, and others tying up along the East River. Not a few shipmasters weighed anchor off the shores of Long Island or New Jersey, whence their human cargo crossed over to New York City.

The arrival of penniless immigrants at New York had for many years burdened the city with their support. They came in a period when the granting of relief to the poor was commonly regarded as a religious function of churches and private philanthropy. Nevertheless, the city maintained an almshouse, a hospital, and several dispensaries, besides giving "outdoor" relief in times of depression, fire, and epidemic. Tolerated as an unavoidable evil and opposed as being uneconomical and tending to increase pauperism, outdoor relief was dispensed only in cases of urgent need.[1] Being the most needy, foreigners crowded the city institutions to such an extent that they were widely considered a menace to society. The statistics of the city almshouse and of hospitals, orphanages, and prisons throughout the state seemed to prove this contention.[2] In the thirties official complaints were voiced about the new and poorer class of newcomers: Europe was "casting upon us the refuse of her *Alms Houses and Prisons*," who wormed their way into New York and threw themselves upon public charity.[3]

Prior to 1847, the subject of the care and support of immigrants was left either to general quarantine and poor laws or to local ordinances. Under the New York State Passenger Act of 1824, every ship captain arriving at the port of New York was required to report to the mayor the name, birthplace, last legal settlement, age, and occupation of each passenger; the master's endorsement of this report, with the signature of two sureties, constituted a bond up to $300 for each alien passenger to indemnify the city in case such immigrants or their children became public charges within two years.[4] As long as immigration remained small, this system worked well enough, but it was not long before the hordes of new arrivals led to flagrant abuses of the bonding procedure. The vagueness of the law and its haphazard application proved irksome to honest shipowners and a boon to the unscrupulous. A class of shrewd, speculative bond brokers appeared, who, for a trifling payment, relieved the shippers of liability. Assuming this liability at prices ranging from ten cents to a dollar per passenger, the brokers profited by the knowledge that they were expected to pay for the bonded passengers only in case of their sickness or destitution.[5] In some cases, however, shippers avoided the brokers by commuting their bonds through flat payments directly to the city of one to ten dollars for each immigrant.[6] "The entire business," wrote a scholarly expert on immigration, "became a private traffic between a set of low and subordinate city officials, on the one hand, and a band of greedy and unscrupulous brokers, on the other. It was a sort of legalized robbery, the headquarters of which was at City Hall." [7]

The city's careless supervision of immigration encouraged shady practices by the bond brokers. As more and more sick and destitute aliens were lodged in the almshouse and other public institutions, some brokers sought to avoid forfeiting the bond money by maintaining their own private poorhouses or contracting with boardinghouse keepers to lodge pauper immigrants. The accommodations thus provided were designed solely to save money. The food was generally insufficient and poor, the clothing wretched, and the upkeep of the premises neglected, while the inmates were subject to callous or abusive treatment. Several of these overcrowded and filthy "hospitals" evoked widespread complaint, and the newspapers teemed with lurid descriptions of them. One of the worst was Tapscott's Poor House and Hospital, situated in the town of Williamsburg across the East River. Rather than subject themselves to the indignities here imposed upon them, individuals were known to have deceitfully gained admittance to the almshouse and Bellevue, the city hospital.[8]

When sick immigrants arrived at New York, the nature of the illness determined the treatment they received. Since 1797 a Marine Hospital on Staten Island had been maintained by the state for quarantining persons with contagious or infectious diseases, but immigrants suffering from noncommunicable ailments usually were not admitted, nor was medical aid provided for those who contracted diseases after their arrival.[9] The Marine Hospital was supported by a head tax levied on passengers and crews of seagoing vessels entering the port, the amount of the tax varying until in 1845 cabin passengers paid two dollars each and steerage travelers fifty cents.[10] Although these moneys were originally intended exclusively for hospitalization, large sums were diverted to other charities by special acts of the legislature.[11] Until the middle of the century, therefore, the destitute, sick immigrant received meager assistance, if any.[12]

To the healthy immigrant the absence of effective regulation was at once apparent. No sooner had a ship appeared in New York harbor than it was boarded by a despicable class of people who seized the opportunity of relieving the stranger of his money and valuables. These were the so-called "runners," agents of individuals and companies in the business of forwarding immigrants to other parts of the country, or agents of boardinghouses near the waterfront, whose principal income was extorted from newly landed foreigners. Besetting the immigrant on board the ship or as soon as he set foot on shore, the runners competed to win his confidence and whisk him to a forwarding or transportation office. In the words of a contemporary report:

The tricks resorted to, in order to forestall a competitor and secure the emigrant, would be amusing, if they were not at the cost of the inexperienced and unsuspecting stranger, and it is but too true that an enormous sum of money is annually lost to the emigrants by the wiles and false statements of the emigrant runners, many of them originally from their own country, and speaking their native language.[13]

Irish runners preyed on the Irish, German upon the Germans, English upon the English, and Americans upon them all. The bewildered newcomer, for example, was shown a neatly printed ticket which he was informed would take him to a given place beyond Albany in a specified manner and at an agreed price. He was then furnished with a steamboat ticket to Albany, where he was to present his passage ticket to the company upon which it was drawn. When the hapless traveler reached Albany, his ticket was protested, or the type of conveyance was changed, contrary to the "agreement." A frequent pretext for not honoring a ticket was that the freight charge on baggage was not paid or that payment was not enough. When the immigrant offered to make good the deficiency, false scales were sometimes used to extort exorbitant freight payments.[14] Originally a local business, the operations of the runners gradually extended beyond the confines of New York, Albany, and other Eastern cities. Forwarding offices began to employ agents in European ports who sold tickets at fancy prices for inland transportation in the United States which proved to be worthless when presented in America.[15]

At New York the foreigner's ignorance of local conditions was a source of prosperity for the immigrant boardinghouses near the waterfronts and along Greenwich Street on the West Side. Many of the lower-class houses sent their own runners to the docks to drum up trade. Assuring the gullible that their services were free of charge, they carted the immigrants' luggage to the boardinghouses for "safekeeping." Their methods are well illustrated by Maguire's account of a young Irish lad who landed in 1848 with a box of tools, a bundle of clothes, and a few pounds in gold: [16]

The moment he landed, his luggage was pounced upon by two runners, one seizing the box of tools, the other confiscating the clothes. The future American citizen assured his obliging friends that he was quite capable of carrying his own luggage; but no, they should relieve him—the stranger, and guest of the Republic—of that trouble. Each was in the interest of a different boarding-house, and each insisted that the young Irishman with the red head should go with him. . . . Not being able to oblige both gentlemen, he could oblige only one; and as the tools were more valuable than the clothes, he followed in the path of the gentleman who had secured that portion of the "plunder" . . . the two gentlemen wore very pronounced green neck-ties, and spoke with a richness of accent that denoted special if not conscientious cultivation; and on his (the Irishman's) arrival at the boarding-house, he was cheered with the announcement that its proprietor was from "the ould counthry, and loved every sod of it, God bless it!"

Room and board were promised at reasonable rates, but the boarding-house keepers induced their guests to stay several days, for which they charged three or four times the rate for the first day. To this sum they added outrageous charges for cartage and storage of baggage. If the boarder could not pay, he was turned penniless into the street, while his belongings were held as security.[17] Not only did such boardinghouse keepers fleece their customers, but they deliberately misinformed them about employment conditions in New York or transportation routes to the West, and they even prevented the stranger from obtaining reliable advice.[18] In 1848 the state legislature recognized the seriousness of the situation and adopted regulations for these boardinghouses, which resulted in some improvement.[19] Charges grew less exorbitant, and some individuals were forced to deliver the luggage they held as "security." However, if boardinghouse keepers could not legally hold their guests' baggage, it could be conveniently "stolen." Outright robbery became more frequent, and in some instances the keepers were suspected of active participation in these thefts.[20]

Until nearly the middle of the century, state control over immigration was so weak as to be almost nonexistent. The city officials who administered the local immigration laws were constantly faced with the problem of aliens who landed in adjoining states and seeped into the city. Perth Amboy was a favorite landing place, and large numbers came by river and canal or overland from Canada and Nova Scotia. Not a few traveled by steamboat from Rhode Island and Connecticut, the captains of these ships not being compelled to report their passengers to the mayor.[21] These clandestine entries into the city, added to the flow of new arrivals directly from Europe in the forties, overtaxed the slender resources of private charitable organizations which attempted to care for the sick and poor. As foreign paupers roamed the streets and filled the almshouse, the charities joined in the popular outcry for some sort of effective state legislation. Newspapers lent their support, revealing that the almshouse commissioner had "been compelled to turn the *dead house* at Bellevue into a receptacle for the living." [22] Immigrant societies, led by a few gifted spokesmen of the foreign-born population, campaigned for a state law. Andrew Carrigan, on behalf of the Irish, and Friedrich Kapp and Leopold Bierwirth, for the Germans, showed outstanding leadership in the movement, which also enlisted the active cooperation of the Whig politician Thurlow Weed at Albany.[23]

At length a bill was introduced in the legislature providing for the establishment of a state immigration commission. The New York City politicians fought it tooth and nail, and, aiming to keep power in their own hands, they sent a delegation to Albany to oppose state control.[24] After a bitter struggle, the lieutenant governor cast the deciding vote, and on May 5, 1847, the state assumed jurisdiction over immigration.

The new law created a Board of Commissioners of Emigration consisting of ten members, six appointed by the governor, the mayors of New York and Brooklyn, and the presidents of the German Society and the Irish Emigrant Society.[25] The board inspected incoming ships, gave advice, aid, and employment opportunities to immigrants, and maintained and supported immigrants who became public charges within five years after landing. Under the new law, the master of every ship was required to file complete data for each voyage at the mayor's office, subject to a $75.00 fine for each omission; shipowners and consignees had to give bond for each passenger, but this obligation could be commuted by the payment of $1.00 per person.[26] The commutation fee was successively raised until in 1867 it was fixed at $2.50, and the bonding system was so amended that the old brokerage practices were completely eliminated.[27]

In applying the greater resources of the state to the protection and assistance of the immigrants, the Commissioners of Emigration faced certain initial difficulties. Runners and several transportation agencies hampered the board for a number of years until they were driven out of business. Authorized to acquire an immigrant landing dock, the commissioners leased a large pier at the foot of Hubert Street but were immediately served with an injunction obtained by outraged residents of the neighborhood who feared inconveniences and lowered property values. Unfortunately, the state supreme court sustained the injunction.[28] Finally, the board itself became involved in politics. It was only seldom that those members appointed by the governor were really interested in their jobs, with the result that the duties fell upon a few shoulders, and the maintenance of German and Irish interests was left largely with the German and Irish members.[29]

Criticism of the board, not without a political tinge, was a regular feature of the Irish press in New York City. The *Irish American* kept up a barrage of accusations involving the "reckless and culpable conduct" of the commissioners, their "extravagant expenditure of moneys of the poor emigrant, in providing fat places . . . for a parcel of loafing doctors *residing in the city*—their committing the lives of the sick to a lot of experimentalizing students—their permitting the desecration of the dead, and many other things, too numerous to repeat." [30] Referring to the "blundering and inefficiency of the Commissioners and the barbarity of their officials," this paper asserted that "hundreds of our people . . . just cast on shore from the emigrant ships, parade, daily, the streets of New-York as *howling beggars*. They sleep, in droves . . . in the station houses; the Commissioners supplying them with bread. In the morning they wander over the city *begging*." [31] Mike Walsh, then Democratic member-elect of the state assembly, made political capital by his blunt charges of inefficiency. "Respectable females," he declared, were "forcibly shoved out like dogs" for proudly refusing the first offer of pittance, and allowed to sit upon benches, "shivering and shaking like so many aspen leaves." [32]

While the *Irish American* was unduly sensitive, some of its criticism was justified. An investigation revealed that the employment agency and lodgings maintained by the commissioners were in a dirty and neglected condition, that there were instances of maltreatment of immigrants and inadequate medical care. Not only were several members of the board indifferent to their responsibility, but others had vested interests. Merchants and shippers, however philanthropic-minded, naturally were interested in profits from the immigrant traffic, yet such persons were appointed to the board.[33] They were "the very men who should not be appointed," complained the *Irish American,* which asked that the commissioners be elected rather than appointed by the governor, a change which would have replaced Whigs with Democrats.[34]

In spite of these charges, and perhaps spurred on by them, the board alleviated the worst abuses of the immigrant trade. It was obvious, however, that few malpractices could be eliminated without a specific landing point for all immigrants arriving by sea from Europe. After the initial failure of the commissioners to lease a pier, agitation was commenced for the use of Castle Garden.

Just off the southern tip of Manhattan Island was a circular stone structure, once a part of the city's fortifications but long used as a place of amusement. Its name had been changed from Castle Clinton to Castle Garden, and here appeared a "long series of Circus Companies, Menageries, Chinese Junks, and monstrosities without number." [35] Here appeared Bosio, Sontag, Alboni, Grisi, Jenny Lind, and other stars of song and stage; here were performed innumerable concerts, operas, and theatricals.[36] This famous old building was converted in 1855 into a landing depot for immigrants, and the shady groves of Battery Park became the site of strange people and strange voices in a strange land.[37]

Castle Garden was of great advantage to the immigrant. He was landed more speedily and more safely than before. He was less subject to the deceptions of swindlers.[38] He might continue his journey without delay from the wharf to his destination: passenger tickets henceforth were obtained from supervised transportation companies with offices at the Garden, baggage was accurately weighed, exorbitant charges and porters' fees were eliminated, and the traveler was informed freely and reliably on travel routes and employment conditions.

Upon entering the large rotunda of Castle Garden, the immigrants registered with a clerk of the Commissioners of Emigration, passed on to a desk where clerks of the transportation companies laid maps before them, helped them choose a route to their destination, and provided them with an order on the official cashier setting forth the number of tickets required, route, passage price, and any additional freight charges. At another desk the cashier issued the tickets. The passengers were then led back to the dock, where they showed the weighmaster the baggage checks which they had received on shipboard; baggage was collected, weighed, and labeled, and freight charges were paid to a collector at the scales. A steamboat then transported passengers and baggage free of charge to the terminals of the various railroad and boat lines.[39]

The emigration commission and the use of Castle Garden as a landing depot relieved the overtaxed benevolent societies which drew their strength from the "foreign" community of New York City. Of these, four had been founded in the eighteenth century: the St. George's Society (English), the St. Andrew's Society (Scotch), the Friendly Sons of St. Patrick (Irish), and the German Society. These associations were not exclusively alien; the St. George's Society, for example, admitted not only natives of England, but their sons and grandsons, British officers and their sons wherever born, and natives of British colonial possessions.[40] With the exception of the German Society, these groups were social clubs with charitable functions of a limited nature. Nationality was the bond of their existence, and controversial subjects were usually avoided at meetings.[41] The members were merchants and professional men of wealth and prominence. At their annual banquets, which were gala social occasions, they toasted patron saints, rulers living or dead, and lands native and adopted, in an atmosphere of jollity and sometimes ostentatious display, which occasionally evoked unfriendly comment in the press. "The 'Friendly Sons'—a sort of Irish 'What-is-it?'—had their celebration," quipped the *Freeman's Journal,* commenting on "their usual amount of joking about the venerable memories of the day."[42]

In befriending the stranger in New York, the English, Irish, Scotch, and German societies were not alone. A French Benevolent Society had been established in 1806 to assist the needy French and Swiss.[43] In 1832 the Swiss, now more numerous, founded their own association, although it did not act independently of the French until 1845.[44] The small Welsh population claimed two St. David's societies, both organized informally in 1835.[45] A Spanish Benevolent Society, supported by Cuban and Puerto Rican merchants, was founded in 1838 to minister to the Spanish-speaking poor of New York, and Spanish persons arriving in the city were forwarded to South America, to the Antilles, and to points in the United States.[46] Among the Jews the oldest and strongest association was the Hebrew Benevolent Society, founded in 1822, but with the augmented immigration from Germany and Poland many new societies sprang up in the forties and fifties. German Jews formed the German Hebrew Benevolent Society in 1843, and a decade later Polish groups similarly served the Polish Jews.[47] The Scandinavian and Dutch communities also had their national clubs, while somewhat later Belgian, French-Canadian, and Italian societies were founded.[48] Smaller and less well-known associations were composed of mechanics, artisans, and others in the humbler walks of life.

The resources of all these groups were utterly inadequate for the support of the thousands of immigrants who applied to them for relief. Funds were quickly exhausted even in prosperous years, while during depressions the societies had no hope of coping with the demands for charity.[49] In the thirties the St. Andrew's Society gave but ten dollars to only the most urgent cases, while the St. George's Society found it necessary to appeal to England for aid.[50] A scheme for the creation of an English emigrant office was abandoned for lack of funds, but the idea persisted.[51]

The emigrant office in New York was distinctly a product of nineteenth-century immigration. Nevertheless, the German Society, since its establishment in 1784, had concentrated on the welfare of German immigrants. Although it resembled the English, Irish, and Scotch societies in its membership of comparatively wealthy merchants and professionals, who enjoyed its *Gemütlichkeit* and social prestige, the German Society showed far greater solicitude for the newcomer. Under the early leadership of Baron von Steuben, it had combated the prevalent system of indentured servitude, assisted emigrants in distress, and promoted emigration from Germany. With the decline of indentured servitude in the early nineteenth century, the society turned to the protection of free German immigrants from rapacious innkeepers, crafty land agents, runners, and fraudulent transportation concerns.[52] The German Society had evolved into a true immigrant aid association.

Small and usually ephemeral groups devoted to aiding immigrants appeared early in the century. Among them were the Shamrock Society and the German Emigrant Society, active during and after the War of 1812.[53] An Irish Emigrant Association was organized in 1817 by Irish exiles of 1798 with the purpose of asking Congress for ten townships in Illinois Territory to be settled by Irish immigrants.[54] Upon the failure of the plan, the society perished.

Immigrant aid societies, in general, had five major functions. They gave advice to the stranger and tried to shield him from the swarms of tricksters waiting to prey on him. They acted as clearinghouses for information about relatives and friends. They gave immediate financial help in cases of serious need. To many able-bodied immigrants, the most important service was the effort to find them jobs, and the employment bureaus of these societies were nearly always besieged with crowds of men and women seeking work. An even greater undertaking was the effort to "keep them moving."

If Horace Greeley said "Go West," so did every immigrant aid association. Frequently, small groups of emigrants banded together, not only for the perilous sea trip, but to build their own little community in the wilderness or to join those who pioneered before them. Whole families, members of colonization projects, particularly among the Germans and Scandinavians, passed through New York. For these newcomers, who were mostly farmers and artisans, New York meant additional expense and waste of time unless they could transfer at once to boat or railroad and shove on to the interior. Scotch, English, and Irish emigrants who chose Canada as their ultimate destination often landed at New York and then proceeded up the Hudson to Albany, thence by way of Rochester to Upper Canada.[55] Irish laborers imported for the construction of public works, Irish and German domestic servants, Scotch farm hands, and many others passed through the Empire City. Adventurers of all nations, dazzled by the lure of California gold in 1849, tarried in New York and sought passage to the West Coast at $100 per person.[56] Others in the city craved, not excitement, but the security of family and friends on the Eastern seaboard.[57] For all these, the immigrant societies gave advice about transportation routes and rates, located missing persons, and established contact with relatives in the interior of the country by communicating with immigrant societies in other cities, such as Boston, Albany, Philadelphia, Baltimore, Cincinnati, St. Louis, and New Orleans; sometimes they helped defray the travel expenses of the poorest immigrants; above all, they warned people not to stay in the Eastern cities, where it was harder to find employment.

The first organization devoid of social functions and with a well-rounded program of immigrant aid was the Emigrant Assistance Society. Avoiding the pomp and ceremony of the earlier benevolent societies, and without any grandiose scheme of land settlement, this body was formed in 1826 to meet the needs of newly arrived Irish laborers. Under the leadership of William J. Macneven, who had been a promoter of the ill-fated Irish Emigrant Association, this new agency directed the incoming strangers to jobs on the roads and canals.[58] Three years later it was supplemented by the Union Emigrant Society, both agencies providing data on wages, permanence of employment, routes and distances to the interior of the country.[59]

Out of these pioneer efforts grew a larger and better known organization, the Irish Emigrant Society. Created in 1841 under the auspices of Bishop (later Archbishop) John Hughes, its promoters were leading Catholics and Protestants; several merchants, philanthropists, and social workers; Thomas O'Connor, the editor and Tammany leader; and

Congressman John McKeon. Aided by a paper devoted to the interests of the Catholic Irish, the *Freeman's Journal,* which stressed the group's Americanism, the society was launched on its long career, despite factional hostility and charges that it was organized by aristocrats.[60]

Since the Irish Emigrant Society was chiefly concerned with the Irish, similar agencies were formed to aid persons of other nationalities. A group of English merchants founded a British Protective Emigrant Society in 1844 with the blessing of the British consul, who was one of its first members.[61] Although half its applicants for employment were English, there were many Scotch and Welsh, while one fourth of the jobseekers were Irish.[62] Struggling with public indifference and lack of financial support, the British Protective Emigrant Society survived for several years by constant appeals for gifts and the presentation of benefit concerts and literary entertainments.[63]

All immigrant aid societies experienced difficulty in raising funds. Some were under suspicion of having "a more tender regard for the *money* of the emigrant, than for their [*sic*] safety and comfort." [64] Not only were they blamed for inadequate attention to destitute aliens, but they were also accused of questionable deals with forwarding companies. Fly-by-night agencies, such as the New York Holland Protection Emigrant Society, were "got up for the purpose of booking passengers," and the agent of the British Protective Emigrant Society was charged, probably unfairly, with receiving a commission for recommending passengers to the forwarding house of Hinds & Company.[65] It is not surprising, therefore, that contributions never measured up to the needs of the societies. A further obstacle was the relative poverty of New York's immigrant communities, which lacked the means of supporting an organization of such wide scope as the Association for Improving the Condition of the Poor. The indifference of native Americans to the small-scale charitable activities among the various nationalities left closed to the immigrant aid societies the resources of the native merchants and manufacturers who supported the A.I.C.P. Finally, it was usually considered the duty of the Catholic clergy to care for needy Catholics, the majority of whom were Irish. The heavy demands upon the Roman Catholic Benevolent Society and St. Patrick's Asylum for girls, founded in 1817 by the Sisters of Charity, led to the creation of the Roman Catholic Orphan Asylum in 1825 and a similar institution in Brooklyn a few years later.[66]

The Catholic Church, however, was utterly unprepared to cope with the rising tide of Irish immigrants in the thirties and forties. New organizations were at last called into existence by the widespread misery of the Irish poor in New York before and during the famine years. To grant relief and to preserve family life among the impoverished Catholic immigrants, the Society of St. Vincent de Paul was organized in 1846; and in the same year Bishop Hughes secured several Sisters of Mercy from Ireland to open a home for the care of destitute immigrant girls.[67] At the same time Catholic churches founded benevolent societies to minister to their poor. The Benevolent Society of St. Patrick's Cathedral held annual festivals, enabling it to donate clothing and cash to the Catholic poor, and to contribute to the Society of St. Vincent de Paul.[68] During these years the Church and the German community faced similar problems posed by German Catholic immigration, but it was not until 1858 that St. Joseph's Asylum was created to care for dependent German children.[69] German Catholic churches, however, performed the customary benevolent functions.

In spite of heroic efforts, the lack of funds and trained personnel limited the ability of the Catholics to alleviate the condition of immigrants of their faith. Protestant churches and charities stepped into the breach, grudgingly, but with an understanding of the imperative need for some kind of action. Alluding to the fact that the Protestants and Jews took care of their needy, the Association for Improving the Condition of the Poor asserted that "excepting the relief of a few orphans," the Catholics made "no corresponding provision for their poor, neither by their churches or otherwise; nor yet assist, by their contributions, those who are engaged in this Christian duty." [70] The Catholic reaction to this unjust charge was a stubborn defense against the much-feared proselytism of Protestantism.[71]

The limited resources of churches, charities, and immigrant societies, and the inability of the local authorities to cope with problems of an immigration unprecedented in history, left the newcomer to his own devices. It was not until mid-century that the state began to regulate immigrant boardinghouses, terminate the bond brokerage system, and eliminate the sharp practices of transportation agents by the establishment of the Castle Garden landing depot. Until then, immigrants were forced to rely upon the warnings and advice of their compatriots or religious kinsmen, who provided in the immigrant community a haven for the helpless strangers and a hearth which reminded them of home.

IV

THE IMMIGRANT SETTLES

DURING THE FIRST FEW DAYS after landing at New York, the immigrant felt lonely and bewildered. Having looked forward with curiosity and hope to his arrival, he now found himself in a land of strangers and strange customs. As one Scotchman put it, if he should die, there would be none to mourn him.[1]

The first concerns of the newcomer were shelter and food. If he had no relatives or friends with whom he could live temporarily, he walked to one of the many boardinghouses in the vicinity of Greenwich Street or the dingy side streets near the East River docks.[2] Despite the evil notoriety of some of these hostelries, most were honestly run. However, nearly all were old buildings with damp cellars and little ventilation, poor sanitary conveniences, and flies, bedbugs, and wharf rats as permanent guests. Frequently, the parlor was a beer cellar, saloon, or grocery and provision store, where the new boarder might see "two barrels of whiskey—one colored red with oak juice and sold for 'first-rate Cognac brandy,' and the other answering with the most limpid assurance to the various demands for gin, Monongahela, or schnapps."[3] The landlord enjoyed greater profits from liquor sales than from room rents, which ranged from fifty cents to three dollars per week, nearly always payable in advance.[4] German boardinghouses sometimes maintained forwarding agencies for their constantly shifting occupants, many of whom sought private lodgings elsewhere at the first opportunity.[5]

The boardinghouse dwellers were predominantly male, but entire families of immigrants sometimes rented the small, single rooms for several weeks after landing. Immigrant families left the boardinghouses as soon as possible and settled in the old private residences which had been converted into tenements in anticipation of their coming. Not only families but single men found it cheaper to rent rooms in tenements, where they shared their quarters with fellow countrymen.[6]

The location of the immigrant communities which grew up in New York was determined by three basic elements: employment, housing conditions, and group consciousness. To find work was one of the first objectives of the newcomer, and he tried to live within easy walking distance of his job.[7] From the Battery north to the foot of Hubert Street on the Hudson, and east to Corlear's Hook on the East River, lay three miles of waterfront crowded with slips and warehouses. The nucleus of large-scale shipping activity was South Street, the shipping merchants' mecca, where the wharves jutted out like rake prongs into the East River. Smaller vessels, chiefly schooners and sloops, tied up in the Hudson, but east of the Battery large ships landed their Western produce from Albany and their lumber, granite, lime, and fish from New England. At Old Slip and Coffee House Slip were vessels southward bound for Baltimore, Philadelphia, Richmond, and other cities where they picked up cargoes of coal, tobacco, cotton, lumber, and naval stores.[8] A floating population of sailors and longshoremen congregated on the docks, and cartmen, porters, and casual laborers trudged with their heavy loads into the side streets. That there were so many laborers in the lower wards was a logical outcome of this employment, and likewise, ship carpenters, caulkers, riggers, ropemakers, sailmakers, and other skilled artisans were dependent upon the shipping trade.[9]

A few blocks from the waterfront, merchants and importers gave employment to ambitious clerks and workmen, native and foreign. Pearl Street, winding along the East Side, was the early home of the wholesale dry goods dealers, who lived above their stores. Boarding with them were clerks, bookkeepers, or junior partners, mostly Americans but including a growing number of English, Scotch, Irish, and Germans. The retail dry goods trade was carried on mostly in William Street. By the middle of the century the dry goods jobbing and importing district had extended to William, Broad, Pine, Cedar, and Liberty streets.[10] Businessmen of other trades established themselves at similar focal points. In 1830 the hatters, fur merchants, and stove dealers centered around Water Street, between Pearl and South; the silk dealers were clustered in Hanover Square, the wholesale druggists in Fletcher Street from Pearl to the East River, and the wholesale grocers in Front Street paralleling South.[11] In the area of the old Beekman marsh known as "the swamp," leather dealers entrenched themselves in the vicinity of Beekman and Ferry streets.[12] Thirty years later these business districts had expanded but remained in the same general areas, and Broadway had blossomed into a promenade of beauty and fashion, lined with bookshops, jewelry, upholstery, hat and cap, tailoring, millinery, and large retail dry goods stores.[13] With the dispersion of trade throughout the lower tip of the metropolis, native and immigrant wine dealers, tavern keepers, confectioners, and grocers plied their trades and bargained with foreign-born importers offering exotic cargoes from Sicily, Madeira, Bordeaux, or the Caribbean.

Because of this ceaseless commercial activity, property values below City Hall rose to phenomenal heights. By 1840 the value of real estate in the First, Second, and Third wards was assessed at one third of the total for Manhattan Island.[14] The speculative value of this land led owners to neglect the upkeep of residential properties which would be torn down and replaced by commercial buildings.[15] Meanwhile, the dilapidated old structures served a purpose: they housed the inpouring immigrant tide. Although the population of the first three wards was small, the proportion of aliens rose from one ninth of the total in 1835 to one fifth in 1845 and three fifths in 1855.[16] During the famine years of the late forties the Irish crowded into the boardinghouses and tenements in the Greenwich Street area, and in the late fifties this vicinity was host to thousands of transient Irish, Germans, Scandinavians, Spanish-speaking peoples, and Italians.[17]

To live in the lower wards required some money. The penniless stranger, wholly without means, could not afford the relative luxury of a boardinghouse. His search for shelter without cost led him to sparsely populated sections north of the settled part of town. In the twenties and thirties Irish immigrants clustered around the "Five Points," a depressed and unhealthy area on the site of the filled-in Collect swamp in the old Sixth Ward.[18] Here, at little or no cost, the poorest of the Irish occupied dilapidated old dwellings and built flimsy shanties with whatever materials they could gather. In the heart of the Five Points was the Old Brewery, erected in 1792 on the banks of the Collect and long famous for its beer. Transformed into a dwelling in 1837, the Old Brewery came to house several hundred men, women, and children, almost equally divided between Irish and Negroes, including an assortment of "thieves, murderers, pickpockets, beggars, harlots, and degenerates of every type."[19]

As early as 1830 the Sixth Ward, and the Five Points in particular, had become notorious as a center of crime, and the riots of 1834–1835 were supposed to have originated in this long-settled Irish neighborhood.[20] The criminality of the area was usually overemphasized, but poverty was widespread, and thousands of law-abiding inhabitants led wretched lives in cellars and garrets.[21] To the original Irish and native population, including Negroes, came new accretions: English, Germans (including Jews), Polish Jews, more Irish; and in the fifties, Italians and laborers and workers in near-by clothing factories, machine shops, and foundries.[22] The ward remained predominantly Irish, however, 42 per cent of its inhabitants in 1855 being natives of the Emerald Isle.[23] By this time an even larger proportion of Irish lived to the east in the built-up, commercial, and industrial Fourth Ward, where they accounted for nearly half the population.[24] Spreading along Water, Cherry, and Monroe streets, they moved north and east. In the Second, Fourth, and Seventh wards facing the East River, the Irish comprised 38 per cent of the inhabitants.[25] These wards served as a distributing point for thousands of refugees from the Emerald Isle, and the easy ferriage across the river brought to Brooklyn an Irish population which spread over an area less severely constricted by land speculation than Manhattan.[26]

As stores, businesses, and dwellings were erected in southern Manhattan, homeless immigrants trudged farther to the limits of the built-up region. They occupied barren areas of rocks and hills, where, as squatters on the land, they erected flimsy one-room shanties and eked out a precarious semirural existence. Thus developed New York's "shanty town." With few exceptions, the shanty dwellers were Irish and German. "Dutch Hill," a steep precipice at First Avenue and Fortieth Street became in the sixties a well-known squatter colony, where the foreign-born inhabitants tended their cows, pigs, goats, and fowl, and worked in near-by quarries and manure heaps.[27] Along the Hudson from Fortieth to Eightieth streets west of Sixth Avenue lived a shanty population of Irish and German ragpickers, cinder gatherers, and laborers.[28] Many of them were employed in grading, paving, and sewering streets, removing rocks, or excavating for building purposes. Some worked in the stables of the city railroads and stage companies or labored in near-by Central Park, which was laid out in the latter fifties. In 1864 the New York *Times* estimated at twenty thousand the number of squatters, who paid neither rent nor taxes.[29]

Whether in shanty town or in the commercial districts, whether along the waterfront or in the Five Points, immigrant settlers drew to their areas others having the same nationality, language, religion, or race. Once a nucleus was established toward which later arrivals were attracted, the cohesive bond resulting from consciousness of similarity tended to replace the magnetic forces of cheap shelter and ready employment. Native prejudice against foreigners furthered the isolation of these communities, and white prejudice against Negroes similarly produced well-defined colored settlements.

Long before the waves of nineteenth-century immigration, the Negroes of New York City had lived in distinctively colored sections. Segregation of the colored community, noticeable as early as 1800, continued long after the legal emancipation of New York's slaves in 1827.[30] Racial prejudice and custom had planted an impenetrable barrier between native whites and Negroes, and a French traveler wrote in 1833 that there was not one trade in the city where colored persons were allowed to work with whites.[31] Negroes were not permitted to sit in any public assembly, court, or church, except in the particular quarter set apart for them—"generally in the most remote and worst situation." [32] What was true of social gatherings was also true of living quarters, except where the poorest foreign immigrants were concerned. In 1825 more than one fifth of the city's Negroes inhabited the Sixth Ward, spreading north and west from the Five Points into the Fifth and Eighth wards; in addition, colored persons were scattered throughout the city, many of them serving white families who had not joined the rush uptown.[33] A decade later, however, few Negroes remained in the lower part of the island, and the Sixth Ward had yielded to the Fifth and Eighth as the center of the colored population.[34] The Negroes established themselves in West Broadway, Thomas, Leonard, Sullivan, Greene, Mercer, and Mulberry streets, where they remained beyond the middle of the century.[35] In curious contradiction to the general trend of migration up the island, the Negro expansion was southward from the Eighth Ward to the Fifth until mid-century, when there was a return movement into the Eighth. The dispersion of the Negroes was effectively blocked on the north by Greenwich Village, with its large proportion of native-born whites and a widely diffused Knickerbocker element which maintained its exclusiveness but not its wealth.[36] To a lesser extent the Washington Square neighborhood also limited Negro migration. By 1860, however, a large colored settlement had appeared far to the north, between Twenty-Sixth and Fortieth streets near the Hudson, and not a few Negroes already had filtered into the Greenwich and Washington Square localities.[37]

As did the colored inhabitants and the Irish, other racial and national groups occupied distinct areas of New York. The coming of the Continental Europeans in the thirties transformed the Empire City into a complex agglomeration of little communities, a few of which showed clearly defined nationality but most of which included a heterogeneous mixture of foreign elements. At the same time, individuals or families of most nationalities established themselves in every part of the city.

Second to the Irish in numbers were the Germans, who originally were scattered in the commercial districts. In all the lower wards the German mercantile population rented rooms and residences, and many German families occupied upper stories of warehouses, stores, and taverns.[38] Although not a few Germans remained south of City Hall, German settlers began moving north in the thirties into Elizabeth Street and the Bowery, veering eastward into the Tenth Ward. So many Germans established themselves here in the following decade that the area was dubbed

"Kleindeutschland." [39] The nucleus of this Little Germany lay between Canal and Rivington streets and included the north-south arteries of Elizabeth, the Bowery, Chrystie, Forsyth, and Eldridge streets; but the German population extended as far as Houston Street, east to Attorney, south to East Broadway in the Seventh Ward, and west to Lafayette in the Irish Fourteenth. [40]

The center of German business activity was in William Street and in neighboring streets above Beekman as far as Pearl. In the forties and fifties the German business area followed the population movement and invaded the vicinity of the Bowery. "As one passes along the Bowery," observed a German in 1847, "almost everything is German." [41] Small German workshops appeared in *Kleindeutschland,* which expanded to the East River and pushed steadily northward in the fifties and sixties. The poorer Germans gathered in dense settlements near the river. Among the artisans and laborers were many German craftsmen whose livelihood depended upon the shipyards and ironworks of the Eleventh Ward. In 1856 nearly twenty-four thousand Germans lived in this ward, or 44 per cent of its total population, while the native Americans and Irish numbered about thirteen and a half thousand apiece. [42] At the same time, the Germans poured into the Seventeenth Ward, which rivaled the Eleventh in the size of its Teutonic population. [43] Although the Germans settled in every ward, they preferred the East Side of Manhattan, where they penetrated to Eleventh Street between Second Avenue and Avenue C, continued their northward march along Third Avenue, and formed isolated communities farther north near the East River. [44] In these northernmost settlements were groups of immigrant ragpickers, called "chiffoniers," whose lives and occupations were comparable to the Irish shanty dwellers. These country-bred Germans searched rubbish heaps for bits of paper or scraps of food, saving what they could and then graduating to steadier employment and more substantial homes. [45]

As did the Irish, the Germans found it simple to cross the East River. Some of them settled among the sons of Erin in Brooklyn village, but a far larger number formed a closely knit German community in Williamsburg, where it was estimated in 1847 that they comprised two thirds of the population. [46] Small German settlements also appeared across the Hudson at Jersey City and Hoboken. Prior to the large migration of "forty-eighters," the Germans of these outlying regions, added to Manhattan's 50,000, gave the metropolitan area a Germanic population of some 80,000. [47]

Although the New York Germans and Irish together surpassed in numbers all other nationalities combined, the English and Scotch constituted the third and fourth largest groups, respectively.[48] Far fewer numerically, they were neither Roman Catholic in religion, like the majority of Irish, nor did they speak a foreign language, like the Ger-

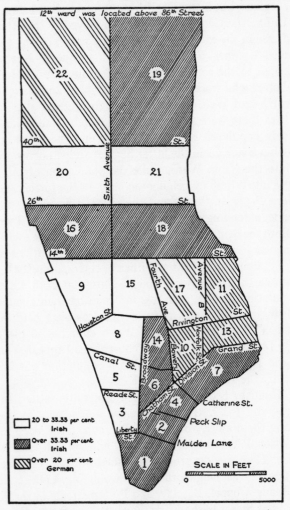

WARD DIVISIONS OF LOWER MANHATTAN, 1855, SHOWING GEO-
GRAPHICAL DISTRIBUTION OF IRISH AND GERMAN POPULATIONS

mans; and this lack of differentiation from native white Protestantism enabled them to mingle with Americans to a greater extent than other nationalities. There is no positive evidence that the English formed any distinct geographical community until the forties, when it seems probable that English laborers and skilled workers settled in the Fourth

Ward.[49] In 1855 nearly twenty-three thousand English lived in all sections of Manhattan. Most of them inhabited the northern part of the settled area, reflecting the uptown trend and the need for labor in the upper regions, but many English continued to live below Fourteenth Street.[50] Unlike the Germans, the English moved to the Hudson side of the island, and in the early sixties a sizable English colony existed in the upper forties between Fifth and Seventh avenues.[51] Nearer the river and somewhat to the south was a considerable district of English and Scotch laborers who worked in factories, stables, and slaughterhouses.[52]

The Scotch and Welsh, as did the English, gravitated to the West Side. In 1825 there were apparently two Scotch settlements, one in the still sparsely populated Fourteenth Ward and the other in the Third Ward. Within a few years the latter had expanded northward along the Hudson into the Ninth Ward, while the population of the Fourteenth spilled over into adjoining neighborhoods.[53] In the forties and fifties the Scotch were dispersed throughout the city but continued to prefer the Hudson side, extending along upper Eighth Avenue to Twenty-second Street.[54] Both the Scotch and the English penetrated the exclusive Greenwich Village in greater proportion to their total populations than did the Irish and Germans, an indication either of their similarity to the native inhabitants or their superior financial status, or both. Of the minute Welsh population there is even less information than about the Scotch and English. In 1827 Welsh religious services were held in Mulberry Street, and in 1833 there were two Welsh churches in the Fourteenth Ward.[55] By 1852 two different Welsh churches had appeared near Broome Street in the Tenth Ward, but the Welsh population was following the pattern set by the English and Scotch.[56]

As the English, Scotch, and Welsh generally settled in the same localities, so did the Latin peoples show a tendency to live together. Constituting the majority of this small group, the French moved early to the Hudson River side of the island and spread north and east in the thirties. Their steady progression northward was marked by little communities in the neighborhood of Columbia College, in Murray, Warren, Reade, Chapel, Barclay, and Fulton streets in the Third Ward and in Thomas Street in the Fifth Ward. By the forties French families were living in Lispenard, Walker, and White streets in the Fifth Ward and an advance guard in Greene Street in the Eighth.[57] The French did not pioneer the advance up Manhattan, for there were few laborers or shanty dwellers among them. The center of French life remained in the West Side below Houston Street, and particularly in Greene, Laurens, Wooster, Broome, White, and Spring streets. From this neighborhood the French reached into the wealthy Washington Square district and across the island into the Seventeenth Ward. By the end of the Civil War the French had joined the movement uptown in settlements from Tenth to Fortieth streets in the west, from Tenth to Twenty-second on the East Side, and in the fifties near Fifth Avenue.[58]

The few Hispanic peoples and Italians were too scattered in the 1820's to form distinct communities, but in the thirties they too gravitated to the West Side, with a vanguard of Italians moving eastward into the Sixth and Fourth wards.[59] Although by mid-century the Latin peoples were sprinkled through the city, the natives of Central and South America, of the West Indies, and of France were most numerous in the western Fifth, Eighth, and Sixteenth wards, in the Fifteenth, and in the eastern Seventeenth and Eighteenth; the Spaniards occupied the same areas except the Fifth and Eighth wards, while the Portuguese and Italians lived in the Fourth and Sixth wards.[60] With the swift increase of Italian immigration, beginning in the fifties, hundreds of poor Italian peasants poured into the Five Points area and the adjoining Eighth Ward.[61]

Of the remaining national groups the Swiss tended to settle among the French and Germans, depending upon their language and associations in Switzerland; the Netherlanders lived in the central and northwestern part of town and among the Germans of the Seventeenth Ward.[62] Scandinavians arriving in the fifties congregated on the East Side, particularly in the Fourth and Seventh wards and in the business districts at the lower tip of the island.[63] A group of Czechs appeared during the Civil War years in Essex, Division, Houston, Delancey, and Rivington streets, where they mingled with the Irish, Germans, Jews, English and Dutch.[64] At the same time, a tiny body of Chinese which had first inhabited Gold and Cherry streets in the fifties filtered beyond the City Hall to Park and Baxter streets at the Five Points, there laying the basis of Chinatown.[65]

The Jews constituted a unique group, for they included a large number of nationalities: native American, English, Dutch, German, Polish, Bohemian, Russian, and a few Spanish and Portuguese.[66] Because of their consciousness of Judaism, their history of segregation in European ghettos, and the early pervasive influence of the synagogue, the Jews had more in common with one another than with Christians who happened to have been born in the same countries.[67] When the Dutch ruled New Amsterdam, the few Jewish inhabitants were required to live in a separate section of the city. Although the law may not have been enforced, there is some evidence of a Jewish neighborhood on Whitehall

Street, probably near the extreme tip of Manhattan.[68] Under British rule after 1664 the Jews voluntarily inhabited a district near their synagogue in Mill Street.[69] For many years thereafter, the majority of Jews settled in Pearl, Water and lower Greenwich streets, but an increasing number moved uptown, where in the 1820's they spread on both sides of Broadway.[70] The richer Jews established themselves west of Broadway on upper Greenwich, Laight, Charlton, Greene, and Wooster streets, while their poorer brethren veered in the opposite direction toward the Bowery, entering Centre, White, Pearl, Franklin, Canal, Broome and Houston streets in the Sixth Ward.[71]

The late thirties marked the first division of the Jewish quarter into distinct neighborhoods based on kinship and country of origin. Beginning about 1837, German, Dutch, and Polish Jews penetrated into Bayard, Baxter, Mott, and Chatham streets; crossing the Bowery, they pushed as far east as Division, Market, and Henry streets. Somewhat later, German and Bohemian Jews poured northward into the German quarter above Grand Street and occupied Ludlow, Attorney, Clinton, Ridge, and Pitt streets, and the lateral arteries of Rivington and Stanton.[72] In the latter fifties this Jewish section expanded as far north as Twentieth Street, while the midtown area, excepting the vicinity of Mott, Bayard, and Chatham streets, was rapidly abandoned. Into this older Jewish locality bounded by Canal, Elm, Mott, and Bayard streets flowed a stream of Polish and Russian Jews.[73] Meanwhile, the wealthier Jews moved north to Thirty-third Street on the West Side, congregating particularly in Fourteenth Street near Seventh Avenue and on Thirty-third Street between Fourth and Seventh avenues.[74] Thus the old ghetto broke apart into newer ones based largely upon nationality and wealth. However, as newly arrived Jews took up residence in the very sections abandoned by those who had become more assimilated, the lower East Side remained Jewish in character long after the Civil War.

Few elements contributed more to the cohesiveness of a group than the compactness of its settlement. Existing customs prevailed with little outside interference, religious beliefs were nurtured in comparative security, and native languages were perpetuated over a long period of time. The immigrant community, like a decompression chamber, represented a place and a time of adjustment from one atmosphere to another. The psychological transition from alien to American was slow, lasting over several generations, but the first and most important stage occurred in the immigrant settlement, where there was a constant struggle between the old and the new.

By the middle of the century New York City rivaled San Francisco and the Western mining towns as a mecca of nationalities. Districts of Irish, Germans, Jews, English-Scotch-Welsh, Dutch, Canadians, French, Latin Americans, Italians, Scandinavians, and others gave the Empire City the aspect of a polyglot boardinghouse. Although lower Manhattan retained its foreign population, the immigrant communities spread uptown with the general population and across the rivers to Brooklyn, Williamsburg, Hoboken, and other settlements in the metropolitan area. Ability to pay the rent, proximity to place of employment, and the cohesive bonds of nationality, religion, and language determined the location of the foreign districts. For many immigrants this implied a squatter life in shanty town. For the majority it implied a prolonged residence in dilapidated tenements and a period of adjustment to the hardships of overcrowding in unsafe and unsanitary surroundings.

V

TENEMENT LIFE

As NEW YORK'S WHARVES BECAME CROWDED with warehouses amid a scene of noisy and ceaseless activity, the wealthier inhabitants moved elsewhere, and their homes passed into the hands of boardinghouse keepers and of real estate agents. White-collar employees and working-men, finding it necessary to live near the docks, warehouses, stores, and workshops, occupied these old dwellings and found them a blessing. However, as property values rose in the lower wards, rents were raised, and those tenants who could afford it followed their former proprietors into the upper wards. The rest sought cheaper quarters in the old neighborhood.

To meet the demand for rooms and apartments, owners and agents converted old homes into tenements by erecting partitions for the accommodation of three or more families. Unscrupulous owners made room for more by dividing their space into "the smallest proportions capable of containing human life within four walls." Beginning in the thirties, immigrant families poured into these reconstructed buildings, the Irish becoming their principal occupants, although in some houses Negroes crowded " from cellar to garret." [1] Thus appeared the first stage in the development of the modern New York slum.

Housing facilities could not keep pace with the incoming tide of foreign workingmen and their families, and the insistent demand for shelter at low rentals resulted in the development of a second type of tenement. When owners discovered that converted dwellings yielded substantial profits in rents, they constructed new buildings designed especially as tenement houses.[2] Usually such a building contained a narrow hall opening from a street or court; on each floor, including the cellar, two suites of rooms opened into the hall. Front and rear rooms of the building contained windows, but the bedrooms and closets in the middle were dark. In most cases there was another tenement in the back yard, frequently altogether enclosed and accessible only through an alley. Alongside these buildings and in the yards were many little, irregular frame structures, some in dilapidated condition, serving partly as sheds and partly as homes for the overflow of the tenements. Such haphazard combinations of front and rear buildings on the same lot created an intricate array of rear courts and alleys, notoriously dark, foul-smelling, and encumbered with accumulations of filth.[3]

As immigration intensified the housing shortage, the insistent demand for rooms and apartments induced owners to rent basements, attics, and even lofts and stables to eager but poor homeseekers. In the seven wards below Canal Street, the gross density of population per acre climbed from 94.5 persons in 1820 to 163.5 in 1850, while the average block density increased from 157.5 to 272.5 in the same period.[4] In the Seventh Ward, with a large Irish population, and the Tenth Ward, which included many Irish and Germans, the average block density rose from 54.5 persons per acre in 1820 to 170.9 in 1840.[5]

A considerable number of immigrants moved into cellars, where rents were cheaper and where, consequently, diverse ages, sexes, races, and nationalities crowded together. In 1843, 7,196 persons were living in cellars.[6] During the great waves of Irish and German immigration, the basement population expanded so that by the middle of the century about twenty-nine thousand persons were living underground.[7] Thereafter, the number of cellar residences decreased as newer and larger tenements were built, and by 1863 it was estimated that only eighteen thousand persons lived in cellars.[8] Typical of overcrowded cellars was a house in Pike Street which contained a cellar ten feet square and seven feet high, with one small window and an old-fashioned inclined cellar door; here lived two families consisting of ten persons of all ages.[9] The occupants of these basements led miserable lives as troglodytes amid darkness, dampness, and poor ventilation. Rain water leaked through cracks in the walls and floors and frequently flooded the cellars; refuse filtered down from the upper stories and mingled with the seepage from outdoor privies. From such an abode emerged the "whitened and cadaverous countenance" of the cellar dweller.[10]

Population could expand only northward on Manhattan Island. This limitation increased the competition for apartments in an area of already inflated property values and drove rentals upward. Immigrants who had lived in cities in the Old World resented the high rents which they were forced to pay and cried out bitterly against the rapacity of landlords. Disillusioned about the city's living conditions, an English workman grumbled that for a New York room with bare, whitewashed walls and no sanitary facilities, the rent was double that in London.[11] As middle-class private dwellings disappeared, the clerical workers and artisans also relapsed into tenement lives.[12]

Tenement houses were rented by the week or month. Many an owner was enriched by charging $3.00 to $13.00 per month for apartments, and seventy-five cents to $1.25 per week for single rooms twelve feet square.[13] In this system of rent gouging, the chief figure was an agent, or sublandlord, who leased a house or group of houses for several years. The owner thereby was assured of an income and relieved of responsibility for direct supervision of tenants, while the agent collected the rents and sometimes saved enough money to purchase the property in a short time.[14] Since the agent was a speculator whose interest was to make as large a profit as he could, he thought in terms of risk and reimbursement, not of tenant welfare. "He measures rooms, and estimates —not their capacities for accommodating human life in health and comfort—but their capability of containing human life to pay the rent." [15]

Despite the fact that many poor tenants frequently moved about in response to changing employment conditions, they were conscientious about paying their rent. The reason was fear of eviction. This possibility placed the tenant at the mercy of the landlord and put rent before fuel and clothing.[16] For those who had acquired a small amount of personal property, the consequences of eviction were disastrous. A wife's property could be seized as well as her husband's and sold on execution for his nonpayment of rent. Only such items as necessary food and clothing, cooking utensils and tableware, fuel for sixty days, a few pieces of furniture, the family pictures, and a few books, including the Bible, were exempt from levy or sale.[17] To insure that rents would be paid, some landlords maintained blacklists of delinquent tenants; evicted persons thus found it difficult to rent new homes.[18]

Newspapers, both native and foreign-language, were full of protests against evictions and high rents. They reported spontaneous meetings of lodgers to combat the inhumanity of the landlords and the raising of rents. At a mass meeting in 1848, tenants demanded that the legislature limit profit in rents to 7 per cent on assessed valuation and put a stop to the practice of ejecting one paying tenant in order to rent to another. They called for a city tax of 3 per cent on all unimproved lots. A proposition before the legislature to incorporate companies of capitalists to build tenements was condemned as tending to encourage the combination of capital for the suppression of the poor. Finally, the formation of a lodgers' league was urged to protect the interests of the tenants against property owners and their agents.[19]

The wide gulf between tenants and owners was emphasized by the unhealthy physical aspects of tenement life. To the immigrant who had been a city dweller in Europe it was no novelty to settle in apartments which lacked proper lighting and ventilation, but the peasant from rural Ireland or southern Germany was forced to make a difficult adjustment to living conditions in New York. Instead of the fresh country air, he breathed the foul miasma of cramped and insalubrious quarters; instead of the surrounding daylight of farm and field, there was little but gloom and darkness. Daylight rarely entered more than one of the two or three rooms in the apartments of the poor, and cross ventilation was usually an impossibility.[20] Samuel Gompers, the immigrant cigar maker and future labor leader, wrote:

Our apartment in Sheriff Street was a typical three-room home. The largest, the front room, was a combined kitchen, dining-room, and sitting-room with two front windows. There were two small bedrooms back, which had windows opening into the hall. We got water from a common hydrant in the yard and carried it upstairs. The toilet was in the yard also.[21]

When water for bathing and washing had to be fetched from street pumps or near-by wells, bodily cleanliness was more of an ideal than a reality. Not only was it impossible to bathe, but insufficient space and air hindered home laundering. To overcome this situation, private philanthropy erected a "People's Washing and Bathing Establishment" in Mott Street in the early fifties.[22] A few years later a *Verein* was formed to crusade for free baths for the German working population.[23] All such ventures failed, however; it is likely that most immigrants bathed in the Hudson, East, or Harlem rivers. One of the chief attractions of Sunday excursions was a swim in the ocean, in Long Island Sound, or in the Hudson above the city, where bathers were free of the polluted waters of lower Manhattan.[24]

The deficiency of water in the tenement areas was largely responsible for the accumulation of filth. Nearly all the old buildings, and many of the newer ones, lacked toilet facilities. Back-yard, wooden privies were common, but they could not accommodate the large number of inhabitants they were intended to serve. Through overuse and improper care, the privies remained a constant menace to health, and their contents, instead of being drained or carried away, frequently overflowed to the surface and created breeding places of disease.

Had the city maintained adequate inspection and control of tenement sanitation, New York might have avoided its reputation for dirtiness. City ordinances provided for the regulation of privies, cesspools, sewers, gutters, and cemeteries, but these laws were poorly enforced, particularly in tenement localities, where complaints proved ineffective. The lack of official supervision was largely the result of maladministration, employment of incompetent health officers, and the fear of infringing upon the presumed rights of private property.[25] Owing to the paucity of sewers, the question of sanitation was of city-wide concern. As late as

1857 only 138 miles of sewers had been constructed in nearly 500 miles of streets, leaving unsewered "nearly three fourths of the city, including some of the most densely populated and filthy portions."[26] Waste water drained into yards and alleys, filled the sinks, and broke into cellars and foundations; some 24,000,000 gallons of sewage matter daily accumulated in such areas and in the gutters and streets of the city.[27]

The streets were cleaned under a contract system which resulted in neglect and avoidance of responsibility. In the absence of a paid municipal street-cleaning force, contractors vied to receive "the highest compensation for the smallest discharge of duty." Imperfectly drawn contracts provided loopholes for evasion, and the spirit of the law was repeatedly violated. The contractors usually subcontracted for the cleaning of the several wards, the subcontractors often letting out further subcontracts; meanwhile, the low wages, uncertainty of pay, and harsh treatment of the laborers who did the actual cleaning contributed to the ineffectiveness of the system.[28] The haphazard removal of garbage forced even cleanly inhabitants to violate the law. They dumped into the streets the contents of their unemptied refuse containers. Since poor women were the usual offenders, sympathetic policemen hesitated to tear them from their families by hauling them off to jail.[29]

In New York, where it was asserted that overcrowding was greater and that there was less concern and expenditure for the welfare of the slum population than in any other large city, the lower wards became the scene of frequent accidents among workingmen and their families. The concentration of shipyards, docks, and manufacturing plants in lower Manhattan exposed the laborer to collisions in cluttered streets, falling timber and brick, and collapsing walls. This peril was likewise an ever present possibility in the tenements and boardinghouses wedged amid factories, slaughterhouses, stables, and lumber and coal yards.[30] When inadequately inspected buildings crumbled on their foundations and antiquated firetraps suddenly were consumed in flame, the danger became real. Where front doors and windows were the only fire escapes, the inhabitants were compelled to "roast or break their necks."[31] Typical of such catastrophes were the $600,000 fire in the Woolsey sugar factory at Clinton and South streets and a frightful explosion in Hague Street, both in the winter of 1849–1850.[32]

Life in the slums was a continual struggle with illness and death. The high incidence of disease in New York was directly related to the sanitary condition of tenement dwellers, of whom a large number were the foreign born or their children.[33] In the crowded immigrant quarters quarantine was an impossibility, and communicable diseases suddenly erupted into epidemic proportions. The Sixth Ward was a center of contagion, typhoid breaking out among the Irish and Germans in 1837, typhus in 1842, and cholera in 1849.[34] Respiratory diseases likewise took their toll. Tuberculosis, pneumonia, and bronchitis were common, and scrofula was called "the great scourge of the pauper population." [35]

That immigrants suffered more heavily from disease than the native population was well known. During the ten years from 1849 to 1859, of all persons admitted to Bellevue Hospital, a public institution, 83.9 per cent were foreign-born.[36] According to the unusually complete report of the city inspector for 1857, three of every five deaths from cancer in that year occurred among the immigrants; tuberculosis took the lives of 656 more immigrants than natives.[37] Deaths from all causes were always proportionally higher among the foreign population than among the natives. More than half of the persons over ten years of age who died in 1840 were immigrants.[38] In the latter fifties aliens accounted for 36.6 per cent of all deaths, but had the city statisticians considered parentage, the number of deaths in immigrant families would have produced a far higher percentage. The mortality of children of foreign parents showed a great excess over those of American parents, an eloquent proof of their poverty and lack of proper medical care.[39] Nearly two thirds of New York City's total mortality in 1857 were children under the age of five, the majority undoubtedly of foreign parentage.[40] A physician of Providence, Rhode Island, wrote:

It is well known that the foreign population, as a class, in this city, and in other cities in this country, are under entirely different sanitary influences from the American population. The greater portion of the foreign population live in a miserable class of tenement houses, with all the want of conveniences, and positively injurious influences of such houses; their social habits are not calculated to preserve health; and a knowledge of the laws of hygiene is entirely wanting among them. Of course, the children of foreign parents are subject to the same injurious influences upon health, and suffer from them more than the parents themselves.[41]

Despite the hospital facilities of the port of New York, diseases were introduced by newly arriving immigrants, and their spread was inevitable in the densely populated tenement districts. The largest annual number of deaths from typhoid, typhus, dysentery and diarrhea occurred during the periods of the greatest influx of immigrants—from 1847 to 1855.[42] Fleeing the famine in their native land, many starving and diseased Irish left the emigrant ships, spread their diseases, and died shortly afterward.

Among the immigrants, the Irish were the chief victims of disease, and Irish-born patients of city institutions were nearly always in the majority. Natives of Ireland comprised 53.9 per cent of New York City's foreign-born inhabitants in 1855, but at Bellevue Hospital, 85 per cent of all the foreign born admitted from 1849 to 1859 were born in Ireland.[43] The comparatively good health of the Germans is in striking contrast with the Irish. While 29.4 per cent of the city's foreign-born population were natives of Germany, only 6.25 per cent of admissions to Bellevue were German-born.[44] Thus the proportion of Germans admitted to the hospital was only one fifth of the proportion of Germans in the total immigrant population of New York. In explanation it was asserted that the Germans were more cleanly and orderly in their living habits, but it is more likely that their generally superior economic status enabled them to live in comparatively comfortable surroundings. Moreover, the German immigrants, as a rule, were not so physically debilitated as were the poorer Irish, particularly those escaping famine in their native land and fortunate enough to survive the horrors of the voyage in tightly packed emigrant ships from Liverpool. The greater financial resources of the Germans were indicated by the statistics of the German Society relating to the annual immigration of Germans at the port of New York.[45] Perhaps for similar reasons other nationalities sent proportionally few persons to Bellevue. The English comprised 6.9 per cent of the foreign born, yet only 4.56 per cent of admissions to the hospital were natives of England; the Scotch accounted for 2.6 per cent of the alien population, yet only 1.78 per cent of the Bellevue admissions were born in Scotland.[46]

As in the case of other diseases, the insanity rate among the foreign born was considerably higher than that of the native Americans, and that of the Irish was by far the highest of the foreign born. Over three fourths of the admissions to the city lunatic asylum on Blackwell's Island from 1849 to 1859 were of alien birth; two thirds of these were natives of Ireland.[47] The resident physician at the asylum admitted his inability to account satisfactorily for the high proportion of foreign insane. "Very few of the indigent insane of this city," he asserted, were

sent to the State Asylum at Utica, and none to Flushing, Hudson, or the Bloomingdale Asylum. Either the ratio of insane is very much less among the natives, or they are kept at their homes. Probably the first supposition is true, and this may arise in part from the shipment of the insane from Europe during a lucid interval.[48]

Nevertheless, it is also likely that many natives had better means of taking care of their insane and at the same time were unwilling that their kin associate with the foreign-born insane at a public institution.

Insanity, apparently, was common among newly arrived immigrants. This phenomenon was attributed to the "privations on shipboard," "the changes incident to arriving in a strange land," and to "want of sufficient nourishment." [49] In 1854 thirty-five of the hundred patients admitted to the Lunatic Asylum and chargeable to the Commissioners of Emigration had been in New York City less than one year, although many were only temporarily deranged and soon recovered.[50] Insanity was prevalent especially among young women, according to one physician, who ascribed it to "the combined moral and physical influences of their leaving the homes of their childhood, their coming almost destitute to a strange land, and often after great suffering." [51]

If physical and mental illnesses could be traced to the conditions of immigration or to existence in New York's slums, ignorance, lack of cleanliness, and inadequate medical care also played their part. Attracted by cheap prices, many poor families bought impure food from hucksters and basement storekeepers.[52] Medical advice was ignored by many, the Irish being the chief offenders.[53] While the Irish exposed their children to inclement weather, the Germans went to the other extreme, confining their sick to overheated rooms and excluding fresh air.[54] Superstition and home remedies were applied to all sorts of common ailments and disabilities. To her bald and toothless son in New York an English mother wrote, "You can have false teeth that is a very common thing and you must get some Castor Oil and rum and rub your head every morning." [55]

Credulous persons were fair targets for the army of charlatans who offered a pill for every ill. Advertisements for patent medicines appeared in nearly every newspaper, particularly in the German papers. For twenty-five cents one could buy a box of Dr. Fubarsch's *Vegetabilische Lebenspillen* for the cure of fever, colds, scrofula, worms, hemorrhoids, and "all delicate female ailments." [56] Van Pelt's Indian Vegetable Salve, costing fifty cents, was for the treatment of "breast ailments," burns, and carbuncles; *Pastilles de Paris* were good for colds and bronchitis; Tarrant's Cordial Elixir of Turkey Rhubarb for indigestion and dyspepsia; "innocent-pills," "blood-cleaning pills," "family pills," and "anti-diarrhea pills" vied with "syrup of naphtha," "lung balsam," and "marshmallow drops" as specifics or cure-alls. At one dollar a box, "Ladies Silver Pills" were "the rich man's friend and the poor man's need."

Despite insufficient medical care, poor immigrant families were not completely without the services of doctors. European physicians, surgeons, dentists, specialists, and midwives offered consultation and aid either free of charge or at nominal fees.[57] Occasionally, these doctors co-operated with immigrant aid societies. In 1843, for instance, thirteen German physicians agreed to treat the poor gratis upon presentation of a certificate of need from the German Society.[58] Besides employing doctors for the free treatment of needy Germans, the society also spent several hundred dollars annually for medicines and paid the bills of the dispensaries which leading Germans founded in the lower part of the city.[59] Ultimately, a German hospital was established in 1866, but only after a long agitation by community-conscious German businessmen, physicians, and philanthropists.[60] Likewise, the dream of a Jewish hospital was slow of realization, and it was not until 1855 that the Jews' Hospital was opened to patients.[61] A Jewish clinic, however, was organized a few years earlier to meet the crying need for free medical service.[62] The Irish failed to develop such a degree of medical co-operation. Overburdened with work among the poor, the relatively few Irish physicians faced an insuperable task of giving medical attention to the multitude of Irish immigrants who could not pay for it. When the Irish fell sick and home remedies did not avail, they sought admission to the city dispensaries and hospitals, where they were nearly always in the majority. The only organized medical aid among the Irish was through their benevolent and fraternal associations, a form of mutual aid common to all immigrant groups.

The helplessness of the immigrant poor was reflected in the large proportion of foreign-born paupers. City almshouse statistics prior to 1849 were unreliable, but during the next decade detailed figures revealed that fully three quarters of all persons admitted to the almshouse were born outside the United States.[63] After the middle of the century, extensive immigration coincided with rising living costs to aggravate the already precarious existence of the newcomer, and in 1852 more than half the needy in all the Atlantic seaboard cities were Irish and German immigrants, mostly day laborers.[64] In the Empire City alone, half of the persons relieved by the Association for Improving the Condition of the Poor were Irish; three eighths, Germans and other nationalities; while only one eighth were born in the United States.[65] Then depression struck. In 1854 and 1855, and again in 1857, the number of indigent poor mounted to unheard-of figures as unemployment stalked the city and mass meetings demanded public works to feed the starving.[66] It was an ominous sign that in the year of Lincoln's election fully 86 per cent of the paupers in New York City were of foreign birth.[67]

Huddled together in teeming tenements, in squalid alleys and court-yards, immigrants came into frequent conflict with the law, particularly in the extremely poor neighborhoods of the Fourth and Sixth wards. Panel thieves operated in the "Dutch" groceries of Duane, Thomas, and Anthony streets and in West Broadway, hardened murderers and harbor thieves congregated in Cherry and Water streets and on the wharves, and gangs of criminal hoodlums like the "Kerryonians" and the "Dead Rabbits" haunted the Five Points and the Bowery.[68] Most immigrant lawbreakers, however, were individuals incapable of organized crime. In the vast majority of cases, they were arrested by the police on charges of petty thievery, drunkenness, or disorderly conduct.[69] Family worries involving illnesses and deaths, the monotony and uncertainties of work in New York, and the isolation and friendlessness of the immigrant were relieved by frequent trips to the tippling shop. Love of liquor, fostered in Ireland by the hopeless outlook of the Irish peasantry, was further encouraged in New York by innumerable bartenders. Nor was hard drinking limited to the children of Erin, for the English and Scotch liked their whiskey too, and the French and Germans, traditionally wine and beer drinkers, included lovers of rum, brandy, and schnapps. Under the influence of drink, desperate and reckless individuals forgot their suffer-ings and their sorrows, committed assault or robbery, and wound up in jail.[70] Of the total number of persons committed to the city prison during the nine years 1850–1858, seven eighths were recorded as "intem-perate," most of them immigrants, unmarried, and between the ages of twenty and forty.[71]

Immigrants were easy prey for policemen who, unwilling to risk their jobs by raiding gambling dens, brothels, and criminal hideouts, kept a sharp eye for slight misdemeanors committed by persons of no political influence.[72] Because of alien habits or unfamiliarity with the English language, some foreigners unintentionally violated city ordinances; others, who happened to be present at brawls and riots, were subjected to arbitrary arrest.[73] As common among the poor as the boisterous conduct of the intemperate was the addiction to petty stealing. The culprits apparently stole needed goods more often than money, and some-times they were arrested merely on suspicion, as is evidenced by this press report:

ARRESTS—John McGorty and Michael Dowd were arrested for stealing a keg of white lead; John McKeeney on suspicion of having stolen $34; Jane Mullen for stealing a wash tub; Mary Donahan stole 34½ yards of calico from the premises of Mr. Taylor, 31 Catharine st.[74]

After their apprehension, the guilty and innocent alike were herded into the overcrowded city prison. Petty offenders mingled with confirmed felons, the sane with the insane, and children with jaded adults reeking of alcohol.[75] During 1859, 23 per cent of the persons arrested in New York City were native Americans, 55 per cent were born in Ireland, 10 per cent in Germany, 7 per cent in England and Scotland, and 5 per cent in other countries.[76] These figures are less significant, however, than the rate of criminal convictions for each nationality. In the courts of special sessions, slightly less than one per cent of the native American population of New York City were convicted in 1859, while 5.5 per cent of the Irish, 3 per cent of the Scotch, 2.5 per cent of the English, 2 per cent of the Canadians, 1.5 per cent of the French, and 1.2 per cent of the Germans were convicted.[77] The high proportions of foreign-born criminals are misleading, however, for the vast majority of crimes were committed by persons between the ages of twenty and forty, and it was this age group which was so largely filled with the foreign born.[78] Among the immigrant groups, the Germans were known for their law-abiding qualities, and the Jews, most of whom were Germans, appear to have had the lowest incidence of criminality. "There are far less charges of crime alleged against the Jews as a class, than against any other equal portion of citizens in our city," reported the *National Police Gazette*. Yet when a Jew was arrested, the newspapers noted that he was a Jew, whereas the creed of others was rarely given.[79]

Dens of gambling and vice dotted lower Manhattan. Despite the ban on lotteries passed by the state legislature in 1832, New York gamblers bought tickets for lotteries in other states, in Cuba, or in Europe, or they turned to the policy game. Negroes were the main victims of this numbers racket, but many immigrant women were also "daily won to its infatuation."[80] There is no evidence, however, that the foreign born gambled more than the natives; Jonothan Green's curious "Report on Gambling" hardly mentioned foreigners.[81]

Prostitution appears to have been almost as common among American women as among immigrants, but in either case poverty was the chief inducement to vice. In their failure to make ends meet, immigrant girls, devoid of family life, walked the streets in despair or drifted into dance halls and brothels, where in some instances they were exploited by women of their own nationality.[82] Of 2,000 prostitutes examined in 1858 at the Penitentiary Hospital on Blackwell's Island—in effect, the city's venereal hospital—762 were natives of the United States and 1,238, or five eighths of the total, were immigrants.[83] The largest proportion was born in British territory: 706 in Ireland, 104 in England, 63 in British North America, 52 in Scotland, and one in Wales, while 257 were natives of the German states, 17 of Switzerland, and 13 of France.[84] More than 45 per cent of these foreign-born prostitutes had lived in the United States less than five years, and of these, 21 per cent were residents of less than one year.[85] Of the 2,000 women, native and immigrant, three eighths were between the ages of fifteen and twenty, and fully three quarters were younger than twenty-six.[86]

Forced by circumstances to spend their formative years amid poverty, vice, and crime, children of the poorest immigrants grew up without family guidance and the restraining influences of church and school. Parents, who were subject to definite social controls in Europe, were unable to assert authority over children whose views of life were gained from experiences with " 'flash-men,' engine-runners, cock-fighters, pugilists, and pickpockets . . . and . . . low theaters." [87] For the boys of the streets, the Golden Rule was an altogether impossible precept, especially when they were "stuck and short" and "had to live." [88] Girls, pitiable and deserted, sometimes the daughters of prostitutes, made a scant living as fruit, nut, and candy peddlers, by petty thievery, or "by more questionable means." [89] Drifting loose upon society, the homeless, friendless, and lawless youth created serious problems of juvenile delinquency in New York as early as the 1820's. The vagrant and criminal children of foreign parentage admitted to the House of Refuge over a period of three decades were far more numerous than those of native parentage.[90] Although specific offenses committed by children were not reported before 1863, nearly all the children sent to the House of Refuge during the four years 1863–1866 were charged with petty larceny and vagrancy; but some were accused of disorderly conduct, assault and battery, manslaughter, rape, arson, forgery, and other crimes.[91]

Such were the living conditions of the foreign born. The New York tenement houses appeared in response to the needs of a growing population in congested lower Manhattan. Crowding into the hurriedly reconstructed dwellings or, later, into specially designed tenements, immigrant families occupied the poorest districts of the city, where life and limb were jeopardized by the failure to enforce housing regulations, the presence of factories and other industries in their midst, the uncleaned streets, the ineffective sewage system, the absence of bathing facilities, the futility of quarantining diseased persons, the widespread ignorance and lack of medical care, and the high incidence of pauperism, crime, vice, and juvenile delinquency. Persons of middle age or older, having little opportunity to rise to a comfortable living standard, eked out a bare existence in the forgotten streets of the lower wards. Younger men and women, more often their children, improved their status and moved to cleaner, safer neighborhoods, vacating their former rooms and flats for occupancy by more recent immigrants. As this process was repeated year by year, the foreign settlements acquired a fluidity made possible by the immigrants' occupational skills and their adjustment to the employment opportunities in New York.

VI

GAINING A FOOTHOLD

Unskilled Labor

ALREADY FAMOUS AS THE GATEWAY to the New World, New York City was receiving by mid-century three quarters of the immigrants from Europe. These newcomers dispersed in every direction, the English, Scots, and Germans settling on the land or joining their compatriots in other cities, and the Irish supplying the brawn for thousands of public works. Despite appearances, only a relatively small proportion of immigrants remained behind to swell the city's foreign population. Over two million alien passengers arrived at New York during the decade of the fifties; yet in 1860 the total foreign-born population of New York and Brooklyn was less than 484,000.[1] Before the famine years, the Irish stream flowed through New York but left behind a backwash of Irish people, which to native New Yorkers semed disproportionately large.[2]

The majority of the German immigrants scattered from the city almost as soon as they landed. Giving a lucrative business to the transportation companies, they pushed westward toward communities in upstate New York, Pennsylvania, Ohio, Illinois, Michigan, Wisconsin, and across the border to Canada. Those having the means, traveled to the distant West —Wisconsin, Iowa, and Missouri—while the poorest entered the factory areas of New England or hunted jobs in New York and other Eastern cities. However, even poor people managed to leave the seaboard to seek out relatives and friends in the interior.[3] During the fifties an even larger proportion of immigrants of nearly all nationalities were prosperous enough to forsake New York for inland towns, farms, and forests. Immigrant remittances helped many of the poorer newcomers to reach their goals and lessened the demands upon the Commissioners of Emigration for relief and medical care.[4] In 1860 slightly more than half of the 105,162 immigrants arriving at the port planned to settle in New York State, but the City Inspector later estimated that only 15,000, or about 14 per cent, chose to stay in the Empire City.[5]

In relation to the native population of the city, however, the actual number of aliens who settled where they landed was large. Over half the population of Manhattan Island in 1855 was of foreign birth; 54 per cent of these were natives of Ireland and 29 per cent had come from the German states.[6] It was a well-known assumption that, despite their rural background, the Irish forsook the land and congregated in American cities; but it was hardly realized that thousands of Germans, English, Scotch, and French lingered in New York for the same reasons. Being most numerous, the Irish attracted the most attention.

From a nucleus of artisans who came to the United States after the Napoleonic Wars, New York acquired a sizable foreign population long before the Irish famine migration of the forties. New York and other Eastern cities then offered the best employment opportunities for craftsmen and attracted later arrivals who might better have remained farmers. Many of the earlier artisans were skilled Scotch-Irish weavers from Ulster, who had farmed at home to raise their own food but became urbanized through employment in the infant textile industry in American cities.[7]

In addition to those who made New York City their destination, many immigrants arrived with little or no money and were forced to remain where they landed. Ignorance and suspicion, soon awakened by the runners and fraudulent "intelligence offices," may have deterred some of the Irish from settling on the land, but poverty was the decisive reason for terminating their journey at New York.[8] In the forties and fifties the city's Irish community was considerably enlarged by extremely poor immigrants who possessed neither the fare for leaving town nor the funds to rent or buy land, had they so desired. With the exception of a few merchants, the wealthier Irish, like the wealthier Germans, heeded the advice of immigrant societies and departed. "The pith and marrow of Ireland, with money and value—averaging between 100 and 5,000 dollars each family—have arrived, within the past two years, in our seaboard cities" remarked the *Irish American* in 1849. "These emigrants do not stop in cities to spend their money and fool away their time. They go directly into the interior to seek out the best locations as farmers, traders, and so forth."[9]

Dislike of farming probably induced others to shun the countryside. Although most of the new arrivals were from the rural districts of Ireland, their knowledge of farming usually was limited to the tending of impoverished potato patches, an experience which gave them a decided distaste for agriculture. Land had so long been associated with oppression in Ireland that the Irish in America were "seldom found felling the forest or turning up the virgin prairie on their own account" but settled at sites of public works, in villages, and especially in large cities.[10] A few enterprising canal and railway workers saved enough to purchase land at nominal prices along the Erie and Lackawanna railroads, but the mass of Irish laborers were rootless unmarried men or husbands who returned in off seasons to their families and acquaintances in New York and other large cities.[11] Many remitted their savings to the Emerald Isle and later returned to the Empire City to meet wives and children sailing westward on prepaid passage tickets to happy reunions in America.[12]

The absence of co-operation among Irish immigrants further thickened the Celtic ranks in New York. Unlike the Germans, Swiss, and Dutch, the poverty-stricken Irish came to the United States as individuals rather than as family groups or bands of colonizers following a chosen leader. The flight from famine did not permit of lengthy advance preparations, and the wretched condition of many who found themselves stranded in New York left them friendless, planless, almost hopeless. Those having the stamina and the financial means for pushing to the interior were handicapped by ignorance of travel conditions; and the initial concentration of the Irish in cities produced few protective associations comparable to those created by the Germans wherever they settled.[13]

The gregariousness of aliens in strange surroundings served to weld them into distinct social entities in New York and other large cities. The Irish adherence to the Roman Catholic faith set the children of Erin apart from the Protestant communities in which they lived and placed them on the defensive. Common memories of the Green Isle provided another bond of fellowship. Thriving upon the Irish love of people and whiskey, Irish saloons and political clubs maintained local loyalties, as did the fire and police forces, with their large Irish memberships. "The Irish are a social people," explained the *Irish American*, "and require great self-denial to induce them to forsake the society of their kindred and kind, and take up their abode in less strictly settled locations, even though sure of becoming prosperous by so doing." [14] In lesser degree this was also true of other immigrant groups who found in Little Germany, Little Italy, and the Ghetto the languages and habits to which they had long been accustomed.

The immigrant communities, moreover, had an important economic function in providing job opportunities not likely to occur elsewhere. Foreign-born importers and tradesmen relied, in most cases, upon the immigrants themselves. Food and liquor dealers in particular found their clientele in the foreign districts of town, where Old World habits persisted and where one could eat Westphalia ham, Magdeburg sauerkraut, Gruyère cheese, tripe *à la Parisienne*, or spaghetti and macaroni.[15] Brewers and distillers, bakers and confectioners, butchers and grocers likewise played prominent roles in the immigrant community. In the many small workshops and stores, foreign-born manufacturers and merchants employed workers who spoke the same language and thereby forestalled the friction which took place among the unskilled laborers.[16]

The fortunes of the immigrant were enormously influenced by the type and duration of his first employment in the New World: to find a job was the most immediate need. In the early decades of the nineteenth century emigrants were advised to take with them certificates of good character or letters of recommendation from prominent persons, usually magistrates or clergymen. Such documents were most effective when addressed to some "respectable" person at the port of debarkation.[17] A fortunate few, usually clerks, bookkeepers, and young merchants, came to New York with letters to importers or wholesalers, who obligingly made efforts to find them positions. A few prominent immigrant merchants who had established themselves in the city's commercial circles took pride in employing newcomers of their own nationality.[18] One of these earlier, financially successful immigrants was Grant Thorburn, a Scotch nail maker, who, after opening a shop in New York at the turn of the century, abandoned his calling and became first a grocer and later a florist. After 1810 Thorburn acquired wealth and fame as the leading seedsman of the city. For many years his store in Liberty Street was a lounging place for immigrant horticulturists and a clearinghouse of job information and advice for newly arrived Scotch gardeners.[19] Mass immigration, however, placed a strain on the benevolence of individuals, and most aliens had to shift for themselves or depend upon private agencies in their quest for work.

So many aliens passed through New York City that it became the largest recruiting center for foreign workers in America. In all the newspapers appeared notices for farm hands, laborers, miners, servants, governesses, nurses, skilled mechanics, and factory hands. Employers, both native and foreign-born, advertised in the immigrant press.[20] Labor contractors made periodical visits to New York, recruited the Irish in the slums, and shipped them to the South and West. German innkeepers hired Germans and carried on a minor forwarding business; and employment agencies mushroomed all over the city, some of them maintaining regular correspondence with factory owners and contractors from whom they received orders to hire and transport immigrants.[21]

As immigrant aid societies sought positions for newly landed aliens, the oldest and most efficient service was provided by the German Society. Many thousands of farmers, laborers, and servants were sent to employers in the interior of the country, but large numbers of artisans were directed to places in the metropolis. In 1853, a year of tremendous German immigration, the society sent weavers to Rhode Island, miners to Virginia, laborers to farms and railroads throughout the United States, and found jobs in New York for cabinetmakers, tailors, shoemakers, metalworkers, and other craftsmen.[22] The Irish Emigrant Society stood in the same relationship to the Irish but was handicapped by their greater numbers and less diversified skills.[23] During the years after 1825 job help was proffered by many smaller agencies, benevolent and mutual aid societies, and political and social clubs of each nationality.[24] Some of these organizations were patronized by foreign consuls residing in the city, and at least one received aid from the head of a European state.[25]

Native philanthropic agencies also grappled with the employment problems of alien workers. Apparently, the earliest was the Society for the Encouragement of Faithful Domestic Servants, founded in 1825; ten years later, the Society for the Promotion of Knowledge and Industry operated an employment office where an overwhelming majority of the job seekers were foreigners.[26] However, the orientation of immigrants was never a major function of such institutions. It was not until mid-century that private American philanthropy undertook the specific task of finding jobs for newcomers regardless of nationality. In 1854 the American and Foreign Emigrant Protective and Employment Society was formed for this purpose and to shield the newcomers from fraud on both sides of the Atlantic.[27] In the succeeding years a number of other organizations facilitated the employment on the land of the city's helpless and crippled poor.[28]

The work of private agencies was considerably lightened when the largest single employment office was opened in 1847 by the Board of Commissioners of Emigration. Through correspondence with labor contractors, the commissioners sent boat and train loads of unskilled immigrants to the interior, and operations expanded so rapidly that in 1850 an enlarged "Intelligence Bureau and Labor Exchange" was established. During its first full year of operation, this office relieved and provided employment for eighteen thousand newcomers. As applications increased, the labor exchange set up branch offices in seven states and became truly national in scope.[29] During the fifties, an average of over fifteen thousand persons a year obtained jobs through the exchange.[30]

In a city of countless boardinghouses, large hotels, and elegant mansions of the elite, servants were in constant demand. Domestic service, in most instances, required few if any previously gained skills and admirably met the needs of transplanted peasant women and girls. Thus, by

1855, nearly one quarter of all the immigrants in the city were household help, "nurses," laundresses, cooks, and waiters.[31] Barred from American households because of ignorance of the English language, Continental Europeans usually turned to their wealthier compatriots already established in New York.[32] A few from the Caribbean and Latin America lived in the homes of the British, Spanish, and French merchants who employed them.[33] Newcomers from the British Isles, on the other hand, were hired by all but the German-speaking families.

Nearly all the domestic servants who came from Great Britain were born in Ireland. Of the ten thousand to twelve thousand estimated to be in New York City in 1846, between seven thousand and eight thousand were said to be Irish, another two thousand Germans, and the rest French, Americans, and a sprinkling of other nationalities.[34] A decade later nearly 80 per cent of the thirty-five thousand foreign-born servants and waiters living on Manhattan were Irish, while the Germans supplied another 15 per cent.[35] Irish servants formed a quarter of the Irish working population, whereas German servants comprised only one tenth of the German workers.[36] This relative paucity of German domestics resulted from the Teutonic practice of migrating in family groups, an impossibility for the thousands of single Irish girls and women who could barely pay their passage or who reached New York only through the philanthropic efforts of others. Once in the Empire City, Irish women were far better off in wealthier private households than as miserable seamstresses living singly in the slums or as laborers' wives forced to sew in order to make ends meet. German families remained together, often using skills such as tailoring which women and children had shared in Europe. Other immigrant women followed the German pattern: domestic service claimed nearly 15 per cent of the Welsh, 16 per cent of the Swiss, 14.5 per cent of the French, and 10.5 per cent of the Scottish working people living in the city.[37] Among workers born in England, the British provinces of North America, and Latin America, about one tenth of each group became servants.[38]

An initial handicap of the Catholic Irish servant girls was the prejudice they encountered in America. Potential employers disliked and even feared their religion, shuddered at "Irish impulsiveness" and turbulence, and were disgusted and morally shocked at the Irish propensity for strong drink. While some Americans preferred to hire natives of specific countries, no other immigrant nationality was proscribed as the Catholic Irish were. In congested cities like New York, the presence of a large Irish population sharpened mutual antagonisms, and discrimination against the children of Erin was flaunted in public.[39] The

Irish boiled with indignation upon reading the hated words, "No Irish need apply," or their equivalent, as in these advertisements:

WANTED—An English or American woman, that understands cooking, and to assist in the work generally if wished; also a girl to do chamber work. None need apply without a recommendation from their last place. *IRISH PEOPLE* need not apply, nor any one that will not rise at 6 o'clock, as the work is light and the wages sure. Inquire at 359 Broadway.[40]

WOMAN WANTED.—To do general housework . . . English, Scotch, Welsh, German, or any country or color except Irish.[41]

All the more obnoxious to the Irish were indications of a preference for the Negro. As the tradition of servitude and the continuing stigma of inferiority prevented most Negroes from pursuing skilled trades, they followed the only course open to them: common labor and the various service occupations. By 1855 some two thousand colored persons were servants, laundresses, cooks, and waiters—over half of all the gainfully employed Negroes.[42] As waiters and coachmen, they were the chief competitors of the Irish, and they sometimes competed with foreigners in menial occupations as whitewashers, carpet shakers, chimney sweeps, and bootblacks.[43] Colored servants were considered more submissive than the Celts, whose reputation for docility under their English rulers was extremely questionable.[44]

Despite the anti-Irish feeling, the great preponderance of Irish house-keepers, nurses, chambermaids, charwomen, laundresses, cooks, and waiters was evidence of a pressing need for them. Good workers usually had no difficulty in getting jobs.[45] Once hired, Irish women found security in the shelter and food provided with such employment, as well as some chance to save money and raise their social status. In the mid-forties wages ranged from $4.00 to $10.00 and averaged $6.00 per month, in addition to free board, lodging, and time for mending and washing. Chambermaids and houseworkers received $5.00 to $6.00 and slop-women $4.00 monthly. Cooks, ladies' maids, nurses, and waiters were better paid, enjoyed more comfortable living quarters, and earned extra compensation if they cared for children.[46]

Although efficient, honest, and virtuous, Irish servant girls astonished even their compatriots by their self-assurance. Poor and uneducated, they reflected in their deportment a newly won status far above the wretchedness of their lot in the Old Country. In New York they often mistook "forwardness if not impertinence" for independence, asserted the *Irish American*,[47] they dressed "too expensively and showily for their calling" and assumed "unbecoming airs." Some forgot themselves "so far as to *hire the employer,* in place of the employer hiring them." [48]

As did the Irish, but in lesser degree, Catholic immigrants from other lands met with religious discrimination in New York. Advertisements for Protestant governesses, cooks, and maids blackballed many French, Germans, and Swiss.[49] Nevertheless, Continental Europeans profited from the vogue of hiring French servants and particularly from the favoritism of an aristocracy of alien merchants.[50]

The employment of women in the Empire City was not limited to domestic service; women were conspicuous in the needle trades. Until the middle of the century, the large majority of seamstresses were American women: wives and widows of mariners, mechanics, and laborers; most of the milliners were also natives, but a sizable proportion was English and French.[51] Dressmakers doing piecework in their homes received $1.00 to $3.00 for each dress, and privately employed seamstresses earned sixty-two and a half cents, seventy-five cents and $1.00 a day.[52] Less independent were the seamstresses in the ready-made clothing industry, who suffered a degradation probably unequaled in any other skilled trade.[53] The competition of country women swarming into the city depressed wages long before the days of immigrant sweatshops. In 1845 the journeymen dressmakers toiled fourteen to sixteen hours a day for the weekly pittance of $1.25 to $1.50.[54] Apprentices worked for six months without wages and frequently paid their employers $10.00 or $15.00 for the privilege of learning the trade.[55]

In the late forties the earlier trickle of foreign women into the sewing trades quickened into a rising flood. The basis of the sweating system had been laid by American employers and American workers, but by mid-century, immigrants not only competed with native labor but contributed as employers to the exploitation of the operatives.[56] Helping to create their own jobs by their demand for cheap dresses, cloaks, and bonnets, the newcomers gradually assumed a dominant role in the sewing trades. By 1855 two thirds of the New York dressmakers, seamstresses, milliners, shirt and collar makers, embroiderers, lace fringe, tassel, and artificial flower makers were foreign-born.[57] Sixty-nine per cent of these immigrants were Irish and 14 per cent German, although in relation to their respective working populations, only 5 per cent of the Irish, English, Scotch, and French and 2 per cent of the Germans (including German Jews) were dressmakers.[58]

The preponderance of Irish seamstresses was a result, not of choice, but of necessity. Single Irish women, unable to find positions as servants, found the sewing trades the only occupations open to them. Some had become familiar in Ireland with the rudiments of dressmaking. Others mistakenly saw in easily learned needlework the road to independence and advancement. Married women, finding it impossible for their families to subsist on workmens' wages in a decade of rising living costs, tried their hand at the needle.

If sewing and domestic service claimed the largest proportion of immigrant women, the rough and heavy labor which contributed so much to the city's material development absorbed more men than any other single occupation. Fourteen per cent of all the gainfully employed immigrants in 1855 were porters and laborers.[59] These were the men who comprised nearly 21,800 of the city's 23,300 unskilled laborers. Negroes, accounting for another 700, were the only natives forced by circumstances to compete on this level with the newcomers.[60] White Americans avoided manual labor, not because they disliked it, but because the foreign born monopolized the work and created for the natives the social and economic incentives to aspire to lighter employment.[61]

In New York, as in other Eastern cities, the majority of laborers were Irish. As early as 1827, a cautious English traveler observed "the lowest stations of the hard-working classes" to be "generally filled by Irishmen, who are as much vilified here, whether justly or not I cannot tell, as in England or Scotland." [62] During the following decades, especially after 1845, thousands of poor Irish longshoremen, congregating at the wharves, followed the orders of their stevedore bosses.[63] The stevedores were skilled men responsible for stowing cargo, while the longshoremen did the heavy work of hoisting freight into and out of the ship's holds. Several shipping houses had their own private longshoremen—Grinnell, Minturn & Co., for example, employing seventy at one time.[64] By 1855 the sons of Erin comprised 87 per cent of the foreign-born laborers in the city.[65] More than one fifth of all the gainfully employed Irish living on Manhattan Island were laborers.[66] In the shipyards and in the warehouses and workshops many Irishmen met their first opportunities. Others labored as quarrymen, blasters, and rockmen in the near-by limestone quarries. Whenever new buildings were erected or old ones repaired, Pat and Mike were on hand, tapped from that reservoir of labor which produced in time many skilled workmen in the building trades.

Immigrants from other lands did not join the ranks of the laboring Irish. In 1855 only about 5 per cent of the gainfully employed Germans, Scandinavians, and Italians, respectively, were laborers.[67] Slightly above 3 per cent each of the Welsh, Scots, and English were laborers, and a mere 2.5 per cent of the French and Swiss, respectively.[68] These newcomers, unlike the Irish, had not fled from disease or famine; some had money, although most were poor. Their most treasured assets were occupational skills adaptable to the industrial, commercial, and agricultural life of the Empire City.

In the immediate neighborhood of New York City, an untold number of immigrants swelled the shifting population of farm laborers. They worked on the prosperous market gardens, orchards, and small farms in the Hudson Valley and on Long Island which sent vegetables, fruits, dairy products, hay, and grain to the New York markets.[69] Scotch and English farm hands performing skilled tasks earned $1.00 to $1.50 per day. The Irish undertook the humbler work at rates of 75¢ to $1.00 per day.[70] At harvest time there usually was a shortage of farm laborers, but in the winter months when their activities slackened, the Irish turned to lumbering, teaming, and odd jobs.[71]

Some of the newcomers became independent farmers. A number of English and Scotch farmers arrived with enough capital to buy their own land; they preferred, however, to settle in upstate New York, the Western states, or Canada.[72] German farmers and their German hired hands played a conspicuous part in the agriculture of the New York area. Upper Manhattan in 1834 had few farms, the wealthy landowners leaving the sod unturned with the knowledge that land values were rising rapidly; but by the outbreak of the Civil War, large sections of former pasture, meadow, and woodland had been brought under cultivation.[73] The advent of German market gardeners hastened this transformation. "With some few exceptions," remarked a census marshal for upper Manhattan in 1855, "the Market Gardens are Cultivated by Germans." [74] Near the Brooklyn shore, from Williamsburg to Astoria, lay gardens and well-tilled farms which had been developed at the turn of the century by imported Germans. Fifty years later these farms were still tended by whole families of Germans—men, women, and children— and cultivated with an intensity and thoroughness rare among the Americans.[75] To the south, a group of successful German farmers in Flatbush became large enough in 1847 to found the first Lutheran Church in East New York, and in Rockland County across the Hudson and in other near-by areas prosperous Germans grew fruit and vegetables for the New York market.[76]

Gardeners, too, obtained employment as the "upper ten" landscaped their residences overlooking the Hudson and Harlem rivers. In 1855 over 90 per cent of the gardeners living on Manhattan were immigrants. The Germans, Scots, and French, who were generally considered superior to American gardeners, were numerous out of all proportion to their respective populations.[77] Single men generally were engaged by the year at wages of $8.00 to $16.00 per month, plus bed, board, and washing. On large estates and at the country homes of middle-class families, they raised vegetables, tended flower beds, and sometimes managed green-houses.[78] By frugal living, it was possible within a few years to rent several acres near the city and become independent market gardeners; conversely, during poor seasons, some market gardeners found it more profitable to return to the status of hired hands.[79]

More independent than gardeners, farm hands, and laborers were the men in occupations concerned with local transportation. As carters, draymen, and teamsters they handled baggage for the incessant flow of travelers, hauled commercial cargoes in the congested business and ware-house districts, carried ice, coal, and wood to domestic consumers, and brick, stone, and earth for construction projects. Of over three thousand foreign-born carters and teamsters in 1855, four fifths were Irish, one eighth German, although proportionally few immigrants entered these callings.[80] The sons of Erin likewise predominated among the immigrant omnibus and stage drivers, hackmen, conductors, and other railroad em-ployees. As private coachmen, they contended, not only with native whites and other English-speaking immigrants, but also with Negroes depending upon the bounty of New York's wealthy families.[81] In an age of horse power the care of animals was entrusted almost entirely to the Irish. Menial work in stables was not a new experience for an agricul-tural people, and additional skills were quickly learned. In 1855, 84 per cent of the immigrant hostlers—nearly all in the city—were born in Ire-land, 12 per cent in Germany.[82] Irishmen also were the keepers of many stables, although in this more dignified position 15 per cent of the foreign-born livery stable keepers were English.[83]

On the rivers, as on the island, foreigners contributed their labor. They played a minor role in river transportation, but the Irish were prominent among them. In the mid-fifties, 71 per cent of the immigrant boatmen, watermen, and ferrymen riding the waves of New York Harbor were natives of Ireland; 9 per cent were born in Germany, and 6.5 per cent in England.[84] The Irish, Germans, and English merely showed superiority in numbers; in relation to population, the Scandinavians were strongest. The few Swedish, Norwegian, and Danish boatmen rep-resented 2.67 per cent of all the Scandinavian working people.[85] These transportation workers were catalysts in the gradual process of urban expansion. The carter at the Battery, the teamster on Bloomingdale Road, the East River ferryman, the cattle drover at Bull's Head landing —these men were vital links in the moving chain of production and trade.[86]

New York's commercial fame obscured the less spectacular but vital role of its industrial population. Immigrant workmen dominated nearly every productive activity, from crude carpentry to the deft handiwork of the violinmaker or lapidary. Of the artisans and factory workers living on Manhattan Island in 1855, three fourths were born outside the United States.[87] Many of the Continental Europeans had partaken of the rural, domestic handicrafts characteristic of southern Germany, Alsace and Lorraine, and the Swiss cantons. The cloth woven by hand-loom weavers, the clothing made by local tailors, and the furniture built by village cabinetmakers were products of men who had spent three to six years of their youth as wandering journeymen. Traveling from town to town in Europe, tailors, linen weavers, cobblers, tanners, curriers and saddlers, tilers, bricklayers, potters, smiths, cabinetmakers, joiners, wheelwrights, and other artisans had learned the trades which they now plied in New York.[88]

New York also sheltered city and seaport folk. Highly trained German cutlers and hardware workers from the neighborhood of Solingen found their way to Manhattan Island and there monopolized the making of surgical instruments.[89] The Herter brothers, later well known as interior decorators, hailed from Stuttgart.[90] Jewelers, confectioners, tailors, cabinetmakers, and piano makers were among the many craftsmen from Paris and London.[91] British and Scandinavian ship carpenters and riggers found employment in the bustling East River shipyards.[92] These were but a few of the artisans who received their apprenticeship on European soil and who became teachers of Americans and immigrants of later generations.[93]

VII

GAINING A FOOTHOLD

Industry

"WE VENTURE TO SAY that One Half (at least) of the mechanics of New York—machinists, turners, ship-wrights, carpenters, cabinet-makers, smiths of all kinds, practical engineers &c., &c., &c., are Irish," wrote the editor of the *Irish American* in 1852.[1] Within five years, the editor of the *Staats-Zeitung* could make as challenging a boast: German bakers and confectioners, he asserted, appeared at every turn, German artisans produced fancy goods and enameled jewelry "which buyers believe to be 'imported,'" and the existence of many large shoemaking, tailoring, and woodworking establishments depended upon German workmen. "Many, if not most of the houses in the eastern portion of the city," he claimed, "have been built by German masons and carpenters . . . and the plumbing, painting, glazing and tin roofing by those who were brought up to the trade in the fatherland."[2]

Proud contentions these, but not silly exaggerations, for each national group was eager to prove the greatness of its contribution to the city's economic growth, and the Irish in particular wished to dispel the common impression that all Irishmen ever did was to dig ditches. The statistics of the state census of 1855 failed to reveal the extent of immigrant participation in the skilled occupations, but an analysis of the marshals' schedules reveals that the foreign born entered every productive calling from routine factory work to the most highly skilled of individual crafts. Certain industries, however, showed phenomenal concentrations of immigrants. In the building trades, the clothing industry, and the working of leather, especially shoemaking, newcomers from many lands found their first opportunities, and a fortunate few advanced toward key positions as contractors, manufacturers, and shop owners. These industries employed more than one quarter of all the gainfully employed immigrants in 1855.[3]

In the building trades, more than half the employees were born outside the United States, and of these, over half were natives of Ireland and one fourth of Germany.[4] The sons of Erin contributed more than three fourths of the foreign-born masons, plasterers, and bricklayers, nearly

half the carpenters, and a third of the painters and glaziers.[5] Over ten
thousand Irishmen and Germans worked in the building industries, rep-

TABLE 1. THE BUILDING TRADES

Nativity	Number for Whom Information Was Available	Percentage of Builders and Building Trades Employees [a] to Total Gainfully Employed of the Same Nationality, 1855
Scotland	798	19.15
Wales	66	14.57
British North America	169	14.06
England	1,333	13.71
Scandinavia	48	8.62
Ireland	7,570	8.56
Germany	3,283	7.17
Italy	34	7.14
Portugal	4	7.14
Bohemia	3	7.00
Switzerland	33	6.95
Russia	4	6.78
Netherlands	20	6.76
Poland	39	6.54
Belgium	5	5.26
France	153	5.00
Latin America	13	4.66
Hungary	3	3.53
Spain	5	3.47
Total foreign born	13,583	8.71

[a] Includes stonecutters and polishers, masons, bricklayers, plasterers, plumbers, roofers
and slaters, painters, varnishers and glaziers, sawyers, and carpenters. Contractors have
been included as builders.

Computed from data derived from the *New York State Census of 1855*, MSS schedules.
Cf. Appendix, pp. 214–217.

resenting 8.6 per cent and 7.2 per cent of their respective working
populations; but the natives of England, Scotland, Wales, and British
North America found even greater opportunities.[6] Nearly one fifth of
the gainfully employed Scots and about 14 per cent of the English, Welsh,
and British North Americans worked in the building trades.[7] Proportionally large numbers of the natives of Scandinavia, Italy, Switzerland,
the Netherlands, Poland, and France also entered these occupations.[8]

Contributing directly to population growth and to the physical development and expansion of New York, thousands of immigrants created their own jobs as building workers. Not only did their invasion of lower Manhattan induce natives to build new homes on the outskirts of town, but their occupancy of slum areas led to the erection of huge barrack-like tenements especially designed to absorb more transplanted Europeans. These newcomers supplied most of the labor for the construction and maintenance of commercial buildings, extension of the avenues, and the adding of new wharves along the Hudson beyond Greenwich Village. As the city moved northward, stonecutters, masons, bricklayers, and carpenters led the way. Stoneyards and carpentry shops abounded in the area above 14th Street in 1855, especially near the shipyards, and above 40th Street many independent carpenters worked by the day for the Third Avenue Railroad.[9]

In the building trades, some immigrants, especially those who spoke English and whose techniques resembled the American, found unique possibilities of bettering themselves.[10] Much of the work was seasonal and therefore gave to the journeyman a mobility which was denied to the more sedentary craftsmen. In the winter, when work was scarce and wages low, many carpenters worked in the shipyards, and masons, plasterers, and bricklayers found better pay when they migrated southward.[11] This lack of local attachment, together with the great demand for construction in the summer months, aided journeymen to become masters and masters to branch out as builders and contractors, owners of quarries, stoneyards, and marble works.[12] Sometimes an immigrant builder was enriched through contracts for public works. Thus Alexander Masterson, a journeyman mason from Scotland, became a builder and architect and made a fortune by obtaining contracts for public buildings.[13] Even ambitious laborers and construction workers, most of whom were from Ireland, advanced to positions as foremen, and some ultimately became independent contractors.[14] Whereas the English-speaking builders and contractors employed English, Irish, and Scotch workmen wherever they were needed, the operations of the German builders were confined to the areas of German settlement, where employers and employees spoke the same language and followed similar technical methods.[15]

If immigrants helped to house New Yorkers, they also clothed them. As in the building trades, every European nation was represented in some branch of the clothing industry. By 1855, some 20,000 foreign-born tailors, dressmakers, hatters, furriers, and clothiers included nearly 13 per cent of the immigrant working population of the city.[16] Although the actual number of tailors of certain nationalities might be small, its significance lay in the relation it bore to the total number of gainfully employed of those nationalities. Thus a mere 202 immigrants from Poland engaged in the manufacture or sale of clothing represented 35 per cent of the Polish-born working population; and whereas more Irish than Germans engaged in these occupations, the proportion of Germans was nearly twice as large.

TABLE 2. THE CLOTHING INDUSTRY

Nativity	Number for Whom Information Was Available	Percentage of Gainfully Employed Clothing Workers and Clothiers to Total Gainfully Employed of the Same Nationality, 1855
Poland	209	35.07
Russia	14	23.73
Netherlands	57	19.26
Germany	8,307	18.15
Hungary	85	17.78
British North America	178	14.82
France	417	13.89
Switzerland	60	12.63
Scandinavia	67	12.03
England	1,111	11.42
Ireland	9,128	10.32
Scotland	388	9.37
Italy	39	8.19
Wales	30	6.63
Total foreign born	20,055 [a]	12.87

[a] Includes 35 natives of Belgium, Spain, Portugal, Bohemia, and Latin America.
This table is based on information obtained from the manuscript schedules of the *New York State Census of 1855*. Included under the heading "clothing industry" are clothiers, dressmakers, furriers, hat- and capmakers, and tailors.

Despite the diversity of the people in the clothing industry, the Irish and later the Germans came to assume the dominant role. Whereas in 1840 the majority of the city's ready-made clothing workers were English, Scotch, and American, the famine migration of the forties left the Irish the most numerous group by the middle of the century.[17] In the custom trade, the English and the Irish advanced to become cutters, foremen, and even manufacturers.[18] At the same time, the work formerly performed by American and Irish women was taken over by German families, whose job lay in putting the garments together.[19]

Tailors were already numerous among the Germans in the early thirties.[20] As ready-made clothes acquired popularity, this type of tailoring offered employment to poor German immigrants; meanwhile, the German master tailors found it difficult to compete with clothing "factories," and not a few surrendered their independence for the security of a weekly wage.[21] While the Irish worked in the back shops of the merchant tailors, most of the Germans toiled at home, assisted by their wives and children.[22] Although the family system was not their innovation, the Germans probably made the first attempt to introduce a division of labor by developing in their homes machine sewing, basting, and other separate but still indefinite divisions of the ready-made clothing industry.[23]

By 1855 the German tailors had surpassed the Irish and formed the largest group of artisans of any single nationality. Nearly nine tenths of all the tailors living in the city were born in Germany or Ireland; of these newcomers the Germans comprised 55 per cent, the Irish 34 per cent.[24] The 6,700 German tailors for whom information was available comprised 14.7 per cent of the German working population, but the Irish tailors, numbering 4,200, accounted for only 4.6 per cent of the Irish workers.[25]

Among the German tailors were many Jews, who played an increasingly conspicuous part in the clothing industry.[26] Jews from Bavaria and Baden took to the needle in New York during the latter thirties, and a decade later were joined by Jews from Prussia, Silesia, and Poland.[27] By 1855 no less than 22 per cent of the gainfully employed immigrants from Poland, mostly Jews, were tailors.[28] Jews from England, France, Switzerland, and the Low Countries, and a few from Russia found their best opportunities as tailors, hat- and capmakers, and "clothiers." [29] Those Jews who came with little or no tailoring experience began as helpers, learned the necessary processes, and advanced to become full-fledged artisans.[30] Others saved enough money to open small "old clo'" shops on Chatham Street.[31]

In the manufacture of ready-made clothing after the middle of the century, wages in New York were generally higher than in Boston, which became a center of factory-made clothes. The New York tailors earned $8.00 to $10.00 a week, nearly twice the wages of the Boston operatives.[32] In the depression years of 1854–1855, however, the New York tailors received $25.00 to $35.00 per month, or the equivalent of $6.00 to $9.00 per week.[33] Women usually earned only half as much as the men. Whereas the male clothing trimmers in six large companies received $30.00 and $35.00 per month in 1855, most of the women earned but $15.00.[34] One employer paid 300 female mantilla makers $17.00 per month, and another firm doled out a monthly pittance of $10.00 to 200 makers of coats, pants, and vests.[35] Most immigrant women received no more than was paid American farm girls, who at least had the advantage of being able to leave their jobs and return to their country homes.[36]

As in tailoring, the manufacture of shoes evolved from the simple stage of the journeyman-master relationship to that of the merchant capitalist, the contractor, and the employee. Until mid-century all labor was done by hand; and when in 1852 the sewing machine was adapted to the making of uppers, only women workers were affected.[37] Customs and retail shop work remained important, but toward the middle of the century mass production was undertaken by merchant capitalists who engaged contractors, who, in turn, hired the journeymen and assigned them to specialized operations.[38] That New York was far behind New England in the production of factory-made shoes was in no small measure due to the presence of highly trained shoemakers and to the pre-eminence of the Empire City as a leather mart.[39] At the outbreak of the Civil War, 56 establishments in the Eighth Ward employed 384 men and 28 women, and 36 shops in the Second Ward engaged 688 men and 165 women, or an average of only 14 per plant in the two largest shoe districts of the city.[40]

Most of the 3,000 shoemakers in the city in 1845 were German, Irish, and French; the comparatively few Americans and English usually specialized in women's shoes.[41] Ten years later nearly all the shoemakers were foreign-born, half of them Germans and one third Irish.[42] As among the tailors, every European nationality was represented, with the natives of Germany, Poland, and France in the leading roles.[43]

TABLE 3. SHOEMAKERS

Nativity	Percentage of Shoemakers to Total Gainfully Employed of the Same Nationality, 1855
Germany	8.13
Poland	5.37
France	5.33
Switzerland	4.84
England	2.88
Ireland	2.04
Scotland	1.74

Computed from data derived from the *New York State Census of 1855*, MSS schedules. For more complete information, cf. Appendix, pp. 214–217.

As skilled immigrant shoemakers poured into New York, poverty and competition for jobs forced many to live wretchedly in cellar shops scantily furnished with bench and tools, a little leather, thread, wax, and sometimes a glass showcase.[44] "There is no class of mechanics in New York who average so great an amount of work for so little money as the journeymen shoemakers," asserted the *Tribune* in 1845:

The Number of journeymen out of employment is also large. . . . There are hundreds of them in the city constantly wandering from shop to shop in search of work, while many of them have families in an absolute state of want. . . . We have been in more than fifty cellars in different parts of the city, each inhabited by a shoemaker and his family. The floor is made of rough plank laid loosely down, the ceiling is not quite so high as a tall man. . . . There is no outlet back and of course no yard privileges of any kind. . . . In this . . . often live the man with his work-bench, his wife and five or six children of all ages, and perhaps a palsied grandfather or grandmother and often both.[45]

Many of these shoemakers were formerly independent craftsmen who, unable to compete with the production of cheap shoes under the contracting system, turned their little shoemaking businesses into repair shops.[46] Others were employed by the contractors, often Irishmen, stigmatized by one workman as "the greatest tyrants in the trade." [47] Although the wages paid by these contractors rose from an average of $4.00 to $6.00 per week in 1845 to an average of $7.00 to $8.00 in 1853, higher prices for food and rent wiped out the apparent gains of the journeymen.[48]

Whereas in the clothing industry and in shoemaking the Irish and the Germans supplied most of the immigrant workers, several important trades were almost completely dominated by German artisans. The historical background of certain industries which employed foreigners, the nature of the work, and the qualifications of the newcomers resulted in the concentration of Germans in the fields of cabinetmaking, piano making, and sugar refining. The art of refining sugar was brought to New York City by German settlers in pre-Revolutionary times, and by the early nineteenth century the industry was almost entirely in the hands of Germans.[49] As New York became a sugar refining center, skilled artisans introduced new techniques from Germany and England and at the same time added to the nucleus of German workers.[50] After the refineries switched to the use of steam, the industry blossomed into a big business, the large refineries hiring in addition to the sugar boilers a host of laborers, maintenance men, machinists, coopers, and box-makers.[51] Ten large refineries employed in 1854 well over a thousand

persons, mostly Germans, in jobs ranging from lowly common labor at
$20 to $30 per month to those of the experienced boilers receiving $1,000
to $2,000 annually.[52]

In even larger numbers the Germans applied their woodworking talents
to the making of furniture, to carving and gilding, and the fashioning of
window blinds. Cabinetmakers were conspicuous among the New York
Germans as early as 1835; and thereafter, although French, Irish,
English, Scotch, Dutch, and Scandinavian workmen entered the trade,
the Germans turned out most of the vast quantity of furniture made in
the Empire City.[53] In 1855 three fourths of the European upholsterers
and cabinetmakers were German.[54] Much of their work was crude and
cheap, but some of it was the elaborately carved and overdecorated
"Parisian fancy furniture" bought by the "up-Townish Ten Thousand,"
many of whom "never think of keeping the same furniture over one
season." [55] Master cabinetmakers, eager to exploit the fashion for French
furnishings, also induced French artisans to come to New York. "The
oldest and most wealthy of the cabinet warehouse-men in this city,"
wrote Nathaniel P. Willis, "has sold out an immense stock of high-
priced articles at auction, and sent to France for models and workmen
to start new [sic] with the popular taste." [56]

Woodworking was carried on in a few large establishments and in
many small, scattered shops, especially along the Hudson River between
Canal and Houston streets and in the German settlements on the East
Side. Before the panic of 1837, cabinetmakers earned $12.00 to $15.00
per week, but during the forties wages sank to $5.00 and $8.00.[57] In 1855,
most of the tiny workshops and all but one of the larger plants employing
at least forty journeymen paid average weekly wages of about $7.00 to
$10.00.[58] As New York consumed vast quantities of cheap tables, chairs,
sofas, beds, and chests, immigrants through sheer necessity allowed
themselves to be exploited. One of the largest furniture firms in the city
employed 140 sofa and chair makers at $28.00 per month, while several
smaller shops paid the pitiful wages of $10.00 and $15.00 per month.[59]

As in the furniture industry, German journeymen came to dominate in
piano manufacturing. Pianos had been commonly made in New York
as far back as 1785, and early in the nineteenth century, English, Scotch,
Welsh, and German piano makers set up their businesses in the Eastern
seaboard cities.[60] Beginning in the twenties, German piano makers came
in such large numbers that by 1840 they had secured a firm foothold in
New York.[61] The coming of these skilled artisans was hardly welcomed
by the native manufacturers. John Osborn, an American maker, complained that foreigners had "pilfered American methods of piano-building

and acoustic development, without any justice or gratitude, but sneer at native Americans and their abstract intelligence . . . which, however, has been in the past effective enough to create a nation, and fearless enough to fight for its honor." [62] If the master piano builders criticized the Germans, the English-speaking workmen disliked them even more. Their rivalry resulted in the formation in 1834 of the first American piano makers' society, which conducted a strike in protest against the employment of German workers.[63] Nevertheless, artisans trained in Germany continued to enter the New York shops, established their own firms, and shared in the transformation of a handicraft industry into a big business.[64] Although many immigrants remained wage earners, a few of the more fortunate individuals opened independent shops ranging in size from small back-yard buildings to the huge Steinway plant built in the 1860's.[65] Some tiny workshops employed only three or four men, but by the mid-fifties several firms hired well over a hundred, and one large company, Lighte, Newton, and Bradbury, reported 164 employees.[66] Aristocrats among cabinetmakers, these craftsmen earned the relatively high wages of $40 to $45 per month, and although some shops paid as little as $28, at least two hundred workmen received $50.[67] Nearly two thirds of the piano makers were immigrants, of whom 61 per cent were German, 11 per cent English, 11 per cent Irish, and the remainder mostly Scandinavian, French, and Scotch.[68]

As in piano making, cabinetmaking, and sugar refining, other industries showed similar concentration of nationalities. In 1845 the journeymen rag-carpet weavers were almost entirely Irish, Scotch, and German; ten years later the same groups, together with the English, included nearly all the immigrant weavers in the city.[69] Germans, dominating many of the handicrafts, accounted in 1855 for nearly all the immigrant cutlers, surgical instrument makers, gunsmiths, and lithographers.[70] Two thirds of the glass cutters were Irishmen, and disproportionately large numbers of watchcase makers were born in France and Switzerland, gold beaters and japanners in England, and ship riggers in the Scandinavian countries.[71]

As New York became a center of printing and publishing, English, Irish, and Scottish immigrants, working first as office help, acquired jobs as journeymen printers. In 1845 one third of the printing house employees were natives of the British Isles and of Canada; only a sprinkling of French and German printers found a livelihood in the city.[72] Most printers were engaged in the publishing of periodicals and books, but some worked in newspaper plants and in job-printing houses. The older and more experienced men earned $500 to $700 per year and the others between $300 and $450, usually at the rate of $5.00, $7.00, and $9.00 per week.[73] Americans retained their hold upon the English language press through the employment of boys who were permitted to work on their own hook after a short apprenticeship. These native "two-thirders" apparently gave the journeymen more competition than the immigrants.[74] By 1855, however, immigrant printers of many nationalities found jobs with foreign-language newspaper publishers, not a few of whom were refugees from the mid-century revolutions in Europe.[75] Bookbinders and book-folders were predominantly American, but a number of skilled English forwarders, marblers, gilders, and stampers appeared in the forties, as well as a few Germans and Irish.[76] After the middle of the century, the number of Irish bookbinders and -folders multiplied, and some Scots also were engaged in the trade.[77]

A larger proportion of British immigrants found jobs in the metallurgical trades, despite the sheer numbers of Irishmen and Germans. Whereas about 3.5 per cent of the gainfully employed Irish and Germans in 1855 were engaged in the heavy metal industries, the Scots boasted 9 per cent and the English and Welsh about 7.5 per cent.[78] The more burdensome tasks were performed by the sons of Erin, especially as blacksmiths and boilermakers, while the British and French, and to a lesser extent the Germans, were lodged in the more skilled callings.[79] Many of these immigrants were employed in foundries and ironworks, most of which were near the East River shipyards. With the shift from sail to steam, the foundries expanded and hired hundreds of men to produce marine engines and boilers.[80] Thus the Allaire works, which in 1829 engaged 200 hands, employed 450 in 1855 and about 1,000 in 1868.[81] The Novelty, the Morgan, the Fulton, the Secor works, and many smaller foundries, blacksmith and machine shops gave work to thousands of boilermakers, founders, machinists, and other metalworkers.[82]

At the site of the shipyards in the Eleventh Ward, and below Corlear's Hook, in the Seventh Ward, a large part of the population was in some way engaged in shipbuilding, repairing, and refitting.[83] In addition to the permanent workers, as many as three hundred shipwrights wandered from shop to shop, spending a day or two on each job. In this army of "floating help" were many journeymen who had completed their apprenticeship and were learning the techniques of the various master craftsmen.[84] Few of the maritime workers—ship carpenters, joiners, spar- and mast-makers, sailmakers, riggers, caulkers, and boat builders —were foreign-born. Nevertheless, in 1855 two thirds of the immigrants (including nearly all the immigrant caulkers) were born in Ireland.[85] Despite the numerical preponderance of Irish and Germans, the Scandinavians and British North Americans capitalized upon their years of experience in the forests and seaports of the north and showed the largest proportions of shipyard workers. Fully one tenth of the gainfully employed Swedes, Norwegians, and Danes, and nearly 6.5 per cent of the natives of Canada, Newfoundland, Nova Scotia, and New Brunswick worked in the maritime trades on Manhattan Island.[86]

Whether in the shipyards, foundries, workshops and warehouses, or in the home, the life of the artisan and factory worker was a tough struggle for existence. The working person rarely knew prosperity in "normal times," and in depression years he faced the specter of unemployment. After the paralyzing panic of 1837, one third of the working population was thrown out of work, and wages fell 30 to 50 per cent from 1839 to 1843.[87] During the next seven years wages remained stationary, but the cost of living was estimated to have risen nearly 50 per cent.[88] In 1853 the *Times* estimated that a workingman in New York City spent $600 a year, of which food, clothing, rent, and household expenses amounted to over $550, while other essential items cost another $15.[89] After a continued rise in family expenses, depression again struck sharply at the wage earner in 1854–1855, causing unemployment and widespread misery.[90] An Associated Working Men's Committee, a pressure group arising spontaneously out of this depression, estimated that 195,000 men, women, and children were in absolute want during the winter of 1854–1855.[91]

The call to arms in 1860 stimulated the tailoring, shoemaking, and metals industries but brought little improvement of living standards. Unemployment ceased, but wages failed to equal the rise in prices.[92] Only by the extraordinary income of military bounties, pay, and allotments, and through charity for soldiers' families unable to provide for themselves, was the working population able to sustain itself.[93]

Nevertheless, in spite of all the difficulties, New York offered chances of advancement to the immigrant. Through hard work and extremely frugal living, the building trades' employee could become a contractor, the clothing worker a shopkeeper or manufacturer, and the cabinetmaker a dealer. Many a newcomer started from scratch, toiled to save every penny, and later set up a small business of his own, hiring his more recently arrived countrymen, who started the process anew.

VIII

GAINING A FOOTHOLD

Trade, Business, and the Professions

IF A LARGE PERCENTAGE OF IMMIGRANTS became artisans and factory workers, many others were retailers, traders, and peddlers. Indeed, one of the surest methods of economic advancement for the newly arrived "greenhorn" was to acquire a basket and a small quantity of wares and peddle them wherever there was a likelihood of sale. Such a start required perseverance but little or no capital. Oswald Ottendorfer, later publisher of the *Staats Zeitung*, began his career in America by "peddling, in utter want and sheer desperation, baskets of gorgeously labeled beverages of doubtful composition among houses of questionable resort."[1]

The vast majority of peddlers were born in Ireland or Germany, many of the Irish selling farm produce and the Germans offering dry goods, clothing, and scores of other manufactured articles. Fruit and vegetable hucksters were mostly Irish women, who hawked oranges, apples, and groceries near the produce markets and on street corners.[2] Unlike the native peddlers from the country, who sold their produce directly from the farms, these immigrants bought their fruit and vegetables from middlemen, and in 1845 several hundred earned $3.00 to $5.00 a week only by haggling over prices with the wives of the working population.[3] Success enabled a peddler to rent a stand at one of the city markets and become a produce dealer or to operate an independent grocery store, where edibles were sold with the more profitable whiskey or brandy.

Irish peddlers always were numerous, but by 1855 the Germans had overtaken them both in numbers and in proportion to population. At the same time, natives of Poland and the Netherlands, although few in number, included many peddlers, whose names gave evidence of the Jews from these countries who took up peddling in America. Nearly all the Polish peddlers were Jews, as were many of the Dutch, while perhaps half of those born in Germany were Jews. In 1855 a minimum of 4 or 5 per cent of the gainfully employed Jews in New York City were peddlers.[4]

Frequently restricted by custom and legislation to petty commerce and shopkeeping in Europe, many Jewish immigrants probably were *Luftmenschen* without any specific vocational skills.[5] Strangers to the

TABLE 4. PEDDLERS

Nativity	Percentage of Peddlers to Total Gainfully Employed of the Same Nationality, 1855
Poland	9.06
Netherlands	4.05
Germany	2.06
France	1.07
Scandinavia	.90
Ireland	.85
Italy	.84

Computed from data derived from the MSS schedules of the *New York State Census of 1855*. For actual numbers of peddlers, cf. Appendix, pp. 214–217.

heavy physical labor of the Irish peasants and knowing nothing of agriculture, these newly arrived unskilled and penniless Jews were assisted by relatives, friends, and even strangers—as long as they were Jews—and encouraged to become peddlers.

When the newly arrived Israelite asks what he shall do to make a living, he is most commonly advised to go and peddle. Accordingly a basket is hastily fixed up, and he is hurried into the country. The country merchants . . . receive them [*sic*] coolly and oppose them step by step. An acrimonious feeling takes hold of the pedlar's heart—he is disappointed and discouraged, and yet he goes on from day to day, changes the basket for the bundle, the bundle for the horse and wagon peddling, and finally emerges a sleek, thrifty merchant. Have the history of one of these men and you have the history of them all.[6]

Like the Irish canal and railroad laborers, many Jewish peddlers left their families in New York and plied their business in distant towns and villages. Although their official residence remained in the Empire City, they returned only for special occasions and for the high holidays, Hanukkah, and Passover.[7] During the middle of the century they were joined by newly arrived Russian Jews who had learned to become glaziers in England while en route to America and who tramped the streets crying "glass put in!" [8]

The itinerant peddlers had their counterpart in the roving German whitewashers, scavengers, ragpickers, and cinder gatherers, and in the 1850's, the Italian fruit and flower hawkers, plaster statuette vendors, organ grinders, and bootblacks. Ignorant of the English language, friendless, fearing to settle as farmers in the country, these newcomers appeared in the slums of the Five Points and the shanty towns on the outskirts of the city.[9] The Germans, some with huge families, lived in abject poverty and occasionally resorted to begging, but perseverance and frugality enabled them to save money and to rise to more dignified occupations.[10] Less independent than the Germans were the Italian children sent out by their parents or by Italian employers on peddling and organ grinding tours. Few Italians owned their organs, but those who did were able to exploit the others, and parents who rented their organs were forced to take advantage of their children, who earned 37.5¢ to 75¢ a day tramping the streets of New York, Boston, and Philadelphia.[11] The comparative fortunes made by the pioneer organ grinders gave rise to the *padroni*, who made a business of importing Italian boys for these tours as wandering minstrels.[12]

The next step upward for the immigrant peddler was the small store. At the lowest level was the secondhand dealer. Old or abandoned buildings, sheds, and shanties near the waterfronts offered the cheapest locations for the dealers in old iron, brass, copper, tin, lead, bottles, rope, and rags. Nearly all the licensed junk shops were operated by Irishmen, who in 1855 comprised 224 of the 245 immigrant junk dealers.[13] As the Irish entered the junk business, the Jews became secondhand clothing dealers. One of the few industries in which in an earlier day the Jews of Europe had been permitted to engage was the selling of secondhand clothing, long an object of ridicule. After legal restrictions were lifted, Jews continued in this occupation, and those who came to New York gained a foothold in the local secondhand trade on Chatham Street.[14] On the same economic level were the pawnbrokers, among whom the Jews were prominent; their shops were concentrated in the Bowery, in Grand, Chatham, and Catherine streets on the East Side and in Greenwich Street with its myriads of poor immigrants.[15]

Of far greater importance to the foreign communities were the thousands of food dealers and retailers who flourished in New York. Immigrant shopkeepers, booksellers, apothecaries, coal, ice, and lumber dealers, important as they were, played a lesser role than the butchers and grocers, dairymen, fruit and produce dealers, and oystermen. It was no accident that in 1855 nearly 4 per cent of the gainfully employed newcomers were food dealers.[16] Immigrant women preferred to trade with people who understood their language, who did business in familiar ways, and who carried in stock those specialities which appealed to the various European peoples. Moreover, the store served a social purpose. Located on the first floor or in the basement of a tenement or boardinghouse, it was a convenient gathering place of tenants and boarders, and it also functioned as a general store, where the "grocer" sold nearly everything needed in the household.[17] Nearly every "grocery" sold liquor, which was the chief source of profit.[18] What the grocery was to the Teutons, the "rum hole" was to the Celts, both affording an atmosphere of conviviality which broke the monotony of the lives of the working people.

Following the great immigration of the Germans in the fifties, New York's familiar corner groceries passed from Irish to German hands.[19] Nearly all the German grocers were immigrants from the mercantile and dairy regions of the lower Rhine valley, the *Plattdeutschen,* or Low Germans. Some were prosperous, owning their own buildings and taking in boarders, but the majority were satisfied with modest but comfortable earnings.[20]

The butchers were somewhat less independent than the grocers. "Men of the most diverse habits, sentiments and opinions," they ranged from slaughterhouse workers to journeymen at the public markets and private shopkeepers.[21] In 1846 journeymen butchers at the Center, Washington, and Clinton markets earned $6.00, $8.00, and $10.00 per month in addition to board and perquisites, and similar wages were paid in the many private meat shops throughout the city.[22] For heavier work, such as that involving the carrying of heavy quarters of beef upstairs at the Fulton market, the butchers received $15.00 to $30.00 per month.[23] When a butcher had learned the business, he rented a shop of his own or, as in some cases where friends could advance the funds, he bought a stand in one of the markets.[24] As early as 1846, half the New York butchers were immigrants, mostly Germans, Irish, and English, and a decade later fully two thirds of the foreign-born butchers were Germans.[25]

Although by 1855 the Irish were more numerous than the Germans as fish and oyster dealers, marketmen, fruit and produce dealers, the Germans easily outnumbered the Irish as food purveyors. As grocers, butchers, and dairymen the Germans were unrivaled, and these three occupations accounted for all but a few of the German food dealers. About 6.67 per cent of the German working population were engaged in these trades, while the Irish claimed but 2 per cent.[26]

Closely associated with the retailers of foodstuffs were the importers and dealers in European delicacies, wines, and liquors. They supplied shopkeepers with such Continental favorites as Westphalia Ham, Dutch herrings, Magdeburg sauerkraut, Göttingen *würste,* German poppy oil, lentils, *paste d'Italia,* anchovies, caviar, and sardines.[27] They dealt regularly in French and German wines, and when in the fifties disease affected

the grapes of western Europe, they imported Hungarian wines.[28] From
Italian merchants the growing Italian population in the sixties bought
its own favorites: Lacrima Cristi, Capri, Felerno, Garrinara, Ghemme,
Lissona, Asti, *vino commune di Napoli,* and other wines.[29]

Other suppliers of immigrant dealers, restaurants, and hotels were a
few enterprising food manufacturers who established themselves in the
vicinity of New York. Parisian confectioners appeared early, and in 1829
a Frenchman set up a chocolate factory in the city.[30] In the fifties A.
Klix advertised the first German coffee and chocolate factory, where he
sold German-style mustard to peddlers, boardinghouses, and inns,
charging them fifty cents a gallon.[31] Shortly after the Civil War, an
Italian was manufacturing spaghetti, macaroni, and vermicelli at a
plant in Brooklyn.[32]

Bakers and confectioners were by far the most numerous of the food
manufacturers. Although most of the earlier bakers were Scotch and
Irish, the proportion of Germans increased rapidly, so that in 1855 the
1,500 German bakers were more than twice as numerous as the Irish and
twelve times as numerous as the Scotch.[33] Jews augmented the number
of German bakers, supplied the Hebrew community with kosher butchers, and in 1859 nine Jewish bakeries used 2,200 barrels of flour in preparing matzoths for Passover.[34] Of the gainfully employed Germans
(including Jews) 3.75 per cent were bakers and confectioners, and sugar
refiners brought the total to 4.3 per cent; only a negligible proportion of
Irishmen were bakers and confectioners, but 3.67 per cent of the Scots,
3.5 per cent of the French, and 3 per cent of the Swiss were thus employed.[35]

The French and Swiss generally were cooks, confectioners, and sometimes proprietors of chocolate shops, bakeries, cafés, and restaurants.[36]
Some addressed themselves primarily to the immigrant population, but
many appealed to native New Yorkers as well. While a small Provençal
bakery catered to the French public in the 1830's, Louis Curtillet offered
to everyone his meat pies, plum puddings, *confection de crême glacées,*
and *punch à la Romaine,* and during the forties J. Pinteux's Café de Mille
Colonnes in Broadway near Duane Street was a lavishly furnished resort
of wealthy Americans.[37] Pinteux's café soon passed into the hands of
Ferdinand Palmo, the Italian impresario, who renamed it the Café de
la Republique in 1848, year of republican revolutions.[38]

Of the immigrant restaurateurs the most famous were the Delmonicos,
Swiss immigrants from the canton of Ticino near the Italian border.
Peter and John Delmonico opened a small confectionery and catering
business in New York in 1825, and shortly thereafter, their nephew

Lorenzo joined them in starting a downtown restaurant with extensive menus, including salads and vegetables, served in the European manner. Lorenzo Delmonico won such recognition as a teacher of gastronomy that experienced cooks left their Parisian kitchens and offered him their services.[39]

Many French restaurants were also "pensions" and "hotels"—glorified eating places with rooms and apartments for rent by the day or week. There were a few large hotels, however, like that of M. Delacroix, who boasted of 80 rooms "richly furnished and decorated" and a dining room seating 200 persons.[40] German "hotels" were advertised in the thirties, but until the middle of the century German businessmen preferred to stay at the more stylish American hotels.[41] Nevertheless, by 1840 three large hotels, more than a dozen inns, and many restaurants and boarding-houses catered to the German population.[42] The leading German hostelry was the Shakespeare Hotel on Duane Street, which became the meeting place of the literati, the professional men, freethinkers, and politicians, and the headquarters of revolutionary propaganda during the German uprisings of 1848–1850.[43] Whereas the Shakespeare charged $3.50 to $4.00 a week for room and board, and Schwarz's hotel on Dey Street charged $3.50, the rendezvous of the German workers, Schafft's Hotel on Chatham Street, demanded only $1.00 to $1.50.[44] By 1855 the Schwarz and Schafft hotels had disappeared, but the enlarged German community was served by five prominent hotels beside the Shakespeare.[45]

Irish hotels were far less numerous than Irish boardinghouses, but as early as 1832 John McDermott advertised the old Sixth Ward Hotel in Duane Street, which, like the Shakespeare Hotel of the Germans, was a rallying point of republicanism.[46] In 1850 another proprietor, Patrick Garrick, announced that the "Sixth Ward Hotel, one of the oldest Packet Ships in port is now at anchor at her old Dock, 41 Duane-street, corner of Centre. She is roomy between decks and has superior Bar Room accommodations, and is in the hands of an experienced Commander."[47] At 135 Fulton Street, Dunlap's Hotel catered to a "constant influx of strangers," charging them $2.00 and $2.50 per week or thirty-seven and a half cents per night.[48] Another Irish hostelry was the Fourteenth Ward Hotel at the corner of Elizabeth and Grand streets, where workingmen met to demand higher wages.[49]

Other nationalities had their stopping places. The English and Scotch found early accommodations at the Pearl Street House, the Albion and Adelphi hotels, the Burns and Waverley houses, all conveniently located in the business district.[50] Levi's Family Hotel, established in 1845, catered for more than a decade to the Jewish population.[51] When Cuban,

Mexican, and Spanish merchants arrived at New York, they stayed at an increasing number of hotels and inns run by their countrymen.[52] During the sixties, as businessmen continued to arrive from Italy, a few Italians ventured to open hotels.[53]

The hotels, inns, and boardinghouses, and hundreds of smaller and less conspicuous eating places, sold liquor to their growing immigrant clientele. Hundreds of naturalized citizens were licensed liquor dealers, but scores of illegal places operated without license.[54] The surge of immigration during the late forties and early fifties created a demand in the foreign sections of the city for liquor, especially among the Germans who congregated with their families in their favorite beer gardens and among the Irish who drowned their sorrows in drink at hole-in-the-wall liquor shops. By mid-century, the liquor traffic became one of the most important in the city. Nearly 5,000 liquor stores and taverns, of which over 700 were unlicensed, were reported by the chief of police in 1850, and within four months the number of licensed liquor dealers had jumped to 5,250 and the unlicensed to 750.[55]

The manufacture and sale of drink lay behind the success of many an immigrant oyster cellar, saloon, boardinghouse, inn, and hotel. Exclusive of "grocers," over 1,700 immigrants, from the rich importer and wholesaler to the proprietor and barkeeper of the smallest waterfront grog shop dealt in alcoholic beverages in 1855, and nearly 300 more were brewers and distillers.[56] When temperance agitation threatened their existence, they banded together in protective associations, as in 1845, when a Liquor Dealers Protective Union was formed.[57] Ten years later, when a state temperance law severely restricted the sale of liquor, this union joined another association whose membership already had swelled to 800.[58] Dealers and hotel keepers, alive to loopholes in the law, retained well-known legal staffs to do battle in the courts, while some openly flouted the law by continuing to sell liquor without a newly required special license.[59] Organizing mass meetings, the liquor men mobilized the strong antitemperance sentiment among the foreign born and ferreted out those who did not oppose the law.[60]

While the English-speaking immigrants consumed whiskey and porter, and the French drank wines and brandy, the Germans preferred beer. German breweries appeared in the 1830's, but it was not until the forties that they introduced lager beer to New York.[61] Native, English, Scotch, and Irish brewers manufactured ale and porter; lager beer, however, was more palatable and lighter in body and alcoholic content, and its adoption in America revolutionized the brewing industry. Joseph Doelger and the Schaefer brothers were among the pioneer brewers of lager in New York, and the continued immigration of the Germans assured their success and that of many other brewers.[62]

The number of German brewery owners was limited, since it took $800 to $1,000 to found a brewery, but they were important figures in the community.[63] Nearly all the breweries were small in size and averaged but five or six workmen apiece.[64] Sometimes the employees learned the art of brewing and became independent brewers, but many were merely laborers carrying out the instructions of the foremen or brewmasters.[65] In the mid-forties, brewery employees earned $4.00 to $12.00 per month in addition to board, lodging, and washing; the higher paid workmen were office employees and foremen, while the majority who earned low cash payments were partly compensated with free beer.[66] Life in the breweries led to the excessive consumption of beer: the working hours were long and completely unregulated. Toiling fourteen to eighteen hours on weekdays, the brewery men also broke the Puritan Sabbath by working six to eight hours on Sundays as well.[67]

The influence of the brewery owners was subtly exerted upon the community. Sometimes a brewer might operate a tavern, but usually his income depended upon the patronage of beer gardens, groceries, hotels, and boardinghouses.[68] Although some brewers took employees into their homes, others boarded their workmen with those establishments which bought their beer.[69] Evidence of the restiveness of German innkeepers under the domination of the liquor interests was an apparently ill-fated attempt to form a joint stock brewery in 1850.[70]

If brewing and baking were among the more important types of immigrant manufacturing, cigar making likewise drew immigrant workers. In 1855 the Germans accounted for four fifths of all the foreign-born tobacconists.[71] In the tobacco industry, as in many others, no sharp differentiation existed between employer and employee: if skilled, an employee might become an artisan-shopkeeper, combining manufacture with sale.[72] Large factories were exceptional, appearing first about the middle of the century.[73]

Although about two fifths of the immigrant working population were engaged as artisans and factory workers, a few rose to prominent positions in the field of manufacturing. The difficulties of the foreign-born manufacturer were formidable, however. Ignorance of the English language in some cases, unfamiliarity with American business methods, and lack of capital limited the newcomer's industrial opportunities. The foreign entrepreneurs "cannot compete here with high capital," averred the *Irish American,* "and with the want of correct knowledge of our mode of transacting business, and the difficulties of pushing his way through a populous community . . . he fails." [74] The marshals of the state census of 1855 recorded less than a hundred foreign-born "manufacturers," about one third of whom were natives of Germany.[75] That the Germans were so conspicuous is not surprising in view of the fact that they had more highly developed skills than the Irish and greater numbers than the English and Scotch.

The Europeans invested their capital in those industries which offered easy sale in an assured market. Makers of cloth and clothing were foremost among immigrant manufacturers, followed by makers of furniture, oils, paints, soap and candles, liquors, and tobacco products. While almost all nationalities and races entered the clothing industry, a number of Jews became furriers and hat and shirt manufacturers, and Scotsmen turned to the making of textiles.[76] Of thirty Scottish-born manufacturers who joined the St. Andrew's Society between 1825 and 1870, seven were engaged in the making of thread and yarn, two made cotton goods, two manufactured hemp bagging, one produced carpets, five made soap and candles, five were distillers, one was a brewer, and two were tobacconists.[77] The census of 1855 revealed at least eight immigrant manufacturers of yarn, cloth, or clothing, including an English and two German silk manufacturers, an Irish and a Scotch cotton manufacturer, an Irish hat manufacturer, a German shirt manufacturer, and an English shoe manufacturer.[78] Others were sugar refiners, brewers and distillers, and manufacturers of tobacco, soap and candles, mats, curled hair, paper boxes, ink, animal charcoal, bone buttons, furniture, pianos, and metal products.[79]

Though dignified by the census as "factories," the workshops of many foreign-born manufacturers employed few workers, usually less than fifty. Many employers hired only a handful of helpers. Thus in 1855 nine men worked at George Moller's charcoal establishment; thirteen, at Herman Rullhausen's sugar refinery; four men and six boys made mats for the Irishman James Cosgrove, and five men produced ink for the Scot James Lightbody.[80] Many would-be manufacturers operated on a shoestring. Instances of failure usually went unrecorded, but probably there were many. In 1853, for example, an ambitious French company bought land near New Rochelle for the erection of a Bohemian glassworks and arranged to import a colony of French artisans, but apparently the scheme soon was dropped.[81] One immigrant who compensated for an early failure was Robert Lyon, an English Jew, who turned from the manufacturing of umbrellas to become editor of the *Asmonean* and the *Mercantile Journal*.[82]

Not all the businesses were conducted on a small scale, however, for in a number of industries, especially toward the middle of the century, several large enterprises prospered under their foreign entrepreneurs. The English piano manufacturer John F. Nunns, for instance, reaped a fortune estimated at half a million dollars, a French cabinetmaker was said to be worth $150,000, and the cotton mill of the Scotsman Alexander Knox, became one of the most important in the state.[83]

Most of the European manufacturers began their career in New York as journeymen or master craftsmen and gradually accumulated enough money to acquire plants and become big employers. Starting as a paper hanger in Pearl Street, Francis Pares, an Englishman, became a paper manufacturer with a large store in Chambers Street.[84] Alexander McDonald, Scottish owner of an umbrella factory, rose from the humble rank of journeyman umbrella-maker, and a more famous Scot, the cabinetmaker Duncan Phyfe, employed fully a hundred men before he died in the middle of the century.[85] As immigrants continued the tradition of combined manufacture and sale, former tailors, cabinetmakers, upholsterers, leatherworkers, and smiths amassed fortunes as dealers in clothing, furniture, hides, carpets, and hardware.[86] The clothing industry offered the best opportunities. One of the city's leading clothiers was P. L. Rogers, an Irish immigrant. Arriving from County Tyrone at the age of eighteen, he apprenticed himself to a tailor, then opened a small clothing store, moved to larger quarters, and by 1850 headed a mammoth six-story establishment at Fulton and Nassau streets, where a thousand employees made and sold both custom- and ready-made clothes.[87]

Some newcomers profited by their mechanical ingenuity. Thus Samuel Downe, a humble brassworker from Cork, invented an improvement in gas meters which led to contracts with half the gasworks in the United States and enabled him, nineteen years after he landed, to employ eighty-six workers in a $125,000 business.[88] A German Lutheran clergyman, Friedrich Geissenhainer, invented a workable anthracite furnace and after patenting the process began the manufacture of iron in 1833.[89] Sometimes clever immigrants utilized the inventiveness of others. In their radical departures in piano making, the Nunns brothers pioneered the innovations of Charles Sackmeister, an itinerant inventor who had been shabbily treated by other piano manufacturers.[90] Industrial know-how sometimes was furthered by family collaboration in business ventures. Usually this was a father-son relationship, as in the Knox cotton mills, the distillery of John Pirney, and the soap establishments of James Buchan and Allan Hay.[91]

Importers, wholesalers, financiers, agents, and salesmen were few in number but the wealthiest and most prominent members of the foreign community. New York's geographical situation and its consequent advantages as a center of trade had attracted European merchants ever since colonial times. Because of the flourishing trade with Liverpool, more businessmen came from England and Scotland than from any other country, many of them acting as agents of British textile manufacturers.[92]

In the early nineteenth century several firms branched out into new ventures, among them the Englishman James Boorman and his Scottish partner, John Johnston, who carried on an extensive business importing dry goods from Scotland, wines from Madeira and Italy, and iron from England and Sweden, and exporting tobacco from Virginia.[93] Nor was mercantile activity confined to the English and Scotch. The shipowner John Flack and the wine merchant Dominick Lynch were Irish, and Alexander T. Stewart, who later made a million in dry goods, was an Ulster Irishman.[94] A few French refugees from the Negro revolt in Santo Domingo, like Louis Salles and Charles Sagory, grew rich from the increasing trade between New York, Le Havre, and Paris.[95] Other foreign merchants, like Caspar Meier from Germany, H. C. De Rham from Switzerland, Frederick Gebhard and his two sons-in-law from Holland, ensconced themselves at New York.[96] In the thirties German Jewish merchants and financiers appeared in the city; August Belmont, representing the Rothschilds, opened his bank in 1837; and eleven years later the Seligman brothers started an importing firm which became a well-known banking house after 1862.[97]

Some of the European commercial and financial magnates were associated only incidentally with the immigrant communities. Many never became American citizens, retained old ties, and returned to spend their dying days in the lands of their birth. The English, Scotch, and French merchants, in particular, kept alive their pride in empire, and despite long residence in New York, their loyalty lay on the other side of the Atlantic.[98] Others pursued international operations on such a large scale that they transcended local attachments. A number of them marketed American securities in Europe. Thus Frederick Gebhard used his wide connections in England, Holland, Germany, and France to advance the interests of the Illinois Central Railroad, of which he was a director, and Charles Hallgarten created in Germany a market for United States Government bonds during the Civil War.[99] Not a few merchants like John Jacob Astor, German-born fur king, were speculators and real estate operators. Some attained wealth from the appreciation of their holdings, especially if they invested in land on Manhattan Island.[100]

Unlike these mercantile moguls, hundreds of lesser businessmen catered directly to the needs of the city's foreign-born population. To the nucleus of northern and western Europeans came Spanish, and Latin American and Portuguese merchants, a few Italians (chiefly Genoese), and natives of Austria and Hungary, Poland and Russia. By 1855 about 1.5 per cent of the foreign-born working population were merchants, financiers, agents, traders, speculators, and salesmen.

TABLE 5. MERCHANTS

Nativity	Number for Whom Information Was Available	Percentage of Merchants, etc.,[a] to Total Gainfully Employed of the Same Nationality, 1855
Spain	27	18.75
Latin America	37	13.26
Portugal	5	8.93
Russia	5	8.47
Holland	22	7.43
Switzerland	29	6.10
Hungary	5	5.88
France	168	5.60
England	454	4.67
Scandinavia	25	4.49
Poland	25	4.20
Scotland	170	4.10
Italy	18	3.78
Wales	17	3.75
British North America	30	2.50
Belgium	2	2.10
Germany	777	1.69
Ireland	452	.51
Total foreign born	2,269 [b]	1.46

[a] Includes merchants, financiers, agents, traders, speculators, and salesmen.

[b] Includes one Czech not tabulated above. Computations are from data compiled from the manuscript schedules of the *New York State Census of 1855.* Cf. *infra*, Appendix, pp. 214–217.

The German merchants, mostly from the Rhineland and the Hanseatic cities, and the Irish, including natives of Ulster, contributed the smallest proportion of their working populations, despite their absolute numerical strength.[101] This evidence of a dearth of commercial opportunities in Germany and Ireland was implied by the higher proportion of merchants among the English, Scotch, and French, and by the fact that Spanish merchants comprised nearly one fifth of the small Spanish working population of New York.[102]

Many of these men dealt in imported fruits and delicatessen products, liquors, and cigars, which were bought by immigrant dealers, food stores, and restaurants. Without large immigrant populations these men would have had no business. On the other hand, some merchants imported Irish linens, German toys, Swiss watches, and French perfumes, drugs, and textile finery in response to the demand of a growing American public.[103]

A vital function of the merchants lay in the financial services which some of them provided. They handled remittances, arranged transportation, and helped businessmen jump the hurdles of a strange language and unfamiliar business practices. In the late 1830's brokers such as Schulz & Bleidorn, G. Sonne, and Philipp Speyer, transmitted letters and money to Europe, sold travel tickets, acted as employment and real estate agents, and imported a few foreign products.[104] During the next decade the expanding immigrant population was served by a host of commission merchants and shipping agents, insurance brokers, currency exchangers, translators, interpreters, and legal advisers, all of whom advertised regularly in the press.[105]

An army of clerks, bookkeepers, and copyists assisted the merchants. Most of the clerks were of the same nationality as their employers and were engaged partly for their knowledge of the language and sometimes for sentimental or family reasons.[106] In 1855 clerical workers comprised nearly 4 per cent of the foreign-born working population.[107] Although four fifths of the immigrant clerks were Germans and Irish, and hundreds more were Englishmen, Scots, and Frenchmen, the natives of Cuba and other Latin American countries and of Spain and Portugal included the highest proportion of clerical workers, many of them undoubtedly employed by companies involved in the Caribbean and Mediterranean trade.[108] The clerks were notoriously poorly paid. In 1846 their salaries seldom averaged more than $250 to $300 per year, but in a few rare instances they earned as much as $600 or $1,000.[109] In a dogged competition for jobs, the immigrant failed to match the sons of the wealthy who, through favoritism and native birth, monopolized the clerical jobs in American mercantile houses.[110]

A small number of professionally trained people brought their specialized talents to the Empire City. Of all classes of immigrants the professionals found the least encouragement in New York. Scholars, lawyers, and artists, proud of their social standing in Europe, frequently found their training to be of little use in materialistic America; and they accepted almost any kind of work at first to keep from starving.[111]

Failure to achieve success sometimes brought bitter disillusionment.[112] Among these intellectuals were refugees from the political turmoil of Europe, especially the revolutions of 1830 and 1848–1849. During periods of unrest and rebellion in Poland, France, Hungary, Italy, Germany, and Ireland, and in their wake, New York harbored small but vocal bands of exiles who kept up their nationalist and republican propaganda.[113] While some returned to their native lands, many remained as teachers, journalists, lawyers, and small businessmen.[114]

Of the professional men who were not refugees, the Germans and Italians were most prominent as musicians. The Italians and French won early American appreciation of their musical abilities, and, as early as 1837, more than a hundred experienced German musicians composed, sang, and played in New York.[115] Italian musicians continued to settle in the city, particularly after the failure of the opera troupe led by Montresor and Da Ponte in 1832–1833, while German social life, with its singing societies, Sunday concerts, and *Sängerfeste* provided a healthy environment for hundreds of Teutonic composers, instrumentalists, and singers.[116] Even in native musical organizations such as the Philharmonic Society, many members were Germans.[117] By the mid-fifties more than half of the foreign-born musicians in New York had come from Germany.[118]

Foreigners dominated the plastic arts. Frenchmen, Italians, Englishmen, and Germans were most numerous as painters, sculptors and engravers, and the English were unrivaled in the arts of photography and daguerreotypy. Germans specialized in portraiture and in fresco painting, while Italian artists included wax figure and plaster statuette makers, whose livelihoods were assured by the demand of the growing Catholic population for religious objects of this nature.

As Catholic and Jewish immigration increased in the late 1830's, priests and rabbis joined the predominantly Protestant clergy, and a decade later a number of German rationalist preachers settled in the city. Missionaries of various sects and Catholic nuns performed charitable and educational duties and swelled the ranks of the clergy. In 1855 nearly half of these people had been born in the Emerald Isle.[119]

Knowledge of the language and American legal practices accounted for the fact that more than half the immigrant lawyers were English and Irish; German lawyers and those from other non-English-speaking countries rarely practiced outside their immigrant communities.[120] Most of the foreign-born architects and engineers were German, while in the sciences and medicine, the English, Germans, and French were prominent as chemists, physicians, surgeons, dentists, and veterinarians.[121]

On the American stage, where English tradition reigned, British actors were common. Likewise, the literary influence of the mother country encouraged English authors to try their luck in the city. The Germans and French established theaters for the production of dramas in their own languages, but their shaky financial foundations offered little hope to immigrant actors.[122]

Teachers, lecturers, linguists, and literary folk represented nearly every European nationality. Irish, English, German, and French journalists and publishers found a niche in New York, and a few distinguished writers and scholars taught in the city's colleges.[123]

In 1855 nearly 2 per cent of the foreign-born working population were members of some profession.[124] The largest proportion was among the Italians, almost two fifths of whom were professional men, mostly musicians and artists.[125] Relatively large proportions of the natives of Belgium, Hungary, Spain, Latin America, France, and Switzerland likewise were professionals, as were 5 per cent of the English and Welsh, nearly 3 per cent of the Scots, and 4 to 5 per cent of those born in the Netherlands, Poland and the Scandinavian countries.[126] Singularly, the Germans and the Irish included the smallest proportions of professional men; they comprised slightly more than 2 per cent of the Germans and only .5 per cent of the Irish.[127] Because the English were socially acceptable, and because Americans still looked to England for intellectual leadership, educated Englishmen were relatively numerous in scientific, literary, and artistic circles at New York. With this exception, however, the largest national groups in the city provided the smallest share of professional people, a clear indication of the dearth of Old World opportunities.

The members of the professions, merchants, and manufacturers comprised an aristocracy aloof from the daily life of the great masses of immigrants. Bridging the gap between them and the manual workers was a middle class of shopkeepers, food purveyors, and liquor dealers, sustained mainly by the ever expanding foreign communities. The majority of the immigrants, whether as laborers, artisans, or factory operatives, gradually were absorbed in the city's economic structure. In the clothing, furniture, and building industries, the newcomers played a major role, while in many other crafts they contributed their technical skills. This participation of immigrants in the industrial and commercial growth of New York intensified the labor struggles of the period and, despite occasional grievous clashes with American workingmen, the foreign born co-operated with the natives in desperate efforts to improve working conditions and to restore the lost dignity of the working people.

IX

IMMIGRANT AND NATIVE WORKERS

As THE OAK DRAWS nourishment from the soil, American labor was sustained and molded by immigrants and their children. Foreigners performed not only rough labor on canals, railroads, and roadways, but joined with natives at their skilled work in factories, workshops, shipyards, and in building construction and maintenance. In the pre-Civil War period, while the United States was experiencing the growing pains of industrialism, native labor was forced to tackle the problem of assimilation and Americanization of these immigrant wage earners. It was "only by the assimilating power of labour organizations," observed John R. Commons, "that they can be brought together in a movement that depends for success on their willingness to stop competition and espouse cooperation." [1] This assimilation and its accompanying race and national conflicts gave character to American labor movements and distinguished them from the European.

The relations of native and foreign labor in the United States usually have been simplified into a formula of competition and strife. While struggles undeniably took place, natives and immigrants showed a fundamental co-operation in their common aspirations. The English arrived early and in large numbers. Skilled workmen who knew the language and customs, they remembered bitter experiences in the labor movement in England, and during the thirties they were influential in American labor struggles. [2] The Irish, not having any labor philosophy in the Emerald Isle, accepted the prevailing labor views in the United States and joined native unions. [3] The Germans, like the English, had taken part in a strenuous labor movement, but unlike the English pure and simple unionism, their organizations in America during the fifties taught radical and socialist unionism and independent working class action. German labor leaders included intellectuals thoroughly familiar with the theoretical and practical aspects of the labor movement. [4] After having participated in the labor agitation in the fatherland, German workmen in the United States became dominant in such occupations as woodworking, baking, brewing, and cigar making. [5] They naturally proceeded to create their own unions, support labor papers, and found political clubs.

Until the late twenties, American workmen had no "labor philosophy."

The early labor unions did not resort to the panaceas which later occupied their attention, and but few individuals expounded the virtues of
co-operation, agrarianism, socialism, or class struggle. In these years
of budding industrial capitalism, a skilled mechanic still had a chance
to become a master in his trade; he did not conceive of the abolition of
the wage system, for to him wages and hours were the most important
issues.[6]

With the organization of workingmen's parties in New York, New
England, and Philadelphia in the late twenties and early thirties, workmen began to champion a series of reforms not directly related to the
issues of wages and hours. Deep currents of discontent flowed through
the industrial and commercial centers, as mechanics and shopkeepers felt
a loss of status in society "in consequence of the inroads and usurpations
of the wealthy and powerful," and the "continued prevalence of irra-
tional, anti-republican and unchristian opinions in relation to the worth
and respectability of *manual* labor."[7] Inspired by the enthusiastic
leadership and fiery zeal of the Scottish-born reformer Frances Wright,
the New York "mechanic" and journalist Thomas Skidmore, and Robert
Dale Owen, son of Robert Owen, more genuine labor leaders attempted
to improve the morale of the rank and file by asserting the unity of the
working classes and demanding reforms which would equalize their opportunities and restore their dignity. Although they disagreed among
themselves as to the most desirable reforms, they urged widespread
education of the poor. To the popular demand for universal education
they added the abolition of imprisonment for debt, the destruction of
licensed monopolies, revision of the militia system, more equitable taxation, mechanics' lien laws to protect workmen from fraudulent contractors, less expensive legal procedures, direct elections by the people,
the abolition of prison labor and of capital punishment, and the suppression of lotteries and intemperance.[8]

Immigrants, especially the English, Scotch, and Irish, played a vital
part in these movements. Having no reason to organize on a separate
basis, the newcomers joined native unions where they produced few
leaders but in some cases supplied the bulk of the followers. They were
prominent among the ship carpenters, who, with the typographers and
printers, took the lead in labor organization.[9] In some cases, immigrants
later became union organizers, like John Samuel, a Welsh glass blower,
who took part in the Philadelphia general strike in 1836 and later organized the glassworkers of that city.[10] A few were intellectuals who
fought on the wage earners' behalf. Perhaps the most conspicuous was

George Henry Evans, editor of the New York *Working Man's Advocate*, devoted follower of Thomas Paine, hard-money enthusiast, and ardent land reformer, who protested against hostility to the immigrant and urged that public lands be given free to Eastern wage earners as inalienable homesteads.[11]

Though reformers might wax eloquent over their pet schemes, the more immediate question of wage rates was the key to the relationship of native to foreign labor. Native unions were unwilling to risk the competition of foreigners. The Typographical Association viewed with alarm the advertisements in British newspapers inducing English and Scotch printers "to leave the comforts of home in the old country."[12] Seth Luther, addressing the workingmen of New England in 1832, accused manufacturers of sending "agents to *Europe* to induce *foreigners* to come here, to underwork *American* citizens, to support *American* industry, and the *American* system."[13] In self-defense, therefore, native associations absorbed persons of foreign birth.

On the other hand, a favorite device of conservatives was to blame immigrants for creating labor disturbances and agitating for higher wages! In the famous conspiracy trial of the journeymen tailors in 1836 the judge maintained that combinations to raise wages were of foreign origin and "mainly upheld by foreigners."[14] Twenty of the tailors tried unsuccessfully to obtain a bill of indictment against the masters. In their defense, the *Union*—the official organ of the New York Trades' Union— announced that only four of the twenty were born in Europe and that they had been in the United States for fifteen or twenty years. The "concerted mode of attributing every demand for an increase in wages on the part of our operatives, to foreigners, is but a degrading and pitiful comment to their sense of independence and intelligence," declared the *Union*.[15] Persons exclaiming loudly against nativist riots were the very ones who tried to "glut their vindictiveness against the common people, by arraying the native born laborer against his fellow being."[16]

The paradoxical position of the foreigner was emphasized in 1836–1837, when an era of wild speculation in bank notes was followed by panic and depression, and when the defection of the workers from Tammany Hall to the Locofocos broke the Democrats' hold on New York City and produced a nativist administration. In these two years, the city witnessed struggles between journeymen and their employers. What were the immigrant—largely Irish—workers to do? "If they go to work at the old price, the journeymen at once cry out 'those d——d Irishmen are always ratting,' and if they 'strike' the employers at once exclaim 'those d——d Irishmen are always uprorious [*sic*],' so that between them all, poor Pat is treated like a football in a ring—every body gives him a kick." [17]

The dozen years of hard times after the panic of 1837 were a period of turbulent conflicts among the working classes. Depressed wages and unemployment nearly put an end to the early aggressive trade unionism.[18] At the same time, immigration recovered from its temporary setback following the panic and began to skyrocket in the mid-forties.[19] Native mechanics and tradesmen manifested extreme bitterness toward their foreign competitors, and violent disputes raged among the immigrants themselves, particularly the Irish and Germans.

In the charged atmosphere of disappointed hopes and dwindling opportunities, the political nativism, or antiforeign sentiment, of the thirties became a virulent economic nativism in the forties. A newspaper calling itself the *Champion of American Labor* appeared briefly in 1847 and blew loudly upon its nativist trumpet. Asserting that alien cheap labor was the only cause of conflict between capital and labor in the United States, the *Champion* would preserve the American workingman from degradation, restore his dignity, and relieve him of the misery and want to which "the pauper laborers of Europe" were accustomed.[20] It would stop the "swarms of needy adventurers, cut-throats and paupers of European jails and poor-houses, that, like the locusts of Egypt," were landing on our shores and enabling New York and Boston shippers to amass fortunes from the immigrant trade.[21]

The primary accusation of native labor was that immigrants lowered general wage levels. It was charged that every family in America was well supplied with foreign cooks, chambermaids, and seamstresses working for wages which would never attract native girls. A shoemaker complained of being thrown out of work three times in one year "by persons just come to this country, who will work for what I can't live on." [22] Responding to handbills printed in their own language, German shoemakers displaced Americans, and German tailors had in five years lowered the price of coats from $5.50 to $2.25.[23] The wages of cabinetmakers fell from $12.00 to $15.00 a week in 1836 to less than $8.00, with the majority probably earning less than $5.00 in 1846.[24] To meet the demand of workingmen and boardinghouse keepers for cheap furniture, German cabinetmakers worked for a pittance, turning out huge quantities of crude beds, chairs, and tables. "There are persons who are constantly on the watch for German emigrants who can work at Cabinet-Making—going on board the ships before the emigrants have landed and engaging them for a *year* at $20 or $30 and their board, or on the best terms they can make," revealed Mike Walsh's *Young America*. "The emigrants of course know nothing of the state of the trade, prices, regulations, &c., &c., and become willing victims to any one who offers them immediate and permanent employment. This it is which has ruined the Cabinet-Making business, and the complaints on the part of the journeymen are incessant." [25] In the building trades, similar grievances were held against the Irish painters, carpenters, and masons who allegedly lowered wage levels.[26]

Another complaint against aliens was that they broke down the apprenticeship system in the skilled trades. Native artisans and tradesmen had long been accustomed to sharp occupational division of labor in which apprentices learned to become journeymen and master workmen and perpetuated a spirit of exclusiveness in each craft. Technological improvements continually weakened the hold of the skilled workmen upon the supply of labor, however, and the new techniques of production led to the employment of unskilled or poorly trained hands.[27] The presence in the city of so many untrained workers led to the charge that a mechanic's reputation no longer guaranteed him a job. House painting ceased to be a monopoly of the painters, one of whom lamented that the trade was "entirely destroyed by carpenters undertaking to perform the work." [28] In several skilled trades, notably the book-folders' and boot- and shoemakers', "the skillful worker just through . . . apprenticehood [was] too often sent adrift to make room for raw hands." [29] By 1845 apprenticing in the shoemaking trade had largely disappeared, and foreign workmen, largely Irish, who had completed their apprenticeship in Europe were being employed in New York at low wages.[30] Skilled workers pointed to the futility of apprenticeship when jobs were taken away by foreigners, and in New York, Brooklyn, Poughkeepsie, and other towns protest meetings demanded the restriction of immigration.[31]

It was undeniable that recent immigrants frequently worked for lower wages than Americans or aliens of long residence in the United States. The Association for Improving the Condition of the Poor observed:

The increased emigration from Europe in late years has operated adversely to the interests of the native laboring and mechanic classes in this city, both by crowding them out of employment, and diminishing the rewards of industry. Needy foreigners accustomed to live upon less than our own countrymen, are enabled to produce articles cheaper and to work for lower wages. With the increase of laborers, the standard of comfortable subsistence had not only been depressed, but wages must continue to fall as competition increases.[32]

From the viewpoint of the newcomer, it was imperative that he find employment in the trade for which he was trained, but failing that, he might take any job offered to him. If he were totally unskilled, he soon picked

up the rudiments of a trade in New York. Economic nativism was, therefore, an expression of the American craftsman's desire to preserve his
monopoly from the determined attempts of immigrants to gain a foothold.[33]

If the white Americans could rise to skilled positions, the Negro Americans found it extremely difficult to rise above manual labor and domestic
service. This situation led to direct competition between the colored and
Irish inhabitants. Both groups vied for favor as personal and domestic
servants: the women as maids, scrub- and washerwomen, seamstresses
and cooks, and the men as laborers and waiters. Most of the smaller
hotels hired colored waiters; the Metropolitan employed about sixty or
seventy and the Stuyvesant House, the Earls, the Clifford, and others
gave work to Negroes.[34] Along the waterfront, the Irish and Negro dock
workers rubbed elbows in mutual antagonism. The Irish were the most
formidable enemies of the Negroes, wrote James Dawson Burn, an
Owenite and keen observer of working conditions in the United States:

I have often heard the nature and condition of the colored people discussed
by my shopmates in America. I have met with a few well-conditioned men
who look upon the blacks as rational beings; but the strongly expressed opinion of the majority was, that they are a soulless race, and I am satisfied that
some of these people would shoot a black man with as little regard to moral
consequences as they would a wild hog.[35]

Race prejudice gave the Irish an advantage over the Negroes and enabled the former to advance to better-paid occupations. The degraded
situation of the colored workers was emphasized by the refusal of journeymen to work with them and by the financial inability of the few
colored employers to hire their own apprentices and journeymen. Even
in the customary Negro occupation of barbering, Frenchmen and Germans were supplanting colored barbers.[36]

To a strong race consciousness was infused a class consciousness, felt
most acutely by the colored population. In 1851 New York City Negroes
held a convention for the purpose of bettering their condition and appointed a Committee on the Social Condition of the Colored Race. "The
enormous combination of capital, which is slowly invading every calling
in the city, from washing and ironing to palace steamers," reported Dr.
James McCune Smith for the committee, "must tend more and more to
grind the face of the poor in the cities, and render them more and more
the slaves of lower wages and higher rents." [37] Negro waiters pioneered
in demanding higher wages and in 1853 received $16 a month to the
white waiters' $12. In this exceptional situation the whites held a meet-
ing to force equalization of their wages; and in the hope of ultimately

obtaining further gains, a Negro delegate to the meeting advised the whites to strike for $18 a month.[38]

More characteristic of Negro-white relations was the deterrent effect of the employment of colored workers in labor disputes involving the Irish. The use of Negroes as strikebreakers inflamed the smoldering passions of the races. When in 1853 the Irish laborers at the Erie railroad depot struck for $1.25 a day and a working limit of ten hours, Negroes allegedly armed with revolvers were hired in their places.[39]

Fights between the Irish and the Negroes were not entirely motivated by race prejudice and economic rivalry. Irish impulsiveness played its part, and the sons of Erin themselves were involved in continual internecine strife. The well-known clannishness of the Irish stemmed from the disabilities they had experienced in the Emerald Isle. In neglecting the Catholic Irishman's education and barring his political and economic advancement, the British government reaped a reward of undying Irish hatred for all things English (including the hapless English immigrant in America). This antagonism turned Irish loyalties inward and created an intense local patriotism which centered upon religion, family, and particular sections of Ireland. Secret societies were organized to settle agrarian difficulties and to annoy the British government, and in America these societies persisted in spite of the opposition of the Catholic clergy.[40] Most numerous among the canal and railroad laborers, these secret associations took their names from the provinces of Ireland, the prominent ones being the "Corkonians," the "Far-Downs," and the "Connaught-Men." Their rivalry produced many a bloody brawl.[41] If a labor contractor were wise, he requested specifically whether he wanted Connaught-Men, Corkonians, or Germans, or English, and he took care to separate the Irish Catholics from the Protestant Orangemen.[42] On the other hand, some contractors encouraged the Irish to fight so that the contractors could abscond with the laborers' wages during the confusion. At an Irish convention in New York, one Michael McQuade, of Utica, declared to his fellow laborers that:

A great many of the contractors have themselves confessed to me that they got up those fights on purpose, in order to evade the payment of the men, and said all they had to do coming on pay-day, was to employ some persons to kick up a row, and that they would be sure to get off from paying at all. I know one man who had what is called "a cold water contract," near Elmira, and I met him one day . . . bringing six barrels of spirits with him to his sections, on carts. . . . Said he, "Monday is pay-day . . . and I have no money for the men, so I do not know what else to do. I must have a fight and that will settle all." [43]

The conditions of labor brought on these affrays. The monotony of ditch digging, grading, and rail laying was broken occasionally by the presence of some passing attraction. When the circus made its appearance, the Irish railway laborers were "always sure to 'take a day's fun.' A fit or bout of drinking was invariably the consequence; and, as invariably, a fight with the negroes who congregated to amuse themselves." [44] Catering to the Irish love of liquor, the contractors opened shanty stores for the sale of rum. While the more prudent workers contracted for board as part of their pay, or received flat weekly rates for their upkeep, most of them fell victim to the system of the shanty store. Unscrupulous subcontractors monopolized the supplies at isolated camps and charged exorbitant prices at these stores. They paid wages in goods and liquor, and the laborers often drank up their wages.[45] The railroads sometimes resorted to equally shady practices: deliberately advertising for more workmen than they needed, they took advantage of the labor surplus to beat down wages. After traveling hundreds of miles, the laborer discovered that he was paid less than originally advertised; he had no alternative but to accept what was offered.[46] Thus, instead of the high wages, fine food, and agreeable accommodations he expected, he found himself working from dawn to dusk at about a dollar a day, or less.[47] Encouraged by the absence of customary restraints, the Irishman revolted. He found himself away from family and friends, absent for many months from association with women, and lacking the spiritual consolation of the clergy. His abnormally boisterous life made the construction camp the scene of many "Irish riots." [48]

Irish rivalries, born of a deep mistrust even of fellow Irishmen, were not peculiar to the common laborers on the canals, railroads, tunnels, embankments, and waterfronts. Suspicions lurked among the "educated mechanics." When an Irish "greenhorn" entered a workshop or factory for the first time, he remained suspect until he revealed from what part of Ireland he had come.[49] The pride which Irishmen took in their intimate friends and associates stimulated occupational rivalries. A large number of the New York cartmen were Irish, more trade-conscious than their American competitors, and the first to organize; yet those on the East Side of Manhattan were rivals of those on the West Side, and the dock cartmen vied with the coal cartmen.[50] Among the city's volunteer firemen, of whom many were Irish, the intense pride of each company produced strong rivalries which sometimes degenerated into battles as the companies fought each other instead of the fires.[51]

If the Irish fought among themselves, they managed to unite in a common front against other nationalities. Clashes between the Irish and the generally peaceful Germans were frequent.[52] Stemming largely from divergences in customs and speech, these national affrays also emphasized economic rivalries, as German laborers competed for employment with the Irish and the Negroes in the cities, and the Irish battled it out with the Germans on the canals and railroads.[53] Both American and Irish workers scorned and hated the newly arrived "Dutchmen" for their humility and willingness to act as strikebreakers.[54] In 1846 some five hundred Irish laborers at the Atlantic Dock in Brooklyn demanded a wage of eighty-seven and a half cents per day and a reduction of working hours from thirteen to ten. The contractors refused, and a strike ensued. Applying to the German Society, the contractors obtained a cargo of freshly landed Germans and ordered the Irish to leave the premises. The Irish staged a sitdown strike by taking possession of the shanties in which they had been living, threatened death to those who would work, and temporarily drove off the Germans by intimidation and violence. The sheriff of Kings County called out the militia, overawed the Irish, and protected the new workers.[55]

In the skilled trades, immigrants participated less often in strike-breaking activities. Newly arrived aliens, it is true, were used as scabs; but the older foreign-born residents tried to induce them to join unions.[56] When workingmen's associations existed, the foreign-born artisans tended to side with the unions rather than with newcomers of their own nationality. During a wave of strikes in 1850 the German shoemakers refused to allow their members to work in shops where their English-speaking brethren were on strike, and they adopted the same wage demands.[57] Naturalized American workers were indignant when they were scorned as foreigners. To the *Champion of American Labor* one adopted citizen wrote:

You intend to shut out the foreigners or naturalized citizens of this country from any benefit that will arise from your plans to get better wages. . . . you use the word *American* very often and nothing at all is said about *naturalized citizens*, but if you think to succeed without the aid of foreigners you will find yourself mistaken; for we are strong and are getting stronger every day, and though we feel the effects of competition from these men who are sent here from the poor houses of Europe, yet [*sic*] if you don't include us to get better wages by shutting off such men, why you needn't expect our help.[58]

Throughout the forties and fifties, despite occasional clashes of races and nationalities, the American labor movement gained adherents from the incoming tides of foreign artisans. Native workingmen aided the immigrants and in turn sought their co-operation. Some unions set up labor exchanges where newly arrived journeymen might register for employment. The Operative Bakers' Union, founded by Americans, Scotch, English, Irish, and Germans, aimed "to advise and protect newly-arrived emigrant Bakers" and established a "Call House," or employment bureau, patterned after those already existing in Scotland.[59] In 1850 the joiners and cabinetmakers resolved to post handbills in immigrant boardinghouses directing newcomers to places of employment at adequate wages and preventing them from falling into the clutches of labor exploiters.[60] Dominated by the Irish, the unskilled laborers admitted members from many lands. The banner of the longshoremen's union was decorated with flags of France, Germany, the Netherlands, Sweden, Ireland, Denmark, Hungary, and Italy, bound together under the American flag and the word "unity." At the top of the banner was displayed the proud challenge: "We know no distinction but that of merit." [61] This recognition of common cause, dictated by self-interest rather than altruism, led to strenuous efforts to adapt the foreigners to American working conditions.

The various nationalities co-operated in efforts to improve their status. In the early stages of union organization, however, it was often necessary to conduct the proceedings in more than one language. The membership of many labor unions included a large number of foreign born; and to overcome the language barrier, the English proceedings were translated for them.[62] When the majority of members could not speak English, the meetings were conducted in foreign languages. In 1850 when 800 of the city's 2,000 cabinetmakers organized, the proceedings were given in German, then followed an English translation, and the constitution was printed in German, French, and English.[63] The upholsterers' union, half of whose 140 members were Germans and the rest Americans, Irish, English, and French, elected a president who spoke German and French, an English and two German secretaries, and a French treasurer.[64] Translations were cumbersome, however, and the resulting inconvenience enhanced friction and jealousy among members of some trades. Sometimes, complete dismemberment was threatened unless the unions divided along linguistic or national lines.[65] The Germans soon formed separate unions which consulted with the parent unions on matters of mutual interest, and some, like the bakers' union, adopted the same constitutions.[66]

In the middle of the century, trade unionism experienced a powerful revival. The gold discoveries in California and the optimism of speculation in a period of rapid industrial expansion produced a boom. Workingmen did not share in the prosperity, however, as prices rose higher than wages and the cost of living reached new heights. "Even of those who have the best wages and earn from $10 to $15 per week," asserted the *Tribune,* "not one in ten saves anything." [67] Labor leaders, spurred by the militant class consciousness of the Germans, sought immediate relief of distressed workers and their families. Their foremost demands were for wage increases and reduction of working hours. The carpenters struck for $1.75 a day. The upholsterers tried to raise their weekly earnings from $7.00 to $9.00, and for those already earning $9.00 an increase of 25 per cent was demanded.[68] In the large majority of shops, the shoemakers were granted an increase from $5.00 to $7.00 a week, and a fair scale of wages was adopted for piecework.[69] The bakers' union, revolting against a sixteen- to eighteen-hour day, demanded a twelve-hour maximum and the limitation of night work.[70] The bricklayers, plasterers, and silversmiths wanted to co-operate with the Germans, and the German hatters, blacksmiths, and wheelwrights sought to co-operate with their American brethren.[71] In 1853 another wave of strikes found the compositors asking for a raise of 15 per cent, the stonecutters 12 per cent or a reduction in the hours of work, German and Irish shoemakers jointly seeking wage boosts, cartmen holding out for twenty-five cents more per day, gilders demanding twenty cents per hour instead of sixteen cents, and many other trades, including the French carpenters, participated in the general attempt to force higher wages.[72]

The unskilled laborers sought to share in the gains by adopting the trade union tactics, and their efforts were supported by the skilled workers. When the laborers struck for $1.12½ a day, a representative of the striking carpenters declared to the Laborers' Union Benevolent Association: "Our interests are identical, one and the same, and we must act in concert to elevate our moral and social condition." [73] In 1854 striking longshoremen were encouraged by the shipwrights, caulkers, and spar-makers, who agreed to prevent journeymen from working until the strike was settled.[74]

Without question the most far-reaching strike was that of the tailors in 1850. In the ready-made clothing industry, which since the early thirties had centered in New York City, the old method of production in which the journeyman tailor worked inside his master's small shop had given way to mass-production methods. Contractors hired workers by the score, and what work was not accomplished in the factory was let out as piecework to be done in the tailors' homes. Women and Irish, German, and Jewish immigrants were prominent in the trade; and their wages were pitifully inadequate to satisfy their minimum needs of food and shelter. Before mid-century the American (mostly of Irish descent) and German tailors were not on the best of terms. However, when the native tailors struck in July, 1850, the two groups buried their differences. They agreed on the same scale of wages, and a tremendous mass meeting in City Hall Park was held on their behalf. Those who continued to work at the old prices were assaulted.[75] The combined action of the tailors resulted in the formation of a union having about two thousand members; and if the strike was otherwise not entirely successful, it cemented the relations of the tailors of different nationalities.[76]

The early fifties found the national groups working together in a frenzy of enthusiasm for the common cause. The cabinetmakers, largely German, but including English-speaking members, planned to reorganize "for the accommodation of all nations." [77] The German blacksmiths and wheelwrights, seeking American co-operation with their Protective Association, declared: "We all belong to one great family—the Workingmen's family." [78] In their effort to establish a co-operative store, the turners appointed a committee, part English and part German. The English-speaking and German bakers met at Hillenbrand's Mechanics Hall in Hester Street and adopted similar policies.[79] In nearly every case, the Germans took the lead; they were especially active in organizing many of the trades into unions and in setting up co-operatives; where unions already existed, the Germans proved to be the most forceful members.[80]

By the middle of 1854 nearly all the effective trade unions had abandoned their dealings with employers as individuals whenever it was possible to deal with them as a group. Through collective bargaining, the unions sought contracts with employers' associations, and if successful, they tried to coerce refractory employers into submission to their terms.[81] Labor's demands centered about long-standing issues of wages, shorter hours, abolition of night work, frequency and regularity of pay, substitution of cash for store pay, restriction of the number and extension of the time of apprentices, better trade conditions, and the closed shop. Whether by trade agreements or by individual settlements, the unions generally secured wage advances and improved working conditions in these years. The business prosperity of the time was a considerable factor in their success, but the workers had in four years achieved by their own efforts disciplined and integrated organizations inconceivable a decade before. If the German, Irish, English, Scotch, French, and other immigrant union members were not entirely responsible, at least they contributed decisively to the new solidarity.

Labor's gains were short-lived. The boom period did not last, and the return of hard times proved too great a burden on the unions; most of them were broken up in the depression of 1854–1855 and the panic of

1857. Wages dropped to new low levels, and unemployment hung like a storm cloud over the city, despite the temporary relief afforded by the return to Europe of disillusioned workmen and by the relative decrease of immigration.[82] The outbreak of the Civil War provided another crisis for those unions which had survived the depressions of the fifties or had been organized afterward. In New York, the interruption of the Southern trade brought in its wake bankruptcies and stagnation in some industries; and with reduced consumption owing to the war, unemployment prevailed. "The number thrown out of employ was at least 25 per cent greater than in any year since 1857," affirmed a contemporary report.[83] Unlike later wars, in which American labor profited, the Civil War was disastrous to the workers, and their situation steadily grew worse. "The condition of the laborer here," explained Mayor Gunther, "is not one promising a fair remuneration under our inflated paper currency. One-half of his wages is absorbed by taxation; and the balance, at the present rates, is about 40 cents in real value to each dollar of nominal payment."[84] Nevertheless, late in 1863 and in 1864, strikes for higher wages and agitation for an eight-hour day spearheaded a new movement which gathered strength in the years to come.[85]

The war ended four decades of struggle for recognition of the dignity of labor and for working conditions commensurate with living costs. Native unions had drawn strength from the foreign born and their children, who filled the ranks with America's needed brawn and technical skill. The Irish, because of their numbers, early dominated the unskilled and certain trades, but they absorbed the American labor philosophy, which was born of the experiences of British unionism and nourished by English and Scotch immigrants. Maintaining separate labor organizations, the Germans exerted little direct influence at first but contributed enormously to the strength of unionism in the fifties. Artisans from other lands were absorbed in the vibrant process of Americanization. Suspicions and antagonisms appeared, yet beneath the divisions of nationality and race lay a consciousness of purpose: the realization of America's opportunity for material well-being.

X

THE GERMAN WORKERS ORGANIZE

NEW YORK WAS THE CENTER of the early German labor movement in America. The mass of German workers lived there, and it was a primary point of contact between the German artisans in the United States and European exiles carrying revolutionary ideas to America. Nevertheless, the class consciousness so characteristic of the German labor agitation spread wherever German workers settled: in Philadelphia, Baltimore, Cincinnati, St. Louis, and, to a minor degree, in Chicago and Milwaukee.[1]

In the twenty years before the Civil War, the German artisans played a highly significant part in labor's battle with capital. Immigrant German workers contributed to the spirit of unrest in the forties and took part in strikes in the trades which they were beginning to dominate: furniture and cabinetmaking, tailoring, and piano making.[2] In a number of occupations the Germans organized social clubs or mutual aid societies, some of which later developed into unions. These *Vereine* were founded by the cabinetmakers, bakers, wood carvers, watchcase makers, upholsterers, bookbinders, gilders, and piano makers.[3] They were the precursors of the strongly class-conscious German unions in the middle of the century.

The *Vereine* were influenced by refugees from abroad who had been active in the secret communist organizations which had sprung up in western and central Europe. The chief spreaders of revolutionary ideas were members of workingmen's self-culture societies and traveling apprentices, many of whom had been harried out of their native countries. Some found asylum in Switzerland. Some, especially tailors, went to London; others gravitated to Paris, where the first German workers' union was founded in 1830.[4] In a few years this secret organization evolved into the *Bund der Gerechtigkeit,* better known as the *Bund der Gerechten* (Society of the Just). Its leading spirit was Wilhelm Weitling until Marx and Engels gained control in 1847.[5] Members of the *Bund* found their way to New York, where they won converts among their fellow Germans. German communists settled in other cities, too, and published propaganda sheets like the *Adoptiv-Bürger* in Philadelphia and the *Anti-Pfaff* and the *Vorwärts* in St. Louis.[6] At first their influence was imperceptible. The New York Germans regarded them as radical

agitators, and the German artisans had little in common with these intellectuals, these "greenhorns," who were unfamiliar with labor conditions in the United States. In time, however, the communists gained adherents.[7]

Beginning in the mid-forties, the German workers were subjected to
the self-assumed leadership of intellectuals and reformers in much the
same way as the English-speaking workers. The agrarian movement was
taken up by the Germans, who had their own George Henry Evans in
the person of Hermann Kriege. A member of the *Bund der Gerechten,*
Kriege came to America in 1845 and immediately organized a branch
of the *Bund* at New York. From this association sprang the *Deutsche
Jung-Amerika Gemeinde* (German Young America Community), which
championed the demands of the American land reformers.[8] Kriege himself was strongly influenced by agrarianism and attuned his earlier
communism to the advocacy of land reform. "If once the soil is free,"
he wrote, "then every honest workingman" will be welcomed as a "blessing to our republic." [9] With naïve optimism, *Jung Amerika* made its first
appeal to the German Society for support. When the conservative merchants of the society contemptuously ignored the request, *Jung Amerika*
sponsored a meeting of German workers at which Kriege and others
spoke, and a *Sozial-reformassoziation* was formed. This Social Reform
Association became a recruiting agency for the parent body, which was
still practically unknown even in the German community.[10] It aimed to
do for the German workingman what Evans' National Reform Association hoped to do for the English-speaking workers; but while
Evans' followers regarded land reform as an end, the social reformers,
being essentially communistic, saw agrarianism only as a means to their
goal.[11] The association maintained a paper, the *Volkstribun,* which,
under the editorship of Kriege, lasted a year.[12] Meanwhile, German land
reform societies sprang up in Milwaukee, Cincinnati, Boston, Newark,
Philadelphia, Chicago, and St. Louis.[13]

The *Jung Amerika* movement was short-lived. While four hundred
to six hundred persons were estimated to have attended meetings of the
reform association, the leaders met with indifference and hostility. Some
of the members became more enthusiastic over the Mexican War than
over land reform or the rights of labor, and they joined the Army. The
organization's few English-speaking members drifted away in response
to the hostile sentiment of natives, who regarded the agitation as un-
American. Kriege himself flirted with Tammany Hall and alienated himself from the more radical reformers, who within two years turned to
another and more profound thinker, Wilhelm Weitling.[14]

Weitling was born and reared in the liberal center of Magdeburg, Germany. As a journeyman tailor, he felt the pangs of poverty; and his active mind rebelled against his masters. He went to Paris, where he became a powerful member of the *Bund der Gerechten,* and crossed into Switzerland, where he preached his philosophy in a Geneva tailor's shop. There he formed communist associations, issued a periodical for workers, and carried on organizational work in Zurich and other cities.[15] Imprisoned and banished from Switzerland and Prussia, Weitling sailed for America in 1847.

Weitling was not unknown to reformers in the United States. He had written in Europe several effective pamphlets, one of which he translated as "The Gospel of the Poor Sinner." After arriving at New York, he hobnobbed with Albert Brisbane and other American Fourierites and revived the radical agitation among the Germans. Under his guidance, a secret organization, the *Befreiungsbund* (League of Deliverance), appeared in New York City and in other German communities as far away as New Orleans and New Braunfels, Texas.[16] Weitling had hardly formed this German-American equivalent for the *Bund der Gerechten* when news of uprisings abroad impelled him to return to Germany as a propagandist and revolutionary agitator. He soon was forced to flee the *Vaterland* and, after a brief stay in England, he landed once more at New York in August, 1849.[17]

Clearly influenced by the writings of Fourier, Weitling's communism was based on moral grounds and deep religious conviction. He believed that in the search for equality and happiness, mankind was shackled by the evils of private property and its offspring, inheritance and money, which had created a modern form of slavery. Capital, wrote Weitling, was originally the property of laborers, who therefore should enjoy what was rightfully theirs. In Weitling's utopia, all would receive a guarantee of support and enjoyment in return for six hours of labor a day; beyond this the enjoyments of each would depend upon the surplus of labor rendered. In keeping with the usual demands of the times, Weitling proposed an elaborate system of public education.[18]

In America, Weitling was best known for his theory of the bank of exchange. Before he came to the United States, Weitling had advocated the common ownership of property and the centralized management of both the production and distribution of goods. In Europe, he and others had preached that such a transformation of society could be achieved only by political revolution; in the United States, however, Weitling found no enthusiasm for the destruction of American political institutions. On the contrary, American workingmen emphasized the need for economic reforms within the existing political framework. Weitling, therefore, abandoned his earlier ideas of ownership and management, retaining only the theory of centralization of exchange. This he emphasized in the form of a "bank of exchange," which, he declared, was "the soul of all reforms, the foundation for all cooperative attempts." [19] Stores for raw materials and finished products should be set up, and paper money should be used as a medium of exchange. To these stores the workers would bring their products and receive in exchange whatever they needed, according to the value of their products. [20]

Within a few months after his second arrival in America, Weitling created an *Arbeiterbund* (Workers' League), with a central organization in New York City. This new association was dedicated to his theories and to the founding and support of "Communia," a communistic colony in Wisconsin, to which territory German immigrants already were flocking. [21] The propaganda organ of the *Bund* was called the *Republik der Arbeiter*. It appeared as a monthly in January, 1850, a weekly from April, 1851, to December, 1854, then again as a monthly until its death in July, 1855. From the beginning it represented Weitling's personal views. [22] In New York, as in other cities, the new league busied itself with plans for implementing the labor exchange, and Weitling himself addressed meeting after meeting of the various trades' *Vereine*. By the autumn of 1850, three groceries, two bakeries, two tailor shops, and a boardinghouse, all in the New York area, were carrying out Weitling's principles. [23] The limited membership of the association, however, showed the indifference of the majority of the German workingmen. From March, 1851, to July, 1856, there were only 967 members of the *Arbeiterbund*. [24]

Nevertheless, one of the binding forces among the Germans was the idea of co-operation. The Germans believed in producers' co-operatives, not merely as an expediency to be used during a strike, but as a guiding principle, as an end as well as a means. [25] Fresh from the turmoil of the mid-century European revolutions, recent immigrants joined the German labor movement in the United States and instilled it with varying anti-capitalistic ideals. These newcomers, whose schemes ranged from visionary utopias to the advocacy of terrorism, envisioned America as a proving ground for their ideas and as a training camp for proletarian forces doing battle throughout the capitalistic world. Compared with the English and the Irish, the Germans were more imaginative, more willing to sacrifice in the present for the sake of the future, more prone to the consideration of grandiose plans. Their idealism was kindled with a glowing faith in the integrity and honesty of their fellow workers. [26]

Weitling did not believe that small producers' co-operatives alone

would relieve the lot of the workingmen; he urged a combination of all
workers and small employers against their common enemy, the powerful
merchant-capitalist.[27] In practice, however, Weitling lent his aid to the
co-operative movement. As a representative of the German tailors, he
appealed to the New York City Industrial Congress in 1850 for funds
to support an Association Clothing Establishment.[28]

During 1850 and 1851, Weitling was the dominant personality in the
German labor movement. He formed the first central organization of
the workers' *Vereine* in New York in 1850, the *Zentral-kommission der
vereinigten Gewerbe* (Central Committee of the United Trades), the
first session of which was attended by delegates chosen by some 2,400
workingmen. More than one fourth of the persons represented were
cabinetmakers, and another third were bakers, shoemakers, upholsterers,
and tailors.[29] Weitling's influence was evident, not only in the proceedings, but in the nature of the organizations which sent delegates.
Among them were a lodge of an American "protective union," or consumers' co-operative, an *Ökonomischer Tauschassociation,* or barter
society with eighty members, and the *Soziale Reformverein* or Central
Social Reform Association, with 200 members comprising the nucleus
of Weitling's followers.[30]

Weitling's labor exchange theory was considered favorably by a few
organizations and accepted in part by others. The *Reformverein* opened
its meetings for the discussion of the bank of exchange, and soon the
German trades began to act. Among the first were the German carpenters,
whose constitution announced a goal of steady work and the full product
of each member's labor, called upon other trades as well as carpenters
throughout the country to form similar associations, and advocated a
common bank of exchange for all trades.[31] At a meeting of carpenters,
cabinetmakers, and shoemakers, over a thousand persons voted to establish a Weitling-inspired *Gewerbe-Tauschbank.*[32]

Weitling was served by a number of devoted disciples who spread his
propaganda. Throughout 1850 Franz Arnold was the most active lieutenant, agitating for banks of exchange in Philadelphia, Pittsburgh, St.
Louis, and other western cities. Weitling's power waned rapidly after
1851, however, owing to defections of men like Arnold and the alienation
of those who opposed Weitling's dictatorial attitude and his refusal to
submit to majority rule.[33] Although he continued to publish the *Republik
der Arbeiter* until 1854 Weitling lost his influence as early as 1852.[34] His
panacea meant less to the German artisans than did practical measures
of immediate benefit, which did not involve tiresome and lengthy organizational work. The rank and file were more attracted to the principle

of simple producers' associations. Unsuccessful attempts to better their working conditions proved to them the need for solidarity, and they listened eagerly to schemes for the setting up of co-operative workshops. If these ventures failed to live long, they might by their competition at least force employers to pay them more.

When the Germans came in contact with the English-speaking workers, they began to lose their ardor for co-operation. In general, American workingmen did not favor producers' co-operatives. While reformers or a few artisans who liked the idea of "self-employment" often persuaded them to adopt resolutions favoring co-operatives, the workers shrank from the actual work of starting the movement. Unlike the Germans, the American trade unionists sought limited immediate objectives through combination for collective action against employers, and they hesitated to follow the example of the Germans by creating large-scale co-operatives involving substantial sections of individual trades.[35] The Industrial Congress which met in New York in 1850 failed to give financial aid to striking German tailors who had requested funds for a co-operative shop.[36] In the same year, German cabinetmakers organized co-operatively, but they could not enlist the support of the Americans. Some of the Germans complained about the lack of sympathy and energy of the American cabinetmakers and of their unwillingness to join the association.[37] Several other similar societies were started by the Germans, and most either failed completely or lingered briefly before disintegrating. By September, 1851, only four German co-operatives existed in New York.[38]

Apart from the reluctance of the English-speaking workingmen to join the co-operative movement, the Germans encountered certain practical hindrances. They lacked capital; while manufacturers could employ newly arrived immigrants at low wages, the co-operative societies were unable to increase their capital in proportion to the increase in immigration. Many of the so-called "productive associations," moreover, were really organizations of small capitalists or master workmen, their members sometimes contributing several hundred or even a few thousand dollars. Other difficulties were the necessity of applying to the legislature for special charters; inexperience in business management; and, occasionally, the restraining influence of religious conservatism, which saw in co-operative shops the "first step to socialism." [39] Realizing the small impression their schemes made upon the native workingmen, many of whom, incidentally, were Catholics, the Germans drifted away from co-operation. In time they adopted American trade union principles, sometimes with more success than their fellow workers.[40]

The defection of the Germans from the principles of co-operation led them toward a more radical type of activity. From 1852 to 1856 a group of refugee intellectuals took advantage of the trade union movement to use the unions as the basis of a general class-conscious organization. The leader around whom these reformers clustered was Joseph Weydemeyer, who has been considered the most prominent German labor agitator in America during those years.[41]

Weydemeyer introduced Marxian socialism to American labor; he was a close follower of Marxian ideas and became Marx's mouthpiece in the United States. Born in Münster, Westphalia, in 1818, he received a good education and served for a time as an officer in the Prussian Army. He began to associate with Marx and Engels at Brussels in 1846, and thereafter remained a faithful disciple. In 1851 he landed at New York, and at once circulated among the German workers. He attempted to combine political and industrial organization through a short-lived revolutionary society called the *Proletarierbund* and the publication of two extremely ephemeral propaganda papers, both entitled *Revolution*, the second of which appeared but twice.[42] It was not long before he matched wits with trade union leaders.

At the instigation of Weydemeyer and a coterie of close associates, a general meeting of the New York German trades was held at Mechanics Hall on March 21, 1853. Its purpose, the formation of a workingmen's alliance, was discussed at length, Weydemeyer demanding political action and the trade unionists desiring merely a central trades council. Weydemeyer was victorious, however, and the meeting adopted a platform which recognized both industrial and political planks. One consequence was the formation of an *Allgemeiner Arbeiterbund*, which later changed its name to the *Amerikanischer Arbeiterbund* to distinguish it from Weitling's association, which still existed.[43] The league made determined efforts to unite the workers regardless of nationality, for the reform of working conditions, and it organized them politically into ward clubs, where delegates were elected irrespective of crafts or trades. In three months eleven of the city's twenty wards had been organized, and branch *Vereine* had been established in Staten Island, Brooklyn, and Williamsburg. Initial enthusiasm waned, however, and the work proceeded haltingly, while outside the New York area the socialists made even less progress.[44]

The program of Weydemeyer's *Arbeiterbund* emphasized current trade union demands: a ten-hour day and the abolition of child labor. It stressed the continuing desire for self-improvement by advocating free higher education for all and state supervision and care of children whose families could not support them. Like all reform movements among the Germans, it sought support by opposing "Sunday" and temperance legislation, a tactic which attracted wide attention among the beer-loving and recreation-conscious Teutonic population.[45]

To spread the Marxian dogma, the Weydemeyer group issued the *Reform,* a daily which was, at least at first, completely proletarian and revolutionary. Ostensibly its editor was Kellner, a refugee from Kassel who had helped publish a socialist daily in Europe. Weydemeyer remained in the background, in accordance with the custom of European revolutionaries of protecting the guiding spirit from governmental complications.[46] The staff of the *Reform* was in close touch with Marxian movements in London and Paris, in Germany and Switzerland, and in all refugee circles.[47] However, the paper did not succeed in winning the confidence of many German workingmen, perhaps largely because of the opposition or studied contempt of the popular *Staats-Zeitung* and other German newspapers. In March, 1854, the sheet was taken over by a company which struggled valiantly and vainly to save it; in a little over a month the *Reform* was but a memory.[48] By the mid-fifties some of the radicals had grown conservative, and many had left New York City to carry on their agitation in the West. When Weydemeyer himself went West in 1856, the Marxians of New York lost their most effective commander.[49]

An attempt was made to reunite the New York socialists the following year at a meeting in Hoboken. On the initiative of F. A. Sorge, Albert Komp, Fritz Jacobi, Fr. Kamm, and others, a communist club was created, embracing principles of the equality of mankind and the rejection of all religious beliefs. Although the group corresponded with Marx in London, with Weydemeyer in Milwaukee, and other socialists elsewhere, the club was not influential, and during the Civil War it suspended its meetings. With the return of peace in the land, the group renewed its activity; and several of its members pioneered the International Workingmen's Association, later known as the "First International," on American soil.[50]

The efforts of these radicals laid the groundwork for the strongly socialistic German labor movement after the Civil War. From a nucleus of intellectuals in the mid-forties, augmented by a stream of revolutionary exiles—the famous "forty-eighters"—the proletarian forces gathered strength to combat the earlier complaisance of the German artisans. The waves of immigration in the middle of the century brought to New York a new generation of increasingly class-conscious workers who provided a fertile field for the experiments of Weitling and the Marxism of Weydemeyer. The refugees exerted no little influence through workers' singing associations similar to those in Europe, through the *Turnvereine* which leaned strongly toward socialism, through several German free schools associated with Weydemeyer's *Arbeiterbund,* through a consumer's union, a mutual fire insurance company, and benevolent and mutual aid societies.[51] After a lapse during the Civil War, the movement revived as high living costs stirred unrest in the mid-sixties. On October 6, 1865, a small group of disciples of Ferdinand Lassalle met in Spring Street to form an *Allgemeiner Deutsche Arbeiter-Verein.* This new society counted among its members many "forty-eighters" and some members of the Communist Club; it wielded considerable power in labor circles and maintained relations with the National Labor Union, an American organization headed by William H. Sylvis, and with the International Workingmen's Association.[52]

The organizational activities of the socialist leaders introduced a new element into American labor struggles. From the beginning the socialists devised tactics of collaboration, at first boring from within, and then capturing unions for their own purposes. They embarked upon a policy of dual unionism when they were unable to win over their more conservative fellow workers. By these methods the German radicals gained such influence that at the end of the Civil War they dominated the German labor movement.[53] Their efforts bore fruit in the organization of the *Vereinigte Tischler* (United Cabinetmakers) after a mass meeting of 500 woodworkers in 1859 at the Halle der Social-Reformer, 281 Grand Street. This successful association became Local 7 of the furniture workers' union, which played a vital role in the New York trades union movement, and finally emerged as Local 309 of the carpenters' union.[54] In 1858 the cigar makers of New York and vicinity formed a society which claimed 325 members, mostly German.[55] The next year the piano manufacturing house of Steinway threatened to fire any workers attending labor meetings; the piano makers accepted the challenge, struck for higher wages, and took steps to form a lasting union.[56] Other German trades, including the turners, upholsterers, printers, ladies' shoemakers, and capmakers were organized in the late fifties and early sixties.[57] Some of these unions, such as the printers', failed because of insufficient funds and internal dissensions, but they provided the backbone of later and more fortunate ventures.[58] A few years after coming to New York in 1863, Samuel Gompers noticed that the *Arbeiter Union,* the central body for the German workers in New York, was more virile and resourceful than the Workingmen's Council, its English-speaking equivalent. The

Germans were more educated and disciplined in European labor movements and were generally associated with the International.[59]

Thus the German labor organizations paralleled the American, gathering strength as class-conscious German immigrants swelled their ranks after 1847. Until mid-century the Germans had kept to themselves, largely because of language difficulties.[60] Thereafter, a strenuous effort toward co-operation was spearheaded by the agitation of the bakers and tailors, and an appreciable number of English-speaking workingmen collaborated with the Germans in these trades.[61] Germans as well as Americans came under the influence of reformers; but, like the Americans, they reverted to simple unionism as the best means of improving their condition. In one respect, however, the Germans differed from their native brethren: they felt more keenly, often through personal experiences abroad, the emotional impact of early communism and of Marxian socialism, and they continued to uphold its principles long after the Civil War.

XI

CONSCIOUSNESS OF KIND

WHEN IMMIGRANTS SET FOOT upon Manhattan Island, they brought with them memories of their old homeland. Past associations and sentimental feeling for the Old Country, involving attachments to region, church, and family, were cohesive elements in the new land to which they had come. Immigrants' letters were filled with intensely personal matters, of births, marriages, illnesses, and deaths in families, news of friends, employment conditions, and local gossip.[1] Homesickness was unashamedly expressed in correspondence and in the press, as amateur poets burst forth with songs of longing for the Fatherland.[2] Stationers and book-sellers offered inexpensive views of European towns, and museums exhibited bas-reliefs and miniature models of mountains, lakes, and cities, which refreshed the foreigners' memories of beloved birthplaces and scenes of childhood experiences.[3] Among the Irish and the Germans, regional loyalties were sustained in New York by social and fraternal clubs like the Sligo Young Men's Association, the *Mecklenburger Mandschiens-Club*, and the *Norddeutsche Gemütlichkeit*.[4] Military organizations were formed by natives of Baden, Bavaria, and the Palatinate, and the more ignorant Irishmen clanned together in secret societies representing Cork, Connaught, Down, and other counties.[5]

When misfortune overtook those who remained in Europe, the national sympathies of immigrants in New York superseded local loyalties. The Irish gave spontaneously and generously to their kinfolk in the Green Isle, sending whatever they could afford—usually small drafts of a few dollars at a time—to stave off starvation in years of lean harvests. During the famine year of 1846, the Irish of New York City transmitted over $800,000 by every packet to every parish in Ireland.[6] Others helped, too: Christians and Jews, natives, Germans, and Frenchmen contributed to a central relief committee in New York, which received over $170,000 in cash, and foodstuffs valued at $70,000.[7] The Irish in America, however, were the most concerned, and for a decade following the famine they sent $19,680,000 to Ireland.[8] When Scottish weavers, carpenters, and dock workers "depended upon human sympathy for their existence" during the depression of 1841–1842, the Scots in New York held public meetings and solicited contributions.[9] The French collected over $2,000 to aid the families of the dead and wounded in the July Revolution and in the forties and fifties sent relief funds to the victims of floods in France.[10] Italian merchants and intellectuals were responsible for raising a fund of $10,000 to relieve wives and children of Italian soldiers who were crippled or killed in the war with Austria in 1859.[11]

Patriotic feelings were aroused by the arrival of royal personalities, as when the French tendered a reception to the Prince de Joinville upon his arrival in New York in 1838, or by the death of national figures like Lafayette, the Duke of Orleans, and the Duke of Wellington.[12] National anniversary celebrations were likewise observed at New York. Every year the Scots met to observe the birthday of Robert Burns, amid poetry, songs, toasts, and speeches, and a number of Burns clubs were formed during the fifties.[13] Wealthy Englishmen celebrated Queen Victoria's birthday, but the Irish commemorated instead the American Fourth of July.[14] In 1859 the Germans held an elaborate *Schillerfeier*, honoring the great German poet with dramatics, concerts, speeches, dances, and illuminations.[15]

The patriotic ferment which pervaded the Continent of Europe after the Napoleonic Wars, like the simmering Irish restiveness under British domination, mingled in the melting pot of New York. The Empire City was the American focal point of the political exiles of Europe. When the influential Professor Sylvester Jordan, of the University of Giessen, was imprisoned for freethinking and reform agitation, New York Germans collected some $600 for the relief of his family.[16] Mazzini's Young Italy movement was spread among the Italians of the New World by Felice Foresti, who in 1841 organized its New York branch, the *Congrega Centrale*, as a center of Italian republican propaganda.[17] Polish exiles in the city agitated for the liberation of Poland, Hungarians sought recruits to fight Austrian despotism, and a small band of Cubans formed juntas to free their island from Spanish rule.[18] Stimulated by political refugees from abroad, the Germans held mass meetings, attended benefits, and joined societies for the collection of money and the dispatch of republican *émigrés* to aid the German revolutionists of 1848–1852.[19] Themes of nationalism, republicanism, and—among the left-wing elements—the unity of the working classes drew together the French, Germans, Italians, Latin Americans, Poles, Hungarians, Irish, and Americans in mass meetings, processions, and dinners celebrating the cause of liberals all over Europe.[20]

The common nationalistic fervor in 1848 heartened the champions of Irish freedom, who nevertheless deplored the anticlericalism of the Continental revolutionists.[21] Indeed, Irish political freedom was closely related to the unhindered operation of the Catholic hierarchy in Ireland. When the Catholic emancipation movement gathered momentum in the twenties, Friends of Ireland associations sprang up in American cities; and the New York group, led by William J. Macneven and Robert Emmet, among others, kept up a vigorous agitation for Irish religious and political liberties.[22] The Friends of Civil and Religious Liberty celebrated the Catholic Emancipation Act in 1829, and thereafter for fifteen years, the Irish in New York supported O'Connell's movement for the repeal of the legislative union of Ireland with England.[23] In 1843 a mammoth Repeal Convention met for three days in the Empire City and planned to organize each state of the Union in a supreme effort to raise money for Repeal.[24] The Irish had complete confidence in Daniel O'Connell, and many of the poorest immigrants eagerly donated their mite of twelve and one half cents or twenty-five cents, but the collapse of the Repeal movement and the appearance of the radical Young Ireland Party divided the loyalties of Irish-Americans.[25] By 1848, the Irish had ceased contributing to Repeal; the more radical turned to the leadership of John Mitchel and T. F. Meagher and established "Directories" in several cities, the New York Directory receiving in a few weeks over $40,000.[26] However, famine in the Green Isle drew from the immigrant Irish the funds which might have sustained the rebellion of 1848, the failure of which ended widespread support of movements to free Ireland.[27]

These nationalistic activities, however, sprang from sources external to the lives of the immigrants. In not a few instances the embers of patriotism were fanned by refugees whose primary interest was in Europe, not America. Genuine immigrants, planning to spend their entire lives in the United States, were more deeply concerned about their everyday existence, the welfare of their families, the future of their children in the new world of opportunity. To satisfy their social and material needs, they founded a wide variety of institutions forming an intricate pattern of group activities which eased the adjustment of Europeans to American conditions.

Man craves companionship and associates with people of similar interests. So it was with the alien, who looked for friends in a friendless new home, social approval in the midst of the contempt of native Americans, and material well-being in a fiercely competitive, materialistic, young nation. In the saloon, the grocery, and the liquor shop, he associated with his fellow foreigners in pursuit of relaxation and the enjoyment of simple pleasures.[28] Hundreds of restaurants, oyster cellars, and "pensions" offered opportunities for business and professional contacts as well. Love of liquor, fostered by the harshness of life in the Green Isle, led Irishmen to the myriads of barrooms of New York or to the more respectable Ivy Green Tavern of Malachi Fallon, Daniel Sweeny's House of Refreshment, or John Keefe's restaurant.[29] Accustomed to the frivolity of the village *Wirtshaus,* the Germans flocked to the beer gardens in New York.[30] One of the largest, and a favorite, was the Atlantic Garden on the Bowery, where both sexes of all ages congregated "amid dense clouds of tobacco-smoke, and hurry of waiters, and banging of glasses, and calling for beer." [31] Like other big German beer halls, the Atlantic contained several bars, a shooting gallery, billiard tables and bowling alleys, and an orchestra. During the forties, the Atlantic catered exclusively to Germans, but by the late sixties it was patronized by crowds of French, Irish, English, Italians, Portuguese, and even Asiatics.[32] The English gravitated to such places as the Richard the Third House, the Brown Jug Tavern, and the Albion Hotel; the Scots gathered at the Blue Bonnet, the Wallace, and the Burns houses; the French, Swiss, and Italians, at the Café de Mille Colonnes, the Restaurant Lafayette, and scores of other eating and drinking places.[33]

At the larger restaurants, "assembly rooms," and hotels, immigrant groups held banquets, parties, balls, and anniversary celebrations. During the summer months, however, they deserted lower Manhattan for the coffee houses of Bloomingdale, Staten Island, Hoboken, and the north shore of Long Island.[34] Excursions and picnics were popular among all nationalities, the Germans developing the habit into an inclusive group activity.

For closer and more permanent associations, the newcomers founded or joined a huge number of fraternal and benevolent societies. In their simplest and most typical form, these were mutual aid societies, much like those already existing in Europe and America. Their members usually were tradesmen, artisans, and laborers, whose meager earnings induced them to band together for protection against the uncertainties of life in an era which saw only the beginnings of life insurance. The mutual aid society provided sickness benefits to its members and paid the funeral expenses of those who died. Although the earliest of these associations appeared in colonial times, the surge of immigration in the nineteenth century greatly increased their size and number. In the twenties, the Irish formed a Hibernian Universal Benevolent Society and a St. Patrick Friendly Society, which were among the first of many similar groups appearing in the next three decades.[35]

Daily occupational contacts led to the formation of mutual aid societies in various trades. Tailors, shipwrights and caulkers, painters, masons, quarrymen, and longshoremen were only a few of those who created benevolent associations, which sometimes increased their bargaining strength with employers.[36] One of the largest of these societies was the Laborers' Union Benevolent Association, formed in 1843. By 1850 its 2,500 to 4,000 members paid monthly dues of twelve and a half cents, the sick received $2.00 per week, and families of deceased members were granted $15.00 for funeral expenses.[37]

Other groups were formed under religious auspices. Catholic churches sometimes organized them for the benefit of their members, and all the earlier Jewish societies developed within the synagogues.[38] Because of the secessions resulting from intrasynagogue controversies in the forties, many Jewish mutual aid societies severed their religious connections as the only means of preserving their membership. Meanwhile, newly formed independent societies appealed to Jews who were unaffiliated with any synagogue and, therefore, ordinarily ineligible for burial privileges.[39]

The functions of some mutual aid associations expanded to include the relief of families of deceased members, and new groups were founded exclusively for the support of widows and orphans.[40] All such organizations were by their very nature exclusive. Because of their limited means, they extended protection only to members and their families; and while they were of little aid to the charitable efforts of the community at large, they nevertheless performed a vital function in giving their members a sense of security and well-being.

Most of the larger benevolent associations, like the St. George's and St. Andrew's societies, and the Friendly Sons of St. Patrick, were composed of wealthy merchants and professional men. Thus it was customary for these groups to help the poor of their own nationalities, but their charity relieved only a minute proportion of the needy, and new societies attempted futilely to accomplish the same ends. In the thirties a few Scotch journeymen bakers formed the Thistle Benevolent Association and by a wise policy of admitting rich Scotsmen increased their membership to nearly two hundred in 1841.[41] By the close of the Civil War virtually every nationality in New York claimed at least one benevolent society.[42]

Fraternal lodges, combining sociability and mutual aid with features of secrecy and the ritualism of oaths, passwords and grips, attracted immigrants from all walks of life. The newcomers created their own orders and also organized chapters of existing fraternities like the Masons and the Odd Fellows. St. Andrew's Lodge, No. 169, under the jurisdiction of the Grand Lodge of Scotland, was active in New York Masonry before 1830, and during the following decades the Germans, the French, and later the Italians established Masonic lodges.[43] The French and Germans organized branches of the Odd Fellows, the Swiss had their Helvetia Lodge, and the Germans formed lodges of the Brothers of Hermann, the Sons of Hermann, the Order of Templars, the Druids, and others.[44] In 1843 German Jews established their first independent fraternal order, the B'nai B'rith, and six years later a similar order, the Free Sons of Israel.[45]

Fraternal association and national consciousness were united in the myriads of sporting and athletic clubs founded by the foreigners. On the waters of New York Harbor, the Hudson and East rivers, and Long Island Sound, immigrants indulged in the popular pastimes of fishing and boating. As early as 1833 an East River Fishing Club was organized by Irishmen, and in 1844 English rowing enthusiasts formed a boat club.[46] On the meadows of Manhattan and Long Island, and at the Elysian Fields in Hoboken across the Hudson, groups of newcomers introduced to New York the national games of Europe. German gymnasts performed as the "Jefferson Tumbling Company" in 1840, a number of Scotsmen created the St. Andrew's Curling Club in 1845, and an Irish hurling and football club was formed to revive that "truly Irish national sport." [47] During the forties and fifties the St. George Cricket Club afforded Englishmen a chance to challenge such "brother amateurs" as the Toronto and the New York cricket clubs.[48]

Some organizations enabled individuals to build and maintain their social position in the foreign community. To be a soldier or a fireman heightened one's prestige among the less favored inhabitants. After midcentury, a number of the city's volunteer fire companies were completely dominated by immigrants, usually Irish but also English and Germans, who formed with the natives innumerable chowder clubs and target companies.[49] For the Germans, at least, the fire companies were not new. Both in Europe and in America, the German *Turnvereine,* or gymnastic societies, acted as volunteer fire companies.[50] Feasting and drinking were an integral part of the fireman's life, and until the temperance movement crept into the firehouses, a barrel of liquor was frequently hauled along with the engine to each fire for the resuscitation of exhausted fire laddies.[51]

More popular than the fire laddies were the glamorous, uniformed militia and target companies composed of workers, shopkeepers, and clerks, both native and foreign. Despite names and appearances, these organizations were really social clubs which afforded recreation and companionship. They lent dignity and prestige to their members, transforming them from forgotten men into proud patriots who displayed their prowess at target excursions and shooting matches, funeral processions, civic ceremonies, Fourth of July and St. Patrick's Day parades. When the men of the Napper Tandy Light Artillery Company marched in their green jackets with yellow braid, light blue trousers with scarlet stripe, and blue caps with braid and tassel, they never failed to win the admiring applause of the Irish onlookers, especially the ladies.[52]

Irish immigrants banded together, frequently naming their companies after Emmet, Mitchel, Meagher, or other national heroes, while the Germans preferred to honor Washington and Jefferson, the French their Lafayette, the Italians their Garibaldi. Some units revealed the regional origin of their members, such as the Bavarian Military Club and the Kilkenny Volunteers, or their occupations, such as the companies of Irish shipwrights and caulkers and the German shoemakers, bakers, brewers, and coopers.[53]

A compelling reason for the establishment of "foreign" military companies was the unwillingness of the native companies to admit immigrants. Thus in 1836, when the New York Cadets resolved to prohibit foreigners from joining the corps, ten Irish members immediately declared their independence and organized an Irish company, the Montgomery Guard.[54] Because the newcomers were rarely admitted to the native units of the state militia, scores of Irish and German companies soon were organized, and although they bought their own uniforms, the state supplied them with arms and equipment.[55] In 1850 some seven hundred men of the Irish Dragoons, Guyon Cadets, Felon Guards, Carroll Light Guard, Sarsfield Guard, Erina Guard, and other Irish companies combined as the "Irish Volunteers" to form the Ninth Regiment of the New York State Militia, the first Irish regiment in America.[56] During the next ten years the Irish companies appeared in such profusion that they dominated the 69th and 75th regiments and were included in the 10th, 11th, 14th, and 70th regiments, while several maintained their independence of the state militia.[57] The galaxy of Irish units, motivated partly by desire to fight a future war for Irish independence, contrasted strangely with the failure of the English to organize a single military body during the entire period.[58]

The colorful uniforms, martial displays, and companionship provided by the militia also attracted hundreds of Germans, Frenchmen, Scots, and Italians, Christians and Jews. Four German companies, averaging eighty men apiece in 1840, included a cavalry troop, artillery, and grenadiers.[59] The oldest of these companies was the Jefferson Riflemen, 38th Regiment of the New York State artillery and formerly the Jefferson Guard, founded in 1835 by a group of Germans headed by the politician Captain Francis Lassak.[60] In the fifties the 3d and 5th regiments were completely German, as were units of the 2d, 4th, 6th, 11th, and 12th regiments.[61] Toward the middle of the century the French and the Scots organized several companies. The Frenchmen formed the *Gardes Lafayette* in 1847, soon absorbed by the 12th and later the 55th regiments of the state militia.[62] The Scottish Guard and the Highland Guards were created in the mid-forties, followed by the Scottish Fusilier Guards and the New York Scottish Highlanders; the latter, organized in 1859, became the 79th New York Highland Regiment.[63] While revolution flared in Italy in 1848, the first Italian unit was organized; led by Captain M. G. Lenghi and the politician Charles Del Vecchio, the company presented a ceremonial sword to the valiant General Giuseppe Avezzana upon his arrival in New York.[64] In 1858 the Italians created a *Guardia Nazionale Italiana*, and a Portuguese company was formed in the following year.[65] Jewish military units, appearing in the fifties, included Troop K—Empire Hussars, the Joseph A. Jackson Guards, the Young Men's Lafayette Association, and the Asmonean Guard, which, however, included Christians.[66] The significance of the immigrant military companies is evident in the fact that in 1853 more than 4,000 of the 6,000 uniformed militia in New York City were of foreign birth. Of these, 2,600 were Irish, 1,700 were German.[67]

Less strenuous but no less effective as a cohesive force were the many social clubs established by foreigners. Most of the benevolent societies, such as the Frendly Sons of St. Patrick, the St. George's, St. Andrew's, and St. David's societies, the French Benevolent Society, and to some extent the German Society, were wining and dining clubs with limited charitable functions. The New York Caledonian Club, founded in 1856, was similar to the older societies but somewhat more democratic.[68] Other groups were completely recreational and had no philanthropic motives, like the Mallow Social Club formed by Irishmen, a society of bald-headed Germans, a Welsh body known as the "Young Cambrians," the Jewish "Harmonie" society, the *Société Lyrique Française,* which gave quarterly banquets, and the *Amis de Gâité,* which conducted annual balls.[69] In the thirties the wealthy English modeled their Albion Club after the fashionable clubs of London, and at their clubhouse in Park Place they gathered for mealtime sociability, billiards, whist, chess, and checkers, gambling only for limited stakes and allowing no games on Sundays.[70] The Germans, with contempt for this austere attitude toward the Sabbath, organized countless singing and dramatic societies which gave performances on Sundays, the Germans' traditional time for jollity.[71]

The social life of the Germans revolved around their innumerable *Vereine,* some of which fostered music, literature, dramatics, or gymnastics, but all of which gave vent to the time-honored Teutonic love of *Gemütlichkeit.* This was the initial impulse of many occupational *Vereine* of shoemakers, painters, turners, cabinetmakers, upholsterers, piano makers, butchers, confectioners, brewers, cigar makers, barbers, waiters, and members of other trades which flourished with the high tide of German immigration in the fifties.[72] It likewise motivated the professional associations formed by German physicians and surgeons in 1846 and 1855, a German pharmacists' reading club in 1851, and two chess clubs which appeared several years later.[73] German amateur dramatic clubs, first treading the boards in New York about 1840, provided the nucleus of the professional German theater.[74] During the fifties several of these theatrical societies performed comedies and vaudeville acts in hotels and beer gardens, and occasionally in theaters, where "a strictly German audience, which if not very elegant, was yet of a perfectly respectable stamp." [75] A German amateur vaudeville performance at the Olympic Theater impressed the sophisticated *Albion* with its "very Germanesque acting, strongly characteristic of low life in the old Vaterland, and full of fun and drollery. The jokes, though rather broad perhaps, were still exceedingly good." [76]

More characteristic of the Germans were singing societies, which presented regular concerts, performed on public occasions, serenaded popular stage and opera stars, and gave benefits for charitable causes. Patterned after the familiar *Liedertafel* of Germany, they appeared first in the thirties but were small, informal, and ephemeral for a full decade until the increasing German population supported larger and permanent *Vereine.*[77] All classes of society enjoyed this form of recreation, the singing club of the impoverished social reformers rivaling in musical attainments the aristocratic and wealthy *Liederkranz,* which gave its first concert in 1847.[78] During the fifties the *Rheinischer Sängerbund,* the *Arion,* the *Yorkville Männerchor,* the *Sängerrunde,* and the *Concordia* were among the leading singing societies; and by 1858 at least seventeen well-known *Vereine* were vocalizing in Manhattan, Brooklyn, Williamsburg, and Hoboken.[79]

More politically minded were the *Turnvereine,* gymnastic societies introduced to New York in 1848 and 1850 by political refugees who had been members of *Turnvereine* in Germany.[80] Organized originally during the dark days of Napoleonic conquest, the turner groups emphasized bodily strength and vigor as a means of creating a united and liberal, republican Germany. In America their interest in German regeneration

was paralleled by their forceful propaganda for free soil and the abolition of slavery.[81] Although the turners' early leaders were intellectuals,
the rank and file were skilled artisans, for whom social activities were
perhaps more vital than political partisanship: the turners gave gymnastic exhibitions, held fencing and shooting matches, sang as glee clubs,
acted in plays, listened to lectures, debated, and drank beer.[82]

The societies of several nationalities in New York organized periodic
large-scale social gatherings. The German *Folksfeste,* reminiscent of
festive occasions in villages and towns of the Old Country, became a
German-American institution in the decade of the fifties. German target
companies marched to their *Schützenfeste,* and civic groups celebrated
the memory of national heroes with popular gatherings on the outskirts
of town.[83] The various *Turnvereine* of New York held their first *Turnfest*
in 1853; and a thousand turners, including hundreds from Washington,
Baltimore, Philadelphia, Albany, Bridgeport, New Haven, and Boston,
gathered for a series of processions, picnics, and performances.[84] In these
same years the German musical societies of scattered communities as-
sembled every summer for their *Sängerfest.* The first took place in Philadelphia in 1850, the next in Baltimore, and in 1852 scores of *Vereine*
including hundreds of singers participated in a gala four-day festival in
the Empire City.[85] New York played host again in 1855 and in 1858, when
278 musicians and 300 singers presented Beethoven's Ninth Symphony
at the Academy of Music on a Sunday evening, paraded through the
streets the next morning, and topped the festivities with a picnic at
Jones' Wood along the East River north of 60th Street.[86]

Like the Germans, other nationalities maintained in colorful ceremonies their time-hallowed traditions. "Clad in the garb of the ancient
Gael," the Scots held annual games on Long Island or at the Elysian
Fields in Hoboken, where members of the Highland Society or the
Caledonian Club played shinty and competed at racing, leaping, throw-
ing, and other tests of strength and skill. These events were climaxed
with a banquet amid songs, recitations, and highland dances.[87] On St.
David's Day, the "National Cambrians" sang Welsh songs, heard the
harp of the Cymri, and watched the Welsh Druids in ancient costume.[88]
The Irish celebrated St. Patrick's Day with dinners, dances, and parades
led by the Irish military companies in full regalia.[89] During the fifties,
however, the enthusiasm of the Irish benevolent and trade societies for
marching on St. Patrick's Day was dimmed by the American condemnation of foreign-born militia as fostering divided loyalties and standing
in the way of the assimilation of adopted citizens.[90]

In the mid-century years, immigrants, like the natives, indulged in speculative ventures, some catching the gold rush fever and forming societies for group migration to California, others investing in land, steamships, railroads, mines, and industrial plants.[91] The less fortunate newcomers, however, sank their savings into the treasuries of building and loan associations, which mushroomed in the New York area. The almost irresistible appeal of these enterprises during the fifties lay in the widespread desire of the poor to secure homes cheaply and conveniently. Following the pattern already in use in England, they banded together, raised funds by subscription, and loaned money to members paying the highest premiums. So great was the demand for money that would-be homeowners sometimes borrowed from several different associations, and in the heat of competition interest rates soared; borrowers were known to have paid discounts of 33.33 per cent in the early phases of building operations.[92] In 1850 a group of French and Swiss planned, apparently without success, to found a little village for workingmen; and two years later a number of Irishmen formed a Village Homestead and Savings Fund Association through purchase of $100.00 shares in monthly installments of $2.00.[93] Land was to be bought and laid out in lots; individual members would obtain land at cost, and as the property was expected to "quadruple in value," the owner had "all the advantage of the speculation." [94] The Germans took part in "a thousand and one" speculations, of which the more important were the German Building Association, the First German Building Loan and Accumulating Fund Association, the German Building Association—Concordia, and the German Building Association in the City of New York.[95]

These immigrant projects looked better on paper than they were in actuality. The difficulty of withdrawing funds and the fines for nonpayment of dues led to frequent charges of mismanagement.[96] Promises of individual purchasers to pay promptly for land were based upon hopes never fulfilled. Sickness, unemployment, and rising living costs completed the ruin of many families who had made partial payments; and by 1856 these ventures, through lack of caution and unsound financing, had lifted $5,000,000 from the pockets of the working classes.[97] Among the building and loan schemes, some were nothing but speculative frauds which, by humanitarian appeals, offered for $20 (or less) lots which turned out to be "a good place for catching fish" or "a bottomless marsh inhabited only by frogs." [98]

After 1850 the wiser immigrants found better places for their money. Ignorance, suspicion, lack of interest, and insufficient funds had prevented the establishment of savings banks until in the winter of 1850–

1851 the untiring efforts of the Irish Emigrant Society secured a charter for an Emigrant Industrial Savings Bank.[99] Most of the bank's depositors, numbering about 2,300, were servants and laborers, but some were well-to-do; their accounts in 1856 averaged $238.56 and ranged from $1.00 to $10,000.00.[100] The Germans were the only other immigrant group to follow the Irish example. For years they talked about a bank, and countless schemes were advanced, but it was not until 1859 that a *Deutsche Sparbank* was opened.[101] Although some of its 3,500 depositors were Americans and Irish, the great majority were Germans, among them a large number of tailors, shoemakers, cabinetmakers, and grocers.[102] By 1860 the combined resources of these two banks amounted to nearly $2,500,000 belonging to more than 10,000 depositors, and four years later they held $6,056,600 belonging to 24,151 persons and organizations, clear evidence of the necessity and the popularity of these institutions.[103]

The group activities of businessmen were not limited to the founding of banks; insurance and shipping were of great concern to them. Early in 1859 the *Germania* life insurance company was formed, and three years later it showed an $18,000 surplus on a capitalization of $200,000.[104] As late as 1865 the *Germania* was the only German life insurance company in the United States, and it busily insured the lives of Germans in all parts of the country.[105] The German demand for other types of insurance was met by the creation in 1852 of an association for the insurance of horses and a $200,000 fire insurance company in 1857.[106] With the development of commerce in the forties and fifties, foreign-born merchants considered the establishment of exclusive shipping services. Several attempts by Frenchmen in New York to create a permanent French steamship line ended in failure, and early Irish plans for a direct steamship service to Galway came to naught; however, in 1858 a Galway and New York Steamship Company was successfully launched; and in the meantime German merchants had fathered two lines, the Hamburg America in 1856 and the North German Lloyd, whose ships began their runs between Bremen and New York in 1858.[107]

Except perhaps the business associations and the military companies, the group activities of the immigrant were necessary tools of adjustment to life in America. In some instances the newcomer adopted or joined institutions already familiar to Americans, such as the militia, the fire companies, building and loan associations, professional and commercial organizations, benevolent and mutual aid societies. These were foreign only in membership. Other immigrant associational activities, like the

Scottish games, the English pursuit of cricket, and the German theatrical, musical, and gymnastic *Vereine,* were deeply rooted in the national cultures of these peoples. The foreigners freely accepted elements of American social and economic life which were compatible with their European experience, but when they found no satisfactory substitute for their own social groupings, they attempted proudly, even defiantly, to preserve their cultural heritage.

XII

CHURCH, SCHOOL, AND CULTURAL ATTAINMENT

EVEN AS NATIONAL CONSCIOUSNESS was emphasized in the New World, an awareness of religious or racial kinship likewise was a cohesive bond in the immigrant community. As in Europe, the churches provided consolation for the individual and, particularly among the Irish Catholics, a rallying point for the group. For thousands of Irish immigrants the only familiar aspect of life in America was the Catholic Church, which also numbered among its communicants Germans, French, Swiss, Italians, and Spanish-speaking peoples. In 1830, according to an estimate of Bishop John Dubois, 35,000 Catholics lived in the Empire City; eleven years later there were between 60,000 and 80,000, and by mid-century, 100,000, of whom perhaps two thirds were Irish.[1]

The role of the Catholic Church as a unifying force appears most clearly in the ever expanding Irish population. When in the twenties and thirties Catholic Irish immigrants began pouring into New York, latent antipathies to "papists" stirred in the minds of Protestant Americans. As in colonial days, the newcomers were accused of adhering blindly to an authoritarian ecclesiastical hierarchy headed by a foreign potentate, the Pope, and creating an ugly menace to the religious and political liberties of the United States. Popular opposition to the Irish, however, was neither entirely theological nor based upon political theory but was mainly social in nature, resting upon the apparently universal contempt for poverty-stricken foreigners as an uncouth, ignorant, and clannish lot.[2]

As masses of impoverished immigrants, overwhelmingly Irish, crowded the almshouse, the jail, and other public institutions, Americans loudly protested the "incautious admission of foreigners," of "assassins and robbers," of "the filth and offscouring of all Europe."[3] American resentment was kindled by the knowledge that many English towns and several Swiss and German states deported or facilitated the emigration of undesirables to the United States and that hundreds of Irish paupers drifted southward from the British maritime provinces where they had been conveniently stranded by transatlantic lumber vessels.[4] Not only were native New Yorkers obliged to support the foreign poor, but the "watch returns" and "police intelligence" of the daily press were filled with Irish names; and the notoriously vicious Five Points became the haunt of the Irish, lending plausibility to the charges that immigrants were responsible for every crime and misdemeanor.[5]

Friendless and insecure in this hostile environment, the innocent Irish found compensation in religion. The Church imparted dignity. It was a symbol of strength with which the individual identified himself and the means of salvation, offering escape from the poverty and cares of the present world into the eternal bliss of the hereafter. Not the fine points of doctrine but the harsh realities of immigrant existence in New York gave strength to the Church and made it the bulwark of the Irish community. Bishop Hughes wrote of the Irishman in New York:

It is only when he has the consolation of his religion, that he feels comparatively happy in his new position. If on the Sunday he can be present at the holy sacrifice of Mass, if he can only see the minister of his religion at the altar and hear the word of God in the language to which his ear was accustomed from childhood, he forgets that he is among strangers in a strange country.[6]

The newcomers' demand for religion outran the ability to pay for it. The poverty of immigrant congregations created financial worries for the trustees of churches and grave social problems for the priests, who held mass in "miserable wooden shanties" or in rented rooms of abandoned buildings in obscure side streets.[7] St. Peter's and St. Patrick's, the only Catholic churches in the city in 1825, utterly failed to accommodate the swelling numbers of the faithful Irish; and the German Catholics were without a congregation until 1834, when Father Raffeiner began to preach in a vacant Baptist church at the corner of Pitt and Delancey streets.[8] In 1834 hardly half the Catholics of New York attended the six Catholic churches, all of which were in debt and at least half of which were thrown into bankruptcy after the panic of 1837.[9] The German Catholic church soon proved inadequate, and another was founded in 1840 to minister to the Germans living on the West Side.[10] As the Teutonic population increased, new congregations were formed, and at the outbreak of the Civil War, German Catholics attended seven of their own churches.[11] The French Catholics had no church until 1841, when Bishop Hughes laid the cornerstone of the Église Française de St. Vincent de Paul.[12] A growing Italian community in the fifties and sixties was too poor to sustain a permanent congregation until 1866, when the Italian church of St. Anthony of Padua was dedicated.[13] It was the Irish, however, who supplied the bulk of the Catholic inhabitants, who dominated the Catholic clergy at New York, and who were the most willing followers of Bishop Hughes, himself an Irishman. Largely through Irish attendance, the fifteen Catholic churches in 1845 more than doubled in the next fifteen years.[14]

The dominance of the Irish clergymen created discontent among the German and, to a lesser extent, the French Catholics. When Bishop Hughes formed a Church Debt Association in 1841 to raise money for the building of new churches, the three German Catholic churches, by remaining coolly aloof, contributed to the failure of the plan.[15] The German priests numbered hardly one tenth of the Catholic clergy in the city in 1854 and, according to the *Staats-Zeitung*, were treated with arrogance and even hate by the Irish bishops.[16] German Catholics tried frequently and vainly to check the power of the bishops, and in 1846 a sensation was created when a German Catholic congregation formally withdrew its allegiance to Rome, an ill-fated secession which failed to survive the overwhelming opposition of Bishop Hughes.[17] The Irish, for their part, were discontented without Irish priests, and because the traditional authoritarian Catholicism was all they had known in Ireland, they supported the actions of the Irish clergy in New York.[18]

In some respects, the Jewish synagogue played a role not unlike that of the Catholic Church. Despite the particularism and petty jealousy of the several congregations of Jews, religion was the great preserver of Hebrew identity. Until almost the middle of the nineteenth century, the congregation was the all-important element in Jewish community life in New York: it controlled matters of birth, marriage, death; it administered dietary laws governing the choice and preparation of food; and every Jewish social, educational, and philanthropic venture originated in the synagogue.[19] As did the Catholics, the immigrant Jews found in their religious faith a spiritual cushion to absorb the shock of transition, and the pervasive influence of Judaism in the voluntary ghettos of New York resembled that of the ancient ghettos of Europe. Nationality, however, divided Jewish loyalty. Before 1825, Jewish religious organization centered in a single congregation, the old Portuguese synagogue Shearith Israel, which in its highly centralized management resembled the Catholic hierarchy and which represented all Jews in the city just as the Catholic Church represented all of its flock. However, as the Catholic system retained and strengthened its authoritarian controls under the powerful personality of Bishop Hughes, Jewish religious organization began to disintegrate when Ashkenazic Jews broke off from the Sephardic regime of Shearith Israel in 1825 to form a new congregation, B'nai Jeshurun.[20] Three years later, German, Dutch, and Polish Jews seceded from B'nai Jeshurun to form Anshe

Chesed, and both congregations lost some of their Polish members, who established Shaarey Zedek in 1835.[21] Thereafter, new congregations were formed by secession from older synagogues, which multiplied by division, and in 1860 some twenty-seven synagogues were supposed to have existed in New York.[22] As each new synagogue assumed exclusive jurisdiction over the lives of its members, the all-inclusive Jewish community organization withered and disappeared.[23]

Despite the structural anarchy of the New York Jewish community in the middle of the century, the Jews as a group retained their separate identity fostered by the tradition of Judaism, the prejudice against Jews, and the existence of well-defined Jewish settlements. Occasional events abroad also aroused the Jews to co-operate in attempts to alleviate the condition of persecuted Jews in Damascus, and starving Jews in Palestine, Gibraltar, and Poland.[24] When in 1858 the Jews of New York heard of the secret baptism of a Jewish child in Bologna and the forcible removal from its parents by the Pope's order, they held one of many protest meetings which eventuated in the formation of a Board of Delegates of American Israelites to secure and maintain Jewish civil and religious rights at home and abroad.[25]

Far less cohesive as a body were the huge numbers of Protestant immigrants, including Episcopalians from England, Presbyterians from Scotland and northern Ireland, members of the Lutheran and Reformed churches of the Germanic countries, and evangelical sects from the British Isles and the Continent. Divided along national lines, the Protestants lacked a universal religious authority like the Catholic Church or a consciousness of kind like that produced by the communal customs of the Jews. Protestant ministers, moreover, were confronted with the paradoxical trends of evangelical sectarianism and of religious indifference. In an attempt to prevent the drift of the English away from the Anglican Church, the Reverend Moses Marcus, chaplain of the St. George's Society, and a group of Englishmen founded the Anglo-American Free Church of St. George the Martyr, which opened its doors in the forties and offered free seats to poor British immigrants.[26] Other English-speaking newcomers joined existing congregations or established their own. During the forties Scots attended the Presbyterian Church of St. Catherine because of its connection with the Church of Scotland, but many of the poorer Scots met in rented rooms as the Fifth Associate Reformed Presbyterian Church, better known as the Scotch Church.[27] As early as 1827 a group of Welsh Congregationalists met at the African Free School Building in Mulberry Street, and during the thirties small bands of Welsh Presbyterians, Baptists, and Methodists worshiped in scattered frame buildings.[28]

French Protestants attended the Église du St. Esprit, the old Huguenot Church of the persecuted French Calvinists who fled to New York and erected a building for worship in 1704. Under the influence of the Anglicanism of eighteenth-century New York, this church adopted the Protestant Episcopal ritual in 1803 but continued to use the French language.[29] In the late forties another French Protestant church appeared briefly, and an evangelical congregation met in the rear chapel of the Dutch church in Fulton Street; by 1864 the city's French inhabitants claimed four churches.[30]

The largest group of non-British Protestants, the Germans, founded scores of churches representing many sects, mostly of varying degrees of Lutheranism. At the close of the Civil War, twenty-two of the twenty-four Lutheran churches in the metropolitan area were German congregations.[31] The oldest was St. Matthew's Lutheran Church, the venerable *Matthäus-Kirche* in Walker Street, dating back to 1748.[32] During the thirties growing numbers of immigrants from southwestern Germany attended the Reformed Church, which conducted services both in English and German; and by 1840 so many newcomers had joined the congregation that it voted to drop the English language.[33] The decree of Frederick William III of Prussia ordering the union of the Reformed and Lutheran churches provoked in these years a religious uproar, not only in Europe, but in America, where echoes of persecution resounded from the walls of newly created congregations. Within the Reformed Church, a fiery controversy raged over the appointment of a Lutheran minister, the abandonment of the Reformed hymn book, and an attempt to foist the Lutheran catechism upon the congregation.[34] This quarrel and others led to sectarian divisions, and, by 1839, six German Protestant churches included two Evangelical Lutheran, one Reformed, an Evangelical Reformed, an Episcopalian, and a Christian (*Allgemeine Christliche*) congregation.[35] Soon there were others. Contemptuously aloof from all forms of *Pfaffentum,* or clericalism, small numbers of intellectuals and freethinkers organized rationalistic *Gemeinde* devoted to ethical principles regardless of creed.[36] At the opposite extreme were the evangelical and theocratic German Mormons who founded a *Verein* at New York in 1853.[37] Thus, for the Protestant Germans, as indeed for all Protestant immigrants, religion was a divisive and not a unifying force; yet, as with the Jews, each congregation afforded spiritual comfort to the individual, gave its members the mark of respectability in the community, held out the companionship of the like-minded and the promise of marriage to hopeful young men and women.

While immigrants erected churches and transplanted to New York familiar forms of worship, their only successful educational institutions were religious schools. Many children of foreigners were completely untouched by the public school system, which was ill equipped physically and ideologically to accommodate the youth of the slums. Although 17,000 children attended the public schools in 1839, it was estimated that more than 12,000 between the ages of four and fourteen went to no school at all.[38] The sons and daughters of impoverished newcomers thereafter augmented the ranks of the uneducated, some working in shops or at home to help support their families, others walking the streets as newsboys, peddlers, beggars, and vagrants.[39] In the Eleventh Ward, with a large foreign population, only 7,000 of a total of 12,000 children between the ages of five and sixteen attended school in the year 1852.[40] Four years later, a census of the area east of Third Avenue in the Eighteenth Ward revealed that nearly half the children between the ages of five and fifteen did not go to school. Half of these were immigrants, and undoubtedly many of those born in the United States were of foreign parentage.[41] In the entire city between 1856 and 1863, at least 30,000 to 40,000 children were untouched by any schools, public or private, secular or religious.[42] The proportion of children attending schools actually dropped 10 per cent between 1850 and 1856, and during the entire decade many pupils attended irregularly.[43]

The common school system of New York City, moreover, was unacceptable to Catholics. Until it was superseded in 1842 by an elected board of education, the administration of these schools was entirely in the hands of the Public School Society, a state-chartered, private, philanthropic body founded by Quakers in 1805; and its members held decidedly Protestant views. Devout Catholics abhorred the absence of formal religious instruction in the public schools and objected to daily Bible readings from a translation which the Church condemned. They complained that the Protestant teachers commented upon and explained the Scriptures in a manner derogatory to Catholicism and that the school textbooks "abounded in false and contemptuous passages respecting the Catholic Church." [44]

Faced with Protestant proselyting in "godless" schools, the Catholics organized a separate parochial school system which combined secular subjects with Catholic teachings and allowed no individual interpretation of the Bible. The clergy conducted classes in church basements and other modest locations, but the shortage of adequate school buildings and competent teachers severely handicapped their efforts.[45] As Irish and German immigrants swelled the Catholic population, the parochial schools were crowded to capacity yet accommodated less than half the Catholic youth of the city. Bishop Hughes estimated, about 1840, that Catholic institutions provided for only 4,000 or 5,000 of the 9,000 to 12,000 Catholic children of school age.[46] In the next fifteen years the number of Catholic school children tripled, yet teachers remained scarce; in 1856 the parochial schools, convents, and seminaries averaged but one teacher for every sixty to seventy-five students.[47] Although the Irish clergy dominated the education of most children of immigrant Catholics, the German churches also created schools, and in 1845 the French church of St. Vincent de Paul opened a primary school with 160 pupils, of whom 115 were French.[48]

Most of the children of Protestant immigrants attended the public schools. Some went to sectarian institutions supported by the churches, a smaller number attended private boarding and day schools, and the sons of the wealthy were sent to Europe for their education.[49] In no case, however, did the foreign-born Protestants erect a complete system of education based upon nationality, nor did they oppose the principle of state-supported public instruction. Children who attended the public schools during the week might imbibe religious teachings from their ministers at Sunday school.[50] Among the Germans, visionary schemes for a system of German language schools to perpetuate the *deutsche Kultur* failed to materialize before 1860, as the city's public schools absorbed their children and assimilated them into American ways.[51] During the forties the Germans agitated for the installation of German teachers in the public schools, an innovation urged by Governor Seward in a famous message to the legislature in 1840.[52] German instructors were appointed, and in 1850 they banded together as a German teachers' association.[53]

The failure of the public and parochial schools to reach many of the poorest children led to the founding of a few free schools by immigrant groups and native charitable societies. In the hope of eliminating vaga-bondage, the French Benevolent Society established a free school in 1834 which, two years later, accommodated ninety French boys and girls.[54] The Germans, in spite of their larger population, failed to support a free secular school until late in 1859, when, after a long agitation, the *Freie Deutsche Schule* opened its doors.[55] At last, the Germans could point to a true and sizable community project: about seven hundred individuals comprised a *Schulverein*, which elected a board of directors to manage, not only an elementary school, but also an evening session **for** those over fourteen years of age.[56] Within a year, the institution claimed an enrollment of over a thousand persons, children and adults.[57] Meanwhile, the Children's Aid Society, an American philanthropic agency inspired by Charles Loring Brace's devoted work among the children of the slums, conducted a "Social and Industrial School" for German girls and an elementary school for the Italian youth of the Five Points.[58]

Although few immigrants could afford to send their children to private schools, the sons and daughters of the merchant aristocracy attended boarding or day schools, where "an assiduous regard for their moral and religious training" was infused into their program of classical and commercial studies. Prior to 1840, such institutions were conducted almost entirely for American, British, and French pupils, but during the next twenty years at least one Spanish and a number of German schools opened their doors. Some, like Bishop's Classical Seminary in New Rochelle and Don Juan Alzamora's *Casa de educacion* at Newburgh, were located in idyllic surroundings, safe from the "vicious allurements of the city." [59] Among the elite of all nationalities French schools were especially popular. One of the oldest of many schools for "young ladies" was Mme Chagaray's; Charles Coudert, Elie Charlier, and Mme Binsse established well-known institutions, and after 1857 Lespinasse and De Lassalle boasted that their *Institution Française,* which prepared boys for college or the counting house, was patronized by "the first French families." [60] Several German private schools appeared in the forties, but it was not until the influx of educated teachers after the mid-century revolutions that such schools took root in New York; the schoolmaster, Rösler vol Oels, attracted seventy pupils within three months in 1850 and 1851, and Rudolph Dulon's school, founded in 1854, increased its enrollment from a mere forty to 250 in less than four years.[61] Such institutions were exceptional, however, and it was asserted that hardly ten German private schools existed in New York City in 1865.[62] During the fifties, the children of the wealthier Irish and Jewish families went to an increasing number of private schools, but the majority of immigrants of all nationalities depended upon parochial or public education.[63]

If formal academic instruction was fragmentary and higher education beyond the reach of most immigrant children, aspiring young men might attend industrial or commercial schools, and adult working people might learn the English language at the public evening schools. During the twenties the commercial schools taught little more than stenography or, at best, combined it with a classical curriculum; but as trade expanded at New York, technical studies were broadened to include bookkeeping and accounting, business correspondence, English composition, mathe-

matics, architectural drawing, and allied subjects.[64] The Mechanics'
Institute opened a school in 1835 which admitted "all classes of the
community," and in 1853 it instituted a course in German.[65] Of far
greater importance to immigrants, however, were the public evening
schools authorized by the state legislature in 1848. Each year, hundreds
of foreign-born working people—Irish, English, German, Scotch, French,
Dutch, Swiss, and Canadian—both male and female, learned the English
language or received vocational training in the evening schools.[66] During
the sixties several institutions created by immigrants entered the
promising field of adult education. The *Freie Deutsche Schule* offered
evening courses in mathematics, chemistry, mechanics, drawing, bookkeeping, and the German and English languages, and in 1863 the *Societa
di Unione e Fratellanza Italiana* founded an evening school for adults,
with instruction in languages, music, drawing and engraving, mathematics, mechanics, and physics.[67]

Through lectures, libraries, literary clubs, art galleries, and the theater,
the intellectual life of the educated European was maintained in New
York. Young men of many nationalities clubbed together in literary and
debating societies, some of which went beyond the aim of self-
improvement and sought to raise the educational level of the immigrant
communities. Irishmen joined the Irving and Moore Literary Association in 1834, the Carroll Club in 1841, the Thomas Davis Club in 1853,
and the Cosmopolitan Literary Club in 1856.[68] Amid music, poetry, and
declamation, an Irish debating society argued in 1858 whether America
had struggled more than Ireland for liberty, and two years later, on a
more serious level, a few Irishmen organized a New York branch of the
Ossianic Society at Dublin, devoted to the publication and translation
of Gaelic manuscripts.[69] Among the Germans, a group of freethinkers,
including Samuel Ludvigh, editor of several rationalist papers named
Die Fackel, formed a reading club in 1845; and as German immigration
increased in the fifties, a *Bildungs-Verein* appeared in 1856 and in 1858
a *Conversations-Club* devoted to lectures and discussions of social and
educational topics.[70] Although a Jewish literary society existed in 1841,
it was not until the fifties that such clubs flourished among the Jews:
workingmen founded the Hebrew Young Men's Literary Association in
1852, parent of the short-lived Philodiscian Society and the better known
Touro Literary Institute.[71] Somewhat later, the French organized similar
groups.[72] In general, these clubs were small, and their popular appeal
rested more upon balls, musicales, and theatrical presentations rather
than upon the quality of their literary attainments.[73]

Of greater consequence to the immigrant community were library associations, formed mostly after the middle of the century. The earliest libraries of the foreign born were the simple reading rooms of the taverns and restaurants, which used European newspapers as bait for customers.[74] Aided by immigrant book importers and publishers, some of these humble ventures developed into lending libraries and provided the impetus for the creation of noncommercial library associations.[75] In 1842 a Catholic library society led a precarious existence, but it was not until 1856 that the New York Catholic Library Association was successfully launched with 300 volumes and eighty newspapers and a membership of about forty young Irishmen or Irish-Americans.[76] The movement for a truly Irish, rather than Catholic, public library, although supported by leading Irish Catholic booksellers, failed to make headway before the outbreak of the Civil War.[77] Among the Jews, wide influence was exerted by the Maimonides Library Association, created in 1850 by the outstanding German-Jewish fraternal organization, B'nai B'rith. In five years, this library group had almost 150 members and a collection of 800 volumes.[78] Other immigrants patronized the Society and Mercantile libraries, well-known native associations, and at the end of the Civil War a French lending library boasted 1,200 books.[79]

Like the libraries, the immigrant book trade developed slowly. Prior to the late forties, the newcomers provided but a limited market for importers of foreign books. A few enterprising booksellers, like the Frenchman Charles De Behr, the Irishman John Doyle, the Scotsmen William Gowans and Robert Carter, and the German Wilhelm Radde, established themselves in the twenties and early thirties as importers and retailers of European works.[80] The proprietors of newspapers also developed a book business as an adjunct to publishing and frequently advertised books and periodicals in their papers. While a small and select reading public paid fancy prices for fine French, Spanish, Italian, and German works, the best English and French books could be bought cheaply; and in 1830 De Behr sold twenty-five cent editions of Voltaire, Rousseau, Molière, Corneille, Bossuet, Pascal, and other classic French authors.[81]

The majority of immigrants, however, were untouched by this literature. They read little more than newspapers, almanacs, and *Volks-Kalender*, romances, prayer books, catechisms, hymnals, and other religious books.[82] For as little as six or eighteen cents, French readers could buy the stories of Balzac or the popular romances of Paul de Kock, whose many sensational pornographic writings were advertised in the German *Belletristisches Journal* in 1856.[83] Religious books reached the masses of immigrants, especially the Catholics, through book dealers and publishers who dealt almost exclusively in devotional literature. As the city's Catholic population increased in the thirties, John Doyle, Fielding Lucas, Edward Dunnigan, and James Ryan issued books for the faithful; and in 1837 the bookbinders Dennis and James Sadlier laid the foundations of what became the largest Catholic book business after the Civil War.[84] Meanwhile, the growing German Catholic population was supplied by Benziger Brothers, agents of a publishing house in Germany, and by Eichthal and Bernhard, who also sold prayer books to German Jews.[85]

During the forties the quickening of commercial and industrial life led to the publication of technical works of interest to immigrants. Handbooks were offered to farmers and householders as well as manufacturers and tradesmen who desired to learn American methods. The Germans, for example, could buy manuals on sugar manufacturing, brewery technique, baking, soapmaking, bookkeeping, commercial dictionaries, and treatises on money, prices, trade, and commercial law.[86] As foreigners pushed through the Empire City on their way to the West, immigrant as well as native booksellers and publishers advertised dictionaries and grammars of the English language and guidebooks crammed with information about the geography and customs of the United States, tabulations of railroad and boat rates, and warnings against the all-too-numerous frauds to which ignorant aliens might be subjected.[87]

During the mid-century years, the influx of political revolutionists, many of them teachers, journalists, lawyers, and doctors, stimulated the book trade among the Germans and the Irish. Booksellers not only imported more volumes, but also embarked upon lucrative publishing enterprises. Educational, scientific, and medical books, and a flood of ephemeral political tracts found ready sale in New York.[88] When Julius Helmich set up a German publishing house in 1847, he found a large market for liberal and radical pamphlets and a growing demand for philosophical, historical, literary, and technical works.[89] The same variety of books filled the shelves of B. Westermann and Company, established in 1848 as the New York branch of the famous Brunswick firm of Georg Westermann.[90] The German classics—especially Goethe, Schiller, and Lessing—found eager buyers; to a lesser extent, the works of Uhland, Freiligrath, Heine, Wieland, Klopstock, and Hoffman von Fallersleben adorned the homes of literary Germans.[91] Among the Irish intellectuals, political, legal, and historical works relating to the Emerald Isle were most popular. In the fifties J. S. Redfield, who issued American editions of Barrington's *Sketches*, Sheridan's memoirs, Meagher's speeches, Sheil's *Sketches of the Irish Bar*, and other "standard works of Irish genius," built a solid reputation as the leading publisher of Irish works.[92] Redfield's success induced the Catholic publishers, the Sadliers, to issue editions of the fiction of William Carleton and Gerald Griffin, and encouraged the Irish bookseller P. M. Haverty to publish volumes of Irish literature, history, and biography, including lives of the Emmets, Taafe's history of Ireland, Mitchel's *Jail Journal,* and the poetry of Brooke and Davis.[93] Such books were bought by an ever larger number of native American citizens, sons of poorer Irish immigrants who never lost their love for Ireland.[94]

As publishers and book dealers raised the intellectual level of the immigrant community, businessmen—usually French and German—collaborated with artists in several ventures of educational importance during the mid-century years. The Parisian art dealers Goupil, Vibert & Co., seeking to develop an American market for European artists, sponsored the founding in 1848 of an International Art Union. Pictures were auctioned every year to members of the Union, a salon was opened for the exhibition of modern paintings, and $1,200 was appropriated for the support of an American artist to be sent abroad for two years' study.[95] When the scheme proved financially unprofitable, Goupil, Vibert & Co. withdrew from its management; yet the Union survived for a brief time.[96] In 1853 a Rheinisch-Belgische Gallerie was opened, at which imported pictures by living German and Belgian artists were displayed, as well as the works of local German artists.[97] Of growing importance during the fifties was the Düsseldorfer Gallerie, which for more than a decade staged exhibitions, especially of paintings by artists of the Düsseldorf school.[98] A rival appeared in 1859 when Wilhelm Aufermann assumed the direction of an International Gallery sponsored by professors at the art academies of Düsseldorf, Dresden, and Berlin.[99] The influence of the art galleries upon the immigrant population was, however, quite limited. Because of their jobs, many art lovers were unable to attend exhibitions on weekdays; and efforts to keep the galleries open on Sundays met with the rigid reproval of the advocates of strict Sabbath observance.[100] Nevertheless, educated foreigners, who were contemptuous of American cultural development, supported the fine arts in New York by introducing to America the works of contemporary European artists.[101]

In the theater the foreign-born professionals played an even more conspicuous role. Before the middle of the century, however, few of the opera singers, actors, and dancers who trod the boards were permanent settlers in New York; yet they gave to the city's stage a proud cosmopolitanism. French dancers, especially M. and Mme Achille and Mme Hutin, introduced the French ballet to New Yorkers during the twenties; a French company from New Orleans performed opera and vaudeville in the late twenties and early thirties; and Italian opera was brought to the city about the same time by the impresarios Da Ponte and Bagioli.[102] British actors came and went with regularity, while in 1840 the German dancer Fanny Elssler was received with acclaim by natives and Germans alike.[103]

Immigrants themselves did not create a professional theater until the forties, and it was not until 1855 that any immigrant company acquired the financial stability to give it permanence. The Germans were first in the field. Beginning in the winter of 1839–1840, a small group of enthusiasts pioneered a German theater, but their efforts met with public indifference, and the experiment languished after a few years of light comedies and vaudeville.[104] Other German companies performed from time to time; in 1852 the "First German Marionette Theater in America" presented *Don Carlos,* and by 1854 New York City boasted four large German theaters: the *Hofburg,* which specialized in German classics and translations of French plays; *Hugo's deutsches Volkstheater,* which twice a week offered romantic dramas by Kotzebue and minor German dramatists (followed by dancing at Mayer's *Concerthalle*); the *Nationaltheater,* with a varied repertory at the Olympic; and Pleyel's *Nationaltheater* in the Bowery, which presented comedies, farces, and musicals.[105] In addition, Brougham's Lyceum occasionally sponsored German performances, and several small *Schauspielunternehmungen* were scattered throughout the city and in Williamsburg across the East River.[106] In the same year, the opening of the *New Yorker Stadt-Theater* marked the beginning of a long era of successful German drama in the metropolis. Although in its early years the *Stadt-Theater* was handicapped by a lack of means, limited repertory, and inefficient management, it steadily won popularity in the ever growing German community and attracted professional actors from Germany. Its decade of performances testified at last to the flowering of the German stage.[107]

Taking their cue from the Germans, Frenchmen made serious attempts during the fifties to establish a theater in New York. Mindless of earlier French failures in the city, a dramatic company directed by Robert Kemp, of the Parisian stage, gave a single performance before disbanding in 1851; and the Ravels, who were then presenting French vaudeville, invited the Kemp troupe to join them.[108] The vaudeville also failed; and although new French companies appeared almost every year during the fifties, each succumbed as the result of internal discord, inadequate finances, and the fact that the French population was too small to support a theater without the co-operation of the American theatergoing aristocracy.[109] In 1858 a French troupe gave a series of one-act comedies and vaudeville performances at the Metropolitan Music Hall on Broadway and at Wallack's Theater, and its early success encouraged the *Courrier des États-Unis* to hope for a permanent French theater.[110] Like its predecessors, however, the company was doomed by its slender resources and failed to reappear the next season.[111] The following year, a Parisian group under the direction of F. Widow and C. Sage sailed to New York, where the sale of season tickets at $25 assured at least a temporary success of the new *Théâtre Français* at 585 Broadway.[112] Again, great expectations soon were dashed: despite the sale of additional subscriptions, the company was financially weak, moved to less pretentious quarters, returned for a last brief stand in Broadway, and finally departed in June, 1860, for the more congenial atmosphere of Canada.[113] Other French actors persevered and, during the Civil War, continued to delight French audiences, winning recognition from German theatergoers as well.[114]

Although the Germans and the French were the only important groups to possess national theaters in New York, the absence of organized theatrical efforts on the part of the English, Irish, and Scots did not imply a lack of interest in the stage. Many English-speaking immigrants attended native dramatic performances, especially when British or Irish actors took part.[115] Englishmen were eager admirers of Macready, whose rivalry with the American, Forrest, touched off the Astor Place riot in 1849.[116] The Irish exerted great influence upon the drama, for their very presence in New York in such large numbers made Irish plays extremely popular; and as early as 1828, an Irish drama was presented in a performance for the benefit of the Catholic Association.[117]

With the growing interest in Ireland and the increase in the number of educated Irish in the city, Irish plays were given more frequently, and Irish or Irish-American actors were in constant demand. John Collins, Irish comedian and vocalist, "delineator of the dashing, rollicking, thoughtless Irishman," performed in a group of popular but hackneyed Irish plays, among them *Irish Honor, The Irish Post, The Irish Ambassador, The Irish Attorney, The Irish Genius,* and *Teddy the Tiler.*[118] Barney Williams was a great favorite, though he applied himself "too studiously to the provocation of the laugh at absurd hits and positions."[119] Other Irish favorites were John Brougham, Redmond Ryan, James Hudson, and Macarthy—"the very embodiment of the Emeralder."[120]

The unfortunate aspect of Irish comedy was the ridiculous light in which the poor and uneducated Irish were cast, as comedians won laughs from American audiences for their portrayal of the ignorant, pugnacious, and drunken Irish buffoon. The illiterate immigrant cared little what the New York aristocracy thought, but the Irish press showed a just resentment. Many Irish actors depended upon the "grossest caricature and most exaggerated misrepresentation," complained the *Irish American*. "Even the great Tyrone Power, himself, could not squeeze out the guffaw, till he had transcended the boundary of nature and gone over into the province of the absurd and ridiculous." [121] Criticism had its effect, and by 1857 Collins was characterizing the Irishmen with dignity and avoiding "that burlesque assumption of blundering stupidity" which had been "foisted upon the stage to please those who desire to see the Irishman only in a ridiculous light." [122]

Thus, the drama and the arts, in which immigrants as participants or spectators played both active and passive roles, gradually broadened the cultural life of the foreign communities. Simultaneously, the libraries, lecture groups, and literary associations, aided by ambitious book importers and publishers, gave birth to an adult education movement among the mid-century immigrants. The great mass of newcomers, however, were but poorly educated and knew nothing of these cultural refinements. Despite the growing attendance at public evening schools and commercial institutes, most immigrants had little time for formal education; and not a few of their children played a continual game of "hookey" from the public schools. With the exception of the Catholics, those who depended upon the Church for educational guidance fell heir to the rivalries and jealousies among the religious congregations. The Church might give cohesiveness to each sect and consolation to the individual, but it failed in its mission as educator. The real tutor of the foreigner was the newspaper which, wittingly or not, educated many thousands of newcomers into the ways of American life.

XIII

THE VOICE OF THE PEOPLE

NEXT TO THE CHURCH AND THE SCHOOL, the newspaper was the most influential social and educational force in the immigrant community. Widely read, passing from hand to hand, and easily available wherever Europeans gathered, the newspapers were at once mirrors of immigrant life and media of adjustment to the habits and customs of America. Each national group supported one or more papers, most of them weeklies, which reflected and expressed the usually inarticulate attitudes, ideas, and aspirations of their foreign-born readers. Vital to the thriving foreign communities were the printed announcements of marriages, notices of the comings and goings of prominent people, of rooms and apartments for rent, and of changed addresses; the columns of shipping and financial news; the advertisements of hotels, inns, boardinghouses, and taverns; cards of merchants, lawyers, doctors, midwives, and nurses; church and school notices; announcements of political meetings; and publicity for parades, picnics, and community undertakings. Through biographical and historical articles, romances, poetry and song, and especially in its columns of European news, the immigrant press appealed in familiar tongues to the multitudes who cherished sentimental attachments to the Old Country. Continental Europeans and Latin Americans were introduced in the French, German, Spanish, and Italian languages to the American social and political scene; and thousands of Irish newcomers gained their first conceptions of America from the *Truth Teller,* the *Irish American,* and the *Citizen.* By keeping alive old loyalties and at the same time asserting a vigorous Americanism, most immigrant newspapers exerted an assimilative force, particularly during the fifties when political crises divided the American people and turned many toward the waiting arms of the anti-immigrant Know Nothing party. In opposition to nativism, the Irish press was first to fight for the cause of adopted citizens.

Irish papers did not flourish in New York until the middle of the century. The poverty and illiteracy of vast masses of the Irish population made Irish-American journalism a desperate gamble until the more educated sons of immigrants and the mid-century influx of professionals enlarged the Irish reading public. The one exception was the *Truth*

Teller, founded in 1825 and the leading Irish newspaper in the city until the fifties, when it was absorbed by the *Irish American* in 1855. For its forthright advocacy of Irish political causes, its defense of the Catholic faith, and its encouragement to the immigrant, it gained wide support, claiming in 1833 a circulation of 3,000.[1] It had no serious competitors, other than the Catholic papers.[2] For a quarter-century, at least half a dozen Irish papers, like the *Emerald* (1824), two versions of the *Irishman* (1824 and 1832), the *Irishman and Foreigner's Advocate* (1835), and the *Irish Volunteer* (1845), vainly struggled against the prestige of the *Truth Teller* and soon vanished.[3]

The late forties and early fifties witnessed a sudden upsurge of Irish journalism as political exiles landed at New York, capitalized upon popular hero worship, and proceeded to beat the drums for an Irish republic. Many of these ventures were dismal failures, such as the *Irish Advocate* which "made two questionable appearances and vamosed." [4] Some ran into trouble with the Church, such as the radical *Nation,* founded in 1848 by the sharp-tongued Thomas D'Arcy McGee, who soon antagonized Archbishop Hughes. Object of the Archbishop's barbed shafts, McGee moved in 1850 to Boston and established the *American Celt,* which, under the merciless attacks of the clergy and the Boston *Pilot,* abandoned its radicalism.[5] Archbishop Hughes also opposed the *Citizen,* started in 1854 by John Mitchel and Thomas F. Meagher, whose agitation for an Irish republic added to their personal followings and built up a large circulation for their new paper.[6] However, clerical disapproval, augmented by Mitchel's tactlessness, drew away thousands of readers; and at the end of a year, Mitchel handed over the reins to John McClenahan, who rejuvenated the sheet and in six months claimed a circulation of 20,000.[7] Meanwhile, Meagher dropped his connection with the *Citizen* but continued to agitate for Irish independence, and in 1856 he founded the *Irish News,* a political paper devoting much space to the Emerald Isle.[8] The *Citizen* and the *Irish News* were important organs of Irish left-wing opinion, but the *Irish American,* established by Patrick Lynch in 1849, was without a doubt the most influential Irish newspaper in New York. As publisher of the *Limerick and Clare Examiner,* Lynch had supported O'Connell's Repeal movement against the radical Young Irelanders and had tried vainly to unite the warring factions; in New York he benefited by the clerical opposition to the Young Ireland extremists.[9] His *Irish American* criticized the Catholic *Freeman's Journal* but did not brazenly wage war against the New York clergy; on occasion it even lauded the Archbishop.[10] In 1852 the *Irish American* claimed 15,000 subscribers; two years later it claimed 20,000;

in 1850, 30,000; and in 1861, despite the Civil War, about 40,000 subscribers in and out of the city.[11]

Irish journalism henceforth was firmly established in the Empire City. Its chief stock in trade continued to be the cause of Ireland and an undying hatred of England; yet invariably the Irish papers professed full loyalty to America and urged their readers to become citizens and to take advantage of the educational and economic opportunities in the New World. Nearly all the Irish journals were strongly political, and each was a stalwart supporter of the Democratic party in the United States, at the same time denying or discountenancing the "Irish vote."[12] Consistently friendly to the working man, the Irish press encouraged the organization of labor and reported sympathetically the news of strikes, unemployment, poor housing conditions, high rents, and the mounting costs of living.[13] It praised the Irish immigrant's contribution to America's material development; it defended him and his faith against the onslaughts of nativism, especially the street preaching of Protestant fanatics like John S. Orr, the "Angel Gabriel," in the 1850's; and it upheld the right of Irishmen to parade in their own militia companies and rejected the charge that Irish-Americans had a dual loyalty which put St. Patrick above Uncle Sam.[14]

A powerful educational force in the community, the Irish papers were strongly conservative in a number of significant respects. They upheld the cause of law and order in America, and, while minimizing the existence of "Irish riots," deplored intemperate and irresponsible conduct among the Irish.[15] Influenced by the authoritarian traditionalism of Irish Catholicism, the papers rejected all schemes for the reformation of society. They upheld commonly accepted ideas of womanhood, marriage, and the family, and ridiculed such innovations as "free love" and the "unfeminine and undelicate gyrations of the Amelia Bloomer class."[16]

Protestant sectarianism, Mormonism, and Millerism were scorned or violently criticized. When Federal troops were sent to subdue the Mormons in 1857, one paper hoped that "the fundamental principles of the country and the Government" would not be "defied with impunity by the lechers and strumpets who are herded in the desert between the Mississippi and the Pacific."[17] Fanny Wrightism, agrarianism, Fourierism, and socialism were likewise severely condemned.[18] In 1830 the *Truth Teller* voiced the conservative creed:

An ultra philosophic female gives lectures upon faith and politics, tells one class of people that they have not all the rights they ought to have, or might have if they pleased, and immediately the *Fanny Wright Party* makes its appearance. A crack-brained enthusiast (or perhaps designing rogue) proposes a general division of property among the people: hence the *Agrarian Party*. A philosopher, not exactly mad enough to require confinement and a straight jacket, thinks that certain rights and immunities are withheld from the labouring classes, and so conjures up a *Working-men's* Party.[19]

Above all, the Celtic journals gave vent to the Irish hatred of abolitionism. For the Irishman, the moral question as to the right or wrong of slavery was unimportant; in view of authoritative judicial decisions forbidding interference with it in the slave states, the Irishman believed that the "maniacal ravings of the traitor Lloyd Garrison" were illegal and would surely lead to the dissolution of the Union.[20] The *Irish American* was "for the Union and nothing but the Union; . . . against all the devils of Abolitionism, Freesoil . . . and every other humbug which the fermentation of bad passions or party purposes is capable of vomiting upon the surface of society."[21] As did most whites, the Irish assumed that the Negro was an inferior being. "An African negro and a Caucasian white man," asserted the *Citizen,* "can never become equal; not having been made so in the scale of creation"; yet the abolitionists tried to free the Negro and opposed the Irish "foreigner," and the *Irish American* wondered why.[22] During the Abolition Riot of 1834 the Negroes, under the protection of "gloomy and giddy-brained puritans," behaved themselves with "a swagger of artificial consequence, and an assumption of equality." "Why," wrote a Catholic editor, "should the sable race of Africa, to whom the inscrutable wisdom of providence has denied the power of intellect, the amenity of the moral affections, and the grace and whiteness of form, presume to enter the lists of human perfection with . . . superior grades of society . . . which they never can attain?"[23] Such views, as well as a possible fear that Irish labor would be overwhelmed by the competition of emancipated Negroes, produced an almost fanatical attack upon abolitionists and all they stood for.[24]

The Germans were less united in their attitudes. The size of the German population and the need for communication in a familiar language contributed to the early development of Teutonic journalism in New York, and German immigrants supported more newspapers than any other national group. By far the most influential German paper in the city was the *New Yorker Staats-Zeitung,* established in 1834; in two decades it attained a circulation of 14,000.[25] Beginning as a weekly, the *Staats-Zeitung* was capably managed by G. A. Neumann, who inaugurated a daily edition in 1842 (though at first it appeared but three times a week), and by Jakob Uhl, who introduced a Sunday edition seven years later.[26] The paper printed long columns of American and foreign news, gave increasing space in the forties and fifties to commerce and finance, literature and the theater; its broad democratic sympathies appealed to workingmen and shopkeepers, and its vigorous editorials supported the Democratic party and the local Tammany organization.[27] Such political partisanship naturally aroused opposition. In 1835 the *Allgemeine Zeitung,* a Whig paper, appeared; in 1846 the *Demokrat,* and in 1851 the *Abendzeitung,* both stanch advocates of the new Republican party in the fifties.[28] The *Schnellpost,* first published in 1843, was primarily concerned with European news and emphasized German politics, literature, and science until 1848, when Karl Heinzen assumed control and turned it into his personal organ of reform.[29] Rudolph Lexow's *Criminal-Zeitung,* also known as the *Belletristisches Journal,* began its prosperous career in 1852, featuring in addition to crime and police news a variety of articles on politics, literature, the theater, art, and music.[30] Less extreme than the *Demokrat* and the *Abendzeitung,* this journal espoused the cause of the Republicans and weaned readers away from the *Staats-Zeitung,* which represented the Douglas Democrats and remained, in fact, the only German paper to back the Democratic party in 1860.[31]

The increasingly diversified interests of the Germans led to the founding of specialized newspapers which appealed to distinct segments of the population. Foremost among these were the commercial journals of the 1850's. Shipping news, detailed market reports, financial items—including reports of dividends, as well as articles of a general nature, filled the columns of the *Handels-Zeitung,* which in 1855 absorbed the seven-week-old *Geschaefts-Bericht.*[32] In the latter fifties Friedrich Gerhard published a *Deutscher Bank Noten Reporter,* which publicized forgeries of securities, and a *Deutsch-Amerikanische Gewerbe Zeitung,* whose editor was at one time secretary of a German trade association in New York.[33] During these years many of the older papers met this competition by enlarging their commercial and financial coverage, and the *Staats-Zeitung* ran a series of special articles on economic conditions in 1855.[34]

If the businessmen relied upon the commercial press, restive intellectuals and dissatisfied workingmen and shopkeepers read short-lived reformist papers which usually were started on a shoestring and were unable to build up large or permanent circulations. F. E. Zerrlaut's *Herold* (1836), a Locofoco sheet, was the first of many German propaganda papers espousing radical causes, and in its trail followed such journals of the left as Fröhlich's *Zeit* and Hermann Kriege's land-reforming *Volkstribun* (both in 1846); Wilhelm Weitling's *Republik der Arbeiter* (1850–1855); Gustav Struve's *Deutscher Zuschauer* (1851–

1852) and his *Soziale Republik* (1858) ; the Marxist *Reform,* edited
by Kellner (1853–1854) ; and Karl Heinzen's several papers, including
the *Deutsche Zeitung* (1851), *Janus* (1852), and the *Pionier,* which
Heinzen started in Cincinnati, brought to New York in 1854 and moved
to Boston in 1859.[35] Some were mouthpieces of the freethinkers, like
J. A. Försch's *Vernunftgläubige* (1838), Samuel Ludvigh's *Wahrheits-
sucher* (1839), and the *Fackel,* which Ludvigh published on several occasions during the forties.[36] The liberal and antislavery principles of the
New York *Turngemeinde* were set forth in the *Turn-Zeitung* from 1851
to 1853, when the headquarters of the socialistic *Turnerbund* was moved
to Philadelphia, and the *Turn Blatt für die Vereine,* a monthly established in Williamsburg in 1856.[37] Even the crusade for women's rights
had its German advocates. From 1855 to 1858 the ardent feminist
Mathilde Wendt carried on the struggle as editor of the *Neue Zeit,* a
woman's weekly.[38]

The majority of Germans, however, were not reformers but easy-going
lovers of *Gemütlichkeit* who held fast to the traditional values of society.
They provided fertile soil for the crop of illustrated family journals
which appeared after the middle of the century. Among the pioneers were
the *Illustrirte Welt* (1853), Dilthey's *Familienblätter* (1858), and
the *Illustrirte Zeitung* (1859) ; and the favor enjoyed by this type of
journalism induced Frank Leslie to issue a German edition of his famous
illustrated weekly.[39] Monthly periodicals also appeared in the fifties.
From 1853 to 1856 the *Deutsche Monats-Hefte* presented a potpourri
of novels and romances, tales of travel, illustrated biographical sketches,
articles on music, drama, trade, and politics, humorous drawings, and
engraved plates of the latest Parisian fashions.[40] The stage received increasing attention, and Eduard Herrmann, the "Regisseur" of the *Stadt-
theater,* attempted to edit a *Theater Journal* in 1854 as an adjunct to
the German drama at New York.[41] Popular science was introduced to the
mechanically minded by the *Schule des Volks* (1858) ; and German
humor burst forth in the witty and satirical *Humorist* (1858) and
the breezy *Frischer Lunch* (1859), whose very name poked fun at the
absorption of English words into the German language.[42]

English, Scotch, and Welsh immigrants had the advantage of being
able to read American papers as well as their own. Most of them could
not afford the price of the *Albion,* sophisticated supporter of British
imperialism, whose readers were educated merchants and professional
people, many of whom were more devoted to England than to the United
States.[43] In 1830, eight years after the *Albion* first appeared, the *Old
Countryman,* catering to the tastes of British workingmen, violently

criticized the conservative views of its rival until in 1836 it gave up the unequal struggle and merged with another English paper, the *Emigrant,* which then became the *Emigrant and Old Countryman.*[44] The *Anglo American,* founded in 1843, appealed to the educated British because it featured literature, biography, articles on drama, music, travel, and English news; but it ceased publication after the death of its editor in 1847.[45] During the early forties the *Scottish Patriot,* soon renamed the *Scottish Journal of Intelligence and Literature,* emphasized fiction and poetry, defended the Scots in America, and printed news of Scotland.[46] The small Welsh population was unable to support a newspaper until 1855, when two sheets were started, the *Drych a'r Gwyliedydd* (Mirror and Watchman) and the *Cambro American,* the latter lasting at least until the Civil War.[47]

The city's tiny Scandinavian population witnessed several attempts to found newspapers, but all perished within a few months, until in the sixties the *Scandinavisk Post* established itself for more than a decade.[48] Appearing in 1863, the *Post* was a political sheet which sought to discredit Abraham Lincoln. Although ably edited by Gustav Öbom, it was maintained only through the support of a German Democratic newspaper corporation, and it probably would have disappeared if it had depended upon Scandinavian support.[49]

French inhabitants read the *Courrier des États-Unis,* a well-printed, carefully edited, and thoroughly cosmopolitan paper appealing for more than a century after 1826 to a world-wide public. Originally a weekly, it became a biweekly, then a triweekly, and finally a daily.[50] Its middle-of-the-road policy, moderate tone, wide news coverage, devotion to literature, and ardent nationalism attracted many readers, and by 1855 it counted 16,500 subscribers.[51] Until the mid-century years, no other French paper succeeded in New York, although several attempts ended in failure, while the *Franco-Américain,* founded in 1846, moved to New Orleans the following year.[52] The *Phare de New-York,* created in 1851, gave considerable space to American news, but within two years it was absorbed by the *Courrier.*[53] Both papers were mildly conservative, but a new tone was given to French journalism at New York when Eugène Quesne founded the *Républicain* in 1853 as the militant organ of French liberalism.[54] The *Républicain* ran into financial difficulties, however, and in 1855 gave way to the *Progrès,* a new liberal daily of which Quesne soon became an editor.[55] Finally, in 1860, the *Messager Franco-Américain* began a prosperous existence as a supporter of Lincoln and the Republican party.[56]

The Hispanic peoples, few in number, were unable to sustain a lasting paper until the *Crónica* was successfully launched in 1848. As early as 1830, three Spanish-language journals, the *Redactor,* the *Mercurio de Nueva-York,* and the *Mensagero Semanal,* were published in New York City for the benefit of Latin American revolutionists and merchants who tarried in the city; but the Hispanic population was neither wealthy nor numerous enough to maintain these papers.[57] About the middle of the century sheets advocating Cuban independence appeared in New York. The *Verdad,* established in 1848 and printed partly in Spanish, partly in English, spread the views of Cuban annexationists and filibusterers as the mouthpiece of the local junta for Cuban freedom. Although circulated free of charge and possibly subsidized by the New York *Sun,* which favored the annexation of Cuba, the *Verdad* found few followers, reduced its size, and seems to have succumbed in 1850.[58] In 1854 the Cuban *El Mulatto* and in 1855 *El Pueblo,* both devoted to "liberty in general," led even briefer lives.[59] During the forties and fifties several apparently short-lived commercial newspapers were printed in Spanish; and during the Civil War years a Latin American importing firm published the *Continental,* a trade journal which also reported the progress of the war and carried cultural and political news.[60]

None of these papers was as successful as the *Crónica,* which survived their competition and lived beyond the period of the Civil War. From the start, the *Crónica* appealed to Latin American merchants and carried many advertisements of Havana businessmen; its news columns dealt chiefly with events in Spain and Latin America; but after the middle of the century it printed more news of the United States and, as did most of the foreign press, supported the Democratic party and opposed nativism and abolitionism.[61] It was at once the medium of expression of the Hispanic community, the leading political and commercial paper in the Spanish language during the fifties, and the chief source of information for Latin American immigrants.[62]

Fewer even than the Spanish-speaking peoples were the literate Italians in New York City who read the *Eco d'Italia* for news of political developments in Italy after the revolution of 1849. The founder and editor of the *Eco* was G. F. Secchi de Casali, a native of Piacenza who came to New York in 1843 and six years later founded a short-lived weekly, the *Europeo Americano,* "for the manufacture of the most perverted and wicked ideas that may suggest themselves to a hot-headed individual and to an ignorant mind encumbered with Utopias and dreams." [63] In plain words, Secchi de Casali was a liberal revolutionist. When his paper failed, he established the *Eco d'Italia,* which soon was opposed, not only by Italian diplomats, but by the followers of Mazzini;

a rival sheet, the *Esule Italiano,* was founded in 1850 by the Mazzinian Felice Foresti and edited by Torricelli, a former Capuchin monk who had turned republican.[64]

The *Esule Italiano* apparently changed its name to the *Proscritto* in 1851 and, under the editorial guidance of A. Maggi and F. Manetta, criticized papal power in Italy and the *Eco* in New York.[65] Perhaps because of its less extreme republicanism, the *Eco* withstood the onslaughts of the *Proscritto* and soon was the only Italian newspaper in the city. Its news was mostly of Italy and Europe; not until the 1860's did it become interested in American happenings and the activities of the Italians of New York.[66] Like the Spanish *Crónica,* the *Eco* was supported by a small group of merchants, as well as men of the professions, not a few of them exiles who chose America as their home but wished to keep in touch with the land of their birth. Unlike the *Crónica,* however, the domestic politics of the *Eco* inclined toward the Whigs and later the Republicans, clear evidence that it represented the attitude of only the wealthy few, while the masses of Italians in the Five Points were too illiterate to care.[67]

As did the national groups, the religious communities maintained flourishing newspapers. The Catholics were first in the field, the *Truth Teller* giving equal importance to politics and religion as early as the twenties and the New York *Weekly Register and Catholic Diary,* which rallied the faithful against nativism by attempting to prove that Catholicism was compatible with civil and religious liberty.[68] During the height of the public school controversy, the *Freeman's Journal* was founded in 1840 to "assert the rights of Catholics against the Common Schools System," and in six months absorbed the *Register* to become the only Catholic paper appealing to Irish immigrants.[69] It claimed 4,500 readers in 1846, and nine years later the New York state census credited it with a circulation of 16,000.[70]

Until after the Civil War, the conservative *Freeman's Journal* was either strongly influenced or completely dominated by Archbishop Hughes. Although it supported O'Connell's Repeal Movement in Ireland, the *Journal* was hostile toward Young Ireland and all the mid-century revolutions on the Continent of Europe.[71] It criticized Young Italy, child of the "impractical plans" and "reckless undertakings" of the "sham patriot" and "political quack," Mazzini.[72] It condemned the exaltation of the power of the state in the manifesto of the rump of German liberals gathered at Frankfurt; it was deeply suspicious of the Hungarian revolt, branding Kossuth as an enemy of the Catholic Church; and it opposed the mid-century Cuban filibusters, noting that German, Swiss, Polish, and Hungarian "vagabonds" joined the Cuban "pirates" in the subversion of law and order.[73] When European radicals flocked to America, the *Freeman's Journal* could not understand the "unreasonable fuss" over men who "behaved so badly at home." [74]

The conservatism of the *Freeman's Journal,* supported as it was by Irish and Irish-American readers, lay in a deeply embedded traditionalism of the Irish Catholic clergy, in the reverence for duly constituted authority, and fear of "despotism of the State over property, industry, and family ties." [75] During the upheavals of 1848–1850, the paper was "a champion of social and political order, of law and obedience and patience, and a beacon of warning against the mad passions that were driving nations and men to their ruin." [76] Its opposition to Kossuth, made particularly evident when the Hungarian visited New York, stemmed from his personification of the Magyar revolution, which "became identified in its bearings and scope with the formidable organization now existing throughout Christendom for the complete subversion of our existing Christian society, both civil and religious." [77] When Thomas Francis Meagher arrived at New York in 1852, the *Journal* welcomed him and praised his defense of Irish priests who were charged with fomenting revolution in 1848; but later, when Meagher attacked the Catholic press, he was called a "framer and utterer of shams." [78] The *Freeman's Journal* battled against all the contemporary movements of social reform. It opposed Fourierism, calling its adherents misguided followers of utopian and sometimes un-Christian schemes; it printed a long communication from a group of German Catholics attacking the philosophies of Weitling and of the German socialists; and it gave vent to a virulent hatred of abolitionism, fostered, in the paper's opinion, by abstract disquisitions of "self-elected expounders of the Divine law, as they understand it." [79] After O'Connell delivered his famous speech upholding abolitionism, the *Journal* believed that the Irish leader was unaware that "two-thirds of the most violent 'Abolitionists' " were "as much skeptics in religion, as . . . bigots in Abolitionism," and that they were "Socialists, Deists, Atheists, Pantheists,—anything but Christians." [80]

Although the *Freeman's Journal* was read chiefly by the Irish or Americans of Irish parentage, it also included Germans on its subscription list; and its influence—in effect, that of Archbishop Hughes—pervaded the German Catholic community.[81] By the middle of the century Catholic papers were established in the German language: the ephemeral *New Yorker Bote* in 1849 and the *New Yorker Sion* in 1850.[82] When Papa Oertel's *Katholische Kirchen-Zeitung* moved from Baltimore to New York in 1851, it soon became the leading German Catholic paper in the city, apparently absorbed the *Sion,* and in 1856 boasted of a weekly circulation of 4,000.[83] Like the *Freeman's Journal*, these Catholic papers were stanchly conservative, bulwarks of traditionalism, and targets of the anticlerical press.[84]

Non-Catholic immigrants also read religious newspapers and periodicals during the late forties and fifties. The Protestant sects supported a few German papers, such as the semiweekly *Lutherische Herold*, established in 1850 or 1851 by H. Ludwig, who in 1855 claimed 1,500 subscribers, and a German version of the American Tract Society's *American Messenger*, founded in 1847 and attaining in eight years a circulation of 27,000 in German-speaking communities.[85] Among the Jews, the leading papers were printed in English, although a German-Jewish weekly, *Israel's Herold*, spent a fleeting existence in 1849, and in the following year the *Hebrew Leader*, printed partly in English, partly in German, was read by conservative German Jews.[86] The first successful Jewish weekly in America was the *Asmonean*, founded in 1849.[87] Despite its emphasis upon Judaism, the *Asmonean* avoided narrow theology and concerned itself with all aspects of Jewish life, urged unity among the Hebrew congregations, and encouraged their cultural and philanthropic activities.[88] For the ever growing numbers of German Jews, the *Asmonean* issued in 1851 a supplement in the German language.[89] For the next six years the *Asmonean* was the only Jewish newspaper in the city; but in 1857 its monopoly was broken by the *Jewish Messenger*, edited by the pupils of Rabbi Samuel L. Isaacs and soon the organ of orthodox Judaism in the Empire City.[90] After the *Asmonean* ceased publication in 1858, the *Messenger* was challenged only by the brief appearance of the *Jewish Record* in 1862.[91] Except in matters which related to Judaism or Jewish community life, the Jewish papers reflected attitudes in all respects similar to those of Protestant gentiles. Immigrant Jews, unlike the Irish but like the Germans, showed a diversity of viewpoints which stemmed from their varied European backgrounds.[92]

Whether Protestants, Catholics, Jews, or freethinkers, whether hailing from Great Britain and the European Continent, or from British America, the Antilles, South and Central America, New York's immigrants were served in the fifties by a fully developed network of "foreign" newspapers.[93] Suspicious natives might argue that the Irish press and the foreign-language press perpetuated old loyalties, promoted dual allegiances, and retarded Americanization, but newspapers and periodicals which could be understood constituted the very lifeblood of the immigrant community. Not only did the papers serve as clearinghouses for the practical and immediate needs of buyers and sellers, renters and tenants, employers and employees, but they contributed immeasurably toward lifting the educational level of their readers, enriched American cultural life with gems of European literature, and, above all, introduced the United States to the European. The newspaper, whether conservative or reformist, was conscious of its task in the field of adult education; and it aided the foreigner's adjustment by fostering community activities, urging naturalization, luring its readers into the arena of domestic politics, and relentlessly waging war upon the Know Nothings and the "fanatics" who demanded strict temperance laws. To stimulate intellectual strivings, the press encouraged mutual improvement societies, and some papers spurred immigrant writers to develop a distinct literature. The Germans, for example, were offered prizes for the best original novels on German life in America, and the Irish were exhorted to form literary and scientific associations and to "band together for the sacred object of giving instruction to the immigrant adult population whom a hard fate deprived of such blessings elsewhere." [94] While immigrants continued to read "foreign" papers, their children shared the heritages of two continents, learned the English language, aped American habits, grew ashamed of what they regarded as the uncouthness of their parents, and ultimately were swept into the whirling current of American life.

XIV

THE FOREIGN VOTE

BECAUSE OF THEIR VOTING STRENGTH, naturalized citizens became a powerful force in the politics of New York City. Political parties deliberately cultivated the immigrants. During the movement for suffrage extension in the 1820's, Tammany leaders, originally opposed to foreigners, saw the potential power of the immigrant vote.[1] After manhood suffrage went into effect in 1827, the Democrats developed a system of recruiting aliens which contrasted sharply with the usually hostile attitude of the Whig party. Tammany politicians warmly welcomed the newcomers, instructed them in political tactics, and made them feel that they shared in the responsibility of government. Immigrants were met at the boat; a "naturalization bureau" was set up at the Wigwam, where aliens were advised and assisted in filling out naturalization papers; and it was common knowledge that many of these adopted citizens voted before they had fulfilled the Federal residence requirement of five years.[2]

Wittingly or unwittingly, the foreigners contributed to the notoriously unscrupulous tactics of the political parties in New York City. Democrats and Whigs, and later the Republicans, perpetrated election frauds; and illegal voting was encouraged by the hiring of immigrants as well as "floaters" from Philadelphia, Albany, and other communities, who were less easily recognized.[3] Both major parties made use of the inmates of the city almshouse, the majority of whom were of Irish birth. For a fortnight prior to an election, agents of the political parties generously supplied the paupers with extra food, clothing, and sometimes party papers.

The morning of the election was a busy time at the Alms House. Officers hurrying to and fro—getting together inmates of the establishment, clad in their new dresses—distributing to them tickets to vote and tickets for grog—putting into their hands nice pieces of silver coin, that they might solace themselves after the arduous labor of depositing their ballots.[4]

During the thirties Tammany effectively organized a system of citywide leadership. It held special meetings for foreigners, who were addressed in their own languages, frequently by well-known immigrants who won the confidence of their audiences.[5] In each ward Tammany leaders sought the person who could win over the foreign vote and made him a man of power and authority, a minor boss who commanded, not only his own henchmen, but the police force in his ward. Through this extralegal form of government arose gangs of political ward heelers who were responsible for most of the violence at local nominating conventions and at elections.[6] One of the most prominent of Tammany henchmen was Captain Isaiah Rynders, a former New Orleans gambler and a power in the Wigwam for twenty years after his spectacular New York appearance in the campaign of 1844. As leader of the Empire Club, he directed the less subtle type of "public relations" of the Democratic party, influenced aspiring politicians, and recruited votes. Rynders and his gang, including a number of popular prizefighters like John Morrissey, met newly landed immigrants, found them homes, and got them jobs. Through ownership or control of saloons, they sometimes started the newcomers in the liquor business.[7]

The cornerstone of political activity was the saloon. Here the immigrant proprietor found himself in a key position as a social leader in his neighborhood. Prominent politicans flattered and aided him. Sometimes they presented him with public office, enabling him to dole out jobs and privileges to his neighbors and to increase his political prestige as well as the patronage of his establishment.[8] As saloon keepers became important cogs in the Tammany machinery, their places served as headquarters of the political gangs and were the favorite meeting places of the politicians.[9] Violence frequently broke out in these taverns, but the police rarely interfered. The policemen were appointed by the aldermen who, in turn, depended for election upon the ward heelers.[10]

Many of these very policemen were immigrants. By 1855 more than one third of the city's policemen were adopted citizens, and of these, three fourths were born in Ireland.[11] Police Chief George W. Matsell, himself born in England, reported that 718 policemen were natives and 431 were immigrants, of whom 305 were Irish, or more than one quarter of the total police force.[12] German-born policemen numbered 52, and 26 were born in England, 11 in Scotland, 7 in France, 4 in Canada, 2 in Nova Scotia, 2 in Poland, 1 in Wales, and 7 elsewhere.[13] Since, with few exceptions, the Democratic party wielded political control of the Empire City in the decades prior to the Civil War, the police supported successive Tammany regimes and remained loyal to Mayor Fernando Wood, who defied a state-created Metropolitan Police in 1857.[14] The "silk stocking" districts of Greenwich Village and Washington Square were patrolled almost entirely by native policemen, whereas the populous "foreign" wards, which usually voted Democratic, were covered by relatively strong forces of immigrant policemen. In 1855 the *Staats-Zeitung* reprinted the following official tabulation of the geographical distribution of the police force by nativity:[15]

TABLE 6. POLICEMEN

Ward	United States	Ireland	Germany	Elsewhere
First	19	37	5	2
Second	28	18		1
Third	45	3		3
Fourth	18	32	3	3
Fifth	44	11	1	1
Sixth	21	32	1	4
Seventh	39	20	1	4
Eighth	41	7	4	2
Ninth	49	2	2	1
Tenth	37	2	2	4
Eleventh	40	7	3	
Twelfth	20	12	1	1
Thirteenth	35	10	3	2
Fourteenth	19	30	3	2
Fifteenth	40	1		
Sixteenth	30	14		2
Seventeenth	33	11	5	4
Eighteenth	36	10	1	3
Nineteenth	29	12		2
Twentieth	29	14	11	3
Twenty-first	42	7		1
Twenty-second	25	13	3	3

As the police were pillars of strength in the Democratic stronghold, so were the volunteer fire companies, whose members had close ties with the saloons. The Black Joke Engine Company No. 33 was a deep reservoir of Tammany talent. Malachi Fallon, whose "Ivy Green" tavern was a recognized rendezvous of firemen and politicians, spent his youthful days as a member of the Black Joke and actively engaged in the politics of the Seventh and Thirteenth wards.[16] "Boss" Tweed, of later notoriety, rose through the ranks of the fire companies, organizing the famous "Big Six" in 1849 and later becoming its foreman.[17] "Honest John" Kelly, son of Irish parents, and somewhat later, Richard Croker, a native of the Emerald Isle, were leading spirits in the volunteer fire companies.[18] As fire laddies, immigrants acquired a social prestige which lifted them out of their humdrum existence as members of the working population. The Irish eagerly joined the social organizations of the firemen, especially the target companies and chowder clubs.[19] Some fire companies were completely dominated by persons with Irish names, and a number of companies were composed mainly of men with German, French, or Dutch names.[20]

These, then, were the avenues to political success: the saloon, the police, and the fire companies. Faithful party workers, including immigrants, were rewarded with labor contracts for city public works or jobs in municipal departments.[21] Although the better positions were handed to natives, many Irishmen won minor departmental offices from the Tammany leaders who depended upon their continued loyalty.[22]

The ability of the Irish in political tactics stemmed from previous experience. An ageless struggle with a hated oppressor had produced in Ireland organizations which carried on widespread underground activity requiring the inculcation of loyalty to leaders. At New York this quality reappeared, as orators and demagogues such as "Slippery Dick" Connolly encouraged group solidarity by playing upon political and religious prejudices to control large blocs of votes.[23] The task of Tammany's Irish underlings was facilitated by the newcomers' ignorance of American political issues and the Irish preference for their own leaders, who not only played upon an anti-English theme, but also attempted to satisfy such immediate needs of the immigrant as food, drink, clothing, shelter, and friendship.[24] Whether for Federal, state, or municipal jobs, the Irish were the leading aspirants among the immigrants. One tenth of the 750 custom house officials in 1856 were Irishmen, mostly in the lesser and poorly paid positions.[25]

Few Germans held political posts before the middle of the century. The heterogeneous character of the New York German population, with its relatively large number of merchants and middle-class shopkeepers, its diverse political backgrounds in Europe, and its division into Protestant, Catholic, and Jewish segments accounted in part for the weakness of German politics. Moreover, the language difficulty, the individualistic tendencies of their leaders, and the indifference of many Germans to political life, at least until the arrival of the forty-eighters, resulted in Tammany's neglect of German demands for political offices.[26] In a pointed editorial in 1841, the *Staats-Zeitung* thundered: [27]

Our city government, notoriously at the mercy of adopted citizens has found room for but *one* officer, the *Regulator of Public Clocks;* out of 85 or 90 Candidates but 4 were naturalized citizens—none of these Germans! Call you that "backing your friends?" If this course be persisted in, the consequences will soon be anything but acceptable to the Democracy at large, about as agreeable to them as it is to us, to be told "you are *Dutch, we* can't understand you!"

German Democrats complained that favors rendered brought neither favors nor offices in return. They vigorously demanded more recognition and, failing to obtain it, they declared their independence of Tammany for a brief period in the summer of 1843.[28]

While a few Germans, English, and Scots won political jobs, immigrants of other nationalities rarely were appointed to office. Exceptional individual appointees may have had influence with their compatriots, such as Charles Del Vecchio, one of the city's fire commissioners in 1839, but their followings could not compare in size with those of the Irish and the Germans.[29] It was not until after the middle of the century that immigrants, even the Irish, received nominations of importance on the Democratic ticket, and these concessions were wrung from Tammany only as a result of factional quarrels within the party and by the rising threat of a combination of nativists and the newly formed Republican party.[30] Thus, in 1856 two Irishmen and a German were elevated to the city council, and an Englishman was elected alderman from the First Ward.[31]

In making nominations for elective offices, party leaders carefully weighed the influence of the "foreign vote." For practical purposes, this meant the Irish votes, which were the most numerous, and the German votes, which also counted heavily. The issues which most deeply aroused the immigrants were nativism and temperance legislation, and by their expressed opposition to both, the Democratic leaders won the loyalty of the vast majority of the Irish and Germans. By 1832 the "Irish vote" was safely in Democratic hands, the result of Tammany's political maneuvering in the twenties. In each of two leading "Irish wards"—the Fourth and Sixth—more than half the inhabitants in 1845 were born abroad; ten years later, naturalized citizens accounted for 72.7 per cent of the voters in the Fourth Ward and 76.7 per cent of those in the Sixth.[32] The Sixth Ward went Democratic in the first popular mayoralty election and thereafter remained consistently Democratic both in local and national elections.[33] In nearly all mayoralty elections and in every presidential election during the forties and fifties, the Fourth Ward and the Fourteenth (also with many immigrants) produced a plurality or majority of Democratic votes.[34] The earliest manifestation of a "German vote" occurred prior to the first popular election of mayor in 1834, when Tammany played host to a gathering of German political refugees who supported the Democratic candidates.[35] When another German assemblage, apparently Whig-inspired, condemned this action, some three thousand persons met at the Wigwam to hear the pleas of John A. Stemmler, Frances W. Lassak, and other German leaders, and to pledge their support to the Democrats.[36] In the election, the Democrats carried the city by a slim margin of 1,800 votes, for which the German Democrats took full credit.[37] Thereafter, the preference of the majority of Germans for the Democratic party was indicated by the political behavior of the Eleventh Ward. In 1845 fully 17 per cent of its inhabitants were born in Germany; ten years later 33.6 per cent, or more than one third, were natives of Germany.[38] The Eleventh was the leading "German" ward, but numerous German-born voters in the Tenth, Thirteenth, and Seventeenth wards helped to produce frequent, if scarcely regular, Democratic victories.[39] This gravitation of the Germans to the Democratic party was not seriously challenged until the middle of the century, when the influx of refugees stimulated intellectual radicalism, anticlericalism, land-reform enthusiasm, co-operationism, and socialism among the German population. These movements were anathema to the organization Democrats, and with the upsurge of antislavery sentiment many German left-wingers became Free-Soilers and in the mid-fifties joined the Republican party, as did the more conservative German Whigs.[40] Despite Republican appeals to the foreign-born voters, a large proportion of the 10,000 German voters in 1855 reflected the views of the Democratic *Staats-Zeitung,* oldest and most influential German daily.[41]

Information about other ethnic groups is meager but enough to indicate their relative unimportance in political organization. All but the English were few in number. With the exception of the Irish Catholics, the English-speaking immigrants rarely took part in local politics until they were fully naturalized.[42] At the polls, the English, Scotch, and Welsh, as well as the French, voted as individuals and showed no solid party allegiance.[43] No "Jewish vote" appeared, probably because many Jews opposed a Catholic "church militant" more than they feared nativism.[44] The Negroes, because of old loyalties, ties with former Federalist slaveholders, and fear of the white workingmen, voted the National Republican and Whig tickets.[45]

The Whigs, vilified as a party of privilege and of opposition to foreigners, nevertheless counted immigrants among their members. German Whigs were well organized by 1840, and in the crucial election of 1844 the German Clay Club in the Seventeenth Ward co-operated with the native Whig committees.[46] Partly because of their association with the native aristocracy, British and French merchants and professional men also voted the Whig ticket.[47]

Like the Whig party, the nativist movements paradoxically enlisted the aid of some foreigners. The Native American party included a number of foreign-born members in 1836, and many citizens of foreign birth were said to have electioneered for Harper in 1844.[48] In the mid-fifties, many Jews voted for Know Nothing candidates.[49] The phenomenon of immigrants favoring nativist nominees and of joining avowedly antiforeign associations arose from an intense dislike of Irish Catholics, who crowded the almshouse and the jails and whose social life revolved around a church which wielded political power and tended to foster Irish cultural isolation.[50] Moreover, the coddling of ignorant Irish peasants for the sole purpose of recruiting votes shocked immigrants long resident in America. Thus one devoutly Calvinistic Scot passionately protested the linking of Irish Catholicism with New York politics:[51]

Our Judas Americans will help drive the Bible from the Protestant schools; and as one good turn deserves another, the whole fraternity of jesuits, friars, cardinals, capuchins, confessors, curates, priests, and pretenders, with the lazzaroni at their backs, will join to raise these Judases aforesaid to the highest offices in the church and state.

The Protestant Irish, moreover, regarded their Catholic brethren with undisguised contempt. Because of their Irish birth, the Orangemen leaned over backward and became ardent nativists. They dominated the American Protestant Association, a secret society in the middle of the century, whose 2,800 local members voted the nativist ticket in 1854.[52] "Wherever there is a street-preaching riot, or an attack on Catholic church or convent," wrote an Irish Catholic editor, "be sure that certain faithful *Irish* Calvinists are foremost among the enlightened Protestants upon the ground." [53]

If the nativists sometimes supported candidates in opposition to the Whigs, the more liberal Democrats occasionally defied their party. Immigrants undoubtedly participated in the early workingmen's political movements which temporarily disrupted Tammany's control of party machinery. Despite the widely publicized "agrarianism" and "infidelity" of the Working Men's party of 1829–1830, some Irishmen probably took part, and at least one member of its executive committee in 1830 was born in England.[54] British immigrants who met in 1831 to oppose monopolies and low wages, and to aid distressed workers in England, probably were champions of the Working Men's party.[55]

The issue of monopolies came to a head in 1836, when the Democratic party split into two warring camps, the conservative Tammany faction and the Locofocos, who soon organized their own party. Undoubtedly, the Locofoco (or Equal Rights) party won the sympathy of many immigrants by its uncompromising struggle against monopoly and its demands that the judges be more responsible to the people and that public lands be reserved for the actual settler. The Germans learned of these ideas through the *Herold,* a Locofoco organ conducted by F. E. Zerrlaut, a political refugee from Baden.[56] In the campaign of 1837 the Tammany leaders were forced to give lip service to Locofocoism, and they supported Levi D. Slamm, Locofoco candidate for the state assembly. Moreover, they cannily enticed the Germans by nominating Francis W. Lassak, popular German Democrat, for the assembly. As a result, the German Democrats agreed to support the regular Tammany slate but adopted a platform which was almost pure Locofocoism, including demands for hard money, abolition of the credit system, opposition to state-licensed monopolies, and impartially chosen juries.[57] Partly through the division of the Democrats, the Whigs won the election in the city; but Lassak received more votes than any other local Democrat running for the assembly and was elected when he again received the nomination a few years later.[58]

The allegiance of the Irish Catholics to the Democratic party was matched only by their loyalty to Bishop John Hughes. Despite his insistence that he kept clear of politics, Bishop Hughes was an influential leader who, by his hold upon the minds of thousands of Irish immigrants, wielded political power. In the early forties this power was put to a test on the school question. The city's public schools were managed by a society decidedly Protestant in membership; the Catholics supported their own schools. When in 1840 Governor Seward recommended schools where pupils and teachers might have the same religious faith and language, the Catholics demanded a share of the school funds.[59] The Public School Society bitterly opposed this claim, the city's Democratic common council denied Catholic petitions, and nativist feelings ran high. Thereupon the Catholics, taking the fight to Albany, publicly denounced the Democratic party leaders for favoring the Public School Society. Four days before the election of two state senators and thirteen assemblymen, Bishop Hughes influenced an Irish Catholic mass meeting to make its own nominations.[60] The resulting "Carroll Hall" ticket polled about twenty-two hundred votes, enough to defeat those nominees not endorsed by the Catholics.[61] Thus for the moment the Irish Catholics held the balance of power. In 1842 the Catholics again nominated candidates in opposition to those "tainted with the aristocratic impurities of the [Public School] Society," but these men withdrew when the Senate at Albany extended the state common school law to New York City.[62]

With the exception of the Carroll Hall episode, the Democrats counted upon continued Irish support, but Tammany was several times forced to counteract the independent tactics of dissident Germans. German workingmen and reformers made a number of attempts to form a separate German political party, all of which failed.[63] When the German land reformers met on the eve of a municipal election in 1845, Tammany politicians tried to control them. Failing this, they obtained from Hermann Kriege, leader of the German group, a pledge of the German vote if Tammany bound itself to work for land reform. This Tammany did at a mass meeting just before the election of 1846.[64] Five years later, delegates of the New York City Industrial Congress were induced to participate in a monster mass meeting at the Wigwam "in favor of Land and other Industrial reform, to be made elements in the presidential contest of 1852." By successfully capturing the Industrial Congress, Tammany prevented the formation of a separate party.[65]

When in the fifties the Democratic party split into "Hard Shell" and "Soft Shell" factions, the German Democrats moved independently. Although the Soft Shells had more influence with the adopted citizens, the Germans objected to the nativists among the Soft candidates in 1854 and produced a "German ticket" by adding their own candidates to the list.[66] Both Democratic factions faced a vigorous Know Nothing opposition, however, which impelled them to join forces in backing Fernando Wood, leader of the Softs and secretly a Know Nothing but with a large German and Irish following.[67] After a campaign notable for its many cliques and office seekers cutting across the usual party lines, Wood was elected by a bare plurality.[68] The party rift widened, however, and in the following year the Germans again threatened to act independently, a move which the native-born politicians forestalled by uniting upon candidates acceptable to the German Democrats.[69]

Despite his earlier nativism, Fernando Wood spared no pains to build up his personal backing among the adopted citizens. Not only did he control the Tammany political machinery, at least until 1858, but he also manipulated the police force until it was superseded by the state-created police.[70] Newly arrived immigrants who promised to vote for Wood were sent to the courts with orders reading: "Please naturalize the bearer."[71] The corruption and favoritism of this regime aroused independents, reformers, nativists, and Republicans who ousted Wood from the mayor's office in 1857 and in the next year elected sixteen of the twenty-four councilmen.[72] Thereafter Wood ceased to be a power in the Wigwam, but his strength with the masses enabled him to establish an independent organization which proved more than a match for Tammany.[73]

Thus ended more than three decades of immigrant participation in the city's politics. During most of the period the growing foreign vote kept Tammany in power but contributed to its factional quarrels and extorted occasional concessions from party leaders. If the large Irish vote revealed the most steadfast adherence to party discipline, the German vote, smaller and less dependable but still a political force, remained largely Democratic until the late fifties. Celts and Teutons joined the native-born Democrats mainly because the Whigs supported nativism, temperance, and Sunday blue laws; and when the Republicans appealed to immigrant antislavery sentiment, the German Democrats were slow to join a movement so tainted with Whiggery and nativism. On the other side of the political fence, an aristocracy of foreign-born merchants and anti-Catholics, notably the Protestant Irish, adopted Whig or nativist viewpoints. The older immigrants, too, were alarmed by the degeneration of city government at the hands of unthinking immigrant voters and unprincipled officeholders. Their protest was rarely effective, for the methods developed by Isaiah Rynders, Mike Walsh, "Slippery Dick" Connolly, "Honest John" Kelly, Fernando Wood, "Boss" Tweed, and others, set a pattern of politics familiar to later generations.

XV

THE MAKING OF AMERICANS

THE CALL TO ARMS in 1861 was a test of the devotion of New York's immigrants to the land of their choice. Whatever their attitudes toward slavery or the victory of the Republican party, the newcomers supported the Union.[1] When sectional differences and inflamed passions thrust Americans into civil war and President Lincoln called for volunteers, the foreign born of all nationalities flocked to the colors. The German turners, with their pronounced antislavery sentiments, and the Young Irelanders, with hopes of American support for a future fight with England, were especially active in forming companies and promoting enlistments.[2] As the foreign born grouped around their chosen leaders in picturesque but undisciplined military units, the New York State Militia soon grew in size. The 69th Regiment consisted mostly of Irishmen, many Germans joined the 5th, 6th, 7th, 12th, and 71st regiments, the 79th Regiment was composed of Scots and the 55th largely of French.[3] Englishmen, Belgians, Swiss, Scandinavians, Poles, Hungarians, Italians, and Spaniards, and individuals of all nations and creeds enrolled in defense of the Union.[4]

With the realization of a long war and the growing need for troops, Federal agents feverishly recruited the immigrants. Enlistments were solicited at Castle Garden, as aliens stepped off the emigrant ships.[5] All sorts of inducements were held out to the newcomer, from whiskey and brandy to lavish dinners and entertainments—often through the "connivance des sirènes de bas étage avec les marchands d'hommes." [6] "Daily experience," wrote Mayor Gunther in 1864, "teaches how easily under the pressure of want or the influence of fraud, emigrants can be forced into the ranks." [7] To these wartime immigrants, many of whom were single men without family ties, the government held out generous bounties.[8] Europeans were recruited in their native lands and imported for service in the Army, and United States consular officials in foreign ports obeyed instructions to stimulate emigration.[9] The American Consul at Dublin was besieged with applications for free passage to the United States by Irishmen who were eager to join the Union Army.[10]

Volunteering at the beginning of the war was enthusiastically approved; submission to the Conscription Act of 1863 was quite another matter. Immigrants who had come to America in search of individual freedom regarded enforced military service as an unconstitutional limitation upon personal liberty; many had come to the New World to avoid serving in European armies, and now they found themselves subject to the draft even if, as aliens, they had declared their intention of becoming American citizens.[11] Above all, they resented the discrimination against the poor in favor of the rich, who, for $300, could buy exemption from military service.[12] Archbishop Hughes was unwilling to see the poor exposed to the dangers of battle, leaving "the wealthy to become wealthier in their quiet homes." [13] Although he grudgingly approved the conscription law, the Archbishop recalled statements made to him that some employers, pleading wartime necessity, shut down their plants to compel Irish Catholics to enlist; that "this pretended necessity was only for the purpose of sending fighting men to the field, by which the neighborhood would be relieved from the presence of workmen of foreign birth; that, in point of fact, as soon as necessity drove that class away, their places were promptly supplied by other operatives." [14] The discontent of immigrant workers, especially the Irish, was vented in assaults upon innocent Negroes, deemed inferior beings, whose emancipated Southern brethren might join in a huge conspiracy to take away the white men's jobs.[15] Early in 1863 a band of Irishmen attacked Negro workers, and Americans, Germans, and Frenchmen were aroused by rumors of the importation of Negroes to displace white workers at lower wages.[16] Immigrants had not fought and supported a war to free the slaves; but when emancipation became an accomplished fact their disillusionment was complete, and their inflamed passions erupted into violence.[17]

The smoldering hatreds of racial antagonism and class consciousness, fanned by the Emancipation Proclamation and the Conscription Act, burst into flame during the hectic week of July 11, 1863, when the enrollment of draftees in New York City set off the well-known draft riots. For several days the metropolis was thrown into an uproar as desperate mobs attacked the registry offices, assaulted and killed Negroes, burned the Colored Orphan Asylum into a shambles of blackened ruins, sacked the homes of antislavery advocates, intimidated peaceful workers and forced them to leave their jobs, and plunged into an orgy of robbery and pillage, while the police and a small military force vainly tried to restore order.[18] The draft riots probably were instigated by Irishmen, and much of the violence was the work of rowdies, thieves, and desperadoes, sadistically intent upon murder and plunder.[19] Immigrants as a class, however, refrained from participation in the tumult. In the fair judgment of the Association for Improving the Condition of the Poor:

The mobs were made up of every variety of persons, including native citizens, who were drawn together by sympathy, excitement, or curiosity, and many, indeed, by fear or force. But the actual perpetrators of lawless violence, as shown by legal investigations, were mostly Irish; and yet it were unjust to include all of that nationality among the rioters. What proportion of them were opposed to the outbreak we have no means of ascertaining; it is, however, certain that many of their number resisted it, and at their own personal risk afforded protection to the persecuted negroes [sic]. A review of the facts, therefore, justifies the conclusion that only a small proportion . . . of our laboring poor either joined the rioters or sympathized with them.[20]

Thus the draft riots were a manifestation, not of immigrant feeling, but of genuine working-class discontent, augmented by fierce racial antipathies characteristic of the war years. Mob violence, aroused by a handful of hooligans, was universally condemned. In no way did the disturbances contravene the devotion of the city's foreign population to the cause of the Union. Remembering economic hardships and governmental restrictions in their native lands, the newcomers had gained an appreciation of their adopted country—an appreciation which weakened old loyalties, loosened the ties of the immigrant community, and stimulated closer contacts with Americans.

The assimilation of Europeans and their children into American life was a slow and continuous process which lasted over several generations. Like water flowing from diverse springs into a huge reservoir ultimately to spill over the dam, an endless stream of newcomers poured into the immigrant communities whose swollen population overflowed the slum barriers into the more desirable native neighborhoods. Meanwhile, a trickle moved in the opposite direction: those who were disillusioned by failure to realize grandiose dreams of getting rich quickly recrossed the Atlantic to die in contentment on native sod.[21] Many of the foreign born, however, spent their lives in the Irish wards, in *Kleindeutschland,* the Ghetto, or Little Italy, especially the older people, for whom the adjustment was most difficult. Unable or unwilling to abandon the languages, habits, and social ties which bound them to the Old World, they adapted themselves only superficially—if at all—to American speech and customs. On the other hand, young immigrants became naturalized citizens, grew politically conscious, acquired native handicraft techniques and Yankee business methods, banded together for mutual improvement, and sent their children to the public schools. In their desire to conform to the native pattern, these newcomers shed their homespun and donned ready-made clothing; only a short time after arriving in America, serving girls cast aside their peasant garb and displayed the latest fashions in female finery.[22]

Contact with Americans brought about changes in the language of the newcomers. To avoid ridicule even the English immigrant had to learn Americanisms of speech: to use "smart" instead of "clever," "sick" instead of "ill," "two weeks" instead of "fortnight," "boss" instead of "master"; to pronounce the letter "h"; and to acquire the limitless vocabulary of colorful American epithets.[23] "The language, although in substance English," explained an immigrant guidebook, "has undergone so many changes, that the man who uses it most correctly according to the idioms of England, is the greatest blunderer in the opinion of an American." [24]

Unfamiliarity with the English language hindered the material advancement of immigrants from Continental Europe. Before 1850 many help-wanted notices, especially for domestic servants, specified that the applicants understand or speak English.[25] A Swede, long a resident of New York City, declared in 1853 that the language difficulty was the greatest handicap of his compatriots. "They cannot communicate with those to whom they apply for employment," he wrote, "for during my twelve years' association with Americans I have found only one who could speak Swedish at all." [26] Immigrants who applied for charity or hospitalization, or who ran afoul of the law, were harassed and sometimes victimized because they knew no English. As a result, the Germans demanded bilingual keepers of almshouses, hospitals, and dispensaries, German interpreters in the courts, and the publication of city ordinances in the German newspapers.[27] One result of the helplessness of non-English-speaking newcomers was the establishment in the fifties of a growing number of English language schools and the occasional offering of free language courses to the immigrant population; educated foreigners, as well, announced their qualifications as teachers of English.[28]

Meanwhile, as immigrants and natives mingled in their workshops, at business, in the taverns, and at political gatherings, proper names were Americanized and English words and phrases were incorporated into foreign tongues. Jacob Fuchs became Jacob Fox, Lichtenstein became Lightstone, and Johann Klein became John Little; as cumbersome or unwanted foreign-sounding names were discarded, the children of immigrants occasionally were christened with the names of George Washington, Benjamin Franklin, and other American heroes.[29] The German disregard of the finer points of the English language first appeared in colonial days among the "Pennsylvania Dutch"; but wherever large groups of Germans settled, a great mass of borrowed words, however distorted, became parts of new German-American dialects. The Germans of New York knew what was meant by "ein mistake," "ein arrangement," "eine profitable Reise (journey)"; they read about "die troubles" of the immigration officials and of a "meeting der Centralpark-Commissioners"; a tavern advertised itself as the "freier lunch" at a time when "Lagerbier wird fashionable"; sailors engaged in a "Matrosenfight" in an era when "der riot" was understood by Germans as well as Irish.[30] Frequently, the English words took foreign forms. Germans knew of "ein 'respectabler' Schwindler," recognized "stockjobberei in der Wall Street," and listened to political "stumpfspeeches." [31]

While this peculiar jargon was best exemplified by the Germans, who comprised the largest single foreign language group in the metropolis, English loan words crept into the speech of other immigrant communities. The *Courrier des États-Unis*, for example, referred to "pertes de steamboats," described "un immense meeting" of Whigs and "un campmeeting" of religious believers, advertised a "rail-road," and sometimes used nouns denoting occupation, like "un watchman" and "les brokers." [32] Eventually, the peoples of many different lands, including the Spanish-speaking inhabitants, the Italians, the Yiddish-speaking Hebrews, the Dutch, and the Scandinavians, borrowed English words best suited to their everyday speech.[33]

These linguistic changes were evidence of culture contacts which persisted even when immigrants deliberately perpetuated European customs and when the wall of nativist prejudices hemmed in the newcomers, strengthening rather than weakening Old World nationalisms in New York. Typical of contemporary criticisms of the immigrant communities was the oft-repeated truism that the foreigners did not "conform to our habits, opinions, and manners" and were "almost as impervious to American sentiments and influences, as are the inhabitants of Dublin or Hamburg." [34] Such a superficial observation ignored the subtle, long-run, assimilating forces of the immigrant press, the public schools, the contempt of the young for the "foreign" habits and speech of their elders, the broadening effect of on-the-job contacts in industry and of workers' collaboration in the labor movement, the participation of the Irish in city politics, and the absence of unity within each immigrant group as a whole.

The immigrant community lacked cohesiveness in several essential respects. A wide gulf separated the educated from the uneducated. European class consciousness reappeared in the Empire City as intellectuals and professionals stood aloof and even mistrusted the masses of their fellow foreigners.[35] Wealthy merchants and manufacturers had little in common with tradesmen, artisans, factory hands, laborers, and servants. A bitterly disillusioned English worker wrote:

Money is the be-all and the end-all in the States. With it you are every-thing, without it nothing. The working man is as much hemmed in the iron circle of his class as with us [in England]; the petty storekeeper even looks down on him, and the "dignity of labour" is both disbelieved in and ridiculed. *I assert that in no country in the world are social distinctions more rigidly en-forced.*[36]

To the aristocratic *Albion,* a woman who married somebody "of a sub-ordinate or a menial class" did what was "at once foolish because of its personal consequences to herself, and wrong because of its relation to the duties which everybody owes to the society of which he or she is a mem-ber." [37] The strivings of organized labor likewise were condemned. "Let it not be supposed that there is any thing harsh in advocating a reduction of labour wages," pontificated the *Albion,* contending that the lowered price of ready-made clothing justified wage cuts.[38] When in 1854 a tailors' protective union tried to force nonunion tailors to become mem-bers, the conservative *Courrier des États-Unis* denounced its "acts of tyranny and persecution." [39] During the depression of 1857 the *Handels Zeitung* noticed "unfortunately, some Germans" among the hungry un-employed agitating in the parks and roaming the streets in search of work and food.[40] In short, the misery of the working classes could not be alleviated by their own efforts; it was an evil inherent in the "social constitution of society." [41]

Another element of disunity among the immigrants was the surviving provincialism which set natives of the same country against one another. The Irish Corkonians, who rivaled the Leinstermen and the Far Downs, had their counterparts in Germany, where the southern Germans hated the *Plattdeutschen* from the lowlands of northern Germany.[42] Catholics from Westphalia, the Rhineland, and Bavaria shunned the Lutherans, Methodists, or members of the Reformed faith, while both were severely criticized by the indifferent, the freethinkers, and the anticlericals.[43] In American politics during the fifties, many German Republicans were Protestant, while the Catholics, generally more conservative, were Democrats.[44]

The wave of mid-century revolutions in Europe split the immigrant communities into warring factions, with radicals disagreeing among themselves upon methods of implementing humanitarian, liberal, and nationalist ideals, the conservatives upholding the causes of monarchy and Catholicism in Europe, and probably many others blithely uncon-cerned with the earth-shaking events of those years. Characteristic of the political ideologies which divided the foreign born was the con-troversy between the German "Grays" and "Greens." The German forty-eighters brought to America fixed concepts of freedom *vs.* slavery and humanitarianism *vs.* barbarism; in the profound belief that in the United States lay the only hope of saving the world for their principles, they sought to reform America and demanded that its people live up to their professed ideals.[45] These educated, reformist refugees, known as the "Greens," belabored the earlier German settlers, the "Grays," for their complacency and love of pleasure at a time when their native land was bleeding in the battle against tyranny. They would have none of the dull indifference of beer-drinking, materialistic Germans; they would lead the Teutonic element in a grand effort to establish a German utopia in the New World.[46] The "Grays" struck back. As champion of the older German element in New York, the *Staats-Zeitung* blasted the *Deutschtüm-ler*, who were more narrowly interested in German affairs than in America. Most German-Americans, it averred, took more pride in being free citizens of the United States than in fighting for the overthrow of German princes.[47] It was the duty of the Germans in America to sympathize with their own oppressed people in the Fatherland but not to follow "revolutionary quacks" who wanted to free Europe with American money, raise standing armies, and unite all persons, societies, parties, and peoples for the suppression of monarchy and tyranny.[48]

The psychology of the "Grays" probably was representative of most immigrants in New York. Enthusiasm for revolutionary movements died down when failure seemed imminent, and no doubt the majority of the foreign born were far more deeply concerned with their personal problems than they were in distant political upheavals. A chief stronghold of conservatism was the Catholic Church. It condemned such popular patriots as Mazzini and Kossuth, who attacked the Roman faith; and plans for a public welcome to Garibaldi upon his arrival at New York were so strongly opposed by the Irish Catholics that the idea was abandoned.[49] When the Italian agitator and former priest, Gavazzi, appeared in the Empire City in 1853 and hotly denounced the Church, he was furiously excoriated by the Catholic *Freeman's Journal;* and when the Papal nuncio, Bedini, visited the city the next year, he was the object of similar invective on the part of the liberals.[50]

The basic conservatism of most of the newcomers, however, was indicated by their dislike of utopian schemes for the reformation of society in America, their hatred of abolitionism, their contempt for feminism, and their defense of traditional morality against the inroads of "free lovers." To the *Albion*, the followers of Proudhon were nothing but "speculative vagabonds who would condemn, confiscate, appropriate, do anything . . . but work for an honest livelihood"; Cabet's Icarian community rested on rotten foundations, was encumbered with unworkable machinery and involved a "thousand absurdities." [51] Irish, English, German, and French newspapers scoffed at the "barefaced attempts of women to unsex themselves," the "fanatical aberrations and blasphemies" of the abolitionists, and showed contemptuous amusement at the religious and reformist conventions which met annually in the metropolis.[52]

For most immigrants the institution of the family was at the very basis of society and therefore to be upheld at all costs. The Catholics, especially the Irish, regarded the family as of divine origin and closely tied to the sacramental system. "If this world is worth living for it is because we enjoy the relations of the family," the *Irish American* philosophized: "because we have children and bring them up in the fear and love of God; because we endeavor to infuse into their young souls the knowledge of an hereafter; without which there is no virtue, there is no propriety, there can be no order." [53] Natives of Continental Europe likewise considered the family to be of the greatest social importance. The French, who discovered a material-mindedness and lack of filial love in American homes, stressed the family as a primary educational unit.[54] The Germans emphasized the role of the family in the inculcation of self-control and modesty, virtues which they claimed American youth sacrificed in favor of greater independence.[55] Among the Jews, the family was a powerful educational influence; and the Scotch Church's close control over marital relations was proof that Puritanical morality was not limited to New Englanders.[56]

The constant appeal for harmonious relations in immigrant households was strongly buttressed by the insistent Catholic opposition to state-controlled education. The inculcation of piety and morality was an essential part of a child's education, and the family was best equipped to give such instruction. While the State and the Church demanded uniformity within their spheres of influence, the family produced diversity "in matters not essential" and prevented individuals from being "as mechanically alike as peas in a peck measure": [57]

God has furnished the fountain and the means of this diversity in the family institution. Wherever family traditions have been cherished, family differs from family in its characteristics. The child takes its notions from its mother, not from its schoolmates. Where the family exists, the teacher is but the partial deputy of the parent, and has no authority to do or to teach anything not directed by the parent.

Conditions in America tended to weaken the family bonds of the Lord's children. As Thomas D'Arcy McGee explained:

In Ireland every son was "a boy," and every daughter "a girl" till he or she
was married . . . they were considered subject to their parents till they
became parents themselves. . . . In America, in consequence of the newness
of the soil, and the demands of enterprise, the boys are men at sixteen. . . .
They all work for themselves, and pay their own board. They either live with
the "boss," "governor," or "old man," or elsewhere, as they please. They may
have respect,—they must have some natural deference for parents, but the
abstract Irish reverence for old age is not yet naturalized in America. . . .
Over half a dozen of these keen, hard, worldly young Yankees, an Irish father
is to preside . . . they go to the public school. They are called "Paddies."
. . . They come home, and they want explanations; and here is, precisely
where the second generation breaks off from the first. . . . If . . . the
family tie is snapt . . . our children become our opponents, and sometimes
our worst enemies.[58]

In view of the stress placed upon the family as a primary social unit,
it is not surprising that immigrants were dismayed to witness the disintegrating effects of life in New York upon that time-honored institution.
Sometimes families were completely abandoned as fathers left the city in
search of railroad or canal jobs. Family quarrels were inevitable among
the poor, for the daily wage of an Irish laborer hardly sufficed for a
single meat dinner for his average-sized family of six or seven persons.[59]
The relative absence of social control over the individual led to breaches
of the marriage bond, and unwanted children were abandoned to become
vagrants, petty thieves, criminals, and prostitutes.[60] Strained relations
between parents and children indicated culture conflicts within the
family. Ashamed of their humble elders, whose rustic manners belonged
to the countryside of the Old World, young people attempted to free
themselves from parental authority, and their independence was mis-
interpreted by the parents as rank ingratitude and overweening pride.[61]
Nor were the parents blameless. Narrow provincialism, so common
among immigrants, alienated many of their children. Because of Irish
factionalism, young Irish-Americans refused to participate in the community enterprises of their elders, saying "I am ashamed to go; this will
end in some quarrel or another, and I don't want to be called Irish." [62]
German provincialism was enhanced by the fact that marriages were
usually contracted by persons of like religion or natives of the same
locality.[63] While mixed marriages occurred in New York, intermarriage
was the exception rather than the rule. Enough cases of intermarriage
took place between Irish Catholics and Protestants, however, to arouse
immigrant leaders. "We meet every day the apostate children of
Irish parents, sons of emigrants, and themselves the worst enemies of
emigrants," lamented Thomas D'Arcy McGee.[64]

Thus, contrary to contemporary utterances, the immigrants were less "clannish" than Americans imagined. As each ethnic group gained in population, national or religious solidarity tended to disintegrate. Differences in class status, varying viewpoints on politics and religion, frequent factional clashes, contact with Americans in the schools, in the factories, in business, in civic enterprises, and in recreational activities eroded the sharp outlines of national consciousness. The newcomers lost old loyalties and acquired new ones as family influences were weakened by conflicting attitudes of parents and children and by marital unhappiness and irresponsibility sometimes born of poverty and ignorance, as immigrants joined nonnational recreational and philanthropic associations, and as doctrinal or national differences shattered the control of the Protestant churches and the Jewish synagogues. What seemed to be a static, unassimilable element of the population was in reality a dynamic source of strength to America; for, as new immigrants arrived in the Empire City they took the places vacated by those who had preceded them in the slow, irregular process of the making of Americans.

Mentally and emotionally, the process began in Europe, when men and women looked with hope toward the New World. Physically, it began with the long and perilous journey to the slum districts of New York. There, amid overcrowded, unsanitary, and unsafe housing conditions—pestholes of disease and death, pauperism and crime—the immigrant community took shape; but while outsiders were criticizing the clannishness of the foreign born, new generations arose ultimately to be absorbed into American life.

In the shanty towns and tenement areas, the great mass of poverty-stricken newcomers led peaceful and uneventful lives. Here were the recruiting grounds of labor contractors and employment agencies. Here dwelt the thousands of laborers who sallied forth each weekday to work on buildings, roads, embankments, in quarries, workshops, warehouses, and along the wharves. Here lived the immigrant needleworkers, less secure than the domestic servants who resided with their employers. In the slums were enacted scenes of exploitation: the beginnings of the sweating system appeared in the sewing trades, where even immigrants lived like parasites upon the toil of their less fortunate brethren. Here were the haunts of the skilled and semiskilled workers who came to dominate the shoe industry, the building trades, cabinetmaking and upholstering, and the highly trained artisans who made surgical instruments, chronometers, or violins. From the dingy side streets also emerged the hawkers, ragpickers, scavengers, whitewashers, carpetbeaters, and organ-grinders. On a higher social plane, the liquor dealers, grocers, marketmen, butchers, bakers, and confectioners plied their retail businesses in the basements or ground floors of tenements. Immigrant boardinghouse, hotel, restaurant, and tavern keepers, brewers, manufacturers, and importers were aided by an army of waiters, chambermaids, cooks, porters, factory workers, clerks, and bookkeepers. Less affluent, but no less influential than the employers of labor was the small professional class of doctors, lawyers, journalists, teachers, ministers, musicians, actors, and artists.

In the rapidly expanding metropolis, some of the poorer immigrants were able to better themselves economically and socially. Although most of the foreign born probably failed to improve their status materially, while some dropped into the most menial occupations, many individuals rose to prominence.[65] Penniless newcomers peddled in the city streets, slowly saved their earnings, and ultimately became small shopkeepers dealing in junk, old clothes, or operating pawnshops. In the ready-made clothing industry, workers rose to better-paid positions, employed other immigrants, or opened clothing stores. In the building trades, ambitious and persistent laborers learned skilled jobs; masons and other skilled workers became contractors and speculated in real estate. Ingenious artisans in other industries, like the piano makers, worked for wages until they were able to establish themselves as independent manufacturers.

Simultaneously, the workingman struggled for a restoration of his lost dignity, and as living costs spiraled upward native labor unions, agitating for higher wages and shorter hours, drew strength from the foreign born. English, Scottish, and Welsh immigrants transplanted British trade unionism to American soil, where its philosophy was absorbed by the Irish. The Germans, however, maintained separate organizations, and their labor movement paralleled the American. Despite language difficulties, mutual suspicions and antagonisms, and competition in the labor market, the Germans lent an emotional drive to the union movement and, by introducing Marxian socialism, gave it a more distinct class consciousness. While their enthusiasm for co-operatives and other panaceas failed to win over the American workers, the Germans collaborated with native unions in the 1850's, their common consciousness of purpose strengthening the cause of organized labor in its formative years.

As trade unions imparted a sense of social solidarity to their members, national consciousness was also a cohesive power. Its persistence led to a variety of associational activities in each foreign community. Fraternal, benevolent, and mutual aid societies, social clubs, target companies and militia corps, and athletic teams were among the most important agencies of adjustment to life in America. Equally valuable were the annual games, ceremonial dinners, picnics, and festivals. In community undertakings, from the creation of hospitals and orphan asylums to the founding of savings banks and building and loan associations, the newcomer developed a sense of civic responsibility. The Church also aided the adjustment of the foreigner, offering social contacts and consolation in this world, salvation in the next. Since many of the churches were heavily in debt, they were unable to meet the pressing obligation of educating the young; most immigrant children went to the public schools, some attended parochial and private schools, and a tiny minority was sent to Europe by wealthy parents. Many children of immigrants never went to school at all: some were peddlers or factory workers supporting their poor families, while others, devoid of guidance, were petty thieves or prostitutes.

In spite of limited educational opportunities, the foreign born indulged in numerous cultural activities. They founded their own libraries, lecture groups, literary societies, debating clubs; they went to evening classes to learn the English language and to acquire vocational or technical skills, and during the fifties they supported art galleries and professional theatrical associations. As immigrant leaders strove to raise the cultural level of their communities, their strongest ally was the "foreign press."

The immigrant newspaper reflected the ideas, attitudes, and aspirations of its readers. Undoubtedly some papers, like the many short-lived radical sheets of the fifties, tried to perpetuate Old World habits of thinking; but the foreign press as a whole performed a useful task in preparing the newcomer for life in America in a language which he understood. In the mid-century years, specialized journals catered to select groups of readers, as commercial sheets and family-type papers responded to the growing wealth and diversity of the foreign community. The rough-and-tumble political battles in city, state, and nation were recorded on the pages of the immigrant newspaper, which in most cases sided with the Democratic party.[66]

Indeed, the majority of adopted citizens were Democrats. As early as the 1830's Tammany leaders began their efficient organization of the immigrant vote. By personal contact with the newly landed foreigner, by facilitating the naturalization procedure, by holding special rallies for foreign-language audiences, by promising the spoils of office to immigrant ward heelers, the Democratic party built up a powerful political machine. It retained immigrant loyalty by opposing nativist or temperance legislation. Despite the occasional support which naturalized citizens gave to insurgent movements and third parties, most of them, especially the Catholic Irish, rarely deserted the Democrats, thanks to the strategic positions of hundreds of socially important saloonkeepers, policemen, and firemen, whose organizational work marshaled the "foreign vote" and enabled the Tammany bosses to feel the public pulse. The immigrants were as essential a part of New York's political pattern as they were of its population.

Thus ended nearly four decades of immigrant life in the expanding metropolis. When the Erie Canal first joined the Empire City with the waters of the West, less than 20,000 (or about 11 per cent) of Manhattan's 166,000 residents were aliens.[67] Thirty-five years later, at the outbreak of the Civil War, the combined population of New York City and Brooklyn exceeded 1,000,000. On Manhattan Island alone, nearly 384,000 (or 48 per cent) of the 805,000 inhabitants were born outside the United States. Among these newcomers, over 200,000 were natives of Ireland; 120,000 were born in Germany, 27,000 in England, 9,000 in Scotland, and 8,000 in France.[68] The Scotch were easily adaptable to American life, the English somewhat less so; because the Irish, Germans, French, and others crossed the Atlantic with habits of thought less like those of the New World, their assimilation extended over several generations.[69] Many brought with them bitter memories of mud huts and evictions, of flooded farm lands, of unemployment and hopeless poverty, of irksome religious restraints, yet they retained sentimental feelings for the Old Country, for relatives and friends left behind. Time, however, lessened the tenacious, old loyalties as the faces of immigrants turned west instead of east. Though the foreign born might rarely venture beyond the pale of New York's ghettos, their children grew more like the Americans, and their children's children became an integral part of America.

APPENDIX I

Note on Census Statistics

AS LATE AS 1865, state and Federal census statistics
were incomplete and far from accurate. "It is vain to
expect even a tolerable degree of accuracy in either
the National or State census until a thorough reform
has been effected, both in the methods and the *personnel* of the work," asserted the Metropolitan Board
of Health in 1867 (New York State, *Assembly Documents*,
IX, No. 122 [1868], 144); "the State [in 1865] employed
its census takers almost upon considerations that
had no regard to accuracy and completeness of results,
and paid the men by the day or for a long period. The
National census [of 1860], on the other hand, incurred
the greatest possible liability to false and excessive returns, by paying the canvassers or takers a
certain sum for each name they put upon their official returns. We know that the superintendent of the
State census was compelled to accept incomplete and
faulty returns, and he had no means for correcting
or supplying defects in the census of 1865."

What was said of these two censuses applies to
earlier censuses; but, while recognizing the limitations imposed upon him, the historian must use the
figures which are available. He can only hope that
they paint, in general, a reasonably accurate picture
of population and economic life. Statistics of "average wages" in the Federal census are open to ob-
jection on three vital points: methods of obtaining
average wages varied widely from census to census;
such an average applied to all grades of labor and
was so general that it cannot furnish definite information about working conditions; and, finally, statistics collected only for one year in every ten make
it difficult, if not impossible, to determine inter-

185

vening wage fluctuations. (Cf. Edith Abbott, "Wages of Unskilled Labor in the United States, 1850-1900," *Journal of Political Economy*, June, 1905, pp. 329-333.) For these reasons I have refrained from any extensive use of wage statistics as reported in the census and I have relied chiefly upon newspapers for wage data pertinent to specific struggles over wages.

For most of the statistical material dealing with ethnic groups and occupations I have relied heavily upon the marshals' manuscript schedules of the *New York State Census of 1855*. I selected the census of 1855 for two reasons: it was the first of the New York States censuses which fully listed nativities; and, secondly, it was taken after the great German immigration of the early fifties. While perhaps slightly more accurate, the Federal census of 1850, which was the first to inquire into nativities, was useless for a consideration of the large German influx. The Federal census of 1860, moreover, was too close to the end of the period under study to provide any suggestion of the city's population in the mid-century years or before. Original manuscript schedules of the state census of 1855 covering New York City are in the office of the County Clerk, Hall of Records, New York City. Their physical condition varies from excellent to very fragile, but I was able to search the entire set of twenty-two volumes (one for each ward) with the exception of a small part of the volume for the Seventeenth Ward. In this volume the pages which included the First and about two-thirds of the Second election districts of the Seventeenth Ward had deteriorated so badly that I was forced to exclude them from my tabulations. However, I do not believe that this small omission affects materially the conclusions reached in this book.

APPENDIX II

Immigration

Table 7: Comparison of Immigration and City Population Growth, 1820-1860, by Decades

Decade	Immigration to Port of New York	City Population Increase[a]
1820-1830	92,884	78,883
1830-1840	407,716	110,121
1840-1850	1,146,241	202,837
1850-1860	1,994,640	298,122

[a]Note that the rate of dispersion from New York City becomes more rapid in each succeeding decade.

Source: Kate H. Claghorn, "The Foreign Immigrant in New York City," *United States Industrial Commission Reports* (Washington, D.C., 1901), XV, 464.

Table 8: Comparison of Immigrants from Great Britain with Immigrants from Germany, 1820-1855

Period	Immigrants from Britain & Ireland	Immigrants from Germany	Proportion of German to British & Irish
1820-1830	81,827	7,729	1:10.5
1831-1840	283,191	152,454	1: 1.75
1841-1845	267,281	105,188	1: 2.5
1846-1850	750,482	329,438	1: 2.33
1851-1855	930,664	647,273	1: 1.5

Source: Kate H. Claghorn, "The Foreign Immigrant in New York City," *United States Industrial Commission Reports* (Washington, D.C., 1901), XV, 464.

Table 9: Immigrants Disembarking at the Port of New York from May 5, 1847, to December 31, 1860, Showing Numbers and Nativities of Those for Whom Commutation and Hospital Moneys Were Paid or Bonds Executed

Country of Birth	1847	1848	1849	1850	1851	1852	1853	1854	1855	1856	1857	1858	1859	1860	Total Nationalities
Ireland	52,946	91,061	112,591	117,038	163,306	118,131	113,164	82,302	43,043	44,276	57,119	25,075	32,652	47,330	1,107,034
Germany	53,180	51,973	55,705	45,535	69,919	118,611	119,644	176,986	52,892	56,113	80,974	31,874	28,270	37,899	979,575
England	8,864	23,062	28,321	28,163	28,553	31,551	27,126	30,578	22,938	23,787	28,622	12,324	10,375	11,361	315,625
Scotland	2,354	6,415	8,840	6,772	7,302	7,694	6,456	4,909	4,240	4,723	5,170	2,718	2,325	1,617	71,535
France	3,330	2,734	2,683	3,462	5,964	8,868	7,470	7,986	4,174	2,984	3,069	1,786	1,532	1,549	57,591
Switzerland	1,947	1,622	1,405	2,380	4,499	6,471	4,604	8,883	3,273	2,559	2,454	1,315	791	1,422	43,625
Holland	3,611	1,560	2,447	1,174	1,798	1,223	1,085	1,466	822	1,666	1,734	348	261	440	19,635
Wales	472	1,054	1,782	1,520	2,189	2,531	1,182	1,288	1,118	1,376	887	566	500	811	17,276
Norway	882	1,207	3,300	3,150	2,112	1,889	377	81	203	438	62	3	36	53	13,793
Sweden	139	165	1,007	1,110	872	2,005	1,630	1,859	304	918	619	237	318	361	11,547
Italy	197	321	602	476	618	359	553	785	667	690	596	669	399	542	7,474
Belgium	551	...	118	230	475	82	34	398	1,201	850	444	253	57	76	4,769
Spain	101	253	214	257	278	471	659	646	457	330	263	146	234	228	4,537
West Indies	299	392	449	554	575	265	...	11	19	225	330	344	416	523	4,402
Denmark	95	52	159	90	229	157	94	102	174	469	453	284	493	495	3,346
Poland	26	79	133	188	422	188	186	169	346	142	245	88	114	80	2,406
Sardinia	...	...	172	165	98	69	72	148	67	426	405	324	164	89	2,199
South America	...	31	33	104	121	120	175	111	112	163	66	92	138	110	1,376
Portugal	34	57	33	65	26	37	237	205	24	30	93	27	45	19	1,176
Nova Scotia	...	...	151	164	81	73	6	128	9	30	40	18	81	23	804
Russia	10	28	38	18	23	33	39	55	20	56	42	19	69	61	511
Canada	...	...	59	61	50	48	...	2	64	57	30	17	25	25	438
Mexico	...	12	23	41	42	23	51	34	20	19	11	13	13	22	324
Sicily	...	...	21	28	12	42	37	58	18	10	26	19	1	4	276
China	...	2	9	11	22	14	53	20	18	8	11	15	4	13	200
East Indies	23	...	34	32	10	18	...	...	5	...	...	7	...	4	133
Unknown	...	95	...	...	...	...	...	...	...	...	...	...	...	...	95
Greece	...	1	6	4	1	11	1	7	3	3	8	2	6	2	55
Turkey	1	...	6	4	4	5	10	6	2	4	...	6	3	3	54
Arabia	...	...	8	...	...	...	...	...	...	...	...	...	...	...	8
Annual Totals	129,062	189,176	220,603	212,796	289,601	300,992	284,945	319,223	136,233	142,342	183,773	78,589	79,322	105,162	2,671,819

Source: Annual Reports of the Commissioners of Emigration of the State of New York, from the Organization of the Commission, May 5, 1847, to 1860 Inclusive ... (New York, 1861), Appendix, p. 288.

Table 10: Avowed Destination of Immigrants Landed at Castle Garden from Its
Opening as a Landing Depot, August 1, 1855, to December 31, 1860

Destination	1855 From Aug. 1	1856	1857	1858	1859	1860	Total
New York................	19,489	55,055	78,585	34,296	40,923	56,131	284,479
Pennsylvania...........	4,469	11,749	16,660	6,708	7,370	9,512	56,468
Illinois................	3,444	11,064	15,750	6,690	3,940	4,077	44,965
Wisconsin..............	4,667	13,327	12,704	4,953	2,441	2,589	40,681
Ohio....................	3,250	7,085	10,054	6,176	4,668	5,195	36,428
Massachusetts..........	2,037	6,494	6,904	3,212	5,119	6,371	30,137
Canada West............	3,346	8,526	9,673	4,218	2,202	1,872	29,837
New Jersey.............	1,119	3,242	3,806	1,922	2,621	3,414	16,195
Unknown................	957	4,187	4,395	1,484	1,726	3,368	16,117
Michigan...............	1,648	3,296	4,108	1,697	1,305	1,478	13,532
Connecticut............	829	2,292	2,974	1,227	1,929	2,579	11,840
Iowa....................	795	2,380	3,775	1,724	664	776	10,114
Missouri...............	434	1,064	2,366	1,690	1,598	1,614	8,766
Indiana................	881	1,388	2,474	1,271	1,122	1,106	8,242
Rhode Island...........	551	1,354	1,389	510	1,001	1,291	6,096
Maryland...............	485	1,164	1,535	907	902	1,014	6,007
Uncertain..............	317	2,113	2,014	483	303	214	5,444
California.............	447	778	877	1,084	1,108	1,141	5,435
Minnesota..............	127	427	1,253	828	542	466	3,643
Utah...................	250	1,579	14	3	740	905	3,491
Virginia...............	292	567	702	548	575	452	3,136
Kentucky...............	183	460	660	520	546	650	2,019
District of Columbia...	202	407	532	336	308	301	2,086
Vermont................	168	250	297	172	198	270	1,355
Louisiana..............	60	171	206	240	255	321	1,253
South Carolina.........	80	178	157	168	185	296	1,064
Maine..................	143	148	186	210	122	142	951
Tennessee..............	72	178	127	165	147	269	898
Georgia................	70	47	167	162	193	178	817
New Hampshire..........	71	177	179	69	131	123	750
Delaware...............	49	81	113	65	117	123	548
New Brunswick..........	2	...	97	75	82	42	298
Texas..................	5	76	55	43	52	63	294
Kansas.................	1	11	25	88	77	92	294
North Carolina.........	11	66	41	52	48	43	261
Mississippi............	6	14	62	21	50	15	168
Alabama................	7	30	21	24	39	45	166
Nova Scotia............	30	2	42	53	14	21	162
Nebraska...............	...	2	27	42	31	46	148
South America..........	25	30	18	14	36	18	141
Cuba...................	...	...	25	32	46	29	132
Arkansas...............	8	30	9	10	16	21	94
Florida................	13	12	5	11	32	17	90
Mexico.................	...	12	1	5	7	9	34
Oregon.................	1	...	7	6	6	13	33
West Indies............	2	11	...	6	5	9	33
New Mexico.............	...	...	5	...	23	1	29
Central America........	...	...	...	3	9	8	20
Canada East............	...	...	...	...	10	5	15
Prince Edward's Island.	...	...	...	3	3	1	7
Vancouver's Island.....	...	...	...	...	1	3	4
Washington Territory...	...	...	...	...	3	...	3
Australia..............	...	1	...	...	...	1	2
Bermuda................	...	...	...	...	..1	..1	2
Sandwich Islands.......	...	...	...	...	...	1	1
Total.................	51,114	141,525	185,076	84,226	85,602	108,682	656,225

Source: *Annual Reports of the Commissioners of Emigration of the State of New York, from the Organization of the Commission, May 5, 1847, to 1860 Inclusive* ...(New York, 1861), Appendix, p. 340.

Table 11: Avowed Destination of German Immigrants Landed at the Port of New York in 1855

Number	Destination
19,489[a]	New York
4,667	Wisconsin
4,469	Pennsylvania
3,444	Illinois
3,346	Canada
3,250	Ohio
2,037	Massachusetts
1,648	Michigan
1,190	New Jersey
829	Connecticut
795	Iowa
551	Rhode Island
485	Maryland
447	California
434	Missouri
292	Virginia
250	Utah
202	District of Columbia
183	Kentucky
168	Vermont
143	Maine
127	Minnesota

[a]A total of 51,114 immigrants reported their destinations, of which only the most popular are listed here. Many of the newcomers who had no special destination announced New York as their goal.

Source: German Society of the City of New York, *Annual Report*, 1855, p. 15.

APPENDIX III

Population

Table 12: Population Growth on Manhattan Island, 1790-1865*

Wards	Date of format'n of the ward	1790	1800	1810	1814	1820	1825	•1830	1835	1840	1845	1850	1855	1860	1865
First...........	....	....	4,320	7,941	7,630	12,085	9,929	11,331	10,380	10,629	12,230	19,754	13,486	17,373	9,852
Second..........	....	....	5,167	8,493	7,439	8,214	9,315	8,203	7,549	6,394	6,962	6,665	3,249	2,507	1,194
Third...........	....	....	6,449	7,426	7,495	9,201	10,801	9,599	10,884	11,581	11,900	10,355	7,909	3,757	3,367
Fourth..........	....	....	6,935	10,226	9,856	10,736	12,240	12,705	11,439	15,770	21,000	23,250	22,895	21,994	17,352
Fifth...........	....	....	9,148	14,744	14,523	12,421	15,093	17,722	18,495	15,159	20,362	22,686	21,617	22,337	18,205
Sixth...........	....	....	13,076	11,286	11,821	13,309	20,061	13,570	14,827	17,198	19,343	24,698	25,562	26,696	19,754
Seventh.........	1791	....	15,394	12,120	10,886	13,006	14,091	15,873	21,481	22,982	25,556	32,690	34,422	39,982	36,962
Eighth..........	1803	....	....	9,128	10,702	13,766	24,285	20,729	28,570	29,073	30,900	34,612	34,052	39,406	30,098
Ninth...........	1803	....	....	4,719	4,343	11,162	10,956	17,333	20,618	24,795	30,907	40,657	39,982	44,385	38,504
Tenth...........	1808	....	....	10,890	10,824	17,806	23,932	16,438	20,929	29,026	20,993	23,316	26,378	29,004	31,537
Eleventh........	1825	....	....	....	....	....	7,344	14,918	26,845	17,053	27,259	43,758	52,979	59,571	58,953
Twelfth.........	1827	....	....	....	....	....	....	11,808	17,053	11,652	13,378	10,451	17,656	27,958	28,259
Thirteenth......	1827	....	....	....	....	....	7,938	12,598	24,437	18,517	22,411	28,246	26,597	32,917	26,388
Fourteenth......	1827	....	....	....	....	....	....	14,288	17,130	20,235	21,103	25,196	24,754	28,080	23,382
Fifteenth.......	1832	....	....	....	....	....	....	....	17,306	17,755	19,422	22,564	24,046	27,587	25,572
Sixteenth.......	1836	....	....	....	....	....	....	....	13,202	22,723	....	52,882	39,823	45,176	41,972
Seventeenth.....	1837	....	....	....	....	....	....	....	....	18,619	27,147	43,766	59,548	72,953	79,563
Eighteenth......	1846	....	....	....	....	....	....	....	....	....	....	31,546	39,415	57,462	47,613
Nineteenth......	1850	....	....	....	....	....	....	....	....	....	....	....	17,866	28,252	39,945
Twentieth.......	1851	....	....	....	....	....	....	....	....	....	....	18,465	47,055	67,519	61,884
Twenty-first....	1853	....	....	....	....	....	....	....	....	....	....	....	27,914	49,017	38,669
Twenty-second...	1853	....	....	....	....	....	....	....	....	....	....	....	22,605	61,725	47,361
Total...........		33,131	60,489	96,373	95,515	123,706	166,086	197,112	268,089	312,710	371,223	515,547	629,810	805,358	726,386

aIn this table one can see the statistical results of some great fluctuations in the population of those wards in which the necessities of commerce and its warehouses supplanted large masses of inhabitants. For example, in the first six wards, which comprised the whole region south of Canal Street, these fluctuations began to be felt as early as 1845, and the effect became more marked in each succeeding census period. In all the wards south of Four-teenth Street, the encroachment of warehouses and factories produced many changes in the state of the population, concentration being the most important.

Source: Second Annual Report of the Metropolitan Board of Health, 1867, New York State, Assembly Documents, IX, No. 122 (1868), 146.

Table 13: Population of New York City by Wards, 1845

Wards	Nativity					Total[b] Foreign	Total Population
	Great Britain and Possessions[a]	Germany	France	Other Parts of Europe	Mexico or S. America		
First........	4,489	992	279	156	38	5,954	12,230
Second.......	1,960	495	221	55	15	2,746	6,962
Third........	3,192	638	413	81	18	4,342	11,900
Fourth.......	8,061	1,253	310	1,092	62	10,778	21,000
Fifth........	5,779	746	525	226	44	7,320	20,362
Sixth........	7,552	1,502	241	366	26	9,687	19,343
Seventh......	6,795	920	60	198	54	8,027	25,556
Eighth.......	6,620	1,160	273	179	37	8,269	30,900
Ninth........	6,320	416	81	42	19	6,878	30,907
Tenth........	3,198	2,281	162	143	28	5,812	20,993
Eleventh.....	4,654	4,626	221	88	17	9,606	27,259
Twelfth......	3,727	982	178	73	29	4,989	13,378
Thirteenth...	4,051	2,076	106	66	3	6,302	22,411
Fourteenth...	6,984	820	139	68	29	8,040	21,103
Fifteenth....	4,492	292	145	218	47	5,194	19,422
Sixteenth....	13,218	2,254	214	137	28	15,851	40,350
Seventeenth..	5,489	2,963	142	89	14	8,697	27,147
Total.......	96,581	24,416	3,710	3,277	508	128,492	371,223

[a]Includes Ireland. The nativities tabulated here are the only ones tabulated in the printed summaries of the census.

[b]My computation.

Source: *New York State Census of 1845* (printed summaries, unpaged).

Table 14: Comparison of Native and Immigrant Population, 1855

Wards	Total Population	Foreign-born		Irish[a] and German[a] Percent of Total Population	
		Number	Percent	Irish	German[b]
First.........	13,486	9,219	68.4	46.0	14.8
Second.......	3,249	1,976	60.9	35.8	10.6
Third........	7,909	3,796	48.0	28.9	9.2
Fourth.......	22,895	16,035	70.0	45.6	4.4
Fifth........	21,617	10,295	47.6	22.5	12.5
Sixth........	25,562	17,828	70.0	42.4	14.9
Seventh......	34,422	17,499	50.8	34.0	9.0
Eighth.......	34,052	14,877	43.7	21.2	11.2
Ninth........	39,982	13,665	34.2	19.7	6.1
Tenth........	26,378	13,433	50.9	13.0	30.3
Eleventh.....	52,979	29,498	55.7	17.5	33.6
Twelfth......	17,656	9,296	52.7	33.0	12.2
Thirteenth...	26,597	12,559	47.3	18.7	22.6
Fourteenth...	24,754	14,200	57.4	36.2	13.3
Fifteenth....	24,046	9,928	41.3	26.1	4.5
Sixteenth....	39,823	18,286	45.9	39.0	5.9
Seventeenth..	59,548	34,422	57.8	24.9	27.3
Eighteenth...	39,509	20,974	53.1	37.1	9.0
Nineteenth...	17,866	9,624	53.8	35.4	10.0
Twentieth....	40,075	24,515	61.2	27.3	16.8
Twenty-first.	27,914	11,516	41.3	29.7	5.4
Twenty-second	22,605	12,205	54.0	25.4	21.0
Total......	622,924	325,646	52.3	28.2	15.7

[a]Cf. *infra*, Table 15, for Irish and German population in each ward.

[b]Includes Prussian.

Compiled and computed from data in the *New York State Census of 1855*, pp. 8, 110-118.

Table 15: Foreign-born Population of New York City by Wards, 1855

Ward						Nativity					
	England	Scotland	Ireland	Wales	France	Belgium	Holland	Germany	Prussia	Austria	Switzerland
First...........	385	72	6,207	2	137	3	17	1,979	11	1	22
Second..........	147	44	1,164	4	58	...	...	344	2	1	38
Third...........	281	59	2,283	4	140	8	12	714	16	2	21
Fourth..........	1,009	289	10,446	57	276	7	44	2,688	95	6	118
Fifth...........	932	341	4,866	29	729	17	46	2,633	64	3	122
Sixth...........	915	187	10,845	8	363	15	71	3,590	220	30	85
Seventh.........	1,455	328	11,777	84	83	4	37	2,989	95	5	16
Eighth..........	1,568	625	7,210	56	757	15	49	3,717	85	11	84
Ninth...........	1,598	855	7,909	77	185	4	83	2,192	54	13	34
Tenth...........	939	174	3,442	62	189	11	23	7,536	445	59	63
Eleventh........	1,227	316	9,291	46	363	1	19	17,763	23	25	24
Twelfth.........	629	165	5,831	20	123	15	25	2,130	19	3	31
Thirteenth......	768	210	4,965	59	205	1	22	5,926	81	25	16
Fourteenth......	823	152	8,961	11	394	5	75	3,236	61	28	28
Fifteenth.......	1,002	423	6,285	47	478	32	22	1,068	25	9	64
Sixteenth.......	1,957	1,359	11,572	111	212	1	57	2,305	64	25	31
Seventeenth.....	1,466	418	14,815	62	676	11	52	16,223	57	41	79
Eighteenth......	1,259	400	14,666	59	288	1	12	3,525	29	11	37
Nineteenth......	610	181	6,320	20	51	2	8	1,789	10	8	25
Twentieth.......	1,885	1,194	12,853	73	294	5	52	7,413	78	19	30
Twenty-first....	946	263	8,287	24	127	5	20	1,480	20	3	8
Twenty-second...	892	432	5,740	20	193	11	10	4,726	32	3	2
Total	22,713	8,487	175,735	935	6,321	174	756	95,986	1,586	331	978

Source: *New York State Census of 1855*, pp. 110-118.

Table 15 (continued)

Ward	Nativity														
	Italy	Spain	Portugal	Poland	Norway	Sweden	Russia	Denmark	Canada	New Brunswick	Nova Scotia	Newfoundland	West Indies	Mexico	S. America
First.........	11	11	2	6	68	87	3	20	36	3	9	...	7	3	1
Second........	7	...	2	1	1	5	1	12	12	5	2	...	6	...	...
Third.........	7	9	1	7	3	4	4	4	39	3	1	...	18	1	1
Fourth........	84	35	21	114	17	73	5	56	70	13	22	30	41	...	5
Fifth.........	51	17	3	30	11	15	6	5	72	14	33	3	87	1	4
Sixth.........	357	28	55	385	5	12	23	1	75	4	13	15	40	1	6
Seventh.......	22	25	18	59	35	100	6	80	91	50	66	13	31	1	8
Eighth........	138	20	7	40	4	27	4	7	175	18	27	8	120	4	10
Ninth.........	10	8	5	27	7	26	5	14	131	20	54	9	65	1	9
Tenth.........	14	12	...	150	1	23	8	24	84	6	28	12	20	1	7
Eleventh......	5	7	2	26	...	19	6	25	162	5	41	...	19	1	1
Twelfth.......	24	1	7	11	2	23	1	5	76	2	26	2	44	7	7
Thirteenth....	6	6	10	42	3	21	2	5	61	20	29	10	22	1	2
Fourteenth....	50	5	2	104	1	5	11	7	76	5	14	5	37	...	...
Fifteenth.....	35	44	5	13	6	28	3	8	93	5	16	1	83	16	16
Sixteenth.....	8	18	5	27	5	19	1	4	180	15	38	5	94	2	16
Seventeenth...	37	28	6	48	13	21	10	11	125	14	35	8	164	2	17
Eighteenth....	61	41	2	20	22	10	6	15	117	5	32	5	81	14	23
Nineteenth....	7	3	2	8	2	2	...	6	56	8	19	2	29	1	6
Twentieth.....	15	15	3	49	1	20	7	5	161	9	21	1	56	2	12
Twenty-first...	17	10	3	19	3	9	...	13	88	9	18	4	50	4	18
Twenty-second..	2	...	2	14	7	5	4	11	60	1	7	...	7	3	1
Total	968	343	163	1,200	227	554	116	327	2,040	234	551	133	1,121	66	170

Source: *New York State Census of 1855*, pp. 110-118.

Table 15 (continued)

Ward	Nativity							Total Foreign-born[a]
	East Indies	Africa	"Turkey & Greece"	"Islands"	Asia	At Sea	Unknown	
First............	...	...	...	1	...	2	113	9,219
Second...........	...	...	2	...	1	...	128	1,976
Third............	...	...	1	...	3	2	148	3,796
Fourth...........	...	2	5	8	36	3	360	16,035
Fifth............	1	3	...	4	3	...	150	10,295
Sixth............	1	4	...	6	...	4	464	17,828
Seventh..........	4	1	2	9	2	3	...	17,499
Eighth...........	1	6	2	2	...	8	52	14,877
Ninth............	1	1	2	3	...	5	258	13,665
Tenth............	4	1	8	2	3	4	78	13,433
Eleventh.........	6	...	...	2	...	6	67	29,498
Twelfth..........	...	4	...	2	2	4	55	9,296
Thirteenth.......	...	1	1	3	...	8	28	12,559
Fourteenth.......	2	1	2	1	...	4	94	14,200
Fifteenth........	2	1	11	4	1	3	79	9,928
Sixteenth........	2	...	1	4	1	5	142	18,286
Seventeenth......	6	...	1	5	...	13	477	14,422
Eighteenth.......	8	2	...	2	3	5	203	20,974
Nineteenth.......	2	8	...	...	1	9	429	9,624
Twentieth........	1	3	...	1	3	11	223	24,515
Twenty-first.....	2	...	2	1	3	4	56	11,516
Twenty-second....	...	...	...	2	2	...	16	12,205
Total	43	38	40	62	64	103	3,620	325,646

[a] Computed by the author.

Source: *New York State Census of 1855*, pp. 110-118.

Table 16: Tenement Houses and Cellars and Their Population in New York City at the Close of the Year 1864

Wards	Total No. of Tenement Houses	Total No. of Families in Tenement Houses	Average No. of Families in each House	Total Population in Tenement Houses	Average Population in each House	Total Cellar Population	Total Population in Cellars and Tenement Houses	Total No. of Tenement Houses without Sewers	Total Population in Unsewered Houses
First.........	250	2,181	8 1/2	8,564	34 1/4+	498	9,062	89	2,606
Third.........	54	310	5 3/4	1,248	24 1/8	57	1,305	28	640
Fourth........	486	3,636	7 1/2	17,611	35 1/4+	346	17,957	151	4,473
Fifth.........	462	2,597	5 1/2	10,370	24 2/3+	836	11,206	293	5,796
Sixth.........	605	4,406	7 1/4	22,401	34 1/3-	496	22,897	214	6,612
Seventh.......	627	4,586	7 1/4	19,293	30 4/5	1,233	20,526	409	10,953
Eighth........	625	3,977	6 1/2	15,630	25 +	1,258	16,888	302	6,530
Ninth.........	596	3,836	6 1/2	14,955	25 1/10	217	15,172	208	4,485
Tenth.........	534	4,487	9	18,140	34-	453	18,583	110	2,953
Eleventh......	2,049	13,433	6 1/2	64,254	31 5/14	1,366	65,620	403	10,026
Thirteenth....	540	3,729	6 3/4	14,997	27 4/8	939	15,936	215	5,089
Fourteenth....	546	4,509	8 1/2	20,008	36 5/8	417	20,425	207	6,202
Fifteenth.....	197	1,358	7	4,970	25-	235	5,205	72	1,237
Sixteenth.....	1,257	7,088	5 2/3	31,500	25+	2,150	33,650	300	7,107
Seventeenth...	1,890	15,974	8 1/3	63,766	34 2/3+	2,441	66,207	155	4,596
Eighteenth....	836	7,267	8 3/4	35,869	42 6/7	230	36,099	98	3,766
Nineteenth....	571	3,632	6 1/2	16,067	28 1/7+	205	16,272	81	1,912
Twentieth.....	1,162	8,344	7 1/3	32,205	27 4/5	1,013	33,218	291	7,968
Twenty-first..	1,026	7,299	7	36,675	35 5/7-	135	36,870	144	4,491
Twenty-second.	996	7,714	7 1/2	31,845	32-	699	32,544	162	3,233

This Table presents the Statistics of Tenement Houses, as reported by the Sanitary Inspectors of the Council of Hygiene, and verified by the Metropolitan Police. The rather meaningless fractions were in the original tables.

The total number of tenement houses, none of which contained less than three families, who hired their apartments by monthly or very brief periods of rental, was 15,511. This exceeded, by 202, the number which the Council of Hygiene as well as the Metropolitan Police had elsewhere given.

The total population of these tenement houses was..................486,000
The total population in cellars was.................................. 15,224
Total in tenement houses and in cellars...........................501,224

Note -- The Sanitary Inspectors of the Twelfth Ward reported that there were 202 tenement houses of the larger class (averaging more than six families in a house) in that Ward. In the same Ward there were 643 inhabited *shanties*, and 710 other tenements of a poor class, but not having three families each, consequently not counted in the statistics of tenement houses.

Source: Citizens' Association of New York, ***Report of the Council of Hygiene and Public Health*** (New York, 1865), p. 349.

Table 17: Nativity of the Population of New York City, 1860

States and Territories	United States Whites M.	F.	Total whites	Free Colored M.	F.	Total free colored	Total born in United States	Countries	Foreign Countries Whites M.	F.	Total whites	Free Colored M.	F.	Total free colored	Total born in foreign countries
Alabama..........	81	106	187	2	5	7	194	German States:							
Arkansas.........	6	7	13	...	...	...	13	Austria..........	942	749	1,691	1	...	1	1,692
California.......	71	73	144	2	5	7	151	Bavaria..........	9,294	9,282	18,576	...	...	...	18,576
Connecticut......	3,994	3,639	7,633	105	158	263	7,896	Baden............	4,651	4,484	9,135	1	...	1	9,136
Delaware.........	113	97	210	67	77	144	354	Hesse............	5,764	5,405	11,169	...	...	...	11,169
Florida..........	32	34	66	1	3	4	70	Nassau...........	541	456	997	...	...	...	997
Georgia..........	171	198	369	10	20	30	399	Prussia..........	7,145	5,697	12,842	...	...	...	12,842
Illinois.........	163	145	308	1	1	2	310	Wurtemberg.......	3,339	3,158	6,497	...	...	...	6,497
Indiana..........	62	56	118	...	...	...	118	German States (not specified)...	32,135	26,935	59,070	4	1	5	59,075
Iowa.............	19	21	40	...	...	...	40	Total Germany....	63,811	56,166	119,977	6	1	7	119,984
Kansas...........	...	2	2	...	...	...	2	Asia.............	36	31	67	2	...	2	69
Kentucky.........	116	116	232	9	7	16	248	Africa...........	23	13	36	5	3	8	44
Louisiana........	226	209	435	6	18	24	459	Atlantic Islands..	19	7	26	2	2	4	30
Maine............	926	722	1,650	11	2	13	1,663	Australia........	14	8	22	...	...	...	22
Maryland.........	782	739	1,521	387	412	799	2,320	Belgium..........	156	113	269	...	...	...	269
Massachusetts....	4,070	3,424	7,494	72	72	144	7,638	British America...	1,972	1,875	3,847	17	35	52	3,899
Michigan.........	115	110	225	2	2	4	229	Central America...	4	7	11	...	...	...	11
Minnesota........	11	7	18	...	...	...	18	China............	46	5	51	...	...	...	51
Mississippi......	34	40	74	...	...	2	76								

Missouri.........	60	55	115	1	2	3	118
New Hampshire....	700	461	1,161	4	5	9	1,170
New Jersey.......	5,836	5,907	11,743	437	729	1,166	12,909
New York.........	184,773	186,393	371,166	3,370	4,498	7,863	379,034
North Carolina...	98	88	186	40	44	84	270
Ohio.............	470	388	858	29	19	48	906
Oregon...........	...	3	3	...	...	...	3
Pennsylvania.....	2,724	2,662	5,386	289	362	651	6,037
Rhode Island.....	571	498	1,069	11	32	43	1,112
South Carolina...	245	290	535	41	38	79	614
Tennessee........	33	38	71	...	2	2	73
Texas............	38	26	64	1	2	3	67
Vermont..........	770	475	1,245	26	35	61	1,306
Virginia.........	538	506	1,044	247	285	532	1,576
Wisconsin........	73	90	163	...	1	1	164
District of Columbia	95	100	195	30	40	70	265
Territories......	7	2	9	...	...	...	9
At sea...........	48	38	86	...	2	2	88
Not stated.......	943	1,011	1,954	36	43	79	2,033
Total...........	209,014	208,778	417,792	5,237	6,923	12,160	429,952

Denmark..........	417	195	612	...	...	...	612
England..........	14,113	12,936	27,049	14	19	33	27,082
Europe (not specified).	6	5	11	...	...	...	11
France...........	4,172	3,877	8,049	15	10	25	8,074
Great Britain (not specified)...	2	...	2	...	...	...	2
Greece...........	13	6	19	...	...	...	19
Holland..........	781	639	1,420	...	...	...	1,420
Ireland..........	86,580	117,120	203,700	20	20	40	203,740
Italy............	926	537	1,463	1	...	1	1,464
Mexico...........	32	21	53	1	...	1	54
Norway...........	192	59	251	...	...	...	251
Portugal.........	106	34	140	3	1	4	144
Poland...........	967	619	1,586	...	...	...	1,586
Pacific Islands..	2	1	3	...	...	...	3
Russia...........	291	176	467	...	...	...	467
Scotland.........	4,941	4,266	9,207	1	...	1	9,208
Spain............	293	116	409	6	1	7	416
Sweden...........	489	177	666	...	...	...	666
Sardinia.........	32	8	40	...	...	...	40
Switzerland......	901	870	1,771	...	...	...	1,771
South America....	84	71	155	11	4	15	170
Sandwich Islands.	3	8	11	...	...	...	11
Turkey...........	15	6	21	3	1	4	25
West Indies......	556	439	995	120	87	207	1,202
Wales............	466	429	895	...	...	...	895
Other foreign countries	1	2	3	...	...	2	5
Total...........	182,462	200,841	383,303	228	186	414	383,717

RECAPITULATION

Born in United States.............	429,952
[a]Born in foreign countries.......	383,717
Aggregate.........................	813,669

[a] 7 Indians included in white population

Source: *Eighth Census of the United States*, 1860, "Population," p. 609.

Health

Table 18: Admissions to Bellevue Hospital for All Causes, 1846-1858

Year	U.S.A.	Foreign	Ireland	Nativity Germany	England	Scotland	France
1846	600	3,000	2,202	470	...[a]	...[a]	...[a]
1847	841	5,700	4,863	444	264	66	...[a]
1848	588	3,209	2,592	252	192	80	...[a]
1849	618	2,496	2,052	193	138	63	...[a]
1850	647	3,081	2,596	175	165	80	...[a]
1851	1,010	4,332	3,698	201	247	87	...[a]
1852	983	4,037	3,482	210	194	69	19
1853	702	4,134	3,587	184	190	65	26
1854	925	5,288	4,482	316	264	111	24
1855	856	4,899	4,242	281	201	69	16
1856	808	4,676	3,958	316	202	78	38
1857	1,032	5,689	4,791	423	238	88	39
1858	1,156	6,769	5,703	537	232	96	64
Total	10,766	57,310	48,248	4,002	2,527	952	226

Percent of foreign-born, 1846-1858:   84.2   6.9
                         1847-1858:   84.8   6.5   4.7   1.7   0.6[b]

[a]Data unavailable for these years
[b]1852-1858

Compiled from *Annual Reports* of the Alms House Commissioner, 1846, pp. 402-403; 1847, App. p. 42; 1848, p. 97; *Annual Reports* of the Governors of the Alms House, 1849, p. 33; 1850, p. 29; 1851, p. 40; 1852, p. 23; 1853, p. 24; 1854, p. 22; 1855, p. 21; 1856, p. 37; 1857, p. 18; 1858, p. 20.

Table 19: Insanity: Admissions to the Lunatic Asylum, 1849-1858

Year	U.S.A.	Foreign	Nativity Ireland	Germany[a]	England	Total Native and Foreign-born
1849	123	336	228	52	29	459
1850	97	294	199	53	25	391
1851	98	343	194	83	30	441
1852	102	393	259	71	35	495
1853	94	393	241	103	19	487
1854	97	389	241	93	21	486
1855	78	293	178	666	19	371
1856	69	297	187	69	21	366
1857	68	258	157	58	14	216
1858	72	283	155	76	24	355
Total	898	3,279	2,039	724	237	4,177

[a]Includes Prussia, Bavaria, Hanover, Saxony, and Austria

Compiled from *Annual Reports* of the Resident Physician of the Lunatic Asylum in *Annual Reports* of the Governors of the Alms House, 1849, p. 109; 1850, p. 91; 1851, p. 114; 1852, p. 96; 1853, p. 83; 1854, p. 121; 1855, p. 103; 1856, p. 193; 1857, p. 201; 1858, p. 152.

APPENDIX V

Pauperism

Table 20: Admissions to the Alms House, May 8, 1849 -- December 31, 1858

Nativity	1849[a]	1850	1851	1852	1853	1854	1855	1856	1857	1858
Ireland	1,006	1,464	1,710	1,654	1,369	1,885	1,949	2,212	2,705	2,544
England	92	145	165	124	105	118	121	156	183	170
Germany	89	94	114	131	96	139	148	148	281	212
Scotland	36	50	59	53	43	49	38	54	71	82
France[b]								17	23	36
Canada[b]								16	30	15
Other Foreign	38	57	85	44	50	55	67	33	36	37
Total Foreign	1,261	1,810	2,133	2,006	1,663	2,246	2,323	2,636	3,329	3,096
U.S.A.	411	545	650	618	535	737	773	723	875	794
Total	1,672	2,355	2,783	2,624	2,198	2,983	3,096	3,359	4,204	3,890

[a]Incomplete: includes May 8 -- December 31.
[b]Data unrecorded before 1856

Compiled from the first ten *Annual Reports of the Governors of the Alms House*, as follows: 1849, p. 28; 1850, p. 21; 1851, p. 11; 1852, p. 11; 1853, p. 1; 1854, p. 1; 1855, p. 1; 1854, p. 1; 1857, p. 1; 1858, p. 1.

APPENDIX VI

Crime

Table 21: New York City Prison Commitments, 1850-1858

Commitments	1850	1851	1852	1853	1854	1855	1856	1857	1858
Total	21,299	21,792	25,365	28,531	30,691	36,264	27,881	27,845	35,172
Natives	5,777	4,901	5,601	6,302	6,966	8,926	6,426	6,567	8,768
"Foreigners"	15,522	16,891	19,764	22,229	23,725	27,338	21,455	21,278	26,404[b]
Married	8,505	9,240	10,766	11,589	11,990	11,894	9,618	9,364	12,569
Single	12,241	11,578	13,399	15,435	17,072	21,275	15,905	16,074	19,411
Widowed	364	728	962	1,100	726	2,080	1,439	1,520	2,010
Unknown[a]	189	246	238	407	903	1,015	919	887	1,182
Temperate	2,446	2,339	2,474	4,399	5,320	3,561	3,084	4,028	4,972
Intemperate	18,853	19,453	22,891	24,132	25,371	32,703	24,797	23,817	30,200
Totally illiterate	9,449	6,837	8,014	9,131	9,931	11,818	9,582	9,568	12,067
Could only read	1,646	4,486	5,242	4,932	3,305	4,633	2,438	2,455	3,651

[a]Includes persons who refused to answer, could not speak English, or were insane.
[b]For a breakdown of this figure, cf. infra, Table 22.

Compiled from reports of the Warden of the City Prison, contained in the *Annual Reports of the Governors of the Alms House*, 1850-1858, as follows: 1850, pp. 50-51; 1851, p. 67; 1852, p. 47; 1853, p. 42; 1854, p. 60; 1855, p. 81; 1856, p. 153; 1857, p. 144; 1858, p. 107.

Table 22:   Prison Commitments of Immigrants, 1858

Nativity[a]	Male	Female	Total
Ireland	10,299	9,363	19,662
Germany[b]	2,611	986	3,602
England	939	414	1,353
Scotland	327	241	568
France	228	41	269
Italy	176	28	204
Canada	127	54	181

[a]Nativities not listed here included: West Indies (44), Poland (40), Wales (27), Nova Scotia (25), Belgium (24), Switzerland (21), Portugal (19), Holland (19), Spain (19), Norway (18), Sweden (16), and China (14).

[b]Includes 44 Prussians (40 males and 4 females) and 1 Bavarian (male).

Source: Report of the Warden of the City Prison, *Annual Report of the Governors of the Alms House*, 1858, p. 109.

Table 23: Convictions in New York City Courts of Special Sessions, 1859

Nativity	Assault, Battery	Vagrancy	Petit Larceny	Drunk, Disorderly Conduct	Disorderly Conduct	Violating Corporation Ordinances	Exposure of Person	Keeping Disorderly House	Malicious Mischief	Total Convictions
U.S.A.	304	1,028	464	1,546	268	12	5	2	6	3,637
Ireland	794	2,382	639	6,648	787	35	4	4	6	11,305
Germany	194	159	189	750	73	20	4	6	5	1,403
England	62	140	83	317	59	4	1	1	1	666
Scotland	17	57	27	145	31	4	..	..	..	281
France	6	12	18	76	..	1	..	..	1	118
Canada	8	25	16	26	1	4	..	..	..	80
Unknown	..	317	201	..	..	14	..	..	..	542
								Total Convictions[b]		
U.S.A.	8.0[a]	28.0[a]	12.8[a]	42.5[a]	7.4[a]	Negligible		0.9[b]		
Ireland	7.0	21.0	5.7	58.8	7.0	"		5.5		
Germany	13.8	11.3	13.5	53.5	5.2	"		1.2		
England	9.3	21.0	12.5	47.3	9.0	"		2.5		
Scotland	6.0	20.3	9.6	51.6	11.0	"		3.0		
France	5.0	10.0	15.0	64.4	3.4	"		1.5		
Canada	10.0	31.2	20.0	32.5	1.3	5.0[a]		2.0		

[a]Percent of total convictions of persons of that nativity.
[b]Percent of total population of that nationality resident in New York City, according to the 1860 census.

Source: Abstract of Sheriff's Returns of Convictions in Courts of Special Sessions in City and County of New York, 1859, New York State, *Assembly Documents*, VI, No. 190 (1860), 121.

Table 24: Ages at Which Crimes Were Most Frequently Committed, 1850

Ages	No. of Crimes
15-20	2,616
20-30	8,908
30-40	6,002
40-50	2,285

Source: Report of the Warden of the City Prison, *Annual Report of the Governors of the Alms House*, 1850, p. 51.

Table 25: Juvenile Delinquency. Nativity of Parents of Children Admitted to the House of Refuge (of the Society for the Reformation of Juvenile Delinquents), 1834-1866

Nativity of Parent	1834	1835	1836	1837	1838	1839	1840	1841	1842	1843	1844	1845	1846	1847	1848	1849	1850
"American"	78	71	52	59	47	57	40	67	59	47	47	55	38	50	39	69	65
Irish	68	60	70	53	62	82	83	91	104	92	88	92	82	91	127	134	195
English	25	18	22	26	16	16	19	18	29	22	22	21	16	12	12	14	26
Scotch	4	2	1	5	2	..	4	6	9	5	5	5	12	7	7	6	9
German	..	8	7	9	10	..[a]	2	8	7	2	14	16	13	15	16	16	23
French	4	1	2	2	4	..[a]	3	2	6	1	1	2	6	6	2	5	5
Colored[b]	30	30	37	32	42	36	..[d]	2	..	..	..	3	..	..	..	..	..
Other[c]	9	8	..	2	2	..	2	2	1	..	..	..	..	1	5	3	..

Nativity of Parent	1851	1852	1853	1854	1855	1856	1857	1858	1859	1860	1861	1862	1863	1864	1865	1866
"American"	53	45	59	66	61	46	80	40	40	68	42	49	68	71	90	100
Irish	163	157	198	207	205	153	277	198	195	240	216	212	311	301	441	455
English	21	21	20	15	15	17	31	10	14	22	19	18	35	30	29	33
Scotch.	4	8	4	5	13	5	5	9	4	10	5	10	7	10	20	11
German	29	24	25	30	29	15	32	35	30	39	39	38	65	53	96	97
French	4	7	1	3	5	2	2	3	6	5	9	10	10	9	6	10
Colored[b]	..	..	..	..	..	..	..	..	..	27	32	17	39	23	43	37
Other[c]	..	4	7	1	1	..	2	6	5	1	1	2	3	5	5	7

[a] In 1839, 8 parents were listed as "French and German."

[b] Includes "African."

[c] Includes Belgian, Danish, Dutch, Hungarian, Italian, Norwegian, Polish, Portuguese, Russian, Swedish, Swiss, Welsh, "Indian," Jewish, and doubtful or unknown nationalities.

[d] In the years 1840-1859 no statistics of "colored" or "African" were presented.

Compiled from *Annual Reports* of the Society for the Reformation of Juvenile Delinquents, as follows: 1834, p. 61; 1835, p. 47; 1836, p. 54; 1837, p. 29; 1838, p. 29; 1839, p. 36; 1840, p. 41; 1841, p. 38; 1842, p. 29; 1843, p. 24; 1844, p. 21; 1845, p. 25; 1846, p. 22; 1847, p. 20; 1848, p. 24; 1849, p. 32; 1850, p. 28; 1851, p. 22; 1852, p. 48; 1853, p. 24; 1854, p. 30; 1855, p. 29; 1856, p. 32; 1857, p. 29; 1858, p. 35; 1859, p. 39; 1860, p. 26; 1861, p. 26; 1862, p. 25; 1863, p. 21; 1864, p. 23; 1865, p. 25; 1866, p. 15.

APPENDIX VII

Occupations

NOTE ON CLASSIFICATION

THE TASK OF correlating the nativities and the occupations of immigrants was fraught with bewildering difficulties of classification. Of the multitude of occupations reported by the marshals of the *New York State Census of 1855*, not a few were ambiguous, unintelligible, or simply illegible. Many occupations were classified according to the type of article produced rather than according to the type of labor actually performed. (Cf. *Instructions for Taking the Census of the State of New York, in the Year 1855*, issued by the Secretary of State... [Albany, 1855], pp. 20-21.) In some instances it was completely impossible to determine the degree or even the type of skill which a worker might have possessed. A reclassification of occupations was clearly necessary. (Cf. Oscar Handlin, *Boston's Immigrants*...[Cambridge, Mass., 1941], pp. 249-250.) After consulting contemporary and present-day occupational dictionaries and encyclopedias and conferring with Professor Paul F. Brissenden, formerly a member of a regional War Labor Board, and with other persons, I arrived at the following scheme of classification:

Agents and Salesmen, including Advertisers, Auctioneers, Brokers, Collectors, Employment and Insurance Agents, Runners

Artisans and Factory Workers
  Bakers, confectioners, and sugar refiners
  Blacksmiths; farriers
  Boilermakers
  Bookbinders, folders, and sewers
  Brassworkers, including finishers, founders, molders; braziers

Button makers

Cabinetmakers and upholsterers; "cane-makers"; mattress, mirror, woodenware makers; "framers"

Coach and wagon makers; carriage makers, coach trimmers, wheelwrights

Coopers, including stave makers

Coppersmiths

Dyers and bleachers

Glassworkers, including blowers, bottlers, cutters

Gunsmiths; stock makers

Hairworkers; feltworkers; wigmakers

Iron molders (These may include molders of other metals and even wood.)

Ironworkers, including founders, rail makers, and other ironworkers except molders

Leatherworkers, including curriers, glovers, harness makers; leather cutters, dealers, dressers and finishers; morocco dressers and finishers, patent leather workers, pocketbook makers, portfolio makers, saddlers, skinners, tanners, trunk makers, wallet makers

Locksmiths and bellhangers

Musical instrument makers, including organ, piano, and violin makers

Oil and paint makers, including camphine, turpentine, varnish, and white lead makers

Packers of pork, spices, tea, and other products

Paper box makers

Papermakers, stainers, rulers

Polishers and burnishers, including "chasers," enamelers, japanners

Potters; crockery and porcelain makers

Precision instrument makers, including chronometer, clock, and watch makers and repairers; "fluters"; gas meter makers; "instrument makers"; surgical instrument makers

Printers; compositors, electrotypers, feeders, lithographers, plate printers, pressmen, stereotypers, typesetters

Refiners, assayers, etc., including "chippers," melters, platers

Smiths (various), including boltmakers, britannia-ware makers, cutlers, die sinkers, file cutters,

hinge makers, leadsmiths, nail makers, needle-
makers, pin makers, plane makers, sawmakers and
filers, screw makers, sieve makers, spike makers,
spring makers, steel makers, tool makers; type-
cutters, finishers and founders; vice makers,
wire drawers and wireworkers

Straw workers; brush and broommakers, basketmakers,
willow ware workers

Textile workers (various), including cloth printers,
cutters, drapers, flaxworkers and dressers, hair
cloth workers, hemp dressers, hosiers, linen
folders, oil cloth makers, patternmakers, ribbon
makers, (cotton) samplers, silkworkers (except
weavers), spinners, wool carders and combers,
woolen- and worstedworkers

Tinsmiths

Tobacconists, including cigar makers and dealers

Turners, carvers, and gilders

Umbrella and parasol makers

Weavers, including silk weavers, carpet makers and
dealers, mat- and rugmakers

Workers in factories and miscellaneous heavy industry (except boilermakers), including agricultural implement makers, cannon makers, grate
makers and setters, grind- and millstone makers,
India rubber makers, matchmakers, mineral and
soda water makers, miners, "operators," pump and
block makers, range setters, riveters, safe-
makers, scale makers, stove makers

Workers in gems and precious metals, including
bracelet maker, diamond cutters, gold and silversmiths, gold beaters and cutters, jewelers, lap-
idaries, pearlworkers, pen and pencil makers,
pencil case makers, watchcase makers

Other artisans: artificial limb makers, "B. stick-
ers," "bagging" workers; makers of beads, bellows,
belts, billiards, blacking; "block letterers,"
makers of braces, bricks, buckles; cage makers,
card makers, casemakers, cement makers, chain
makers, "coasters," combmakers, cork cutters,
envelope makers, fan makers, feather workers,
fender makers, "finesters," fishing tackle makers,
"fly netmakers," "gloating" workers, gluemakers,

"hame makers," hosemakers, indigo and ink makers, kit makers, lamp black makers, lampmakers, last makers, lath makers, "liners," mechanics (not specified), military equipment makers, millwrights, model makers, mold makers, pipe makers, powder makers, putty makers, pyrotechnists; makers of reeds, retorts, rings, rules, rulers; sack binders, saleratus makers, saltmakers, sandpaper makers, seal makers, shot makers, soda water apparatus makers, stainers, stampers, starch makers, taxidermists, truss makers, waterproofers, wax bleachers, whaleboneworkers, whip makers

Brewers and Distillers, including Cordial Makers, Maltsters

Building Trades Workers
Builders and contractors, including bridgebuilders, dock builders
Carpenters, including joiners, lathers, sash and blind makers, shingle makers
Masons, bricklayers, and plasterers
Painters, varnishers, and glaziers, including grainers, imitation marble workers, paper hangers, sign makers
Plumbers
Roofers and slaters
Sawyers, including woodcutters, planers
Stonecutters and polishers, including stone setters, flag setters, "flaggers," pavers

Clerks; Accountants, Copyists, Telegraph Operators

Clothing workers
Dressmakers and seamstresses, including artificial flower makers, embroiderers; fringe, tassel, and gimp makers; lacemakers, milliners, pocket makers, quilt makers, sewers, shirt and collar makers
Furriers; fur dressers
Hatters, including hat- and capmakers, hat finishers, trimmers
Shoemakers, including bootmakers, crimpers, gaiter binders
Tailors, including mantua and mantilla makers, pants makers, vest makers

Domestic Workers
  Cooks
  Domestic servants
  Housekeepers; janitors
  Laundresses
  Nurses, including "assistant nurses," "leechers"
    and "cuppers," midwives
  Waiters

Engineers

Financiers, including Bankers, Bank Officers

Government Employees, including Custom House Officials,
  Mail Agents, Postmasters

Laborers and Porters
  Laborers, carpet shakers, "day's work" laborers;
    miscellaneous unskilled jobs: bill posters,
    blasters, drillers, firemen, furnacemen, house
    movers, label cutters, lamp lighters, quarrymen,
    "rock men," spike drivers
  Porters, errand boys, office boys, messengers

Machinists

Manufacturers of bonemeal, cotton, cloth, gutta percha,
  hair, patent medicines, perfume, plaster; ship-
  builders; soda manufacturers

Maritime Workers
  Boat builders
  Caulkers
  Chandlers; soap- and candlemakers
  Riggers, rope- and cord makers, stay makers
  Sailmakers; awning makers
  Ship carpenters, including borers, fasteners, join-
    ers, mast and spar makers

Merchants, including Importers

Policemen

Professional Workers
  Actors and performers, including dancers, equestri-
    ans, magicians, riding masters
  Architects
  Artists, including colorers and colorists, design-
    ers, engravers, fresco painters, glass stainers,
    map makers, plaster figure makers, portrait painters

210

Authors

Clergy, including missionaries, nuns

Lawyers, including "counselors"

Musicians

Physicians and surgeons, including "bonesetters," dentists, oculists, veterinarians

Teachers, including linguists, professors, schoolmasters, and certain specialists, e.g., "mathematicians"

Other professional workers, including botanists, chemists, draftsmen, editors, engineers (civil and military), fortunetellers and astrologers, geologists and mineralogists, lecturers, librarians, naturalists, news collectors, notaries public, opticians, photographers and daguerreotypers, phrenologists, poets, publishers, reporters, surveyors

Proprietors and Custodians

Hotel and boardinghouse keepers; innkeepers

Proprietors of baths, bowling alleys, museums; stage proprietors, theater managers, and showmen; quarry owners; inventors and patentees

Restaurant keepers, victualers

Superintendents (various), including baggage masters, dock keepers and wharfingers, foremen, inspectors, overseers, sextons, superintendents and matrons of asylums, etc.; "warehouse" and "storage" men

Watchmen

Service Occupations

Barbers; hairdressers

Undertakers

Other service occupations, including bootblacks, glove cleaners, hat cleaners, "honesters," piano tuners, "refrigerator men," "renovators," scissors and knife grinders, sweeps, tinkers, whitewashers

Shopkeepers and Dealers

Clothiers, including clothing store keepers, merchant tailors

Dry goods dealers

Food dealers, including butchers; dairymen and milk

dealers; fish dealers; fruit dealers; grocers, marketmen (and women); millers; oystermen and dealers; pork cutters; produce dealers; dealers in or makers of coffee, mustard, pickles and preserves, smoked meats, spices and vinegar.

Peddlers; traders

Retail shopkeepers, including apothecaries, booksellers; dealers in charcoal, china and crockery, coal, hardware, ice, junk, lumber, marble, music, paper, oil; ironmongers; lime burners and dealers; pawnbrokers; stationers; stone and brick dealers; toys and "fancy goods" makers and dealers, wood dealers, wool dealers

Wine and liquor dealers, including barkeepers and tenders, importers of liquor, "publicans," saloon keepers, tavern keepers

Speculators; "Gamblers"

Workers in Transportation and Related Jobs
Boatmen, including ferrymen, pursers, stewards, watermen
Cartmen, draymen, and teamsters
Drivers, coachmen, and hackmen
Expressmen; forwarders
Hostlers and grooms
Railroad employees, etc., including brakemen, car drivers, conductors, signalmen, switchmen, timekeepers
Stable keepers
Stevedores; longshoremen

Miscellaneous Occupations
Drovers
Farmers
Fishermen and hunters
Gardeners, florists, and nurserymen
Organ grinders, rag pickers, rag cutters, scavengers, "bouquet makers," newsboys
Prostitutes (obviously very few were reported)
Students
Unclassified minor occupations (heterogeneous and numerically insignificant)

Table 26: Number and Percentage of Gainfully Employed
Immigrants of Each Nationality, 1855

Nativity	Total Population	Number Gainfully Employed	Percent
Ireland	175,735	88,480	50
Germany	97,572[a]	45,764	47
England	22,713	9,725	43
Scotland	8,487	4,142	48
France	6,321	3,022	48
British North America	2,958[b]	1,201	40
Poland	1,200	596	49
Scandinavia	1,108[c]	557	50
Italy	968	476	50
Switzerland	978	475	49
Wales	935	453	48
Netherlands	756	296	40
Latin America	1,357[d]	279	20
Spain	343	144	41
Belgium	174	95	55
(Hungary)	331[e]	85	26
Russia	116	59	50
Portugal	163	56	34
(Bohemia)	331[e]	43	13
China	64[f]	15	23
Total foreign-born	322,279	155,963[g]	43

[a] Includes Prussia.

[b] Includes Canada, New Brunswick, Nova Scotia, and Newfoundland.

[c] Includes Norway, Sweden, and Denmark.

[d] Includes West Indies, Mexico, and South America.

[e] Natives of Austria, Hungary, and Bohemia were ignored in the printed census summaries. The numbers of Hungarians and Bohemians gainfully employed represent my tabulations from the original manuscript schedules.

[f] "Asia"

[g] Exclusive of Negro immigrants. There were 3,688 gainfully employed Negroes, both native and immigrant.

Compiled and computed from data in the printed and manuscript versions of the *New York State Census of 1855*.

Table 27: Occupations of Gainfully Employed Immigrants, by Nationality, 1855

Occupational Classification	Ireland	Germany	England	Scotland	France	Poland	Scandinavia	Switzerland	Wales	Italy	Netherlands	Latin America	British North America	Spain	Portugal	Hungary	Russia	Belgium	Bohemia	China	Total Foreign-Born	Negro	Total Native and Foreign-Born
Bakers, confectioners	861	1,987	147	151	105	2	9	14	3	8	4	3	21	...	1	2	...	5	...	...	3,323	3	3,692[c]
Blacksmiths	1,339	530	144	84	25	1	4	4	5	...	5	...	13	...	...	...	...	...	5	...	2,159	1	2,642[b]
Boilermakers	246	20	14	6	3	...	...	...	2	...	...	...	6	...	...	...	...	...	...	...	297	...	...
Bookbinders & folders	373	143	80	43	4	3	...	1	2	3	2	1	17	...	...	...	...	...	...	...	672	...	1,315[c]
Brassworkers	168	52	41	41	10	1	...	...	2	...	1	1	4	1	...	...	...	...	...	...	322	...	442[c]
Cabinetmakers;upholsterers	408	2,153	104	56	112	11	17	6	4	9	14	3	2	2	...	3	...	...	...	...	2,917	5	3,517[b]
Coach & Wagon Makers	238	137	39	13	8	...	...	2	3	...	1	1	9	1	...	...	...	...	...	...	447	...	757[c]
Coopers	413	269	27	14	15	...	2	1	1	...	1	2	1	1	...	...	...	...	...	...	753	6	1,018[c]
Coppersmiths	75	55	11	3	...	...	1	...	...	...	...	...	1	...	...	...	...	...	...	...	146	...	207[c]
Dyers, bleachers	32	41	17	20	15	...	...	1	1	1	1	...	...	...	...	...	...	...	...	...	129	...	163[c]
Glassworkers	84	20	14	2	18	1	...	...	1	1	1	...	...	...	...	...	...	...	...	...	141	...	143[b]
Gunsmiths	43	51	22	3	3	...	...	...	...	...	1	1	...	...	...	...	...	...	...	...	123	...	126[c]
Hairworkers	26	13	7	2	2	...	1	...	...	...	1	...	...	...	...	...	...	...	...	...	52	...	80[c]
Iron molders	162	42	51	27	6	1	1	1	12	...	...	...	8	...	...	...	...	...	...	...	311	2	593[b]
Ironworkers	150	45	43	16	6	...	...	1	1	1	...	...	3	...	...	...	...	...	...	...	265	1	256[cd]
Leatherworkers	416	391	91	26	30	2	4	2	2	2	1	4	9	...	1	...	...	1	...	...	980	...	1,386[b]
Locksmiths	60	220	35	7	6	3	2	2	...	1	1	...	3	...	...	...	...	...	...	...	338	...	394[c]
Musical instrument makers	61	324	70	19	24	3	29	4	2	5	...	...	7	...	...	...	2	1	...	...	553	...	836[b]
Oil & paint makers	29	18	10	1	1	...	...	...	...	...	...	1	...	...	...	...	...	...	...	...	60	2	302[c]
Packers	32	14	5	3	...	...	...	...	...	...	...	1	2	...	...	...	1	...	...	...	58	...	63[c]
Paper box makers	47	131	3	2	5	...	1	4	...	...	...	...	1	...	...	...	...	...	...	...	194	2	228[b]
Papermakers	44	23	30	5	2	...	1	1	...	...	1	...	...	...	...	...	...	...	...	...	107	...	143[c]
Polishers, burnishers	119	35	33	3	9	1	1	4	...	3	...	...	7	...	...	1	...	...	...	...	215	...	400[b]
Potters; porcelain makers	19	33	99	2	1	...	...	...	...	...	...	...	...	...	...	...	...	...	...	...	64	...	46[cd]
Precision instrument makers	58	180	62	24	31	12	4	26	...	3	1	...	3	...	...	...	1	1	1	1	407	2	607[b]

Occupation	1	2	3	4	5	6	7	8	9	10	11	12	13	14	15	16	17	18	19	20	21	22	A	B	Total
Printers	519	237	195	96	25	6	2	3	2	5	4	6	7	39	3	..	..	1	1	2	..	2	1,151	2	2,077[b]
Refiners, assayers, etc.	28	27	17	1	3	..	2	1	..	..	..	1	..	2	..	..	..	1	..	..	..	..	84	..	168[b]
Smiths (various)	123	89	49	18	14	..	..	..	4	..	..	..	..	..	..	..	..	..	1	1	..	1	298	1	595[b]
Strawworkers, brush and broommakers	135	146	46	12	13	2	1	1	1	1	..	1	..	4	..	1	..	..	..	..	..	..	364	8	470[b]
Textileworkers (various)	100	132	90	40	5	11	2	..	2	7	..	2	..	2	..	..	..	4	2	1	1	..	392	1	210[d]
Tinsmiths	263	230	82	17	17	..	1	2	1	3	..	..	..	4	..	17	..	..	..	..	..	..	619	5	897[c]
Tobacconists	100	1,227	73	7	24	10	..	..	5	..	5	15	30	2	..	2	..	4	2	1	1	1	1,535	8	1,996[c]
Turners, carvers, gilders	163	585	71	24	50	2	5	1	2	1	5	2	..	2	..	4	3	3	1	2	..	3	926	1	1,126[c]
Umbrella makers	157	25	22	2	3	..	4	..	8	2	5	..	..	7	..	..	1	1	..	..	..	..	213	..	270[c]
Weavers	434	135	97	114	9	..	1	..	..	1	..	..	..	7	..	..	..	..	..	..	..	..	794	..	677[d]
Workers in factories and misc. heavy industry	99	150	48	10	3	30	..	1	..	2	..	1	..	3	8	..	1	..	..	..	..	..	323	..	207[d]
Workers in gems and precious metals	177	483	133	40	88	..	8	35	8	1	9	10	2	10	..	1	..	4	2	2	2	..	1,037	6	1,705[b]
Other artisans	244	179	82	34	30	2	5	1	5	7	..	2	..	8	..	1	1	1	1	2	1	..	595	4	757
Brewers & distillers	52	190	15	10	18	..	1	1	1	..	2	..	..	1	..	..	..	..	1	1	..	..	292	1	360[c]
Builders & contractors	207	17	47	14	4	4	..	..	..	2	2	1	..	3	..	..	2	..	1	..	1	..	300	1	849[b]
Carpenters	2,230	1,664	443	258	77	..	24	16	24	23	7	7	5	95	..	3	2	2	..	1	..	..	4,863	12	7,531[b]
Masons, bricklayers, plasterers	2,203	336	203	82	1	33	..	..	5	19	1	4	..	15	..	1	3	..	..	4	..	..	2,870	3	3,634[c]
Painters, varnishers, glaziers	1,070	905	403	122	45	..	16	11	16	11	17	5	7	33	1	..	1	3	1	2	..	..	2,685	1	3,485[b]
Plumbers	430	46	94	76	3	..	..	..	..	1	..	3	1	8	..	1	3	..	..	..	..	..	662	..	1,053[b]
Roofers & slaters	28	12	13	15	..	1	1	..	1	1	..	..	..	..	..	..	..	..	..	1	..	..	71	1	78[c]
Sawyers	151	94	24	7	3	..	..	3	..	2	..	..	..	4	..	..	2	..	..	..	..	..	291	10	293[b]
Stonecutters & polishers	1,251	209	106	224	20	1	2	2	6	6	7	..	..	11	..	..	..	..	1	1	2	..	1,841	..	1,914[b]
Clerks	2,135	2,249	766	290	138	25	36	25	37	37	10	19	48	96	16	7	7	4	9	3	1	3	5,921	18	13,929[b]
Dressmakers, seamstresses	4,559	935	505	194	167	32	21	30	2	11	11	19	4	104	4	7	4	4	5	1	..	..	6,606	111	9,819[b]
Furriers	28	82	15	1	3	5	2	..	..	..	..	..	..	..	..	..	5	..	..	..	..	..	144	..	120[pd]
Hatters	289	422	67	12	41	32	4	1	4	2	4	8	2	6	1	1	2	5	2	2	1	..	892	..	1,422[c]
Shoemakers	2,121	3,721	280	72	160	13	2	23	2	8	8	9	6	25	3	3	7	2	7	3	1	..	6,491	13	6,745[c]
Tailors	4,171	6,709	501	175	203	32	13	25	17	17	24	29	1	62	2	4	1	8	1	1	..	..	12,109	19	12,609[c]
Cooks	504	114	20	11	79	8	1	1	4	7	4	7	1	5	3	8	..	2	7	5	1	..	749	151	755[cd]
Domestic servants	23,386	4,493	665	369	266	8	27	58	27	67	5	4	..	82	4	..	4	1	6	5	1	..	29,470	1,025	31,749[c]
Housekeepers, janitors	154	34	41	8	6	1	1	1	1	2	1	1	..	6	1	3	1	..	1	..	..	..	262	7	..
Laundresses	1,758	167	36	28	18	2	2	2	2	3	3	2	2	7	..	2	5	1	..	6	5	..	2,025	366	2,563[c]
Nurses	485	56	52	20	6	2	2	14	2	2	2	5	2	5	..	..	6	1	..	..	..	..	635	13	656[b]
Waiters	1,491	271	113	66	66	1	2	2	1	5	5	..	..	15	6	..	1	..	..	..	..	..	2,006	499	..
Engineers	157	50	105	53	6	..	..	6	2	6	1	1	4	18	5	..	..	..	..	..	..	..	408	3	867[c]

Table 27 (continued)

Occupational Classification	Ireland	Germany	England	Scotland	France	Poland	Scandinavia	Switzerland	Wales	Italy	Netherlands	Latin America	British North America	Spain	Portugal	Hungary	Russia	Belgium	Bohemia	China	Total Foreign-Born	Negro	Total Native and Foreign-Born
Financiers	2	4	4	2	3	.	.	1	.	.	.	2	3	.	.	.	.	.	.	.	18	...	251[c]
Government employees	74	27	20	7	5	.	.	2	1	1	.	.	.	.	.	.	.	3	1	.	140	...	657[b]
Laborers	17,426	1,870	245	102	53	8	20	2	8	20	4	1	19	.	1	1	.	.	.	.	19,783	536	20,238[d]
Porters	1,474	330	66	32	23	2	8	2	8	3	2	2	5	.	.	.	1	1	1	.	1,966	176	3,052[c]
Machinists	398	361	218	152	45	4	4	10	5	2	2	10	20	3	.	3	.	.	.	.	1,237	...	1,714[c]
Manufacturers	26	32	19	17	1	.	.	8	1	1	.	.	1	.	.	.	.	.	.	.	98	...	207[b]
Boat builders	22	3	2	2	.	.	.	.	.	.	.	.	5	.	.	.	.	.	.	.	34	1	99[c]
Caulkers	84	6	10	2	2	.	3	.	.	.	1	1	.	2	2	.	3	1	.	.	119	...	378[c]
Chandlers	103	66	17	15	1	.	1	.	5	1	4	.	2	.	.	.	.	.	.	.	207	1	317[c]
Riggers	142	76	84	30	2	.	34	1	.	.	.	1	6	2	3	5	4	3	.	.	393	.	482[b]
Sailmakers	70	10	23	5	2	.	3	.	5	.	2	.	3	.	1	.	.	.	.	.	120	2	281[c]
Ship carpenters	372	67	101	53	7	.	15	.	5	15	2	2	53	2	2	.	.	.	.	.	681	1	1,146[c]
Merchants	278	627	326	127	149	20	21	25	14	.	16	25	22	26	4	5	1	6	1	2	1,705	2	6,299[b]
Policemen	292	46	30	13	5	1	1	.	.	5	1	1	4	.	.	2	.	.	.	.	393	...	1,164[c]
Actors, performers	34	20	58	2	5	.	1	17	.	.	1	1	7	3	.	2	.	3	.	.	141	...	231[c]
Architects	5	19	19	1	4	.	.	1	1	64	1	1	1	.	.	4	.	6	.	.	53	...	117[c]
Artists	76	211	100	33	55	.	11	1	4	1	1	2	6	2	2	2	1	1	.	.	589	1	898[b]
Authors	4	.	5	1	.	2	.	1	.	.	1	2	.	2	.	1	.	.	.	.	13	...	34[c]
Clergy	88	39	30	15	3	.	3	1	6	.	3	4	2	2	3	1	1	1	.	.	202	12	393[c]
Lawyers	40	18	24	8	7	.	.	1	1	.	1	5	6	1	1	2	.	.	.	.	115	1	1,112[c]
Musicians	57	274	62	2	18	3	.	1	.	95	1	.	5	5	3	2	2	2	.	.	528	15	746[c]
Physicians, surgeons	113	228	94	26	45	8	6	6	2	2	2	9	5	1	1	4	2	6	.	.	566	6	1,469[b]
Teachers	125	116	58	14	71	5	1	4	6	10	2	10	17	5	1	2	2	4	.	2	452	13	1,356[b]
Other professional workers	31	66	66	13	27	5	1	7	5	3	.	4	19	.	1	2	1	.	.	.	234	13	556[b]
Hotel & boardinghouse keepers	291	238	98	20	48	3	17	7	5	5	3	2	5	5	2	2	1	4	.	.	758	14	1,723[c]
Proprietors (various)	6	1	8	1	1	.	1	.	.	1	.	1	.	.	1	1	1	.	.	.	18	...	64[b]
Restaurant keepers	40	84	15	1	5	.	3	3	.	3	3	.	3	.	.	.	.	.	.	.	163	5	241[b]
Superintendents (various)	84	32	26	8	1	.	2	3	.	1	3	2	5	1	.	.	.	1	.	.	166	8	329[b]
Watchmen	88	21	13	3	1	.	6	.	.	.	1	3	2	1	1	3	1	.	.	.	136	2	160[c]
Barbers, hairdressers	68	608	57	19	40	13	7	5	1	.	.	.	3	.	3	1	.	1	.	.	854	78	997[c]
Undertakers	22	7	10	.	1	.	.	1	.	29	1	.	.	1	.	.	.	.	.	.	41	1	123[c]
Other service occupations	15	29	11	3	6	.	.	.	.	.	1	.	.	.	.	1	.	.	.	.	64	153	154[d]

216

Occupation																					
Clothiers	81	159	23	6	3	16	8	...	1	...	4	1	1	1	...	...	...	...	304	1	403[c]
Dry goods dealers	132	139	39	22	5	7	11	...	...	2	...	...	2	1	2	...	2	...	362	31	8,300[b]
Food dealers	1,817	3,045	217	58	55	54	5	5	15	2	4	5	24	4	...	3	2	3	5,274	11	1,915[c]
Peddlers; traders	753	941	51	12	32	26	1	1	2	4	12	9	2	2	3	3	1	1	1,878	11	2,646[d]
Retail shopkeepers	916	442	247	63	51	1	11	11	14	11	14	2	23	2	3	2	1	...	1,835	4	1,626[c]
Wine & liquor dealers	891	650	98	16	54	1	11	1	5	1	5	...	...	...	...	...	1	...	1,758	12	199[c]
Speculators; "gamblers"	94	22	10	...	...	...	...	1	1	2	4	2	10	2	2	2	...	...	130	2	1,190[b]
Boatmen	313	40	28	12	8	...	13	...	...	2	4	...	11	1	...	...	...	4	438	73	5,498[c]
Cartmen, draymen, teamsters	2,505	380	141	63	27	2	10	2	2	12	1	1	18	2	1	1	2	...	3,185	55	1,741[c]
Drivers, coachmen, hackmen	805	57	69	14	9	...	...	...	1	1	1	1	12	1	1	1	1	...	972	102	189[b]
Expressmen	15	5	5	1	...	...	...	...	1	...	...	...	1	...	...	...	1	...	27	1	317[c]
Hostlers; grooms	262	36	4	2	2	...	...	...	1	...	...	...	1	1	...	1	...	1	309	4	317[c]
Railroad employees & other trans. workers	76	24	14	2	1	...	.1	...	1	...	1	...	2	...	...	...	...	...	119	...	523[c]
Stable keepers	71	3	14	1	1	...	...	1	...	1	...	...	3	...	1	...	1	...	93	1	191[c]
Stevedores	190	7	22	...	...	6	6	...	1	...	...	...	1	1	...	1	...	...	232	16	155[c,d]
Drovers	94	14	6	3	3	...	...	...	...	...	...	...	1	...	...	...	1	...	119	...	197[b]
Fishermen; hunters	42	51	3	6	6	...	1	1	2	2	...	2	2	...	...	...	...	1	108	7	193[c]
Farmers	5	2	3	1	1	...	...	...	...	...	...	1	...	...	...	...	...	...	16	4	85[c]
Gardeners, florists, nurserymen	192	273	43	43	32	1	1	2	1	2	2	...	...	...	...	...	...	...	592	4	645[c]
Organ grinders, rag-pickers, scavengers	19	324	4	1	2	...	...	13	...	...	...	...	...	...	...	...	1	...	364	1	388[b]
Prostitutes[e]	74	22	13	6	1	...	...	2	...	6	2	...	4	3	...	...	...	...	122	10	...[c]
Students	20	4	7	6	1	...	...	...	...	...	...	...	...	...	...	1	...	...	50	1	653[c]
Unclassified minor occupations	67	19	13	3	2	2	1	...	...	...	2	...	2	...	1	...	1	1	112	4	...

[a] The figures in this column are based upon the printed summaries of the *New York State Census of 1855* and are not directly comparable with my tabulation of the occupations of the foreign-born based upon data in the manuscript schedules of the same census. Limitations of time and expense precluded my tabulating the native-born whites. Differences of occupational classification, the inaccuracy of the census, and my exclusion of data in a small portion of the manuscript schedules account for the discrepancies which appear when my summaries are compared with those of the printed census. I have attempted to interpret these classifications in the light of my own tabulations.

[b] Summaries of four or more distinct occupational classifications in the printed census.

[c] Exact figures appearing in the printed census, or summaries of less than four distinct occupational classifications.

[d] Obviously too small. Cf. *supra*, note [a].

[e] Of little statistical value, for obvious reasons.

Compiled from data in the manuscript schedules of the *New York State Census of 1855*.

Table 28: Occupational Grouping of Immigrant Workers, 1855

Occupational Grouping	Percent of All Gainfully Employed Immigrants
Domestic servants, cooks, waiters, laundresses, nurses........	22.38
Laborers and porters..	13.96
Clothing industry: tailors, dressmakers, furriers, hatters, clothiers..	12.87
Building trades...	8.71
Leatherworkers, boot- and shoemakers..........................	6.79
Commerce: merchants, agents, speculators, financiers (1.46%).. Commerce: clerks.................................... (3.88%)..	5.34
Heavy metalworkers..	3.92
Food dealers..	3.38
Dealers and retailers (other than food and liquor) including peddlers, drovers, dry goods dealers..............	2.69
Cabinetmakers, upholsterers, turners, carvers, gilders........	2.47
Cartmen, draymen, etc...	2.04
Bakers, confectioners, sugar refiners.........................	2.01
Professional..	1.86
Liquor industry: manufacturers or sellers....................	1.32
Maritime workers...	0.60
	90.34
Other occupations..	9.66
	100.00

Of all gainfully employed immigrants more than 40 percent were artisans
and factory workers, including a few who might have operated small stores.
This figure was derived from the number of immigrants in the following
occupational groups of my classification:

Bakers, barbers, blacksmiths, boat builders, bookbinders, brassworkers,
button makers, cabinetmakers, carpenters, caulkers, chandlers, clothiers, coach makers, coopers, coppersmiths, dressmakers, dyers, engineers, furriers, glassworkers, gunsmiths, hairworkers, hatters, iron
molders, ironworkers, leatherworkers, locksmiths, machinists, masons,
musical instrument makers, oil makers, painters, paper box makers,
paper makers, plumbers, polishers, potters, precious gem workers, precision instrument makers, printers, riggers, roofers, sailmakers, sawyers, ship carpenters, shoemakers, smiths (various), stonecutters,
straw workers, tailors, textile workers (various), tinsmiths, tobacconists, turners, umbrella makers, undertakers, weavers; also other
artisans (miscellaneous) and factory workers in heavy industry (miscellaneous).

Computed from data in the manuscript schedules of the *New York State
Census of 1855.*

Table 29: Immigrant Laborers,[a] by Nativity, 1855

Ireland	17,426
Germany	1,870
England	245
Scotland	102
France	53
Scandinavia	20
Italy	20
British North America	19
Wales	8
Poland	8
Netherlands	4
Belgium	3
Switzerland	2
Hungary	1
Bohemia	1
Latin America	1
Total	19,783

Compiled from the manuscript schedules of the *New York State Census of 1855*.

Table 30: Immigrant Domestic Servants,[a] by Nativity, 1855

Ireland	23,386
Germany	4,493
England	665
Scotland	369
France	266
British North America	82
Wales	67
Switzerland	58
Scandinavia	27
Latin America	21
Poland	8
Belgium	6
Italy	5
Bohemia	5
Netherlands	4
Portugal	4
Spain	3
Hungary	1
Total	29,470

Compiled from the manuscript schedules of the *New York State Census of 1855*.

[a]For Negro laborers and domestic servants, cf. Appendix VII, Table 27.

Table 31: Relative Status of First and Second Generations, Sixth Ward, 1855

Parents Nativity and Occupation	Their Children Born in the United States Occupation
Ireland	
Laborer	Book-folders (2)
Laborer	Laborer
Laborer	Masoh[a]
Laborer	Brass founders (2)
Laborer	Pocketbook maker; dressmaker
Laborer	Seamstress
Laborer	Clerk[a]
Laborer	Milliner; book-folder
Laborer	Clerk[a]
Laborer	Carpenter[a]
Laborer	Machinists (2)[a]
Laborer; laundress	Stonecutter; book-folders (2)
Porter	Fender maker[a]
Porter	Laundress
Porter	Bookbinder
Porter	Laborer
Porter	Plumber[a]
Laundress	Clerk[a]
Laundress	Lawyer;[a] Policeman;[a] Porter
Tailor	Clerks (2);[a] dressmaker
Tailor	Student
Tailor	School teacher; varnisher
Tailor	Laborer
Tailor	Dressmaker
Seamstress	Weaver
Shoemaker	Carpenter
Shoemaker; laundress	Chair maker
Liquor dealer	Dressmaker
Liquor dealer	Machinist
Liquor delaer	"Apprentice"
Liquor dealer	Dressmaker; milliner
Boardinghouse keeper	Dressmaker
Boardinghouse keeper	Seamstress
Boardinghouse keeper	Cooper
Victualer	Silver burnisher[a]
Fruit dealer	Laborer
"China ware"	Gas fitter;[a] locksmith[a]
Boatman	Printer[a]
Bottler	Clerks (2)[a]
Pencil case maker	Pencil case maker
Coach maker	Fringe makers (2)
Brass founder	Seamstresses (2)
Chandler	Metal roofer; plasterer
Locksmith	Vest maker
Weaver	Laborer
Silk hatter	Clerk[a]
Watchman	Teacher[a]
Cartman	Laborer
Nurse	Silversmith; music teacher; parasol maker
Germany	
Tailor	Coppersmith
Tailor	Drug clerk
Lacemaker	Baker; clerk
Butcher	Butcher; clerk
Turner	Turner
Instrument maker	Clerk
"Mechanic"	Instrument maker;[a] glass engraver[a]
Clerk	Dressmaker
Musician	Clerks (2)
"Speculator"	"Speculator"
England	
Barber	Clerk[a]
Paper hanger	Boardinghouse keeper[a]
England; Netherlands	
Clothier	"Chaser"
England	
Machinist; boardinghouse keeper	Machinist
Engineer	Book-folder; pressman
France	
Butcher	Butchers (2); glass cutter; cook
Wax figure maker	Sailor
Boardinghouse keeper	Cigar maker
Scotland	
Jeweler	Jewelers (2)
Supt. of Outdoor Poor (N.Y.C.)	Clerk
Austria	
Liquor dealer	Clerks (2)
Poland; England	
"Dealer"	Dressmaker; milliner; baker
Italy; Ireland	
Laborer; laundress	Painter[a]
Newfoundland	
Printer	School teacher
East Indies	
Cigar importer	Musician

[a]Indicates an apparent rise in status.

Compiled from data in the manuscript schedules of the Sixth Ward, *New York State Census of 1855.*

Table 32: Relative Status of First and Second Generations, Tenth Ward, 1855

Parents Nativity and Occupation	Their Children Born in the United States Occupation
Germany	
Laborer	Clerk[a]
Laborer	Type founder[a]
Tailor	Tailor
Tailor	Vest makers (2)
Tailor	Printer; dressmaker
Shoemaker	Shoemaker
Shoemaker	Silver plater[a]
Shoemaker	Gilder
Cabinetmaker	Butcher
Cabinetmaker	Quill maker
Carpenter	Trunk maker
Cigar maker	Cigar maker
"Segars" [presumably Cigar maker]	"Segars"
Baker	Clerk[a]
Grocer	Seamstress; teacher[a]
Victualer	Victualer
Beer garden keeper	Dressmaker
Beer garden keeper	Tailor; gunsmith;[a] artificial flower makers (3)
Hatter	Clerk
"Dry goods"	"Dry goods" (2)
Lawyer	Lawyer[b]
Germany; France	
Paper stainer	Dressmaker
Germany; U.S.A.	
Saw-filer	Dressmaker; tailor
Ireland	
Laborer	Turner;[a] parasol maker[a]
Laborer	Dressmaker
Laundress	Printer[a]
Cartman	Cartman; clerk;[a] ship carpenter[a]
Tailor	Tailor; chair maker; painter
Shoemaker	Cutter; seamstress
Grocer	Grocer; bookkeeper;[a] clerk;[a] insurance agent[a]
Carpenter	Carpenter
Cabinetmaker	Varnisher
Painter	Painter
Scale maker	Scale maker; milliner; "type factory" worker
Collector	Dressmaker; clerk
Agent	Harness maker; painter; clerk; marketman
Undertaker	Librarian[b]
Boardinghouse keeper	Printers (3)
"Dry goods"	"Dry goods"
England	
Seamstress	Seamstress
Seamstress	Jeweler;[a] milliner; "mechanic"
Nurse	Seamstress
Tinworker	Servant
Mason	Hat trimmer
Blacksmith	Gold cutters (2)
Tailor	Dressmaker
Butcher	Butcher
Scale maker	Clerk
Machinist	Iron moulder; artificial flower maker
England; Ireland	
Carpenter	Painter; tailor
England; United States	
Printer	Bookbinder
Scotland	
Carpenter	Cartman; upholsterer
Scotland; Ireland	
Machinist	Clerk
France	
Engraver	Milliner
France; United States	
Tailor	Clerk[a]
Wales	
Agent	Parasol maker
Newfoundland	
Laundress	Painter;[a] trunk maker[a]
United States; England	
Shoemaker	Shoemaker
Sash maker	Carpenter
Artist	Clerk
Tobacconist	Clerk
United States; Ireland	
Painter	Cooper; vest maker

[a] Indicates an apparent rise in status.
[b] Undoubtedly in error. These individuals were only sixteen years of age.

Compiled from data in the manuscript schedules of the Tenth Ward, *New York State Census of 1855.*

APPENDIX VIII

Immigrant Land Owners in Two Selected Wards

Table 33:   Gainfully Employed Immigrant Land Owners in the Sixth
Ward (Chief "Irish" Ward), by Nativity, 1855

Nativity	Number
Ireland	87
Germany	70
England	11
Scotland	4
France	3
Switzerland	3
Poland	2
Wales	1
Denmark	1
Spain	1
Total	183[a]

[a]Does not include 35 immigrant land owners who were not gainfully employed.

Compiled from data in the manuscript schedules of the Sixth
Ward, *New York State Census of 1855*.

Table 34:   Gainfully Employed Immigrant Land Owners in the Tenth
Ward (Area of Many Nationalities, especially German),
by Nativity, 1855

Nativity	Number
Germany	124
Ireland	43
England	25
France	8
Switzerland	7
Wales	3
Scotland	2
Canada	2
Portugal	2
Denmark	1
Poland	1
Hungary	1
West Indies	1
Total	220[a]

[a]Does not include 15 immigrant land owners who were not gainfully employed.

Compiled from data in the manuscript schedules of the Tenth
Ward, *New York State Census of 1855*.

APPENDIX IX

Table 35: Native and Naturalized Voters and Aliens, 1855

Wards	Native Voters	Naturalized Voters	Aliens
First	570	1,425	6,062
Second	500	290	1,384
Third	2,069	694	2,765
Fourth	922	2,459	10,785
Fifth	1,962	1,471	7,462
Sixth	686	2,263	13,010
Seventh	2,767	2,649	12,344
Eighth	2,992	1,910	10,783
Ninth	5,133	1,976	9,346
Tenth	2,160	1,476	10,218
Eleventh	2,763	3,612	21,237
Twelfth	957	787	7,864
Thirteenth	2,120	1,852	8,784
Fourteenth	1,246	1,954	10,275
Fifteenth	3,091	1,292	7,406
Sixteenth	3,350	2,173	13,495
Seventeenth	3,229	3,689	26,780
Eighteenth	2,774	2,345	15,677
Nineteenth	1,022	1,460	6,507
Twentieth	2,437	3,045	14,441
Twenty-first	2,262	1,993	8,136
Twenty-second	1,161	1,889	8,027
Totals	46,173	42,704	232,788

Source: *New York State Census of 1855*, p. 8.

NOTES

Chapter I

1. Immigrants from Poland, although proportionally few, were almost entirely Jewish. Most of them stayed in New York City, some 1,200 Polish-born persons being listed by the *New York State Census of 1855*. Asiatic immigrants appeared in the fifties, among them Chinese coolies imported for manual labor, but few Chinese lived in New York. Between 1,000 and 1,500 were supposed to be living in the city in 1855, but the state census showed only 80 persons born in Asia and an additional 43 in the East Indies. *New York State Census of 1855*, p. 118. For items on the Chinese in New York, cf. *New Yorker Staats-Zeitung* (hereafter referred to as *Staats-Zeitung*), May 26, 1855; *Courrier des États-Unis*, May 23, 1855.

2. Marcus L. Hansen, *Atlantic Migration, 1607–1860* . . . (Cambridge, Mass., 1940), p. 120.

3. Oscar Handlin, *Boston's Immigrants, 1790–1865* . . . (Cambridge, Mass., 1941), p. 35; *Hints on Emigration* . . . (London, 1828), p. 43.

4. Hansen, *op. cit.*, p. 142.

5. *Ibid.*, pp. 143–144.

6. *Ibid.*, p. 239.

7. *Ibid.*, p. 240; cf. John H. Clapham, *Economic Development of France and Germany, 1815–1914* (Cambridge, England, 1921), p. 87.

8. Hansen, *op. cit.*, p. 240.

9. John H. Clapham, *Economic History of Modern Britain* . . . (Cambridge, England, 1926–1938), I, 114–116; Élie Halévy, *History of the English People* . . . (New York, 1924–1926), I, Book II, 192–193, 207–208.

10. J. L. and Barbara Hammond, *Village Labourer, 1760–1832* . . . (4th ed.; London, 1936), pp. 73–75; Stanley C. Johnson, *History of Emigration from the United Kingdom* . . . (London, 1913), pp. 40–44.

11. Hansen, *op. cit.*, p. 131; Halévy, *op. cit.*, I, Book I, 219–221.

12. David Stewart, *Sketches of the Character, Manners, and Present State of the Highlanders of Scotland* . . . (2d ed.; Edinburgh, 1822), I, 156–160.

13. Florence E. Janson, *Background of Swedish Immigration, 1840–1930* (Chicago, 1931), pp. 49, 55; Theodore C. Blegen, *Norwegian Migration to America* (Northfield, Minn., 1931–1940), I, 167–170.

14. Janson, *op. cit.*, pp. 116, 149; Blegen, *op. cit.*, p. 174.

15. William Howitt, *Rural and Domestic Life of Germany* (Philadelphia, 1843), pp. 26–27; Hansen, *op. cit.*, pp. 211–215; Gustav Schmoller, *Zur Geschichte der deutschen Kleingewerbe im 19. Jahrhundert* (Halle, 1870), pp. 133–134.

16. Hansen, *op. cit.*, p. 286; Marcus L. Hansen, "The Revolutions of 1848 and German Emigration," *Journal of Economic and Business History*, II (August, 1930), pp. 647–648, 654–656. Cf. John A. Hobson, *Evolution of Modern Capitalism* (London, c. 1916), p. 18.

17. Hansen, "The Revolutions of 1848 and German Emigration," *op. cit.*, pp. 653–654.

18. Hansen, *Atlantic Migration*, p. 294.

19. *Ibid.*

20. *Ibid.*, pp. 295–296.

21. J. L. and Barbara Hammond, *Rise of Modern Industry* (5th ed., rev.; New York, 1937), p. 89.

22. Hansen, *Atlantic Migration,* pp. 221–222.

23. Robert F. Foerster, *Italian Emigration of Our Times* (Cambridge, Mass., 1919), pp. 124, 323–326. Early Italian settlers in the United States took advantage of the impoverishment of Italy after the revolutions of 1848 and 1849 and imported Sardinian professional beggars under contract. Charles L. Brace, *Dangerous Classes of New York* . . . (New York, 1872), pp. 195–197; Children's Aid Society, *Fourth Annual Report,* 1857, p. 16; *Eco d'Italia,* May 10, 17, 24, 31, 1851.

24. Hansen, *Atlantic Migration,* p. 222.

25. *Ibid.,* pp. 222–223.

26. Handlin, *op. cit.,* p. 44.

27. *Ibid.,* pp. 44–45.

28. *Ibid.,* p. 45, citing Sir William Petty, *Tracts Chiefly Relating to Ireland* . . . (Dublin, 1799), pp. 351, 352; George O'Brien, *Economic History of Ireland in the Seventeenth Century* (Dublin, 1919), p. 175; and *Irish National Almanack for 1852* . . . (Dublin, 1851), p. 31.

29. Clapham, *Economic History of Modern Britain,* I, 57–62.

30. Handlin, *op. cit.,* p. 48. Cf. Friedrich Engels, *Condition of the Working-Class in England in 1844* (London, 1892), pp. 90–94.

31. William F. Adams, *Ireland and Irish Emigration to the New World* . . . (New Haven, 1932), pp. 10, 164–167.

32. *Truth Teller,* June 30, 1827, quoting *Limerick Post* (n.d.); Adams, *op. cit.,* pp. 238–239.

33. Adams, *op. cit.,* pp. 49–50; Handlin, *op. cit.,* p. 55.

34. Adams, *op. cit.,* pp. 222–223, 238–239. The earlier emigration was largely from Ulster and Tyrone; the new movement was from Cork, Kerry, Galway, and Clare. Handlin, *op. cit.,* p. 55.

35. Adams, *op. cit.,* pp. 215–217; Handlin, *op. cit.,* p. 49.

36. Handlin, *op. cit.,* p. 50. Cf. [O. C. Gardiner], "Foreign Immigration: its Natural and Extraordinary Causes. . . ." *American Whig Review,* VI (Nov., 1847), 461–462, 644.

37. Hansen, *Atlantic Migration,* p. 266. Cf. Frances Morehouse, "The Irish Migration of the Forties," *American Historical Review,* XXIII (April, 1928), 582–587.

38. Hansen, *Atlantic Migration,* pp. 250–251. Chapter xi has a vivid description of the "flight from hunger." Cf. Morehouse, *op. cit.,* pp. 579–592.

39. Hansen, *Atlantic Migration,* p. 294.

40. *Hints on Emigration,* p. 30.

41. Johnson, *op. cit.,* p. 257.

42. *Ibid.,* pp. 51, 80–81.

43. *Ibid.,* p. 59.

44. Cf. *Consular Letters,* Bremen, August 31, 1831, State Department Archives; Edith Abbott, *Historical Aspects of the Immigration Problem* (Chicago, c. 1926), pp. 147–148. In Sweden the government did not actually prohibit emigration but frowned upon it. Janson, *op. cit.,* p. 154.

45. This, and the attraction of California gold, resulted in the beginnings of migration from Austria-Hungary, especially the province of Bohemia, in the fifties. Hansen, *Atlantic Migration,* p. 299. Thomas Čapek, *Čechs (Bohemians) in America* . . . (Boston, 1920), pp. 28, 33–34, 40.

46. "Foreign Paupers: Message from the President of the United States . . . ," *House Documents,* 25th Congress, 2d Session, X, No. 370 (1837–1838), 11, 13–14; Johnson, *op. cit.,* p. 19; Hansen, *Atlantic Migration,* pp. 128–129. English parishes contracted with passenger brokers to facilitate the departure of persons willing to emigrate. "Report from the Secretary of the Treasury, relative to the Deportation of Paupers from Great Britain . . . ," *Senate Documents,* 24th Congress, 2d Session, I, No. 5 (1836–1837), 10–12.

47. Johnson, *op. cit.*, p. 19.

48. Hansen, *Atlantic Migration*, p. 287.

49. *Ibid.*, pp. 287–288. Cf. "Foreign Paupers . . . ," *loc. cit., passim.*

50. Hansen, *Atlantic Migration*, p. 138.

51. *Ibid.*, p. 140.

52. *Ibid.*, p. 141. Subdivision of land and English competition in the textile industry induced heavy Swiss emigration, particularly from the canton of Glarus. Jules Duval, *Histoire de l'emigration européenne, asiatique et africaine au xixᵉ siècle* (Paris, 1862), pp. 145–149.

53. George M. Stephenson, *History of American Immigration* . . . (Boston, c. 1926), pp. 55–56.

54. Blegen, *op. cit.*, pp. 44–47, 56.

55. *Ibid.*, pp. 24–36, 46–47, 161. In Norway, hard times and high taxes weighed heavily upon the small farmers, the class from which many of the Quakers and the Haugeans were recruited. *Ibid.*, pp. 47–48.

56. George M. Stephenson, *Religious Aspects of Swedish Immigration* . . . (Minneapolis, 1932), pp. 56–59, 72–73; Janson, *op. cit.*, pp. 177, 180–181.

57. Stephenson, *op. cit.*, pp. 89, 94–97, 102, 119–121.

58. *Ibid.*, p. 96; Hansen, *Atlantic Migration*, p. 296.

59. Hansen, *Atlantic Migration*, p. 122.

60. *Ibid.*, p. 126.

61. *Ibid.*, pp. 272–273.

62. *Ibid.*, pp. 289, 304. Jonas Heinrich Gudehus, *Meine Auswanderung nach Amerika im Jahre 1822* . . . (Hildesheim, 1829), pp. v–vi, adverts to the desire to escape military service as a cause of emigration. A student of later German emigration denied that many Germans left to avoid military service. Ernest Bruncken, "How Germans Become Americans," reprinted from the *Proceedings* of the State Historical Society of Wisconsin (Madison, 1898), p. 3.

63. Cf., e.g., S. H. Collins, *Emigrant's Guide* . . . (4th ed.; Hull, 1830), p. 27; Gottfried Duden, *Bericht über eine Reise* . . . (Elberfeld, 1829), *passim.*

64. For a discussion of these clubs, cf. Hansen, *Atlantic Migration*, pp. 149–150.

65. Carl Wittke, *We Who Built America* (New York, 1939), pp. 104–108.

66. Cf. Wittke, *op. cit.*, pp. 101–104. George M. Stephenson, "When America Was the Land of Canaan," *Minnesota History*, X, No. 3 (September, 1929), 237–260; G. Poulett Scrope (ed.), *Extracts of Letters from Poor Persons Who Emigrated Last Year to Canada and the United States* (3d ed.; London, 1832); Edward E. Hale, *Letters on Irish Emigration* (Boston, 1852); Blegen, *op. cit.*, Vol. II.

67. Cf., e.g., the report of the Emigration Society in Frankfurt, cited by *Citizen*, August 30, 1856. For a favorable report, cf. *Deutsche Schnellpost*, July 17, 1844, quoting the Mannheim *Abendzeitung* (n. d.).

68. William C. Smith, *Americans in the Making* . . . (New York, 1939), pp. 28–31; Hansen, *Atlantic Migration*, pp. 154–155; Janson, *op. cit.*, p. 127.

69. Cf. Harry Jerome, *Migration and Business Cycles* (New York, 1926), *passim; True Emigrants Guide* (New York, 1844), p. 85.

70. Intangible and personal factors are suggested by Smith, *op. cit.*, pp. 3–4.

Chapter II

1. Le Havre imported cotton, Bremen tobacco; emigrants were the return cargo. In the thirties the former city was the more important embarkation port, but of the more than 43,000 emigrants from Germany in 1844, nearly 20,000 embarked at Bremen and only 16,000 at Le Havre. *Deutsche Schnellpost*, May 21, 1845. In the fifties Hamburg approached Bremen as an emigrant port, and in 1854, the peak year of German emigration, 76,875 persons passed through Bremen, while 50,819 left by way of Hamburg, or more than twice the total of the previous year. *Staats-Zeitung*, March 24, 1855. Of

German immigrants landing at New York, the majority sailed from Le Havre, Bremen, and Antwerp, in that order, in the 1840's, and in the 1850's from Bremen, Hamburg, and Le Havre, in that order, while thousands more sailed from Liverpool and London. German Society of the City of New York, *Annual Reports, 1845–1860, passim.*

2. Marcus L. Hansen, *Immigrant in American History* (Cambridge, Mass., 1940), p. 31.

3. Of the 223,078 who sailed in 1850 from the United Kingdom, 165,828 departed from Liverpool, 31,297 left from Irish ports, and 11,448 from cities in Scotland. Most of those embarking at Liverpool were Irish. Edward E. Hale, *Letters on Irish Emigration* (Boston, 1852), p. 7.

4. *Irish American,* April 29, 1854.

5. Hansen, *Atlantic Migration,* p. 183.

6. Passenger lists of vessels arriving at the port of New York during 1825 and 1835. Treasury Department Archives, Washington, D.C. Cf. Hansen, *Atlantic Migration,* pp. 184–185.

7. *Freeman's Journal,* March 11, 18, 1843. Cf. Hansen, *Immigrant in American History,* p. 32.

8. *Annual Reports of the Commissioners of Emigration of the State of New York* (New York, 1861), pp. 226–227, 380–381; Anton Eickhoff, *In der Neuen Heimath . . .* (New York, 1884), Appendix, p. 51; *Staats-Zeitung,* August 21, 1852; *Freeman's Journal,* March 11, 18, 1843.

9. Hansen, *Atlantic Migration,* pp. 197–198. Francis J. Grund, the United States Consul at Bremen, reported in 1842 that the Bremen brokers and ship owners had agents all over Germany "to catch all they can on the road." *Consular Despatches,* Bremen, February 10, 1842, State Department Archives, Washington, D.C.

10. Hansen, *Immigrant in American History,* p. 33.

11. Wittke, *We Who Built America,* p. 114; Hansen, *Immigrant in American History,* pp. 32–33.

12. *Annual Reports of the Commissioners of Emigration,* pp. 10, 12; *Report of the City Inspector,* 1847, p. 104. Cf. "Steerage Passage on Immigrant Vessels," *Senate Executive Documents,* 43d Congress, 1st Session, No. 23 (Washington, D.C., 1873); Edith Abbott (ed.), *Immigration; Select Documents . . .* (Chicago, c. 1924), pp. 6–58. Chapters on the Atlantic passage appear in Wittke, *op. cit.,* Friedrich Kapp, *Immigration and the Commissioners of Emigration of the State of New York* (New York, 1870), Robert G. Albion, *Rise of New York Port* (New York, 1939), and Hansen, *Immigrant in American History.*

13. Albion, *op. cit.,* p. 12.

14. *Ibid.,* p. 13.

15. *Ibid.,* p. 14.

16. The customary emphasis upon the canal as the source of New York's commercial greatness overlooks the fact that the city already had a well-established trade. In the year of the opening of the canal, the value of New York's exports reached $35,000,000, nearly one third of the total for the whole country; its imports, valued at $49,000,000, amounted to half the total for the United States. Important as was the movement of Western produce to the Eastern seaboard, the inland shipments from New York of manufactures and imported goods remained a cornerstone of the city's prosperity. Cf. *ibid.,* pp. 13–15.

17. James Grant Wilson (ed.), *Memorial History of the City of New York . . .* (New York, 1892–1893), III, 335.

18. Albion, *op. cit.,* Appendices II and III, pp. 390–391. The figures refer to the entire state but are virtually those of New York City. *Ibid.,* p. 390.

19. A. C. Flick (ed.), *History of the State of New York* (New York, 1933–1937), VI, 152–153.

20. *Ibid.,* p. 155.

21. Flick (ed.), *op. cit.,* VI, 340.

22. Albion, *op. cit.*, pp. 241–242.

23. *Ibid.*, pp. 245, 248–249.

24. Allan Nevins (ed.), *Diary of Philip Hone, 1828–1851* (New York, 1936), *passim*.

25. Albion, *op. cit.*, pp. 257–258.

26. Philip Hone showed a deep-seated hatred and contempt for the Irish. "Irishmen," he wrote, were "the most ignorant, and consequently the most obstinate white men in the world, and I have seen enough to satisfy me that, with few exceptions, ignorance and vice go together. . . . These Irishmen, strangers among us . . . decide the elections in the city of New York." *Diary*, p. 190. Cf. *ibid.*, p. 327.

27. Flick (ed.), *op. cit.*, VI, 238; Victor S. Clark, *History of Manufactures in the United States* (New York, 1929), I, 438–448.

28. Flick (ed.), *op. cit.*, VI, p. 239. Cf. Clark, *op. cit.*, pp. 448–463. For apprentices and children at factory labor, cf. New York State, *Assembly Documents* (1832), Vol. IV, No. 308.

29. Flick (ed.), *op. cit.*, VI, p. 240.

30. *Ibid.*, p. 193.

31. Edwin T. Freedley, *Leading Pursuits and Leading Men* (Philadelphia, 1854), p. 89.

32. *Ibid.*, pp. 91, 93.

33. *Ibid.*, p. 93; Jesse E. Pope, *Clothing Industry in New York* (Columbia, Mo., 1905), p. 13. Contrary to a common assumption, the Germans did not introduce the family system of production, which was in use before they came. *Ibid.*, p. 24.

34. Pope, *op. cit.*, pp. 12–19, 28.

35. Freedley, *op. cit.*, p. 89.

36. Flick (ed.), *op. cit.* VI, 64. Chapter xiv of Arthur M. Schlesinger, Jr., *Age of Jackson* (Boston, 1945) is a good treatment of radicalism in New York about 1830.

37. Flick (ed.), *op. cit.*, p. 65.

38. For the Locofoco party, cf. pp. 168–169.

39. *Letters from John Pintard* . . . (New York, 1940), II, 184–185.

40. New York Association for Improving the Condition of the Poor (hereafter referred to as A.I.C.P.). *Fifteenth Annual Report*, 1858, pp. 32–33.

41. Kate H. Claghorn, "The Foreign Immigrant in New York City," *Reports of the Industrial Commission* . . . (Washington, D.C., 1901), XV, 452.

42. *Report of the City Inspector*, 1834, quoted by Robert W. De Forest and Lawrence Veiller (eds.), *Tenement House Problem* . . . (New York, 1903), I, 71.

43. *Census of the State of New York*, 1825 (unpaged); *ibid.*, 1845 (unpaged); *ibid.*, 1855, p. 8.

44. *Eighth Census of the United States*, 1860, "Population," pp. 335, 337.

45. For the introduction of brick buildings, cf. *Picture of New York* . . . (New York, 1828), p. 153; John Finch, *Travels in the United States of America and Canada* (London, 1833), p. 17.

46. Benson J. Lossing, *History of New York City* . . . (New York, c. 1884), pp. 345–355; Mary L. Booth, *History of the City of New York* . . . (New York, 1859), p. 748.

47. Astor wrote many letters warning lessees that their policies were about to expire or informing them what insurance companies were on his approved list. Kenneth W. Porter, *John Jacob Astor, Business Man* (Cambridge, Mass., 1931), II, 950.

48. Lossing, *op. cit.*, p. 227; Augustine E. Costello, *Our Firemen* . . . (New York, 1887), chaps. xlvii and xlviii, *passim*.

49. Cf., e.g., Finch, *op. cit.*, p. 35.

50. Most of the city's residents depended upon rain water and the city pumps. *Sturtevant MSS*, p. 9. (New York Public Library).

51. *Ibid.*

52. Booth, *op. cit.*, pp. 723–724.

53. James Hardie, *Description of the City of New York* (New York, 1827), pp. 302–305; Lossing, *op. cit.*, p. 239.

54. Augustine E. Costello, *Our Police Protectors* . . . (New York, 1885), p. 102.

55. Lossing, *op. cit.*, pp. 666–667; Costello, *Our Police Protectors*, pp. 137–138, 140–142.

56. A.I.C.P., *Sixteenth Annual Report*, 1859, p. 50.

57. Claghorn, "The Foreign Immigrant . . . ," *op. cit.*, pp. 452–453; John H. Griscom, *Sanitary Condition of the Laboring Population of New York* (New York, 1845), pp. 16, 18, 20–45.

58. David M. Schneider, *History of Public Welfare in New York State, 1609–1866* (Chicago, 1938), pp. 160–167; Lossing, *op. cit.*, p. 308; Booth, *op. cit.*, pp. 733–734.

59. Griscom, *op. cit.*, pp. 43–44. For a discussion of the city's failure to control epidemics in slum areas, cf. New York State, *Senate Documents* (1850), III, No. 92, especially 9, 42.

60. Of the native population in 1830, some 16,000 were Negroes, but as a result of migration elsewhere the colored population actually declined to about 15,000 at the outbreak of the Civil War. George E. Haynes, *Negro at Work in New York City* (New York, 1912), p. 47.

61. Kapp, *Immigration and the Commissioners of Emigration*, p. 12.

62. Flick (ed.), *op. cit.*, VII, 25–26, 52.

63. *Ibid.*, p. 43.

64. Friedrich Kapp, *European Emigration to the United States* (New York, 1869), p. 6.

65. Cf. Appendix, p. 187.

66. Francis Lieber, *Stranger in America* . . . (London, 1835), I, 207.

67. Alexander Marjoribanks, *Travels in South and North America* (London, 1853), p. 306.

Chapter III

1. Schneider, *History of Public Welfare in New York State*, pp. 246–247; New York City, Governors of the Alms House, *First Annual Report*, 1849, p. 7.

2. Flick (ed.), *History of the State of New York*, VII, 44–46. Cf. Edith Abbott, *Historical Aspects of the Immigration Problem*, pp. 559 ff; Edith Abbott, *Immigration: Select Documents* . . . , pp. 110 ff.

3. New York City, Commissioners of the Alms House, Bridewell and Penitentiary, *Annual Report*, 1837, in *Documents* of the Board of Aldermen, 1837, No. 32, p. 221.

4. *New York State Laws*, 1824, chap. 37; Kapp, *Immigration and the Commissioners of Emigration*, pp. 44–45. The masters of ships arriving from points in New York State were excluded from the provisions of the act.

5. Kapp, *op. cit.*, pp. 45–46. From 1828 to 1836 brokers assumed liability at a flat rate of two dollars per ship, regardless of the number of passengers. *Ibid.*, cf. *Annual Reports of the Commissioners of Emigration* . . . (New York, 1861), pp. iii–iv; Schneider, *op. cit.*, pp. 304–305.

6. Kapp, *op. cit.*, p. 46.

7. *Ibid.*, pp. 46–47. All the money from the commuted bonds, until 1842, was received by a certain John Ahern in the office of the clerk of the Common Council and later clerk to the mayor. Ahern kept no regular account books. He paid over his receipts to the clerk of the Common Council, who likewise kept no memorandum of fees or of passengers accounted for. *Ibid.*

8. *Ibid.*, pp. 50–59; Schneider, *op. cit.*, pp. 304–305; *Report of the Select Committee to Examine . . . the Trusts . . . of the Commissioners of Emigration*, New York State, *Assembly Documents*, II, No. 34 (1852), 170–173, 226–250.

9. Kapp, *op. cit.*, p. 125; *Annual Reports of the Commissioners of Emigration*, pp. iii–iv.

10. *New York State Laws*, 1845, chap. 227; Schneider, *op. cit.*, p. 303.

11. Schneider, *op. cit.*, p. 303; E. P. Belden, *New York: Past, Present, and Future* . . . (New York, 1849), p. 101.

12. In 1848 a state "emigrant refuge" and hospital was opened at Ward's Island in the East River. Under the jurisdiction of the recently created Commissioners of Emigration, it received immigrant patients not suffering from communicable diseases. Cf. *Annual Reports of the Commissioners of Emigration*, pp. 20–24; Kapp, *op. cit.*, pp. 125–129.

13. *Annual Reports of the Commissioners of Emigration*, p. 380.

14. *Report of the Select Committee appointed to Investigate Frauds upon Emigrant Passengers arriving in this State*, in New York State, *Assembly Documents*, VIII, No. 250 (1847), 3–4. It was estimated in 1849 that one fifth of the money spent by immigrants for inland transportation fell into the hands of runners. D. R. Thomason, *Hints to Emigrants* . . . (London, 1849), p. 93. Cf. Christoph Vetter, *Zwei Jahre in New-York* (Hof, Bavaria, 1849), pp. 32–41.

15. Memorandum of November 1848, *op. cit.*, pp. 380–381.

16. John F. Maguire, *Irish in America* (4th ed.; New York, c. 1887), p. 190.

17. *Report of the Select Committee . . . to Investigate Frauds upon Emigrant Passengers . . .* , pp. 2–3.

18. *Annual Reports of the Commissioners of Emigration*, p. 29.

19. *New York State Laws*, 1848, chap. 219. However, complaints continued to be voiced. The *Irish American*, June 22, 1850, reported that an immigrant had been charged $18 for one night.

20. *Annual Reports of the Commissioners of Emigration*, p. 27.

21. Commissioners of the Alms House, Bridewell and Penitentiary, *op. cit.*, p. 221; New York City, Alms-House Commissioner, *Annual Report*, 1847, p. 11; *Albion*, June 17, 1837.

22. There were so many paupers at the almshouse and Bellevue Hospital that it was necessary to lodge them in the cellars and garrets, the chapel, and the "dead house." New York City, Board of Assistant Aldermen, *Documents*, 1847, No. 30, p. 373. Cf. *Courier and Enquirer*, January 29, 1847.

23. Kapp, *op. cit.*, pp. 85–86; Wittke, *We Who Built America*, p. 126.

24. Kapp, *op. cit.*, pp. 85–95.

25. In 1851 a petition of the St. George's Society for the appointment of its president as one of the commissioners was denied on the ground that, while the Irish and German members were justified by the large immigration from Ireland and Germany, an additional appointment would be the entering wedge for all other immigrant societies to make the same request. New York State, *Senate Documents* (1851), Vol. II, No. 24, *passim*.

26. *New York State Laws*, 1847, chap. 195, as amended.

27. *Ibid.*; Kapp, *op. cit.*, pp. 97–98.

28. *Annual Reports of the Commissioners of Emigration*, p. 25.

29. Anton Eickhoff, *In der Neuen Heimath* . . . (New York, 1884), Appendix, p. 49.

30. *Irish American*, January 25, 1851. "Desecration of the dead" refers to the board's practice of permitting autopsies on the bodies of immigrants who died while under its jurisdiction.

31. *Irish American*, January 27, 1850. Cf. the issue of February 17, 1850, which urges centralization, lower salaries, and less waste.

32. *Irish American*, January 3, 1852.

33. *Report of the Select Committee to Examine . . . the Trusts . . . of the Commissioners of Emigration . . .* , *op. cit.*, pp. 8, 10, 12.

34. *Irish American*, January 10, 1852.

35. *Tribune*, July 13, 1855.

36. Mary L. Booth, *History of the City of New York* (Special limited ed.; New York, 1867), II, 758.

37. Castle Garden remained the central immigrant landing point until Ellis Island superseded it in 1892.

38. *New York State Laws*, 1855, chap. 474.

39. *Annual Reports of the Commissioners of Emigration*, pp. 409–410.

40. *Constitution of the St. George's Society* (New York, 1853), p. 21. Cf. George A. Morrison, Jr., *History of the Saint Andrew's Society* . . . (New York, 1906), p. 11.

41. Morrison, *op. cit.*, p. 38. The Friendly Sons of St. Patrick, having members of different religious and political faiths, ignored matters of religion and politics until the influx of Catholic Irish in the fifties. Richard J. Purcell, "The Irish Contribution to Colonial New York," Part II, *Studies* (Dublin), XXX, No. 117 (March, 1941), 116; Lossing, *History of New York City*, p. 189.

42. *Freeman's Journal*, March 28, 1863. Cf. *European*, March 25, 1837.

43. *Courrier des États-Unis*, January 10, 1829.

44. Letter from Henry Escher, Librarian of the Swiss Benevolent Society, to George H. Baker, Librarian of Columbia College, May 11, 1899, bound with the Society's annual reports for 1851–1886, now in the Columbia University Library.

45. Lossing, *op. cit.*, p. 581. The St. David's Benefit Society had 350 members in 1857. *Daily Tribune*, March 3, 1857.

46. *Courrier des États-Unis*, January 19, 1847.

47. *Asmonean*, March 2, 1855; *Staats-Zeitung*, November 11, 1854; Lossing, *op. cit.*, p. 126.

48. *Deutsche Schnellpost*, January 25, 1845; *Skandinavia*, January 15, 1847; *Courrier des États-Unis*, September 28, 1857; *Albion*, January 14, 1860. Cf. *Francis's New Guide to the Cities of New York and Brooklyn* . . . (New York, 1857), pp. 121–123.

49. Paupers from Hesse-Darmstadt arriving at New York in 1846 were so numerous and in such pitiful condition that the German Society was unable to help them. *Staats-Zeitung*, October 17, 1846.

50. *Albion*, June 3, 1837.

51. [St. George's Society], *History of St. George's Society of New York from 1770 to 1913* ([New York], 1913), p. 38.

52. Rudolf Cronau, *Denkschrift zum 150. Jahrestag der Deutschen Gesellschaft der Stadt New York* (New York, 1934), pp. 26, 72–74; Eickhoff, *op. cit.*, p. 2 and Appendix, *passim*.

53. Flick (ed.), *op. cit.*, VII, 23; Hardie, *Description of the City of New York*, pp. 291–292. The German Emigrant Society, created in 1814, was distinct from the German Society.

54. For the activities of this association, cf. Thomas F. Meehan, "New York's First Irish Emigrant Society," United States Catholic Historical Society *Records and Studies*, VI, Part II (December, 1912), 202–211.

55. Alexander C. Buchanan, *Emigration Practically Considered* . . . (London, 1828), quoted by Robert Mudie, *Emigrant's Pocket Companion* (London, 1832), pp. 195–196. Some 6,000 of the 41,000 immigrants arriving at New York in 1833 were supposed to have found their way into Canada. *Emigration; Practical Advice to Emigrants* . . . (2d ed.; London, 1834), p. 118.

56. Thomason, *op. cit.*, p. 117. Cf. Thomas Čapek, *Čechs (Bohemians) in America*, pp. 28, 33–34, 40.

57. Although thousands sailed directly from Europe to Boston, Philadelphia, Baltimore, and other American ports, the concentration of the immigrant trade at New York made this route more regular and dependable. By 1852 three fourths of the immigrants arriving in the United States landed at New York. Hale, *Letters on Irish Emigration*, pp. 21, 24.

58. Meehan, "New York's First Irish Emigrant Society," *op. cit.*, p. 211.

59. The Union Emigrant Society tried to obtain from the city a portion of the immigrant commutation money, but the Common Council refused to grant the request, and the Society died for lack of funds. Letter from William J. Macneven to Robert Hogan, December 11, 1839, printed in the *Freeman's Journal*, August 29, 1840.

60. Richard J. Purcell, "The Irish Emigrant Society of New York," *Studies* (Dublin), XXVII, No. 108 (December, 1938), 585–587.

61. *Albion*, June 22, 1844.

62. From November 1844 to November 1847, 1,600 persons applied for jobs; 880 were English, 422 Irish, 205 Scotch, 67 Welsh, and 26 were from Canada and Nova Scotia—who might have been any of these nationalities. During this period about 15,000 sought travel information. *Albion*, December 18, 1847.

63. *Albion*, June 7, 1845, June 12, 1847, January 15, 1848, December 22, 1849; *Anglo American*, January 17, 1846. A short-lived Welsh emigrant aid society was founded in 1843. *Anglo American*, November 4, 1843, November 1, 1845. *The New-York City Directory for 1853–1854* (Appendix, p. 73) refers to a Netherlands Society which "ceased for want of sufficient support." A German *Volksverein* had better success in the 1840's because it confined its activities mainly to giving advice and information and did not offer financial aid. Vetter, *op. cit.*, p. 43.

64. *Report of the Select Committee . . . to Investigate Frauds upon Emigrant Passengers . . .* , p. 6.

65. *Ibid.*, pp. 37, 92–95; Purcell, "The Irish Emigrant Society of New York," *op. cit.*, p. 595; *Irish American*, September 30, 1849. Cf. *Truth Teller*, September 3, 1831.

66. Francis E. Lane, *American Charities and the Child of the Immigrant . . .* (Washington, D.C., 1932), p. 104; Schneider, *op. cit.*, pp. 190–191; Hardie, *op. cit.*, p. 292.

67. The Society of St. Vincent de Paul was patterned after its parent body of the same name, founded in Paris in 1833. Alexander Johnson, "The Society of St. Vincent de Paul," *St. Vincent de Paul Quarterly*, X, No. 2 (May, 1905), 169, 173; Helen M. Sweeney, *Golden Milestone 1846–1896 . . .* (New York, 1896), p. 15. From 1849 to 1854 the House of Mercy sheltered 2,323 and found jobs for 4,852 girls. *Ibid.*, p. 21.

68. *Irish American*, February 26, 1859, December 21, 1861.

69. Lane, *op. cit.*, pp. 107–108.

70. A.I.C.P., *Thirteenth Annual Report*, 1856, p. 25.

71. Cf. pp. 140, 169.

Chapter IV

1. Annie C. Cochran, *Christian Publisher: Life and Work of Robert Carter* [New York (1891)], p. 41; "John Stokes's American Diary," *National Review*, CXI, No. 659 (January, 1938), p. 80; A. Gallenga [Luigi Mariotti], *Episodes of My Second Life* (London, 1884), I, 49; *Emigrant's True Guide . . .* , p. 93.

2. To the European, New York's most peculiar institution seemed to be the boardinghouse, and many a traveler remarked about its prevalence and its influence on society. The cheapest, of course, were inhabited chiefly by sailors and newly arrived immigrants.

3. [George G. Foster], *New York in Slices . . .* (New York, 1849), pp. 84–85.

4. *Ibid.*

5. Thomas B. Gunn, *Physiology of New York Boarding Houses* (New York, 1857), pp. 256, 258. Cf. Francis Wyse, *America, its Realities and Resources . . .* (London, 1846), II, 385.

6. Gunn, *op. cit.*, pp. 255–256.

7. Cf. Edward E. Pratt, *Industrial Causes of Congestion of Population in New York City* (New York, 1911), pp. 14–15.

8. *Albion*, *Rise of New York Port . . .* , pp. 126–130, 134–142, 222; Lossing, *History of New York City*, pp. 214–215.

9. Citizens' Association, *Report of the Council of Hygiene . . .* (New York, 1865), pp. 15, 100, 112, 174.

10. Albion, *op. cit.*, p. 266.

11. Lossing, *op. cit.*, p. 214.

12. *Ibid.*; Flick (ed.), *History of the State of New York*, VI, 215–216.

13. Albion, *op. cit.*, p. 266.

14. D. T. Valentine, *Manual of the Corporation of the City of New York*, 1841–1842, p. 49.

15. Cf. *Report of the Council of Hygiene*, p. 15.

16. Computed from statistics of the New York State censuses of 1835, 1845, and 1855.

17. *New York State Census of 1855*, pp. 110–111.

18. Claghorn, "The Foreign Immigrant in New York City," United States Industrial Commission, *Reports*, XV, 452.

19. Herbert Asbury, *Gangs of New York* (New York, 1939), pp. 13–15; Norman Ware, *Industrial Worker 1840–1860* (Boston, 1924), p. 15, citing New York *Tribune*, June 19, 1850.

20. Claghorn, "The Foreign Immigrant in New York City," *loc. cit.*, p. 452.

21. In his *Gangs of New York* (p. 9), Herbert Asbury erroneously assumed that the bulk of the Sixth Ward population devoted itself almost exclusively to vice and crime, but Nathaniel P. Willis (*Prose Works* [Philadelphia, 1855], p. 583) wrote of the decent people in the Five Points.

22. Hyman B. Grinstein, *Rise of the Jewish Community of New York, 1654–1860* (Philadelphia, 1945), p. 32; *Longworth's American Almanac . . .* for the years 1825–1826 and 1842–1843, *passim;* Chamber of Commerce of the State of New York, *Annual Report*, 1861–1862, pp. 204, 206, 207; *New York State Census of 1855*, pp. 110–111. In smaller numbers, nearly every other European nation was represented in the Sixth Ward.

23. Computed from statistics of the *New York State Census of 1855*. Of the 25,562 inhabitants of the ward, 10,845 were natives of Ireland. In 1864, the Citizens' Association stated that "the Irish" constituted 74 per cent and the "American population" less than 5 per cent of the ward's inhabitants. *Report of the Council of Hygiene*, p. 77. Obviously, "the Irish" included American-born children of Irish parents, for the Irish-born comprised only 37.4 per cent of the ward's population in 1865. Computed from data in the *New York State Census of 1855*, p. 110.

24. 10,446 out of a total of 22,895, or 45.6 per cent. Computed from data in *New York State Census of 1855*, p. 110.

25. *Ibid.* Although the Irish settled in all sections of Manhattan, they seemed to prefer the East Side of the island. Between 14th and 26th streets east of Sixth Avenue, 37.2 per cent of the residents were Irish. Claghorn, ("The Foreign Immigrant . . . ," *loc. cit.*, p. 458), remarks that the Irish were found more frequently on the West Side, but this is disproven by the 1855 census statistics: including even the central Sixth, Fourteenth, and Fifteenth wards, the West Side Irish population extending northward from Liberty Street to 86th Street numbered 78,524; the East Side Irish inhabitants from Maiden Lane to 86th Street numbered 85, 173.

26. Thomas Adams, *et al.*, *Population, Land Values and Government* (New York, 1929), pp. 57–58.

27. *Report of the Council of Hygiene*, p. 286. Germans, popularly known as the "Dutch" (a corruption of *deutsch*), gave the hill its name, but the squatters were mainly Irish. Brace, *Dangerous Classes of New York . . .* , p. 152. For a map showing the limits of the built-up region of Manhattan, cf. p. 21.

28. *Report of the Council of Hygiene*, pp. 286, 292–293, 303.

29. *Ibid.*, p. 303.

30. George E. Haynes, *Negro at Work in New York City* (New York, 1912), pp. 48, 144.

31. E. S. Abdy, *Journal of a Residence and Tour in the United States . . .* (London, 1835), I, 358.

32. [James Boardman], *America and the Americans* (London, 1833), p. 311.

33. *New York State Census of 1825*.

34. *New York State Census of 1835*. The loss in the Sixth Ward is accounted for by the fact that the northern part of the Sixth became the Fourteenth Ward in 1827. The

Fourteenth continued to gain in strength as a Negro locality but never equaled the growth shown in the Fifth and Eighth wards.

35. *Longworth's . . . Directory*, 1832–1833; MSS note of introduction of a colored woman from Joseph Curtis to Mayor Lawrence, on the occasion of the riot of 1834, dated July 12, and now in the possession of the New York Historical Society. This note refers to "many families of colour" in the neighborhood of Sullivan Street; *Staats-Zeitung*, April 7, 1860, New York *Herald*, July 15, 16, 1863. The *Anglo-African*, August 22, 1863, gives addresses of victims of the draft riot of that year.

36. At the time of the Civil War, only slightly more than one fifth of the Village dwellings were tenements, a fact which indicates the degree to which immigrants and Negroes were excluded. *Report of the Council of Hygiene*, pp. 120–121.

37. *Eighth United States Census*, 1860, population schedule, p. 337. Although the population of Manhattan increased steadily throughout the nineteenth century, the Negro population showed an expansion only until 1840. Thereafter the number of Negroes on the island fell from 18,600 to 15,000 by the outbreak of the Civil War, owing, probably, to the aroused hostility to Negroes during these years of abolitionist activity. In Brooklyn, however, the Negro population increased from 2,000 in 1840 to 5,000 in 1860. Haynes, *op. cit.*, pp. 46–47.

38. Advertisements in the *Schnellpost*, 1845–1847, of rooms and apartments for rent.

39. Fritz A. H. Leuchs, *Early German Theatre in New York, 1840–1872* (New York, 1928), p. 3; Arthur Pound, *Golden Earth* (New York, 1935), pp. 202–203; Claghorn, "The Foreign Immigrant . . . ," *loc. cit.*, p. 461.

40. Leuchs, *op. cit.*, p. 3. Other "German" streets were Division, Walker, Grand, and Delancey. *Longworth's . . . Directory*, 1842–1843.

41. Franz Löher, *Geschichte und Zustände der Deutschen in Amerika*, (Cincinnati, 1847), p. 298.

42. A.I.C.P., *Thirteenth Annual Report*, 1856, pp. 52–53; Frederic W. Bogen, *Annual Report* (New York, 1854), p. 5.

43. *Staats-Zeitung*, September 17, 1853; *New York State Census of 1855*, pp. 110–118.

44. *New York State Census of 1855*, pp. 110–118; Leuchs, *op. cit.*, pp. 3–4; *Staats-Zeitung*, November 23, 1850.

45. Claghorn, "The Foreign Immigrant in New York City," *loc. cit.*, p. 461.

46. Löher, *op. cit.*, p. 298.

47. *Ibid.*

48. Excluding the Jews, who were not enumerated as such by the censuses.

49. The English are particularly elusive. Early census figures do not enumerate the English as such, and there are no available contemporary estimates of the English population of New York. The few English boardinghouses, taverns, and restaurants which advertised in the *Albion*, the *Anglo American*, and the *European* between 1828 and 1848 were scattered over several wards, but a number appeared in or near the Fourth Ward in the forties.

50. Especially in the Fourth, Seventh, Eleventh, and Seventeenth wards on the East Side and the Eighth and Ninth on the West. *New York State Census of 1855*, pp. 110–118.

51. The *Parish Register* of the Church of St. George the Martyr, a church attended by English immigrants, lists names and addresses of communicants, beginning in 1859. The addresses for the years 1859–1863 show that of 70 persons, 18 lived in 45th Street, 11 in 47th Street, 8 apiece in 44th and 46th Streets, 7 apiece in 43d and 36th, and 5 apiece in 38th and 48th Streets, nearly all between Fifth and Seventh avenues.

52. Brace, *Dangerous Classes of New York . . .* , p. 174; *Report of the Council of Hygiene*, pp. 240–241, 246.

53. *Longworth's . . . Directory*, 1825–1826; List of members of the Reformed Presbyterian Church, January 1833, in volume II of this church's *Records*. This church was known as the Scotch Church, and its communicants were almost entirely Scotch.

Although the membership list does not include addresses, the names were checked as far as possible with *Longworth's Directory* for 1832–1833 and 1833–1834 and showed that 30 out of 51 persons lived on the West Side, mostly in the Ninth Ward and others in the Fifth, Eighth, and Sixteenth. Cross, Murray, Hammond, Hudson, Amos, and Hamersley streets, and upper Eighth Avenue marked the residences of many Scots in this area. Scotch boardinghouses and taverns were scattered: the Caledonian House in Gold Street, John O'Groat's House in Essex Street, and the Lady of the Lake Tavern in Roosevelt Street were all on the East Side, but the Burns House in Liberty Street, the Waverly House in Fulton Street, the Weavers' Arms Tavern in Hudson Street, and the Rob Roy House at the corner of Greenwich and Hammond streets were all on the West Side. Advertisements in *Old Countryman*, August 11, 18, 1831, January 1, 1834.

54. *Longworth's . . . Directory*, 1842–1843; *New York State Census of 1855*, pp. 110–118.

55. Hardie, *Description of the City of New York*, p. 164; *Longworth's . . . Directory*, 1835–1836, p. 741.

56. *Map of New York City*, 1852, in New York Public Library; *New York State Census of 1855*, pp. 110–118.

57. *Longworth's . . . Directory*, 1825–1826, 1832–1833, 1842–1843; advertisements in *Courrier des États-Unis*, 1843–1848, of rooms and apartments for rent, French pensions, and private residences.

58. *Augustin P. Maugé, Directory Français . . .* (New York, 1864); *New York State Census of 1855*, pp. 110–118.

59. *Longworth's . . . Directory*, 1825–1826, 1832–1833, 1842–1843. It is impossible to form conclusive judgments about the Spanish and Portuguese peoples, for the directories did not distinguish between residences and business addresses; moreover, Spanish and Portuguese Jews were included, although it is likely that they had more in common with the native, English, Dutch, German, and Polish Jews than with the Catholic Spanish and Portuguese.

60. *New York State Census of 1855*, pp. 110–118.

61. *Ibid.;* Brace, *op. cit.*, pp. 194–197; Francisco Moncada, "The Little Italy of 1850," *Atlantica*, January, 1933, p. 160.

62. *Longworth's . . . Directory*, 1832–1833, 1842–1843; *Rode's New York City Directory, for 1853–1854*. It was necessary to assume that the Dutch immigrants could be differentiated from the Knickerbocker element by the humbler occupations of the former.

63. *New York State Census of 1855*, pp. 110–118. By the end of the Civil War, "Swedes, Danes, &c." were living in the Third Ward, showing the normal progression uptown. *Report of the Council of Hygiene*, p. 5.

64. Čapek, *Čechs (Bohemians) in America . . .* , p. 40; Samuel Gompers, *Seventy Years of Life and Labor* (New York, c. 1925), I, 25.

65. *Courrier des États-Unis*, May 23, 1855; *Staats-Zeitung*, May 26, 1855; Gunn, *op. cit.*, p. 275; Junius H. Browne, *Great Metropolis: A Mirror of New York* (Hartford, 1869), pp. 97–98; Louis J. Beck, *New York's Chinatown* (New York, c. 1898), pp. 11–12. Other nationalities included persons born in Canada, New Brunswick and Nova Scotia, numbering some 2,800 in 1855 and settling among the English and Scotch. In all probability, the Canadian French lived with the European French. The Belgians likewise chose areas where French was spoken. Persons born in Newfoundland were probably of Irish parentage for they followed the Irish into the Fourth, Sixth, and Seventh wards. *New York State Census of 1855*, pp. 110–118.

66. I have used the term nationality to indicate birthplace.

67. Cf. pp. 137–138.

68. Grinstein, *op. cit.*, p. 30.

69. Nearby streets on which Jews lived were Stone, Beaver, Broad, Marketfield, Hanover Square, and Broadway. *Ibid.*, pp. 30–31.

70. *Ibid.*, p. 31.
71. *Ibid.*
72. *Ibid.*, p. 32.
73. *Ibid.*, pp. 32–33.
74. *Ibid.*, p. 32.

Chapter V

1. New York State Assembly, *Report of the Select Committee appointed to Examine into the Condition of Tenant Houses in New-York and Brooklyn* (Albany, 1857), p. 22. Cf. *Emigrant and Old Countryman,* September 27, 1837, which describes the slum conditions of the thirties.

2. The first such house, said to have been built in 1833, was a four-story building with a suite of rooms on each floor. Charles H. Haswell, *Reminiscences of New York* (New York, c. 1896), p. 332.

3. *Report of . . . the Condition of Tenant Houses in New York . . .* (1857), p. 23; Claghorn, "The Foreign Immigrant . . . " United States Industrial Commission, *Reports,* XV, 453.

4. Thomas Adams, *et. al., Population, Land Values and Government (Regional Survey of New York and Its Environs,* II, 54. Figures were computed from federal census reports for the seven wards. Average block density, which is more significant because of the elimination of street and park areas, was computed on the assumption that streets below Canal totaled 40 per cent of the gross acreage exclusive of parks. *Ibid.* For statistics of the city's tenement house population in 1864, cf. Appendix, p. 197.

5. *Ibid.*, p. 56. In this computation, streets were assumed to cover thirty-two per cent of the gross area excluding parks. By 1860, however, the population density of lower New York had begun to decline in the face of extension of the avenues northward and easier access to the upper part of Manhattan. *Ibid.*, pp. 54, 57.

6. *Staats-Zeitung,* March 4, 1843, citing statistics from the City Inspector's annual report.

7. A.I.C.P., *Sixteenth Annual Report,* 1859, p. 46.

8. A.I.C.P., *Twentieth Annual Report,* 1863, p. 38; Claghorn, "The Foreign Immigrant . . . ," *op. cit.,* p. 453.

9. Griscom, *Sanitary Condition of the Laboring Population of New York,* p. 10.

10. *Ibid.* Many old houses in lower Manhattan had been built before streets were raised and paved and the dock frontage was extended farther into the water. The lower floors of such buildings were two or three feet below the surface of the pavements. Cf. Claghorn, "The Foreign Immigrant . . . ," *loc. cit.,* p. 451.

11. *London v. New York; by an English Workman* (London, 1859), pp. 3–4.

12. Citizens' Association, *Report of the Council of Hygiene,* p. lxxiii.

13. *Report of . . . the Condition of Tenant Houses in New-York . . .* (1857), pp. 15–19.

14. Griscom, *op. cit.,* p. 6.

15. *Report of . . . the Condition of Tenant Houses in New-York . . .* (1857), pp. 12–13, 19.

16. *Ibid.*, p. 20. Poor tenants were said to have paid their rent more punctually than many middle-class families. *Ibid.*, p. 19.

17. New York State, *Senate Documents,* III, No. 81 (1841), 4. After many petitions for its enactment, a law in 1842 extended the exemption of household furniture and working tools. New York State, *Senate Documents,* I, No. 43 (1843), 1. Cf. New York State, *Assembly Documents,* 7, No. 145 (1842), 5.

18. *Herald,* February 7, 1848.

19. *Staats-Zeitung,* February 26, 1848; *Herald,* February 24, 1848. Rent protest meetings were held as early as 1837. Cf. *Staats-Zeitung,* July 19, 1837.

20. Griscom, *op. cit.,* p.7.

21. Gompers, *Seventy Years of Life and Labor,* I, 493–494.

22. Showers cost five or ten cents, a swim cost three cents and up, and washing and ironing privileges cost three cents an hour. Over fifty thousand persons used the establishment during its first six months of operation. *Irish American*, June 26, 1852; *Citizen*, January 21, 1854. However, it was not patronized by enough persons to make it self supporting, according to Lillian Brandt, *Growth and Development of A.I.C.P. and C.O.S.* . . . (multigraphed; New York, 1942), p. 57.

23. *Staats-Zeitung*, daily ed., July 1, 1858.

24. The accumulation of sewage deposits around the slips and docks is discussed in James E. Serrell, *Compilation of Facts representing the present condition of the Sewers* . . . (New York, 1866).

25. For the inefficiency of the city's health administration and the question of public health control vs. private property inviolate, cf. Griscom, *op. cit.*, pp. 29, 43–44, 48; *Annual Report of the City Inspector*, 1844, pp. 684–685.

26. A.I.C.P., *Fourteenth Annual Report*, 1857, p. 25.

27. A.I.C.P., *Sixteenth Annual Report*, 1859, p. 50.

28. *Report of the City Inspector*, 1862, pp. 11–15, in Board of Aldermen, *Documents*, Vol. XXX, No. 4 (1863). For complaints of the operative masons against subcontracting in the building industry, cf. *Tribune*, May 9, 1850.

29. Board of Aldermen, *Documents*, XXI, No. 12, 247–256.

30. Cf., e.g., *Tribune*, May 21, 1850. For further discussion of industrial plants in residential areas, cf. *Report of the Council of Hygiene*, pp. xcii–xcvi, 27; *Reports of the City Inspector*, 1844, pp. 683–684, and 1856, pp. 196–206.

31. *Report of the Council of Hygiene*, p. 190; *Tribune*, September 16, 1851.

32. *Staats-Zeitung*, December 29, 1849, March 16, 1850; *Asmonean*, February 15, 1850.

33. Cf., e.g., *Report of the City Inspector*, 1857, p. 215; Metropolitan Board of Health, *Second Annual Report*, 1867, pp. 219–231; A.I.C.P., *Eleventh Annual Report*, 1854, pp. 22–27; Claghorn, "The Foreign Immigrant . . . ," *loc. cit.*, pp. 450–452.

34. Griscom, *op. cit.*, pp. 16, 18. In the cholera epidemic of 1849, 880 deaths occurred in the Sixth Ward, more than in any other ward. Governors of the Alms House, *First Annual Report*, 1849, p. 99.

35. Griscom, *op. cit.*, p. 20. For the more numerous ailments of those admitted to the public Bellevue Hospital, cf. Alms-House Commissioner, *Annual Report*, 1846, pp. 404–408.

36. The percentage, which excludes a negligible few of unknown birthplace or who were born at sea, was computed from statistics in the first ten annual reports of the Governors of the Alms House, 1849–1859. The Governors superseded the office of Alms-House Commissioner, whose reports are available but incomplete and unreliable.

37. *Report of the City Inspector*, 1857, pp. 182, 183. As compared with 1,078 natives, 1,734 immigrants died of tuberculosis. This disease was nearly twice as fatal to Negroes as to whites, a reflection of the living conditions of the former, which were comparable to those of the foreign born. *Ibid.*, p. 185.

38. *Report of the City Inspector*, 1840, p. 639. "Foreigners" comprised 51.3 per cent of the total, native whites 43.3 per cent, and the remainder were colored, mostly native but including some from the West Indies.

39. *Reports of the City Inspector*, 1857, pp. 178–179, and 1860, p. 13, in Board of Aldermen, *Documents*, Vol. XXV, No. 9, and Vol. XXVIII, No. 5.

40. *Report of the City Inspector*, 1857, pp. 178–179. In the absence of statistics on parentage, the inspector made this reasonable supposition.

41. *Ibid.*, p. 215.

42. *Report of the City Inspector*, 1860, pp. 230, 245–246. "The ratio of mortality from those diseases varied almost exactly according to the emigration; when there were the largest arrivals of emigrants, it will be found that these maladies were the most fatal. Since 1855 the emigration has largely decreased, and so, also, proportionally, have the fatal effects of these diseases. The largest number of deaths from Small Pox that ever

occurred in this city in one year was in the period of the greatest emigration." *Ibid.*, p. 230. Cf. Claghorn, "The Foreign Immigrant . . . ," *loc. cit.*, pp. 450–451.

43. This percentage of admissions to Bellevue was computed from statistics in the first ten annual reports of the Governors of the Alms House. Cf. *supra*, n. 36. The percentage of natives of Ireland living in New York was computed from statistics of the *New York State Census of 1855*, pp. 110–118.

44. *Ibid.*

45. German Society of the City of New York, *Annual Reports* (*Jahres-Berichte* . . .), 1847, p. 1; 1850, p. 3; 1854, pp. 4, 19; 1864, p. 8; 1865, pp. 9–10. Most of these German newcomers went west or dispersed to other localities in the Middle Atlantic States. Of course, some poor Germans remained in New York City; these included helpless paupers such as those shipped to America in 1847 by the Grand Duchy of Hesse Darmstadt and the penniless political refugees during and after the unsuccessful German revolutions of 1848–1850. *Ibid.*, 1847, p. 2; 1851, p. 2.

46. Computed from data in the *Annual Reports* of the Governors of the Alms House, 1849–1859, and the *New York State Census of 1855*, pp. 110–118. Cf. *supra*, nn. 36 and 43. Natives of France admitted to Bellevue were first enumerated in 1852, and from that year until 1859, the French comprised .6 per cent of admissions, as compared with a French population representing 1.9 per cent of the city's immigrants in 1855.

47. Computed from data in the reports of the Resident Physician of the Lunatic Asylum, in the *Annual Reports* of the Governors of the Alms House, 1849–1859. The Irish constituted almost exactly one half of all admissions to the asylum, both native and foreign.

48. Governors of the Alms House, *Fifth Annual Report*, 1853, p. 70.

49. Governors of the Alms House, *Sixth Annual Report*, 1854, p. 106; cf. their *Third Annual Report*, 1851, pp. 58–59.

50. Governors of the Alms House, *Sixth Annual Report*, p. 106.

51. Governors of the Alms House, *First Annual Report*, 1849, p. 130.

52. *Report of the City Inspector*, 1856, in Board of Aldermen, *Documents*, XXIV, No. 11, 203–204; but cf. Griscom, *op. cit.*, p. 20.

53. *Report of the Council of Hygiene*, p. 342.

54. *Ibid.*, pp. 315, 342.

55. Harriett Lawrence to Thomas Lawrence, an English tailor, August 20, 1856, MSS letter in the New York Public Library.

56. This and the following examples are only a few extracted from the *Criminal-Zeitung*, March 17, 1854.

57. Advertisements in *Irish American*, December 7, 1850, October 8, 1853; *Citizen*, February 4, 1854; *Staats-Zeitung*, March 1, May 3, 1837, December 18, 1839; *Courrier des États-Unis*, October 3, 1829, August 21, 1833.

58. *Staats-Zeitung*, March 11, 1843.

59. German Society, *Annual Report*, 1848, p. 1; Eickhoff, *In der Neuen Heimath*, appendix, p. 54.

60. *Staats-Zeitung*, September 3, 1836.

61. *Asmonean*, October 3, 1856.

62. Grinstein, *Rise of the Jewish Community* . . . , p. 555.

63. Computed from data in the *Annual Reports* of the Governors of the Alms House, 1849–1859. For detailed statistics, cf. Appendix, p. 201. The almshouse reports prior to 1849 were unreliable as to the average number of inmates: fictitious figures were given which were much too large. Weekly enumerations of admissions were begun only in 1849, when the Alms House Commissioner was superseded by a Board of Governors. Governors of the Alms House, *First Annual Report*, 1849, p. 6.

64. A.I.C.P., *Ninth Annual Report*, 1852, p. 25.

65. *Ibid.*

66. For detailed figures on almshouse admissions during these years, cf. p. 201.

67. A.I.C.P., *Seventeenth Annual Report*, 1860, pp. 55–56.

68. For panel thieves, cf. *National Police Gazette,* October 4, 1845; Herbert Asbury, *Gangs of New York,* pp. 193–202; for "sin along the waterfront" and the "river pirates," cf. *ibid.,* pp. 46–86; for the gangs, cf. *Irish American,* April 5, 1851, July 11, 1857; *Courrier des États-Unis,* February 13, 15, 18, 1864; Asbury, *op. cit.,* pp. 21–22, 28, 116; Brace, *Dangerous Classes of New York* . . . , pp. 93–95, 317. Self-defense clubs were organized by workingmen and clerks for protection against hoodlumism. *Daily Tribune,* January 27, 30, 1857.

69. Francis Wyse, *America, its Realities and Resources* . . . (3 vols.; London, 1846), III, 32; Bogen, *Annual Report,* p. 6; *Staats-Zeitung,* November 23, 1850, March 15, 1851, citing reports of the Chief of Police covering the period from July 15, 1845, to March 15, 1851; *Belletristisches Journal,* November 26, 1858. During 1854, this paper listed arrests of Germans each week; most instances were of petty thievery or robbery. Drunkenness and disorderly conduct were far more common than petty larceny. Cf., e.g., New York State, *Assembly Documents,* VI, No. 190 (1860), 121. For statistical details, cf. Appendix, pp. 202–204.

70. "Intemperance is only the unnatural solace of . . . desperate and reckless individuals." George G. Foster, *New York Naked* (New York, [185–]), pp. 122–123.

71. Computed from data in the reports of the Warden of the City Prison, in the *Annual Reports* of the Governors of the Alms House, 1850, p. 50; 1851, p. 67; 1852, p. 47; 1853, p. 42; 1854, p. 60; 1855, p. 81; 1856, p. 153; 1857, p. 144; 1858, p. 107.

72. "There are stringent ordinances against encumbering the streets and sidewalks, against hanging signs further from stores than a certain distance, against selling lottery tickets and keeping policy offices, against driving quicker than a certain rate through the streets. . . . They are not put in force, although the police are bound by law to enforce them. Let a policeman make a descent on one of the lottery or policy shops in Broadway, and the chances are against his holding office another year." *Herald,* February 6, 1848. For the inefficiency of the police and the problem of immigrant criminality, cf. J. W. Gerard, *London and New York: Their Crime and Police* (New York, 1853), p. 8.

73. *Criminal-Zeitung,* December 24, 1852, January 7, 1853.

74. *Daily Tribune,* April 25, 1850.

75. Reports of the Warden of the City Prison, in *Annual Reports* of the Governors of the Alms House, 1850, p. 48; 1851, pp. 58–59.

76. A.I.C.P., *Seventeenth Annual Report,* 1860, pp. 55–56. The New York Prison Association reported 41,299 city commitments for 1863. Of these, 30,822, or approximately three fourths, were "foreigners"—"about the usual proportion." A.I.C.P. *Twenty-first Annual Report,* 1864, pp. 47–48.

77. Computed from figures in the abstract of sheriffs' returns of convictions in Courts of Special Sessions in the city and county of New York during the year 1859, New York State *Assembly Documents,* VI, No. 190 (1860), 121, and statistics of population of New York City, *Eighth Census of the United States,* 1860, "Population," p. xxxii; cf. Appendix, pp. 198, 204.

78. Governors of the Alms House, *Second Annual Report,* 1850, p. 50; "Immigrants in general contribute less than their quota to the criminal population of the United States when correction is made for variations in the age composition of the immigrant population." Edwin H. Sutherland, *Principles of Criminology* (3d ed., rev.; Chicago, c. 1939), p. 123. Unfortunately, there are no specific and reliable tabulations of age levels among immigrants at New York in the pre-Civil War period; however, in 1850 fully 14,910 of the 21,299 persons committed to the city prison were between the ages of twenty and forty, and since a total of only 5,777 native Americans were committed, it is reasonable to infer that most of the 15,522 "foreigners" were in the twenty to forty age bracket. Report of the Warden of the City Prison, in the *Second Annual Report* of the Governors of the Alms House, 1850, pp. 50–51.

79. *National Police Gazette,* July 11, 1846. Jews occasionally committed crimes against property but rarely against persons. (Grinstein, *op. cit.,* p. 259.) It might be expected

that Jewish shopkeepers would be penalized as criminals for working on Sundays although they observed the Hebrew Sabbath. I have discovered no such instances, although in 1858 a New York judge sentenced a Jew who refused to come to court on Saturday but who worked on that day. Jacob R. Marcus (compiler), *Index to Americana in Foreign-Jewish Periodicals (1806–1938)* (typescript in New York Public Library [Cincinnati, n.d.]), II, 338, citing *Archives Israelites* ([Paris], 1858), p. 469. For the criminality of the Germans, Cf. Bogen, *op. cit.*, p. 6. For the French, cf. *Courrier des États-Unis*, August 21, 1845. For the Italians, Cf. Children's Aid Society, *Fourth Annual Report*, 1857, p. 16. The Italians, who were generally peaceable, seem to have been arrested frequently by the police. According to the *Eco d'Italia*, December 30, 1865, one Italian was arrested for every 3.5 Irish and every 2 Germans; yet only 8,000 Italians lived in the city in 1865, as compared with 161,000 Irish and 109,000 Germans. (*New York State Census of 1865*, pp. 130–131.) During the fifties Italians were not known to quarrel among themselves, rarely were drunk, and apparently did not steal. Children's Aid Society, *op. cit.* The number of Italian lawbreakers was insignificant; most of them probably were arrested for vagrancy. For other national groups, information is fragmentary and inconclusive.

80. *National Police Gazette*, October 4, 11, 1845. Cf. lottery advertisements in *Criminal-Zeitung*, March 19, 1858. February 15, 1861, May 2, 1862; *Staats-Zeitung*, April 14, 1860; *Courrier des États-Unis*, August 2, 1862; *Eco d'Italia*, January 7, 1865. The city's few Chinese gambled for pleasure rather than for gain, according to the Reverend Peter Stryker, *Lower Depths of the Great American Metropolis* (New York, 1866), pp. 5–6.

81. Jonothan H. Green, *Report on Gambling in New York* (New York, 1851), *passim*.

82. William W. Sanger, *History of Prostitution . . .* (New York, 1858), pp. 465, 468, 488, 524, 527, 577; *First Annual Report of the Executive Committee of the New York Magdalen Society* (Philadelphia, 1831), pp. 4, 22; Theodore Griesinger, *Lebende Bilder aus Amerika* (Stuttgart, 1858), pp. 148–156, describing notorious houses of prostitution in Mercer Street. Others were in Reade, Duane, Church, Leonard, and Elm streets (*National Police Gazette*, May 1, 1847). These places were frequented largely by Americans, but immigrants hardly needed special bawdy houses in their slums of dark and crowded tenements and poorly supervised boardinghouses. The lower wards moreover, afforded innumerable waterfront groggeries and basement brothels. *Report of the Council of Hygiene*, pp. 10, 26, 37.

83. Sanger, *op. cit.*, pp. 456, 460.

84. *Ibid.*, p. 460. On the theory that one fourth of the prostitutes died or otherwise left New York City each year, the Commissioners of Emigration estimated a ratio of 1 prostitute to every 250 immigrants. *Ibid.*, p. 461.

85. *Ibid.*, p. 463. Not only were the conditions of transit to America and life in the metropolis unfavorable to female morality, but depraved individuals continually arrived from Europe, many having been "sent here by charitable (?) associations or public bodies in foreign lands, as the most economical way to get rid of them. Many of these females [became] mothers almost as soon as they [landed] on these shores . . ." and their daughters became prostitutes. *Ibid.*, pp. 459, 464–465.

86. *Ibid.*, p. 452. The majority of those over thirty kept brothels. *Ibid.*, p. 453. In 1858 an estimated 6,000 prostitutes lived in New York City. Ibid., pp. 456, 579; *Staats-Zeitung*, November 10, 1858.

87. Brace, *op. cit.*, p. 98; *Staats-Zeitung*, January 12, 1850.

88. Brace, *op. cit.*, p. 103.

89. First Circular of the Children's Aid Society, March 1853, quoted in Brace, *op. cit.*, p. 91; *Staats-Zeitung*, January 12, 1850.

90. Society for the Reformation of Juvenile Delinquents, *Annual Reports*, 1834–1862, *passim*. The Society's House of Refuge sheltered vagrant and delinquent children mostly between the ages of ten and sixteen. Perhaps because of their tendency to migrate in family groups rather than as individuals, the Germans appear to have shown less ju-

venile delinquency than the English-speaking immigrants. For statistics, cf. Appendix, p. 205.

91. Society for the Reformation of Juvenile Delinquents, *Annual Reports*, 1863, p. 26; 1864, p. 21; 1865, p. 24; 1866, p. 25.

Chapter VI

1. *Annual Reports of the Commissioners of Emigration* . . . (New York, 1861), appendix, p. 288; *Eighth Census of the United States*, 1860: "Population," pp. xxxi–xxxii.

2. The small percentage of Irish remaining in the Empire City is indicated by Richard J. Purcell's "The Irish Emigrant Society of New York," *Studies* (Dublin), XXVII, No. 108 (December, 1938), 593.

3. German Society, *Annual Reports*, 1847, 1855, Cf. *ibid.*, 1850, 1853, 1854, 1864, 1865. According to the records of this society, 19,489 of 51,114 German immigrants debarking at New York in 1854 gave their destinations as New York State, but a large number of these were really uncertain of their goals and often left the city after a few days. *Ibid.*, 1855, p. 15. For reported destinations of these Teutonic immigrants, cf. Appendix, p. 190.

4. *Annual Reports of the Commissioners of Emigration*, pp. 76, 196. For a short time after the opening of Castle Garden as a landing point, the cash means of the immigrants were recorded. The average was $68.08 per person, but reliable subsequent information showed that large amounts had been concealed. Had full admission been made of the funds in the newcomers' possession, "the average would have been at least double the amount reported." *Ibid.*, Appendix, pp. 345–346. Cf. *Citizen*, January 24, 1857.

5. *Report of the City Inspector*, 1861, in Board of Aldermen, *Documents*, XXIX, No. 4, p. 30.

6. *Census of the State of New York*, 1855, pp. 117–118.

7. Adams, *Ireland and Irish Emigration* . . . , pp. 104–108; Arthur H. Cole, *American Wool Manufacture*, (Cambridge, Mass., 1926), I, 368; Clark, *History of Manufactures* . . . , I, 400.

8. Cf., e.g., Children's Aid Society, *First Annual Report*, 1854, p. 4.

9. *Irish American*, August 26, 1849. Cf. *Tribune*, July 7, 1849.

10. A.I.C.P., *Fifteenth Annual Report*, 1858, p. 37; *Seventeenth Annual Report*, 1860, pp. 50–51. John O'Grady, "Irish Colonization in the United States," *Studies* (Dublin), XXIX, No. 75 (September, 1930), 393–394; Letters from Dr. D. W. Cahill in *Freeman's Journal*, March 31, May 12, 1860.

11. For the purchase of land by Irishmen, cf. O'Grady, "Irish Colonization . . . ," *op. cit.*, p. 389; *Freeman's Journal*, February 27, 1841.

12. *Irish American*, February 11, 1860, citing figures from the Boston *Pilot*.

13. O'Grady, "Irish Colonization . . . ," *op. cit.*, pp. 390–394; *Old Countryman*, November 25, 1835; *Freeman's Journal*, June 21, 1845; *Irish American*, May 19, 1860; Thomason, *Hints to Emigrants* . . . , pp. 68, 74–75; German Society, *Annual Reports*, 1845–1865, *passim*.

14. *Irish American*, September 7, 1853.

15. Cf., e.g., advertisements: *Staats-Zeitung*, March 17, 1837; *Handels-Zeitung*, October 31, 1857; *Courrier des États-Unis*, November 18, 1828, January 21, 1841; *Eco d'Italia*, March 18, 1865.

16. Cf. pp. 104–107.

17. James Stuart, *Three Years in North America* (2d ed.; Edinburgh, 1833), II, p. 511; Calvin Colton, *Manual for Emigrants to America* (London, 1832), p. 65.

18. Cf., e.g., Peter Ross, *Scot in America* (New York, 1896), pp. 232, 268; [Oelrichs & Co.], *Caspar Meier and his Successors* . . . (New York, 1898), pp. 30–31, 34, 36, 75–76; "John Stokes's American Diary," *loc. cit.*, p. 80.

19. Ross, *op. cit.*, p. 241; Grant Thorburn, *Fifty Years' Reminiscences of New York* . . . (New York, 1845), p. 286.

20. Cf., e.g., *Truth Teller*, March 29, 1828; *Emigrant*, May 1, 1833; *Irishman and Foreigner's Advocate*, July 15, 20, 1835; *Staats-Zeitung*, January 4, May 4, 1837; July 22, 1843, April 22, 1858; *Deutsche Schnellpost*, April 1, June 6, 1846, February 17, 1847; *Albion*, March 20, 1841; *European*, April 22, June 3, 1837; *Scottish Patriot*, April 18, 1840; *Courrier des États-Unis*, July 30, 1831, September 22, 1832; *Eco d'Italia*, April 19, 1851.

21. Wittke, *We Who Built America*, p. 134; New York *Tribune*, September 22, 1842; C. Büchele, *Land und Volk der Vereinigten Staaten von Nord-Amerika* (Stuttgart, 1855), p. 561; *Criminal-Zeitung*, September 22, 1854.

22. German Society, *Annual Report*, 1853, p. 4. The Society's placement statistics, as presented in the annual reports, are as follows:

1846: 2,200	1850: 9,427	1854: 6,485	1858: 1,098	1862: 540
1847: 4,743	1851: 9,427	1855: 2,603	1859: 1,160	1863: 1,161
1848: 2,430	1852: 5,956	1856: missing	1860: 1,218	1864: 840
1849: 4,954	1853: 9,435	1857: 1,833	1861: 459	1865: 712

The figure for 1851 is undoubtedly erroneous, probably a repetition of the previous year's total. In general, however, the Society's records were kept with meticulous care. They present the fullest description of immigrant aid in the years prior to the Civil War. The annual reports for 1845–1865, complete with the exception of the year 1856, are in the possession of the Society.

23. From May 1845 to May 1846, this society found positions for only 2,688 of its 5,506 applicants. Nearly all were placed in jobs requiring little or no skill. Irish Emigrant Society, *Fifth Annual Report*, printed in *Freeman's Journal*, May 30, 1846. The author was denied access to the minute books of the Society.

24. Cf., e.g., the Emigrant Assistance, the Union Emigrant, and the British Protective Emigrant societies, the British American Association, the *Allgemeine Wohl-fahrts-verein*, the *Société Démocratique*, and the Caledonian Club. Thomas F. Meehan, "New York's First Irish Emigrant Society," United States Catholic Historical Society, *Historical Records and Studies*, VI, Part II (December, 1912), 211; Purcell, "The Irish Emigrant Society of New York," *op. cit.*, pp. 585–587; [R. Waller, E. F. Beddall, and H. A. Racker], *Sketch of the Origin, Progress, and Work of the St. George's Society of New York, A.D. 1786 to 1886 . . .* (New York, 1887), p. 9; *Albion*, April 20, 1833, June 22, 1844; *Staats-Zeitung*, April 14, 1841; *Courrier des États-Unis*, November 25, 1848; Charles W. Liddel, *History of the New York Caledonian Club* (five volumes of unpublished typescript, 1935, in the possession of the club), I, 62.

25. *Albion*, June 22, 1844; *Courrier des États-Unis*, June 28, 1842. Louis Napoleon gave nearly $1,000 to the French Benevolent Society, ostensibly as evidence of his interest in its work. *Courrier des États-Unis*, November 5, 1850.

26. Isaac N. P. Stokes, *Iconography of Manhattan Island, 1498–1909* (New York, 1915–1928), Vol. V, Column 1647; Board of Aldermen, *Documents*, 1835, No. 34, pp. 141–144.

27. Although its activities were curtailed severely by the depression of 1854–1855, the society attempted to relieve unemployment in New York by sending job-hunters to the country. *Staats-Zeitung*, March 4, December 23, 1854; *Irish American*, January 20, 1855; *Asmonean*, July 6, 1855.

28. An "American Industrial Association," organized in 1858, paid transportation expenses upon promise of reimbursement out of future earnings, but its limited funds prevented large-scale assistance. *Staats-Zeitung*, daily ed., June 9, 1858. For the private efforts of the philanthropist Vere Foster, the "Irish Pioneer Emigration Fund," and the "Women's Protective Emigration Society" in sending Irish girls to farms in the West, cf. *Irish News*, February 14, June 20, 1857, February 20, 1858; *Freeman's Journal*, January 20, 1855; *Citizen*, July 28, 1855, September 26, 1857.

29. *Annual Reports of the Commissioners of Emigration*, pp. 6–7, 60. The main office at 25–27 Canal Street grew so crowded that in 1851 the Commissioners leased an

adjoining building and a new five-story structure at 140 Centre Street. Dissatisfaction with the treatment accorded the applicants, and the commissioners' neglect of the physical conditions in these offices led to the continued formation of new private agencies. New York State, *Assembly Documents*, 1852, Vol. II, No. 34, p. 10.

30. *Annual Reports of the Commissioners of Emigration*, pp. 78–79, 116. Irish laborers, German farmers and farm hands of both sexes were in great demand in the west, and the Commissioners sometimes received twenty to thirty requests in a single day for German domestic servants. During the Civil War, however, the office limited itself to supplying servants in New York City. *Staats-Zeitung*, September 15, 1855; Kapp, *Immigration and the Commissioners of Emigration* . . . , p. 115.

31. Computed from data in the MSS schedules of the *New York State Census of 1855*. Waitresses were few, most of the waiters being men. Although "governesses" have been considered as servants, coachmen and gardeners have been excluded in this computation because it frequently was impossible to determine whether they were independent or privately employed. The census marshals enumerated "drivers, coachmen, etc." and "gardeners and florists" and probably included waiters as servants. For statistics on these occupations, cf. Appendix, pp. 214–217.

32. Cf., e.g., Francis J. Grund, *Americans in their Moral, Social, and Political Relations* (Boston, 1837), pp. 66–67, 73.

33. MSS schedules. *New York State Census of 1855*.

34. *Young America*, January 24, 1846. This estimate included all types of female servants from nurse and lady's maid to scullion and women of all work. Brooklyn and other nearby centers of population were not included in this estimate.

35. Computed from data in the MSS schedules of the *New York State Census of 1855*. "Nurses," cooks, and laundresses have been included.

36. Computed from data in the MSS schedules of the *New York State Census of 1855*. Cf. Appendix, p. 219. Among the Irish the number of servants exceeded the number of laborers by one fourth—a striking contrast with the less advantageously situated Boston Irish, half of whom were laborers and only 15 per cent servants. Cf. Handlin, *Boston's Immigrants* . . . , p. 240.

37. Computed from data in the MSS schedules of the *New York State Census of 1855*. Cf. Appendix, p. 219.

38. *Ibid.*

39. According to the *European* (December 3, 1836), bias against the Irish was confined almost entirely to the cities, and farmers were not swayed by mob feelings. Cf. *Freeman's Journal*, July 29, 1854; *Criminal-Zeitung*, July 15, 1853.

40. *Truth Teller*, December 28, 1833, quoting the *American* (n.d.) By comparison, no invidious distinction was intended in advertisements for a "German cook," a "French nurse," an "Italian chambermaid," or an "English governess." Cf. the demand for Scottish female house servants in Albany (*Citizen*, June 24, 1854) and a request from the South for mechanics who "must be Scotch." *Emigrant*, May 1, 1833.

41. *Irish American*, May 28, 1853, quoting the *Daily Sun*, May 11, 1853.

42. Computed from data in the MSS schedules of the *New York State Census of 1855*. Cf. Appendix, pp. 214–217.

43. *Ibid.* As barbers, the Negroes contended with the Germans and Irish, but as dressmakers they probably were employed by persons of their own race.

44. [James Boardman], *America and the Americans* . . . , pp. 35–36; *Tribune*, May 3, 1853; *Irish American*, November 9, 1856; *Courrier des États-Unis*, May 13, 1853. An English observer rightfully attributed the Negroes' humility to "the circumstances of their helpless and degraded condition." [James D. Burn], *Three Years Among the Working-Classes in the United States during the War* (London, 1865), p. xiii. For favorable comment on Irish waiters at New York, cf. William Ferguson, *America by River and Rail* . . . (London, 1856), p. 52.

45. Thomason, *Hints to Emigrants*, p. 17.

46. *Young America*, January 24, 1846. A tacit understanding among servants regard-

ing wages, privileges, and working conditions was fostered by employment agencies, to which the women paid regular fees long after they had been hired. *Ibid*. For other evils of the system of "registry offices," cf. *Irish American*, September 10, 1853.

47. *Irish American*, November 29, 1856. Cf. *ibid*., July 7, 1855 for a defense of Irish servants as virtuous and industrious.

48. *Ibid*. Cf. Boardman, *op. cit.*, pp. 35–36.

49. Cf., e.g., *Evening Tattler*, August 26, 1841; *Herald*, February 1, 1853; *Staats-Zeitung*, daily ed., April 22, 1858; *Courrier des États-Unis*, January 7, February 7, 1865. The few Jewish servants in New York were employed exclusively by Jews, native and immigrant. Cf. advertisements for Jewish cooks, *Jewish Messenger*, October 12, 1859. In searching the MSS schedules of the *New York State Census of 1855*, I found no recognizably Jewish names among the immigrant servants living in what seemed to be Christian homes.

50. For example: a German importer employed four servants in 1855—German, Irish, English, and Welsh; Napoleon Bunel had eight Irish and four German servants in his French hotel, and a candle manufacturer from France engaged an Irish and three German servants. MSS schedules of the *New York State Census of 1855:* "Sixth Ward, 4th election district"; "Fourteenth Ward, 1st election district"; "Seventeenth Ward, 9th election district." Many other instances could be cited. Pages of the MSS volumes were un-numbered, so these references must remain general.

51. *Young America*, August 23, November 22, 1845.

52. *Young America*, October 11, 1845; *Daily Tribune*, September 3, 1845; Ware, *op. cit.*, p. 49.

53. Cf. Chapter II, pp. 17–18; Chapter VII, pp. 75–78; Ware, *op. cit.*, p. 49; Theodor Griesinger, *Freiheit und Sclaverei* . . . (Stuttgart, 1862), p. 275; C. L. Fleischmann, *Erwerbszweige, Fabrikwesen und Handel der Vereinigten Staaten* . . . (Stuttgart, 1850), p. 336; [C. S. Flint, *et al.*], *Eighty Years' Progress in the United States* . . . (Hartford, Conn., 1868), I, 309–310.

54. *Young America*, October 11, 1845; *Daily Tribune*, September 3, 1845; Ware, *op. cit.*, p. 49. These wages are, of course, exclusive of board.

55. *Ibid*. Sometimes this fee was waived if the apprentice agreed to work for a full year without pay.

56. In 1853 an Irish woman was discovered to be exploiting four girls by paying them no wages except their food for six days a week. For this and other instances of sweating, cf. *Daily Tribune*, June 8, 1853; Isaac A. Hourwich, *Immigration and Labor* (New York, 1912), pp. 362–365.

57. Computed from occupational statistics, *New York State Census of 1855*, pp. 178–195 and statistics compiled from the MSS schedules of the same census, the latter in order to determine the number of foreign born in each occupation. Errors resulting from inconsistencies and omissions are minor, and I do not think that correction would change substantially the conclusion. Cf. Appendix, pp. 214–217.

58. Computed from data in the MSS schedules of the *New York State Census of 1855*. In relation to the gainfully employed of each nationality, the persons born in Canada, New Brunswick, and Nova Scotia together included the largest proportion of dress-makers—8 per cent. The Dutch and Swiss followed with 6 per cent. Of immigrants from Poland, 5 per cent were dressmakers, nearly all of these being Jews. *Ibid*.

59. Computed from data in the MSS schedules of the *New York State Census of 1855*.

60. *Ibid*.

61. Cf. *Irish American*, May 27, 1854; Hansen, *Immigrant in American History*, pp. 160–161.

62. Mark Beaufoy, *Tour through Parts of the United States and Canada* (London, 1828), pp. 15–16. Cf. D. W. Mitchell, *Ten Years in the United States* . . . (London, 1862), pp. 147–148; Griesinger, *op. cit.*, pp. 362–364.

63. The printed summary of the *New York State Census of 1855* enumerates steve-

dores but not longshoremen, who were considered as laborers. The 155 stevedores obviously were the supervisors. In the MSS schedules, the author counted 232 stevedores and longshoremen, but this figure includes a mere fraction of the number of longshoremen, most of whom reported their occupations as laborers.

64. Albion, *Rise of New York Port*, p. 223.

65. Computed from data in the MSS schedules of the *New York State Census of 1855*.

66. *Ibid*. This large proportion of Irish laborers was insignificant, however, when compared with the Irish laborers who comprised 48 per cent of the Irish working population of Boston in 1850. Cf. Handlin, *op. cit.*, Appendix, p. 240, Table XV. Whereas in Boston poor transportation facilities immobilized the laborer, New York's geographical situation enhanced his dispersion; moreover, New York's varied industries and commercial activities and the heterogeneity of the population provided less of an economic and social barrier to Irish well-being than existed in Boston.

67. Computed from data in the MSS schedules of the *New York State Census of 1855*. Persons born in British North America, largely of Irish, English, and Scotch parentage, supplied 2 per cent, and those born in Poland 1.67 per cent of the laborers. *Ibid*.

68. *Ibid*.

69. For these farms, cf. *New York Farmer*, VII, 161, 193, 229 (June, July, August 1834); P. W. Bidwell and J. I. Falconer, *History of Agriculture in the Northern United States, 1620–1860* (Washington, 1925), pp. 228, 260–261; Stuart, *Three Years in North America*, II, 504–505, 509; *Courrier des États-Unis*, October 17, 1862 and advertisements: April 5, 16, 1862.

70. Knight, *Mechanic's and Labourer's Guide*, quoted in *Emigrant's Hand-Book and Guide to the United States; or England and America Contrasted* (London, n.d. [after April 1848]), pp. 16–17; Bidwell and Falconer, *op. cit.*, p. 275.

71. Bidwell and Falconer, *op. cit.*, p. 275.

72. Letter of Dr. D. W. Cahill in *Freeman's Journal*, March 31, 1860; Pound, *Golden Earth*, p. 201; Helen I. Cowan, "British Emigration to British North America, 1783–1837," University of Toronto *Studies; History and Economics*, IV, No. 2 (n.d., 1928), 123. In the mid-thirties the rapid development of Canadian land and resources resulted in the disappointment of prospective settlers looking for cheap land and dampened the sentimental preference of the English and Scotch for Canada. Nevertheless thousands continued to pass through New York *en route* to new homes in the West. Cf. Marcus L. Hansen, *Mingling of the Canadian and American Peoples* (New Haven, 1940), pp. 112–113; *Scottish Patriot*, June 6, 1840.

73. *New York Farmer*, VII (August, 1834), 225; [Isaac S. Lyon], *Recollections of an ex-Cartman* (Newark, 1872), p. 6.

74. MSS schedules of the *New York State Census of 1855*, remarks of James A. Baldwin, marshal of the Twelfth Ward, 4th election district. The printed summary of this census lists totals of 193 farmers and 644 "gardeners and florists" living on Manhattan Island. In the MSS schedules the author counted 108 foreign-born farmers and 592 gardeners and florists. Farmers and gardeners on Manhattan were but a fraction of those who worked in the vicinity of New York.

75. Thorburn, *Fifty Years' Reminiscences* . . . , p. 224; *Staats-Zeitung*, October 6, 1855; Wyse, *America, Its Realities and Resources* . . . , I, 42. In 1842 Orange Judd began publishing at New York a German edition of his *American Agriculturist*. Cf. advertisement in *Staats-Zeitung*, daily edition, July 1, 1858.

76. Historical Records Survey, *Inventory of Church Archives in New York City; The Lutherans* (New York, 1940), p. 28. Some of the Rockland County immigrants were comparatively wealthy. One of them erected a brewery on his farm, supplied beer to his local community, and made deliveries to New York. Another was prosperous enough to return to the city to run a hotel in Bleecker Street. Among the wealthier Germans living in the city, some owned farms upon which they passed their leisure

time as amateur farmers. *Criminal-Zeitung,* July 11, 1856. For advertisements of farms, cf., e.g., *Deutsche Schnellpost,* April 12, May 10, 1845.

77. Conclusions derived from data in the MSS schedules of the *New York State Census of 1855.* For the superiority of European gardeners, particularly Scots and Germans, cf. E. H. M. Cox, *History of Gardening in Scotland* (London, 1935), pp. 199–210; Colton, *op. cit.,* pp. 157–158; Thorburn, *Fifty Years' Reminiscences* . . . , p. 286; *Emigrant and Old Countryman,* November 25, 1835; A. B. Faust, *German Element in the United States* . . . (Boston, 1909), II, 62–63; Wittke, *op. cit.,* p. 398.

78. Knight, *Mechanic's and Labourer's Guide, loc. cit.,* pp. 16–17; Grant Thorburn, "Hints to Gardeners . . . ," in his *Forty Years' Residence in America* . . . , p. 249; Wyse, *op. cit.,* III, 53–54.

79. The products of the German market gardens in one section of upper Manhattan in 1855 were "barely Sufficient to pay Expences, and Support their families, Drough & Disease being the principal cause of failure. Some have abandoned their Gardens . . . others have a prospect of an Abundant Crop . . . [and a number] have turned their Attention to Gardning this Spring, & their prospects are verry encourageing." Comments of the marshal of the Twelfth Ward, 4th election district, in MSS schedules of the *New York State Census of 1855.*

80. Computed from data in the MSS schedules of the *New York State Census of 1855.* Two and eight-tenths per cent of the Irish and 2.65 per cent of the Welsh working people provided the largest national contingents of cartmen and teamsters. *Ibid.*

81. *Ibid.,* especially the Thirteenth and Sixteenth wards. Few Germans became coachmen. Cf. Appendix, pp. 214–217.

82. Computed from data in the MSS schedules of the *New York State Census of 1855.*

83. *Ibid.*

84. *Ibid.* These percentages apply only to persons who lived on Manhattan Island, but there is no reason to believe that the inclusion of Brooklyn, Williamsburg, and other nearby settlements would materially change the proportions.

85. *Ibid.* English and Scotch engineers, some of them operating steamboats, accounted for 12.8 and 11.3 per cent of the gainfully employed English and Scotch, respectively. *Ibid.*

86. Cf. [I. S. Lyon], *Recollections of an ex-Cartman,* pp. 6–7.

87. Computed from data in the MSS schedules of the *New York State Census of 1855.* Some 87,000 persons, of whom 67,000 were foreign-born, were engaged in the skilled and semi-skilled occupations.

88. Howitt, *Rural and Domestic Life of Germany* . . . , pp. 54–57; Herbert Heaton, *Economic History of Europe* (New York, 1936), pp. 335–340; Hansen, *Atlantic Migration,* pp. 220, 222, 225, 239–241. In village and farm households, women spun hemp or flax, and knitted stockings, and children helped in the domestic chores. Howitt, *op. cit.,* pp. 27, 91.

89. Heaton, *op. cit.,* p. 344; MSS schedules of the *New York State Census of 1855.* Cf. Appendix, pp. 214–217. For advertisements of surgical instrument makers, cf., e.g., *Staats-Zeitung,* January 4, 1837, January 7, 1843.

90. *Dictionary of American Biography,* VIII, 596–597.

91. Cf., e.g., advertisements in *Courrier des États-Unis,* January 10, 1829, December 15, 1830, May 9, 1832, April 2, 1834; *Redactor,* July 20, 1829; Moses Y. Beach, *Wealth and Biography of the Wealthy Citizens of the City of New York* (13th ed.; New York, 1855), pp. 31, 57; Haswell, *Reminiscences of New York by an Octogenarian,* p. 270.

92. MSS schedules of the *New York State Census of 1855.*

93. Cf. Heaton, *op. cit.,* pp. 343–352; *Clark, History of Manufactures* . . . , I, 399–400; Wittke, *op. cit.,* pp. 237–238, 392–401.

Chapter VII

1. *Irish American,* November 20, 1852, but cf. the issue of January 1, 1853.

2. *Citizen,* May 23, 1857, which printed a translation of an undated *Staats-Zeitung* article not preserved in the *Staats-Zeitung* file at the New York Public Library.

3. Computed from data in the MSS schedules of the *New York State Census of 1855.* Cf. Appendix, pp. 214–218.

4. *Ibid.* Cf. A.I.C.P., *Ninth Annual Report,* 1852, p. 22; *Irish American,* March 25, November 20, 1852, May 7, 1854; *Citizen,* May 23, 1857.

5. Computed from data in the MSS schedules of the *New York State Census of 1855.*

6. *Ibid.*

7. *Ibid.* Carpentry claimed nearly 8 per cent of the gainfully employed British North Americans, 6.25 per cent of the Scotch, 4.5 per cent of the English, and 4.33 per cent of the Scandinavians, whereas less than 3 per cent of the Irish and German working-men, respectively, were carpenters. The leadership of the Scots is shown by the fact that 12 per cent of all the immigrant stonecutters and polishers, 13 per cent of the plumbers, and 4 per cent of the painters were born in Scotland, yet there was only one Scotch worker for every twenty-two Irish or every eleven German. *Ibid.* The presence of so many Scottish stonecutters may be explained, perhaps, by the prevalence of stone houses in barren parts of Scotland.

8. The building trades claimed 8.6 per cent of the gainfully employed Scandinavians, 7.1 per cent of the Italians, 6.95 per cent of the Swiss, 6.8 per cent of the Dutch, 6.5 per cent of the Poles (including a number of Jews), 5 per cent of the French, and a smattering of others. *Ibid.*

9. MSS schedules of the *New York State Census of 1855,* "Manufactures," and re-marks of the marshal of the Ninth Ward, 2d election district. Many sawyers lived in the Eleventh Ward, where they were employed in sawing logs and timber in the ship-yards. Some four hundred sawyers plied their calling in this area and across the river in Brooklyn and Williamsburg. *Daily Tribune,* April 19, 1850.

10. For American techniques, cf. Peter Nicholson, *Mechanic's Companion* (Phila-delphia, 1863), which used the terminology of the building trades in London. German masons criticized native methods of masonry but were warned by a fellow German to follow American techniques. C. L. Fleischmann, *Erwerbzweige . . . ,* p. 216.

11. Cf. Wyse, *America, Its Realities and Resources . . . ,* III, 11, 18.

12. Cf. *Register of the St. Andrew's Society of the State of New York* (three pam-phlets, n.p., 1922–1923) Second Series, Part II, pp. 38, 40, 50, 58, 61.

13. *Ibid.,* p. 38; Beach, *Wealth and Biography of the Wealthy Citizens of the City of New York* (13th ed., New York, 1855), p. 51.

14. Cf., e.g., *Who's Who in New York City and State* (1st ed.; New York, 1904), p. 386; Beach, *op. cit.* (6th ed.; New York, 1845), p. 26. Information about con-tractors during the pre-Civil War period is meager. The MSS schedules of the *New York State Census of 1855,* Manufactures: Twelfth, Sixteenth, Eighteenth, and Twenty-first wards, contain data for William H. Hanlon, Edward Riley, and Dennis Henessey, all contractors, and for the marble works of Robert Cahill, Boyle and Lander, "Michel" Rigney, and John Meighan. I was unable to ascertain the birthplaces of these men, but their names indicate that some of them probably were born in Ireland.

15. Cf. *Citizen,* May 23, 1857, which printed a translation of a *Staats-Zeitung* article no longer available. Cf. *supra,* n. 2. From the MSS schedules of the *New York State Census of 1855,* I tabulated 300 builders and contractors. Of these, 207 were born in Ireland, 47 in England, 17 in Germany, 14 in Scotland, and the remaining 15 in France, Canada, Wales, Italy, Portugal, Spain, and the Netherlands. Cf. Appendix, pp. 214–218.

16. Computed from data in the MSS schedules of the *New York State Census of 1855.* Cf. Appendix, pp. 214–218.

17. Claghorn, "Foreign Labor in the Clothing Trade," *United States Industrial Commission Reports*, XV, 324; Hourwich, *Immigration and Labor*, p. 364.

18. Jesse E. Pope, *Clothing Industry in New York* (Columbia, Mo., 1905), p. 27. Cutters and foremen were directors of the industry next in rank to the manufacturers. *Ibid.*

19. *Ibid.*

20. Cf. St. Matthew's Lutheran Church, *Marriage Records,* 1833–1836.

21. *Staats-Zeitung,* July 14, 1849; Griesinger, *Freiheit und Sclaverei* . . . , pp. 268–269.

22. Griesinger, *Lebende Bilder* . . . , p. 286; Claghorn. "Foreign Labor in the Clothing Trade," *loc. cit.,* p. 324.

23. Claghorn, "Foreign Labor in the Clothing Trade," *loc. cit.,* p. 324; cf. Pope, *op. cit.,* p. 27.

24. Computed from data in the MSS schedules of the *New York State Census of 1855.* The Germans also were strongest among the hatters, furriers, and clothiers, but the Irish retained their hold on dressmaking. *Ibid.* Cf. Griesinger, *Lebende Bilder* . . . , p. 40; [James D. Burn], *Three Years Among the Working-Classes* . . . , p. 184; *Courrier des États-Unis,* March 8, 1864.

25. Computed from data in the MSS schedules of the *New York State Census of 1855.* The German tailors, of course, included "tailoresses," who were considered in this computation. Although there was probably considerable overlapping of functions, I thought it better not to include "seamstresses" and "dressmakers." Cf. Appendix, pp. 214–218.

26. Fleischmann, *op. cit.,* p. 334; Pope, *op. cit.,* p. 27.

27. Grinstein, *Rise of the Jewish Community* . . . , pp. 127–128; Max J. Kohler, "German-Jewish Migration to America," American Jewish Historical Society *Publications,* No. 9, 1901, pp. 87–105. According to Kohler, restrictions on the marriage and the commerce of the Jews led to the migrations of the late thirties. *Ibid.,* p. 96. For Polish Jews, cf. *Freeman's Journal,* December 13, 1845.

28. Computed from data in the MSS schedules of the *New York State Census of 1855.* Nearly all the immigrants from Poland were Jewish, and at least one tenth—probably many more—of those from Germany were also Jews. Unfortunately for the student of immigration, neither state nor federal census tabulated Jews as such. However, when searching the MSS schedules of the 1855 census, I tabulated separately those natives of Germany and Poland whose complete names seemed obviously Jewish. All others were excluded from this tabulation. I was aware of the pitfalls of judging race or nationality upon the basis of names, and it seemed preferable, therefore, to err conservatively by excluding immigrants who probably were but might not have been Jews.

29. MSS schedules of the *New York State Census of 1855.* Cf. Appendix, pp. 214–218. For Russian Jews, cf. J. D. Eisenstein, "The History of the First Russian-American Jewish Congregation," American Jewish Historical Society *Publications,* No. 9, 1901, pp. 63–74.

30. Claghorn, "Foreign Labor in the Clothing Trade," *op. cit.,* p. 325.

31. Citizens' Association, *Report of the Council of Hygiene,* p. 77; D. T. Valentine, *Manual of the Corporation of the City of New York* (New York, 1843), p. 268.

32. Handlin, *Boston's Immigrants* . . . , p. 83.

33. MSS schedules of the *New York State Census of 1855,* "Manufactures: Second, Third, Fourth, Fifth, Eighth, and Tenth wards."

34. *Ibid.,* Third Ward.

35. *Ibid.,* Fourth and Fifth wards. Brooks Brothers paid three hundred male operatives $25 and four hundred female workers $12; Hanford & Brothers paid its men $25 and its women $15, and although P. L. Rogers paid men $48, the women received only $15. *Ibid.,* Second and Seventh wards.

36. One exceptional instance was the payment of an average of $25 per month to three thousand women making ladies' and children's clothing for S. Chambers. These women probably were more skilled than most of the female tailors. *Ibid.,* Fifth Ward.

37. John R. Commons, "American Shoemakers 1648–1895. A Sketch of Industrial Evolution," *Quarterly Journal of Economics,* XXIV, No. 1 (November, 1909), 72. Most of the inventions before the Civil War were aids rather than substitutes for skill. The slow development of factory production was accelerated only by the adoption of the pegging machine in 1857 and the McKay sole-sewing machine in 1862. *Ibid.,* pp. 72–73; cf. Ware, *Industrial Worker,* 1840–1860, p. 38.

38. Commons, "American Shoemakers . . . ," *op. cit.,* p. 62. Although some entrepreneurs "put out" material to journeymen working in their homes, others began to employ the men in their warehouses as cutters, fitters, and pattern makers. *Ibid.* cf. Fleischmann, *op. cit.,* pp. 341–345.

39. By mid-century, immigrant tanners, curriers, harness makers, trunk makers, pocketbook makers, patent leather and morocco workers, in addition to the far more numerous boot- and shoemakers, swelled the number of artisans in "the largest emporium of foreign hides in the world." MSS schedules of the *New York State Census of 1855* (cf. Appendix, pp. 214–218); James L. Bishop, *History of American Manufactures* (3d ed., Philadelphia, 1868), II, 425; Fleischmann, *op. cit.,* p. 90; [C. S. Flint *et al.*], *Eighty Years' Progress . . . ,* I, 317, 324. The leather districts coincided geographically with the shoe districts. Cf. chapter iv, p. 38. For the New England boot and shoe industry, cf. Blanche E. Hazard, *Organization of the Boot and Shoe Industry in Massachusetts before 1875* (Cambridge, Mass., 1921), and for immigrants in the shoe industry at Boston, cf. Handlin, *op. cit.,* pp. 79–80.

40. Chamber of Commerce of the State of New York, *Fourth Annual Report,* 1861–1862, pp. 201–202.

41. *Young America,* October 18, 1845, which estimated the number of shoemakers in the city at 2,000. The *Daily Tribune,* September 5, 1845, gave the exaggerated figures of 5,000 to 6,000, which have been accepted by Ware (*Industrial Worker,* p. 45). Unless the *Tribune's* figure included the entire metropolitan area, including Brooklyn and Williamsburg, its inaccuracy is evident. The *New York State Census of 1855* (p. 179) listed 6,745 boot- and shoemakers, a figure which included many immigrants who settled in the city between 1845 and 1855. Such a small increase as 700 or even 1,700 in that decade seems quite unlikely. I have raised the estimate of *Young America* by a full third to account for a maximum number of entrepreneurs, contractors, masters, etc.

42. MSS schedules of the *New York State Census of 1855.* Cf. Appendix, pp. 214–217.

43. Computed from data in the MSS schedules of the *New York State Census of 1855.* Cf. Appendix, pp. 214–217.

44. *Young America,* October 18, 1845.

45. *Daily Tribune,* September 9, 1845; Ware, *op. cit.,* p. 45.

46. Griesinger, *Freiheit und Sclaverei . . . ,* p. 269.

47. *Tribune,* May 3, 1853, Cf. [Flint *et al.*], *op. cit.,* I, 324.

48. *Young America,* October 18, 1845; *Daily Tribune,* May 7, 1853; Ware. *op. cit.,* p. 46.

49. *Staats-Zeitung,* May 6, 1854; Paul L. Vogt, *Sugar Refining Industry in the United States* (Philadelphia, 1908), p. 6. Vogt treats the development of the industry in New York but does not mention the role of the Germans.

50. *Staats-Zeitung,* May 6, 1854. Of the 38 refineries in the United States in 1831, 11 were in New York City and 8 in Buffalo; 11 were in Philadelphia, 3 in Boston, and 3 in New Orleans. Sugar boiling was a highly skilled operation until about 1840. Vogt, *op. cit.,* p. 14.

51. Bishop, *op. cit.,* II, 359–360, 532, 594; III, 151, 153; Flick [ed.], *History of the State of New York* (New York, 1933–1937), VI, 233–234.

52. *Staats-Zeitung,* May 6, 1854, which states that 1,500 persons were employed by these companies. The industrial statistics of the state census of 1855 showed 1,628 employees in 14 sugar and syrup refineries. (Printed summary, p. 356.) These were not only sugar refiners but employees of all kinds. Although the printed summary of the census listed only 132 "sugar refiners," a search of the MSS schedules disclosed 360 for-

eign-born "sugar bakers" and "sugar refiners," of whom 265 were born in Germany. Some of them may have been confectioners, but most undoubtedly were skilled employees in refineries. MSS schedules of the *New York State Census of 1855*. Cf. Appendix, pp. 214–217.

53. For German cabinetmakers in 1835, cf. St. Matthew's Lutheran Church, *Marriage Records,* 1833–1836, now in the library of the New York Historical Society; Christoph Vetter, *Zwei Jahre in New-York* . . . (Hof, Bavaria, 1849), p. 156; Traugott Bromme, *Nordamerika's Bewohner* . . . (Stuttgart, 1839), p. 275. The *Daily Tribune,* April 26, 1850, estimated at two thousand the number of German cabinetmakers in the city.

54. Computed from data in the MSS schedules of the *New York State Census of 1855*. Cf. Appendix, pp. 214–217. Likewise, nearly two thirds of the foreign-born wood turners, ornamental carvers and gilders were Germans. *Ibid.* In 1850 the German joiners' association, with a thousand members, was the largest trade union in the city. *Daily Tribune,* May 23, 1850.

55. *Young America,* February 14, 1846.

56. *Prose Works of N. P. Willis* (Philadelphia, 1855), p. 691. The well known cabinetmaker, Duncan Phyfe, was forced to lower his standards of workmanship by the competition of what he called "butcher furniture" after 1830. Cf. Walter A. Dyer, *Early American Craftsmen* (New York, 1915), p. 57. Some Gallic cabinetmakers grew rich upon the vogue of things French, and one Henry Bruner achieved the honor of a place in Moses Beach's catalogue of wealthy citizens, Beach, *op. cit.* (13th ed.; New York, 1855), p. 16.

57. *Young America,* February 14, 1846.

58. Based upon figures of $30 to $40 per month from data for twenty-two wards, MSS schedules of the *New York State Census of 1855,* "Manufactures." By 1860 most of the shops were in the area between Canal and Grand Streets on the south and 14th Street on the north. In the eastern part of this area, comprising the Eleventh, Thirteenth, and Seventeenth wards, many Germans were among the 1,092 individuals working in 70 chair and cabinet furniture shops. The Eighth Ward on the West Side, however, included 31 plants employing 742 cabinetmakers. Chamber of Commerce of the State of New York, *Fourth Annual Report,* 1861–1862, p. 205. Cf. *Daily Tribune,* April 25, 1860; Citizens' Association, *Report of the Council of Hygiene* . . . , p. 40.

59. MSS schedules of the *New York State Census of 1855,* "Manufactures"; Eleventh Ward (5th election district), Fifth Ward (3d election district), and Seventeenth Ward (4th election district).

60. Daniel Spillane, *History of the American Pianoforte* . . . (New York, 1890), pp. 70, 101–102.

61. *Ibid.,* p. 104. German piano makers predominated in Baltimore and showed strength in Philadelphia, two other cities with sizable German populations. Cf. Fleischmann, *op. cit.,* pp. 361–364.

62. Spillane, *op. cit.,* p. 156.

63. *Ibid.,* pp. 188, 201.

64. By 1840, 38 per cent of all pianos made in the United States were produced in the Empire City. Flick (ed.), *History of the State of New York,* VI, 213–214. After the middle of the century, several of the leading New York piano firms were conducted by Germans, but in Boston, where Jonas Chickering held sway, the Germans made considerably less headway. Cf. Handlin, *op. cit.,* p. 88.

65. Spillane, *op. cit.,* pp. 189, 235, 290, 292–293, 312–313. Frederick Mathusek, born in Mannheim in 1814 and trained in the best shops of Germany, Russia, Austria, and France, came to New York after the revolutions of 1848 and figured prominently in the industry for the next forty years. The Bavarian, Albert Weber, arrived in New York at the age of sixteen and six years later, in 1852, founded the famous house of Weber. Another expert piano maker, George Steck, emigrated from Hesse-Cassel, landed at New York in 1853, and developed a prosperous business. The best known of these German piano makers was Henry Englehard Steinway, born in a little village in the Harz

mountains, who in 1853 rented a small rear building in Varick Street and produced square pianos at the rate of one a week. The Steinway firm soon moved to larger quarters in Walker Street, and in 1859 bought an entire block on Lexington Avenue between 52nd and 53rd streets, where a new building was erected. *Ibid.*, pp. 227, 228, 235; Lossing, *History of New York City,* pp. 680–682.

66. MSS schedules of the *New York State Census of 1855,* "Manufactures," especially the Fourteenth Ward, 4th election district. The firm of A. H. Gale employed 110 men and turned out 650 pianos every year, and Jno. B. Dunham engaged 102 men to produce 600 pianos yearly. At this time Steinway & Sons was still a small company employing only 30 men. *Ibid.*, Seventeenth Ward, 8th election district, and Fourteenth Ward, 6th election district.

67. MSS schedules of the *New York State Census of 1855,* "Manufactures." It is difficult to determine exactly what each "piano maker" did; in addition to his knowledge of cabinetmaking, he underwent some degree of specialized training. The type of specialization varied. The firm of William Muller, for example, employed ten men at $45 to make piano cases alone, and A. E. Brooks paid sixty men $39 apiece to make piano legs. *Ibid.* Eighteenth Ward, 2d and 3d election districts.

68. Computed from data in the MSS schedules of the *New York State Census of 1855.* Cf. Appendix, pp. 214–217.

69. *Ibid.; Young America,* December 6, 1845; in 1845 a few individuals "owned" nearly all the manufacturing plants; the "boss" owned the looms and fixtures, bought the materials, rented the workshops—usually cellars—and employed the journeymen at piece work. Weavers, working twelve hours a day in winter and ten in summer, earned an average of $4 a week. *Ibid.*

70. MSS schedules of the *New York State Census of 1855.* Cf. Appendix, pp. 214–217.

71. *Ibid.*

72. *Young America,* Oct. 25, 1845.

73. *Ibid.*

74. *Ibid.*

75. Cf. pp. 145–146.

76. *Young America,* September 13, 1845, which estimated the foreigners at not less than 16 per cent.

77. MSS schedules of the *New York State Census of 1855.* Cf. Appendix, pp. 214–217.

78. Computed from data in the MSS schedules of the *New York State Census of 1855.* Slightly more than 5 per cent of the British North Americans and 4.5 per cent of the French entered these occupations. Cf. Appendix, pp. 214–217.

79. In 1855, 1.5 per cent of the Irish working population were blacksmiths. (Many Germans also were blacksmiths.) Among the more skilled, 3.67 per cent of the gainfully employed Scots and 2 per cent of the English were machinists, and 2.67 per cent of the Welsh were molders. German machinists, locksmiths, and tinsmiths, comprising 1.75 per cent of the German working population, applied the technical skills they had acquired in Europe. *Ibid.*

80. Cf. Citizens' Association, *op. cit.,* pp. 27, 105, 174.

81. Albion, *Rise of New York Port,* p. 149; MSS schedules of the *New York State Census of 1855,* Manufactures, Seventh Ward; Bishop, *op. cit.,* II, 262–263, III, 125. Until after the Civil War New York's eminence in the marine engine and boiler industry was surpassed only by Glasgow, Scotland. Cf. Albion, *op. cit.,* p. 148.

82. In the middle of the century the Novelty works, which stretched from 12th to 14th streets, employed over 1,000 men, including 359 machinists, 248 iron founders, and 242 boilermakers, who received an average of $1.50 for a long day's work. Albion, *op. cit.,* p. 150.

83. MSS schedules of the *New York State Census of 1855,* "Manufactures." There were, of course, shipyards across the East River; in 1855, 31 ship building establishments in New York and Kings Counties (including Brooklyn and Williamsburg) employed over 2,300 hands. In addition, 65 plants were engaged in sailmaking, sparmaking, rigging,

blockmaking, "shipsmithing," boatbuilding, "steamboat finishing," and the making of tree-nails, blocks, capstans, and windlasses. Albion, *op. cit.*, p. 300.

84. Albion, *op. cit.*, p. 302; MSS schedules of the *New York State Census of 1855,* remarks of the marshal of the Seventh Ward.

85. MSS schedules of the *New York State Census of 1855.* Cf. Appendix, pp. 214–218.

86. *Ibid.* Most of the Scandinavians in these trades were riggers (6 per cent) and ship carpenters (2.7 per cent); some 4.5 per cent of the natives of British North America were ship carpenters, joiners, mast- and sparmakers. *Ibid.* Sawyers, mostly Irish and German, were not included in this computation because many were not involved in shipbuilding. Allowance must also be made for the fact that in dull seasons some house carpenters worked on ships.

87. Ware, *op. cit.*, p. 26.

88. *Ibid.*, pp. 31–34; *Daily Tribune,* November 14, 1850 (cf. *ibid.*, May 14, 1850); John R. Commons *et al., History of Labour in the United States* (New York, 1918–1935), I, 487. The retail prices of foodstuffs during the seven years from 1848 to 1854 were tabulated in the *Daily Tribune,* February 21, 1854, and are reprinted in Ware, *op. cit.*, p. 31. For wage rates and wholesale prices, cf. data on New York City establishments in the Aldrich Report: "Wholesale Prices, Wages, and Transportation," United States, *Senate Reports,* 52d Congress, 2d Session, No. 1394 (Washington, 1893).

89. Adapted from the yearly budget printed in the *Times.* November 8, 1853. The *Tribune,* May 27, 1851, printed a budget for one week for a family of five: expenses amounted to $10.37.

90. *Daily Tribune,* February 21, 1854; *Irish American,* December 23, 1854; *Citizen,* December 23, 1854, January 20, February 3, 1855; Booth, *History of the City of New York,* II, 756–757.

91. Schneider, *History of Public Welfare in New York State . . . ,* p. 269.

92. From 1861 to the end of 1863 the average wage increase in all trades was about 25 per cent, or less than half the increase of prices. E. D. Fite, *Social and Industrial Conditions in the North during the Civil War* (New York, 1910), p. 184.

93. *Ibid.*, p. 185.

Chapter VIII

1. M. J. Becker, *Germans of 1849 in America* (Mt. Vernon, Ohio, 1887), p. 43.

2. Colton, *Manual for Emigrants . . . ,* p. 63; *Young America,* November 1, 1845.

3. *Young America,* November 1, 1845.

4. This percentage has been computed upon the basis of tabulations of immigrant peddlers from the manuscript returns of the state census marshals in 1855. I assumed, on the basis of names, that all of the 54 Polish peddlers and half of the 941 German, 51 English, 32 French, and 12 Dutch peddlers were Jewish. These nationalities, together with the Irish, comprised all but 25 of the 1,843 immigrant peddlers for whom information was available. A total of 570 peddlers thus appears to have been Jewish. Of the Jewish population of New York City in 1855, estimated at 30,000 (cf. Grinstein, *Rise of the Jewish Community . . . ,* p. 469), 45 per cent, or 13,500 were assumed to be gainfully employed. Of these, the 570 peddlers comprise 4.22 per cent. Undoubtedly some Jews with less characteristic names have been excluded from this computation; yet even if all the immigrant peddlers for whom information was available, except the Irish, were considered to be Jews, they would represent only 8 per cent of the Jewish working population.

5. Cf. Grinstein, *op. cit.*, p. 129. Grinstein argues: "If these men had known any craft, they would at least have attempted to follow their vocations. Since they did not do so, we may assume that they had no training in any craft whatever." *Ibid.*

6. Letter from Dr. Waterman, *Asmonean,* May 4, 1855. For an Irishman's opinion of German and Jewish peddlers, cf. the letter from Michael Coogan, *Irish American,* July 20, 1853.

7. Grinstein, *op. cit.*, p. 411; cf. Max J. Kohler, "German-Jewish Migration to America," American Jewish Historical Society *Publication* No. 9, 1901, pp. 96–97.

8. J. D. Eisenstein, "The History of the First Russian-American Jewish Congregation," American Jewish Historical Society *Publication* No. 9, 1901, pp. 68, 72.

9. Cf. Citizens' Association, *Report of the Council of Hygiene*, pp. 292–293; Löher, *Geschichte und Zustände der Deutschen in Amerika*, p. 299; MSS schedules of the *New York State Census of 1855;* "Seventeenth Ward, 7th election district; Twenty-second Ward, 3d election district"; Children's Aid Society, *Fourth Annual Report*, 1857, pp. 15–16; Charlotte Adams, "Italian Life in New York," *Harper's Magazine*, LXII (April, 1881), 677–680.

10. Griscom, *Sanitary Condition of the Laboring Population of New York*, p. 39 (n.); A.I.C.P., *Twelfth Annual Report*, 1855, p. 41; Löher, *op. cit.*, p. 299.

11. Children's Aid Society, *Fourth Annual Report*, 1857, pp. 15–16, *Tenth Annual Report*, 1863, p. 28; Brace, *Dangerous Classes of New York* . . . , pp. 194–196; Giovanni Schiavo, *Italians in America before the Civil War* (New York, 1934), pp. 203–204; Foerster, *Italian Emigration of Our Times*, p. 323.

12. Lane, *American Charities and the Child of the Immigrant* . . . , pp. 10–11.

13. MSS schedules of the *New York State Census of 1855;* D. T. Valentine, *Manual of the Corporation of the City of New York*, for 1843–1844, p. 268.

14. They also sold cheap new clothing which was thrown on the market by jobbers and was destined for the South and West. Pope, *Clothing Industry in New York*, pp. 6–8; Griesinger, *Freiheit und Sclaverei* . . . , p. 266. Some Irish also dealt in secondhand clothing. MSS schedules of the *New York State Census of 1855*, "Twentieth Ward, 2d election district."

15. Valentine, *op. cit.*, p. 267.

16. MSS schedules of the *New York State Census of 1855*, Cf. Appendix, p. 218.

17. Griesinger, *op. cit.*, p. 265.

18. In 1855 twenty of the twenty-four groceries in the 5th election district of the Tenth Ward sold liquor, while the marshal of the 2d election district of the Nineteenth Ward remarked: "Almost every grocery retails liquor." MSS schedules of the *New York State Census of 1855*.

19. Thomas L. Nichols, *Forty Years of American Life* (new ed.; New York, 1937), I, 390; cf. Löher, *op. cit.*, p. 299.

20. Griesinger, *op. cit.*, p. 265.

21. *Young America*, February 7, 1846, noted that the butchers seldom acted together to advance their interests. In 1837 they complained of too many middlemen in the cattle market and resolved not to pay the prevailing high prices for cattle at the Bull's Head market, but apparently their efforts were unsuccessful. *Staats-Zeitung*, March 9, October 4, 1837.

22. *Young America*, February 7, 1846.

23. *Ibid.*

24. *Ibid.*

25. *Ibid.;* computation from data in the MSS schedules of the *New York State Census of 1855*.

26. MSS schedules of the *New York State Census of 1855*. Nearly 3.5 per cent of the foreign-born working population dealt in foods. Cf. pp. 214–218.

27. Advertisements, e.g.: *Staats-Zeitung*, May 17, 1837; daily ed.: April 30, May 1, 1856; *Criminal-Zeitung*, March 17, 1854; *Handels-Zeitung*, daily ed.: October 31, 1857; *Courrier des États-Unis*, March 22, 1828, January 21, 1841, January 6, 1860; *Eco d'Italia*, January 7, 1865.

28. *Staats-Zeitung*, September 16, 1854.

29. *Eco d'Italia*, January 7, 1865.

30. *Courrier des États-Unis*, January 10, 1829.

31. *Criminal-Zeitung*, March 17, 1854; *Staats-Zeitung*, daily ed.: May 1, 1856.

32. *Eco d'Italia*, March 18, 1865.

33. To this figure must be added nearly 500 German confectioners and sugar refiners. MSS schedules of the *New York State Census of 1855*. Cf. Appendix, pp. 214–217. In 1834 the 300 members of the Bakers' Trades Union Society, comprising nearly all the bakers in the city, earned $7 and $8 a week. By the middle of the century the eighteen to twenty-hour day had been reduced to sixteen and eighteen hours, but wages remained the same and working conditions were notoriously unpleasant. *Man*, June 9, 10, 1834; *Staats-Zeitung*, May 18, 1850; *Tribune*, April 25, May 23, 1850.

34. For advertisements of bakers and butchers, cf., e.g., *Jewish Messenger*, July 3, September 11, 25, 1857. Much of the bakers' matzoths was shipped to other points; for the example cited, cf. Jacob R. Marcus (compiler), *Index to Americana in Foreign-Jewish Periodicals*, II, 342.

35. Computed from data in the MSS schedules of the *New York State Census of 1855*. Cf. Appendix, pp. 214–217.

36. Cf. advertisements, e.g., *Courrier des États-Unis*, March 9, July 19, 1828, June 15, 1836; November 12, 1840, January 3, 1850; *Phare de New-York*, May 10, 1851; *Républicain*, May 7, 1853; cf. Maugé, *Directory Française passim*.

37. *Courrier des États-Unis*, advertisements: January 7, 1835, June 15, 1836, November 17, 1840; Haswell, *Reminiscences of New York by an Octogenarian*, pp. 388–389.

38. *Courrier des États-Unis*, June 1, 1848.

39. *Dictionary of American Biography*, V, 226–227.

40. This was the National Hotel, *Courrier des États-Unis*, May 25, 1831. For other French pensions and hotels, cf. *ibid.*, advertisements, e.g., June 19, 1830, April 23, 1840, March 19, 1850, January 3, 1853, February 20, 1856, February 1, 1865.

41. *Staats-Zeitung*, June 23, 1855.

42. Anon., *Winke über Auswanderung besonders nach Nord-Amerika* (Zwickau, 1849), pp. 24–26; cf. *Staats-Zeitung*, March 22, May 10, 1837.

43. *Winke über Auswanderung . . .* , pp. 24–26; *Staats-Zeitung*, June 23, 1855.

44. *Winke über Auswanderung . . .* , pp. 24–25.

45. The Hotel Dietz, formerly the Prescott House, at Broadway and Spring Street; Held's Hotel at the corner of Bayard Street and the Bowery; the Hotel Jegel at 47 Barclay Street; Bühler's Hotel, formerly the St. Louis, at the corner of Chambers and Church Streets; and the Hotel Konstanz, 218 William Street. *Staats-Zeitung*, June 23, 1855. Cf. *Handels-Zeitung*, July 17, September 19, 1855; [J. H. Kleefisch], *Die Stadt New York und Umgebung* (New York, 1858), p. 31.

46. *Truth Teller*, March 17, 1832; cf. *European*, September 4, 1836.

47. *Irish American*, December 7, 1850.

48. *Irish American*, January 11, March 29, 1851.

49. *Truth Teller*, January 26, 1833; *Plebeian*, November 10, 18, 1843.

50. *Albion*, May 15, August 21, 1830; *Old Countryman*, August 18, 1831, January 1, 1834; *Scottish Journal of Intelligence and Literature*, April 23, 1842. Most of the wealthier British visitors stayed at American hotels.

51. In 1856 this hotel, hardly more than a boardinghouse, was at 110 Bleecker Street. *Asmonean*, April 25, 1856; cf. *Jewish Messenger*, advertisements, July 3, 1857.

52. *Crónica*, October 27, 1849, April 27, 1850, May 27, 1858, January 14, 1863; *Continental*, October 11, 1862; *Guia de Nueva York y los Estados Unidos . . .* (New York, 1856), p. 152.

53. *Eco d'Italia*, April 5, 1862, January 7, 1865. At the same time two Negro hotels advertised in the Negro press. These were the Globe and the Empire State. *Anglo African*, January 3, 1863.

54. After 1839 licenses were not granted to aliens for taverns and liquor stores. *Revised Ordinances of the Mayor, Aldermen and Commonalty* (New York, 1856), p. 516; *Staats-Zeitung*, November 23, 1850; MSS schedules of the *New York State Census of 1855*. After enumerating stores, groceries, and taverns, one census marshal commented: "This does not include all the drinking holes in the District by a long shot but I

cannot call them Inns or Taverns." *Ibid.*, remarks of the marshal of the Fourteenth Ward, 3d election district.

55. *Staats-Zeitung,* November 23, 1850, March 22, 1851; cf. *Irish News,* May 9, 1857.

56. MSS schedules of the *New York State Census of 1855.* Cf. Appendix, pp. 214–217.

57. *Staats-Zeitung,* April 21, 1855.

58. *Ibid.; Criminal-Zeitung,* May 25, 1855.

59. *Albion,* April 21, 1855; *Daily Tribune,* April 4, May 11, 1855.

60. *Staats-Zeitung,* May 26, July 7, 1855; *Handels-Zeitung,* May 2, 1855; *Progrès,* April 14, 1855. Cf. *Staats-Zeitung,* daily ed.: October 17, 19, 22, and 27, 1853. The state law of 1855 was declared unconstitutional in the following year. Cf. John P. Arnold and Frank Penman, *History of the Brewing Industry and Brewing Science in America* (Chicago, 1933), p. 161.

61. For early German breweries, cf. advertisements in *Staats-Zeitung,* January 4, 1837, December 18, 1839, August 3, 1842.

62. Arnold and Penman, *op. cit.*, pp. 57, 61, 76, 192, 196 ff; [F. & M. Schaefer Brewing Co.], *Our One Hundredth Year,* 1842–1942 (New York, 1942), *passim.* In 1855, 60 per cent of all the foreign-born brewers and distillers came from Germany. Nearly all the Germans were brewers, while the Irish and French usually were distillers. MSS schedules of the *New York State Census of 1855.* Cf. Appendix, pp. 214–217.

63. Büchele, *Land und Volk der Vereinigten Staaten von Nord-Amerika,* p. 429; Arnold and Penman, *op. cit.*, p. 77.

64. Hermann Schlüter, *Brewing Industry and the Brewery Workers' Movement in America* (Cincinnati, 1910), pp. 92, 96.

65. Cf., e.g., Frederick Schaefer, who was employed in Sebastian Sommers' brewery, and John Eichler, who was Jacob Ruppert's brewmaster; these two men later went into business for themselves. Arnold and Penman, *op. cit.*, pp. 192, 225; Otto Spengler, *Das deutsche Element der Stadt New York* (New York, 1913), p. 33.

66. Schlüter, *op. cit.*, pp. 90–91, 93–94. The census statistics of the pre-Civil War period did not discriminate as to the types of brewery workers, and wages of foremen, office workers, and laborers were lumped together. *Ibid.*, p. 91.

67. *Ibid.*, pp. 92–93.

68. Cf. advertisements in *Staats-Zeitung,* December 18, 1839, January 7, 1843.

69. When wages rose during the Civil War, some brewery owners discontinued boarding their men, paid them $40 or $45 per month, and directed them to particular boardinghouses. Schlüter, *op. cit.*, p. 93.

70. Each member was entitled to one vote, except persons holding ten shares, who had two votes. Profits and losses were to be equally divided. Of the two hundred shares offered at $50 each, sixty were sold in a brief burst of enthusiasm, but apparently nothing further came of the scheme. *Tribune,* July 12, 15, 20, 1850.

71. MSS schedules of the *New York State Census of 1855.* Cf. Appendix, pp. 214–217.

72. Jacob H. Hollander and George E. Barnett [eds.], *Studies in American Trade Unionism* (New York, 1912), p. 47; Fleischmann, *op. cit.*, pp. 86–87. Most cigar makers, however, failed to better themselves. *Ibid.*, p. 87.

73. The *Deutsche Tabak-Fabrik* in Chrystie Street, established by Welle and Mayer in 1843, prospered for a decade in the preparation of smoking and chewing tobacco and snuff. Cf. advertisement in *Criminal-Zeitung,* March 17, 1854. A minimum of $2,500 was required to open a sizable tobacco business. Fleischmann, *op. cit.*, p. 87.

74. *Irish American,* May 1, 1852.

75. MSS schedules of the *New York State Census of 1855.* The use of the word "manufacturer" was quite arbitrary, however, and the immigrant's definition of his occupation usually was accepted. It is likely, therefore, that some "manufacturers" did not deserve that rank and that others, who in this study have been considered as "artisans" did a large enough business and employed enough men to warrant consideration as "manufacturers." Cf. Appendix, pp. 214–217.

76. For the Jews, cf. advertisements in *Asmonean,* October 26, November 2, 1849.

77. *Register of the St. Andrew's Society of the State of New York* (three pamphlets, n. p., 1922–23), Second Series, Parts I and II; Third Series; *passim.* The remaining five were manufacturers of looms, leather goods, earthenware, and white lead, and one shipbuilder. *Ibid.*

78. MSS schedules of the *New York State Census of 1855.*

79. *Ibid.*

80. MSS schedules of the *New York State Census of 1855,* "Manufactures: Seventh Ward, 6th election district; Sixteenth Ward, 5th election district; Twentieth Ward, 5th election district; Twenty-second Ward, 3d election district." Cf. the brewers, p. 91.

81. *Courrier des États-Unis,* June 7, 1853; *Tribune,* June 6, 1853.

82. *Asmonean,* March 12, 1858.

83. Beach, *op. cit.,* pp. 16, 57; *Register of the St. Andrew's Society* . . . Second Series, Part I, pp. 22, 24; Flick (ed.), *History of the State of New York,* VI, 196.

84. Beach, *op. cit.,* p. 58.

85. *Ibid.,* p. 52; Ross, *Scot in America,* p. 254; Dyer, *Early American Craftsmen,* p. 51.

86. Beach, *op. cit.,* pp. 26, 31, 40; [William Armstrong], *Aristocracy of New York* (New York, 1848), p. 10.

87. *Irish American,* January 22, 1853.

88. *Citizen,* December 9, 1854; MSS schedules of the *New York State Census of 1855,* "Manufactures, Sixteenth Ward, 3d election district."

89. A. B. Gold, "History of Manufacturing in New York City, 1825–1840" (unpublished master's thesis in Columbia University Library, 1932), pp. 44–45.

90. *Ibid.,* pp. 72–73. For further examples, cf. *ibid.,* p. 99, and Beach, *op. cit.,* p. 31.

91. *Register of the St. Andrew's Society* . . . , Second Series, Part I, pp. 22, 27, and Part II, pp. 45, 51, 52; Third Series, p. 8.

92. Albion, *Rise of New York Port,* p. 238; cf. [St. George's Society], *History of St. George's Society of New York from 1770 to 1913* ([New York], 1913), *passim;* Morrison, *History of Saint Andrew's Society* . . . , *passim.*

93. Morrison, *op. cit.,* p. 98.

94. Albion, *op. cit.,* pp. 238–239.

95. *Ibid.,* p. 239; Frances C. Childs, *French Refugee Life in the United States, 1790–1800* . . . (Baltimore, 1940), pp. 190–194.

96. Albion, *op. cit.,* pp. 239–240; [Oelrichs & Co.], *Caspar Meier and his Successors* . . . (New York, 1898), *passim;* Gustav Körner, *Das deutsche Element in den Vereinigten Staaten von Nordamerika, 1818–1848* (Cincinnati, 1880), pp. 102–103.

97. Körner, *op. cit.,* p. 113; *Encyclopedia of Contemporary Biography of New York* (New York, 1878–90), II, 69–75.

98. Cf., e.g., David Macrae, *Americans at Home* (Edinburgh, 1870), I, 67; Lieber, *Stranger in America,* I, 39; Gunn, *Physiology of New York Boarding Houses,* p. 244; Ernst O. Hopp, *Federzeichnungen aus dem Amerikanischen Leben* (Berlin, n.d. [c. 1878]), p. 55; *Citizen,* January 14, 1854; *Freeman's Journal,* October 5, 1854. For the aloofness of the richer German merchants, cf. Löher, *op. cit.,* pp. 298–299; Gustav Struve, *Diesseits und Jenseits des Oceans* (Coburg, 1863), p. 2.

99. *Handels-Zeitung,* July 22, 1865; Albert M. Friedenberg, "Charles L. Hallgarten," American Jewish Historical Society *Publication,* No. 31, 1928, p. 188; cf. [Oelrichs & Co.], *Caspar Meier* . . . , pp. 38–39.

100. Cf. Beach, *op. cit.,* pp. 4, 9, 16, 45, 47, 58. The millionaire John Lafarge, once an agent of Napoleon, held much Manhattan real estate (*ibid.,* p. 45); William Radde, German book publisher and importer, and John Jacob Astor, fur merchant, had vast landed interests. *Brown Book: a Biographical Record of Public Officials of the City of New York for 1898–9* (New York, 1899), pp. 73–74; *Staats-Zeitung,* April 14, 1860; Körner, *op. cit.,* p. 98.

101. For biographical sketches of German merchants, cf. Theodore Lemke, *Geschichte des Deutschtums von New York von 1848 bis auf die Gegenwart* (New York, 1881), *passim*.

102. For names of Spanish and Latin American merchants, cf. [Alvarez and Grediaga], *Guia de Nueva York* . . . , pp. 153–154.

103. Cf., e.g., advertisements, *Irish American*, October 21, 1849, January 14, 1854; *Irish News*, April 12, 1856; *Citizen*, January 7, 1854; *Staats-Zeitung*, December 18, 1839; *Asmonean*, October 26, November 2, 1849; *Jewish Messenger*, July 17, 1857; *Courrier des États-Unis*, September 12, 1840, January 3, 1850; Hopp, *op. cit.*, p. 54.

104. Cf., e.g., advertisements, *Staats-Zeitung*, January 4, 11, 1837, December 18, 1839.

105. Cf. almost any issue of the *Handels-Zeitung* during the 1850's; *Staats-Zeitung*, January 1, 1848, December 30, 1854, April 14, 1860; *Courrier des États-Unis*, November 26, 1829, August 29, 1846; *Républicain*, May 7, 1853; *Progrès*, January 2, 1855; *Citizen*, January 14, 1854; *Irish News*, April 12, 1856; *Jewish Messenger*, July 3, 1857; *Continental*, January 1, 1863; *Eco d'Italia*, March 3, 1865.

106. Cf. Griesinger, *op. cit.*, p. 264; Grund, *Americans in Their Moral, Social, and Political Relations*, pp. 73–74.

107. More exactly: 3.88 per cent. Computed from the MSS schedules of the *New York State Census of 1855*.

108. From 11 to 17 per cent of the Latin Americans, Spanish, and Portuguese, 8 to 10 per cent of the natives of British North America, Belgium, and Hungary, 7 to 8 per cent of the English, Welsh, and Scots were clerks. Between 6 and 7 per cent of the natives of the Netherlands, the Scandinavian countries and Russia, were clerks; slightly above 5 per cent of the Swiss, 4 to 5 per cent of the Germans, French, and Poles, 2 per cent of the Italians, and 1.5 per cent of the Irish were clerks. *Ibid.* Some of the Germans, however, were "clerks" in grocery stores.

109. Wyse, *America, Its Realities and Resources*, III, 25–26; Löher, *op. cit.*, pp. 298–299.

110. Wyse, *op. cit.*, pp. 25–26.

111. Cf., e.g., Eickhoff, *In der Neuen Heimath*, Appendix, p. 58; Claghorn, "The Foreign Immigrant . . . ," United States Industrial Commission *Reports*, XV, 474; Colton, *op. cit.*, pp. 162–168.

112. Eickhoff, *op. cit.*, Appendix, p. 58; Th. Kfn., "Ueber einige Zweige der Kunst in Amerika," *Atlantische Studien von Deutschen in Amerika* (Göttingen, 1853–1857), I, 1853, 95–109; Theodor Raufmann, "Die Kunst in Amerika, mit besonderer Beziehung auf Malerei," *ibid.*, VIII, 1857, 209–224. "Raufmann" probably is a misprint of "Kaufmann"; if so, the same man was the author of both articles.

113. Cf. "Erinnerungen und Erlebnisse eines Achtundvierzigers," *Pionier*, II, No. 1 (October, 1899), 35–42 (This was an "Illustrirter Volks Kalender" published by the New York *Volkszeitung*.) ; Ernest Bruncken, "German Political Refugees in the United States during the Period from 1815–1860," *Deutsch-Amerikanische Geschichtsblätter* (Chicago, 1904), pp. 30, 31, 42; Löher, *op. cit.*, pp. 281–282; Eickhoff, *op. cit.*, pp. 24–25; Körner, *op. cit.*, pp. 74–75; *Staats-Zeitung*, January 24, 1852, May 13, 1854, tri-weekly edition: September 9, 1842; Thomas D'Arcy McGee, *History of the Irish Settlers in North America* (6th ed.; Boston, 1855), p. 190; *Irish American*, February 14, 1852; *Albion*, July 1, 1848, August 25, 1849; Childs, *French Refugee Life* . . . , p. 192; *Courrier des États-Unis*, July 9, 1834, June 26, 1851, September 18, 1852; *Républicain*, April 17, 1854; Schiavo, *Italians in America* . . . , p. 214; F. Moncada, "The Little Italy of 1850," *Atlantica*, January 1933, pp. 160–161; *Tribune*, March 24, 1848.

114. Cf., e.g., Körner, *op. cit.*, p. 105; Eickhoff, *op. cit.*, p. 25; McGee, *op. cit.*, p. 190; Schiavo, *op. cit.*, p. 214; *Staats-Zeitung*, November 16, 1850; *Citizen*, January 20, 1855; *Scottish Journal of Intelligence and Literature*, February 5, 1842; *Herald*, January 26, 1848.

115. *Staats-Zeitung*, July 12, 1837.

116. Schiavo (*op. cit.*, p. 241) refers to the early Italian musicians.

117. Frederic L. Ritter, *Music in America,* pp. 271–274; Leuchs, *Early German Theatre in New York, 1840–1872,* p. 10; George C. D. Odell, *Annals of the New York Stage* (New York, 1927–1945), IV, 679 ff.

118. Computed from data in the MSS schedules of the *New York State Census of 1855.*

119. *Ibid.;* Schiavo, *op. cit.,* p. 254.

120. MSS schedules of the *New York State Census of 1855,* Cf. Appendix, pp. 214–217; anon. *Asmodeus in New-York* (New York, 1868), p. 105, refers to the large number of Irish lawyers in the city. For German lawyers, cf. Fleischmann, *op. cit.,* p. 533.

121. MSS schedules of the *New York State Census of 1855.* Cf. Appendix, pp. 214–217; *Staats-Zeitung,* November 16, 1850; *Criminal-Zeitung,* March 30, 1855. German chemists conducted laboratories for the making of fine pigments and dyestuffs. Freedley, *Leading Pursuits and Leading Men . . . ,* p. 132.

122. Fleischmann, *op. cit.,* p. 390; cf. pp. 146–148, 214–217. This was in addition to the German *Liebhabertheater,* or amateur theatrical organizations.

123. For example: Francis Lieber, Charles M. Nairne, Da Ponte, and Foresti at Columbia; Foresti and Georg Adler at New York University, and Isaac Nordheimer at Union Theological Seminary, to mention only a few. Cf., e.g. Körner, *op. cit.,* pp. 103, 117–121, 172; Schiavo, *op. cit.,* pp. 256–258; Ross, *op. cit.,* pp. 295–297; Howard R. Marraro, "Pioneer Italian Teachers of Italian in the United States," *Modern Language Journal,* XXVIII (November, 1944), 555–582.

124. Computed from data in the MSS schedules of the *New York State Census of 1855.*

125. *Ibid.*

126. *Ibid.*

127. *Ibid.*

Chapter IX

1. Commons, *et al., History of Labour in the United States,* I, 9–10.

2. David J. Saposs, "The Role of the Immigrant in the Labor Movement," *Amalgamated Illustrated Almanac* (New York, 1924), p. 150; George E. McNeill, *Labor Movement: the Problem of Today* (Boston, 1887), pp. 247, 334–336, 343, 626.

3. Saposs, "The Role of the Immigrant . . . ," *op. cit.,* p. 150.

4. *Ibid.*

5. *Ibid.*

6. Commons, *op. cit.,* p. 125. For the later reform agitation, cf. Ware, *Industrial Worker, 1840–1860.*

7. *New England Artisan,* October 18, 1832, and Samuel Whitcomb, Jr., *Address before the Working-Men's Society of Dedham, Delivered . . . September 7, 1831,* p. 6, quoted by Arthur M. Schlesinger, Jr., *Age of Jackson,* p. 133.

8. Schlesinger, *op. cit.,* p. 134; Commons, *op. cit.,* pp. 177–178; Joseph Dorfman, *Economic Mind in American Civilization, 1606–1865* (New York, 1946), II, 641–649. Some demands were voiced, however, for a shorter working day and for the regulation of child labor in factories. Commons, *op. cit.,* pp. 177–178.

9. F. A. Sorge, "Die Arbeiterbewegung in den Vereinigten Staaten," *Neue Zeit* (Stuttgart), IX, Part I, No. 16 (1890–1891), 500. Sorge, however, overstates the case for the immigrant, asserting that excepting the typographers, shoemakers, and part of the building trades, native workers played but a small role in the movement. *Ibid.* His main point is borne out by the roster of a carpenters' union organized in 1833 which included at first predominantly English, Irish, and Scotch names and which within three years included a number of German names. *Constitution and By-Laws* of the New York Union Society of Journeymen House Carpenters, MSS in the New York Public Library, to which is appended a list of members from 1833 to 1836.

10. Commons, op. cit., II, 25 n.

11. Born in England in 1806 of lower middle-class family, Evans sailed for America at the age of fourteen. After serving as a printer's apprentice in Utica, he moved to New York City, where in 1829 he began editing a short-lived *Working Man's Advocate*. With the revival of unions in 1844, Evans started a new paper of the same name. In his doctrine of natural right to the soil, Evans welcomed class conflict and appealed to workmen to enlist against a propertied class. Evans was the creator and leading spirit of an agrarian National Reform Association, which sought pledges from politicians in return for workingmen's votes. Among Evans' associates in New York was Thomas A. Devyr, an Irish agrarian agitator who fled to the United States and supported the anti-rent movement in upstate New York. Commons, *op. cit.*, I, 237 n., 522–532; Lewis Masquerier, *Sociology: or the Reconstruction of Society, Government, and Property* (New York, 1877), pp. 93–99.

12. George A. Tracy, *History of the Typographical Union* (Indianapolis, 1913), p. 68.

13. Quoted by Commons, *op. cit.*, I, 174.

14. *Ibid.*, p. 410.

15. *Union*, June 10, 1836.

16. *Ibid*. Among the unskilled, the majority of "riots" were really the outcome of unorganized strikes over wage rates or because some contractor absconded with the laborers' wages. In 1836 the ship laborers, riggers, and stevedores struck for wage increases and tried to force others to quit their jobs, but the police intervened, and a riot ensued. Commons, *op. cit.*, I, 416–417.

17. *European*, April 8, 1837.

18. Commons, *op. cit.*, I, 487. The slight recovery in 1843 and 1844 did not alter the general conclusion of hard times, which lasted until after the discovery of gold in 1849. *Ibid.*

19. Cf. Appendix, pp. 187, 188.

20. *Champion of American Labor*, April 3, 1847.

21. *Champion of American Labor*, July 17, 1847. The reference to "cut-throats" and "adventurers" was intended to apply to communist refugees from Germany.

22. *Champion of American Labor*, May 1, 1847.

23. *Champion of American Labor*, April 3, 1847.

24. *Young America*, February 14, 1846.

25. *Young America*, February 14, 1846. Cf. *Daily Tribune*, November 11, 1845.

26. *Champion of American Labor*, April 3, 1847.

27. Abdy, *Journal of a Residence and Tour in the United States of North America, from April, 1833, to October, 1834*, I, 77; *Working Man's Advocate*, August 17, 1844; *Young America*, October 25, 1845; *Tribune*, May 11, 18, 1850. This did not apply to the shoemaking trade, however. The adaptation of the sewing machine to the making of uppers in 1852 did not affect the journeymen cordwainers because the sewing of uppers had been the work of women. The flood of inventions in the fifties—tin patterns for cutting, adjustable lathes, machines for heel making, lasting, and sandpapering—proved to be aids rather than substitutes for skill. The pegging machine was not introduced until 1857 and the McKay sole-sewing machine until 1862. John R. Commons, "American Shoemakers 1648–1895; a Sketch of Industrial Evolution," *Quarterly Journal of Economics*, XXIV, No. 1 (November, 1909), 72–73.

28. *Champion of American Labor*, April 24, 1847.

29. *Young America*, September 6, October 8, 1845.

30. *Young America*, October 18, 1845. In 1850 the German cigar makers considered a three year apprenticeship plan but rejected it as leading to the creation of a caste system. *Tribune*, May 11, 1850.

31. *Champion of American Labor*, April 3, 17, 24, 1847.

32. A.I.C.P., *Ninth Annual Report*, 1852, p. 22.

33. Vetter, *Zwei Jahre in New-York*, pp. 156–157; [George Nettle], *Practical Guide for Emigrants* . . . (London, 1850), pp. 28–29; *Irish American*, January 1, 1853.

34. Haynes, *Negro at Work in New York City*, pp. 67-68; [James Boardman],

America and the Americans, p. 35; *Truth Teller,* May 28, 1831; *Young America,* January 24, 1846; *Irish American,* June 9, 1860.

35. [James D. Burn], *Three Years Among the Working-Classes* . . . , Chapter xiv, *passim;* cf. *ibid.,* pp. 22–23; *Tribune,* February 1, June 17, 1850.

36. *Staats-Zeitung,* April 7, 1860.

37. *Tribune,* March 20, 1851, quoted by J. R. Commons, *et al., Documentary History of American Industrial Society* (Cleveland, 1910–1911), VII, 96–99.

38. *Herald,* March 31, 1853, as cited by the *European,* May 2, 1857. The strike ensued but was unsuccessful. Some employers retained their best waiters at increased wages and fired the rest, replacing them with Negroes or women, *Tribune,* April 26, May 3, 1853.

39. *Irish American,* July 9, 1853. In 1863 Irish longshoremen assaulted Negro strikebreakers. McNeill, *op. cit.,* p. 126.

40. R. J. Purcell and J. F. Poole, "Political Nativism in Brooklyn," *Journal of the American Irish Historical Society,* XXXII (New York, 1941), 16.

41. Henry A. Brann, *Most Reverend John Hughes* (New York, 1892), p. 89; Francis Lieber, *Stranger in America,* I, 236; *Tribune,* February 11, 1850, September 4, 6, 1851; *Citizen,* February 21, 1857; *Irish American,* February 28, 1857.

42. Edward E. Hale, *Letters on Irish Emigration,* p. 34.

43. *Irish American,* July 31, 1852. The fight ensued, as planned; many of the workmen ran away, and of the hundred and fifty men only thirty demanded payment. According to McQuade, the contractor acknowledged making $1,500 clear profit out of the job. *Ibid.* For other examples of contractors "clearing out" before paying their men, cf. *Irish American,* April 3, 1852.

44. *Irish American,* November 1, 1851.

45. *Ibid.*

46. Handlin, *Boston's Immigrants, 1790–1865,* pp. 77–78.

47. *Irish American,* January 31, April 3, 1852.

48. Commons *et al., History of Labour* . . . , I, 416–417.

49. Letter printed in *Irish American,* March 12, 1853.

50. *Irish American,* December 18, 1852.

51. Costello, *Our Firemen* . . . , pp. 119, 123, 751–754; *Tribune,* January 28, 1857.

52. Occasionally, however, violence broke out in purely German disputes. In 1850, for example, the use of strong-arm methods by striking German tailors resulted in a "very unhappy and barbarous conflict" with the police, as stones, clubs, knives, and pistols were freely used. *Irish American,* August 10, 1850.

53. Marjoribanks, *Travels in South and North America,* p. 410. In Baltimore the free Negroes complained of German immigrants, who did cheaper and better work. Hale, *op. cit.,* p. 54. For Irish-German struggles, cf. also *Counsel for Emigrants, and Interesting Information* . . . (Aberdeen, 1834), p. 48; *Staats-Zeitung,* January 11, 1851.

54. "Erinnerungen und Erlebnisse eines Achtundvierzigers," *Pionier,* II, No. 1 (October 1, 1899), 40.

55. *Staats-Zeitung,* April 25, 1846; *Freeman's Journal,* April 25, 1846; *Weekly Tribune,* May 2, 1846; *New Yorker Volkszeitung,* 25th Anniversary Issue, February 21, 1903, p. 8. "It is very regretful," commented the *Staats-Zeitung* (April 25, 1846), "that German workers can be found who are willing to stand in the way of the just demand for a 10 hour day."

56. Commons *et al., History of Labour* . . . , I, 597.

57. *Tribune,* April 16, 1850.

58. *Champion of American Labor,* April 17, 1847.

59. *Tribune,* March 28, April 15, 29, 1850. Largely German, the unions of smiths, wheelrights, joiners, and cabinetmakers offered advice and assistance to immigrants. *Tribune,* April 27, May 23, 1850.

60. Similar information was to be sent to the principal newspapers of Germany so that emigrating journeymen might be forewarned. *Tribune,* April 27, 1850.

61. *Times,* July 1, 1854. A Laborers' Union Benevolent Association, founded in 1843, had several thousand active members in 1850. *Tribune,* June 10, 1850. Cf. p. 183.

62. Commons *et al, History of Labour* . . . , I, 589–590.

63. This was the largest workingmen's organization in the city. *Tribune,* April 26, May 25, 1850. In time the German woodworkers maintained their identity and handled their own affairs. *Staats-Zeitung,* April 2, 1853.

64. *Tribune,* April 20, 1850. The journeymen watchcase makers found it necessary to choose a vice president who spoke French. *Ibid.*

65. The first cigar makers' local, established in 1852, went to pieces in six months because of suspicion and ill feeling between English and German elements. J. H. Hollander and G. E. Barnett, *Studies in American Trade Unionism,* p. 51; McNeill, *op. cit.,* p. 597. Cf. the earlier failure of the cigar makers to co-operate. *Tribune,* June 20, 1850.

66. Tribune, April 23, 1850. The French established their own carpenters' union, but nothing is known of this organization.

67. *Tribune,* July 20, 1850. Cf. *ibid.,* May 14, 1850.

68. *Tribune,* April 20, 1850.

69. *Tribune,* April 16, 1850.

70. *Tribune,* April 16, 1850; *Staats-Zeitung,* May 18, 1850.

71. *Tribune,* May 31, June 19, 22, July 1, 1850.

72. *Tribune,* April 19, 24, 26, 1853; *Courrier des États-Unis,* April 7, 13, 1853.

73. *Irish American,* May 19, 1850; *Staats-Zeitung,* April 18, 1850.

74. *Citizen,* April 8, 10, 29, 1854.

75. *Tribune,* July 19, 25, 29, 1850.

76. Cf. Commons *et al., History of Labour* . . . , I, 590.

77. *Tribune,* April 20, 1850.

78. *Tribune,* June 22, 1850.

79. *Tribune,* April 12, 23, 26, 1850.

80. *Tribune,* April 20, 22, 23, 30, May 11, 31, July 1, 1850.

81. Commons *et al., History of Labour* . . . , I, 606.

82. This was largely the result of increased employment opportunities in England and on the continent, the depletion of the English labor market by the Irish famine emigration to America, and the demands of the Crimean War for manpower. Immigration at the port of New York fell from over 300,000 in 1854 to 78,000 in 1858. *Annual Reports of the Commissioners of Emigration,* Appendix, p. 281.

83. A.I.C.P., *Eighteenth Annual Report,* 1861, p. 17.

84. Letter of Mayor C. Godfrey Gunther to John Williams, General Agent of the American Emigrant Company, September 14, 1864, in *Report on Emigration by a Special Committee of the Chamber of Commerce of the State of New York* (New York, January 5, 1865), p. 23.

85. *Courrier des États-Unis,* November 11, 1863, March 8, 16, July 15, 1864; Hermann Schlüter, "Ein deutscher Arbeiter-Verein in New York," *Pionier,* 1906 (an "Illustrirter Volks Kalender" published by the *New Yorker Volkszeitung*), p. 55.

Chapter X

1. Hermann Schlüter, *Die Anfänge der deutschen Arbeiterbewegung in Amerika* (Stuttgart, 1907), pp. ix-x; F. A. Sorge, "Die Arbeiterbewegung in den Vereinigten Staaten," *Neue Zeit* (Stuttgart), IX, Part I, No. 24 (1890–1891), 775.

2. Schlüter, *Die Anfänge* . . . , p. 128. The movement was not thoroughly classconscious but consisted of a series of attempts to ameliorate the conditions of work under the existing economic system.

3. Sorge. "Die Arbeiterbewegung . . . ," *loc. cit.,* Part II, No. 33 (1890–1891), p. 198.

4. Schlüter, *Die Anfänge* . . . , pp. 17–19; Herman Schlüter (same author, with

Americanized given name), *Lincoln, Labor and Slavery; A Chapter from the Social History of America* (New York, 1913), p. 70.

5. Schlüter, *Die Anfänge* . . . , p. 18; Commons, *et al, History of Labour in the United States,* I, 534. The *Bund's* ideas were characterized by Marx as a "mixture of French-English socialism and German philosophy." *Ibid.*

6. The *Adoptiv-Bürger,* which appeared very briefly in 1846, was probably the first German workers' paper in the United States. Schlüter, *Die Anfänge* . . . , p. 19. For the St. Louis papers, cf. Commons, *op. cit.,* I, 534.

7. Schlüter, *Lincoln, Labor and Slavery,* p. 70.

8. *Ibid.,* pp. 70–71; Schlüter, *Die Anfänge* . . . , p. 20. Evans' second *Working Man's Advocate,* begun in 1844, became the organ of the National Reform Association and was renamed *Young America.* This name, with its German equivalent, *Jung Amerika,* was popular in an era which witnessed the rise of Young Italy, Young Ireland, Young Germany, and other liberal movements. It was significant, however, that in all these agitations actual workingmen were less aroused than middle-class intellectuals.

9. *Volks-Tribun,* May 9, 1846, quoted in Commons, *op. cit.,* I, 489.

10. Schlüter, *Die Anfänge* . . . , pp. 22–23.

11. Cf. Commons, *op. cit.,* I, 534–535.

12. Schlüter, *Die Anfänge* . . . , pp. 26–27.

13. Commons, *op. cit.,* I, 535.

14. Schlüter, *Die Anfänge* . . . , pp. 24–26, 40–46. At a meeting in Brussels, Marx, Engels, and other communist leaders resolved that Kriege was not a communist and that his *Volks-Tribun* compromised communism in Europe as well as in America. *Ibid.,* p. 29.

15. *Young Germany. An account of the Rise, Progress, and Present Position of German Communism; with a memoir of Wilhelm Weitling* . . . (London [1844]), pp. 3–9; Commons, *op. cit.,* I, 512–513.

16. Frederick C. Clark, "A Neglected Socialist," *Annals of the American Academy of Political and Social Science,* V (March, 1895), 722–730; Schlüter, *Die Anfänge* . . . , pp. 49–50.

17. Clark, "A Neglected Socialist," *op. cit.,* p. 730; cf. Schlüter, *Die Anfänge* . . . , pp. 50–70.

18. Clark, "A Neglected Socialist," *op. cit.,* pp. 83–85.

19. *Republik der Arbeiter,* March 1850, quoted in Commons, *op. cit.,* I, 514.

20. *Republik der Arbeiter,* October 1850, paraphrased in Commons, *op. cit.,* I, 514.

21. Clark, "A Neglected Socialist," *op. cit.,* p. 730. The colony lived until 1853, when it went the way of all the utopian experiments, largely as the result of difficulties over land titles. As one of Fourier's German disciples in America, Weitling was connected briefly with a colony of Fourierites in Clayton County, Iowa, founded by Heinrich Koch, a German watchmaker whose radical politics landed him in jail. After his release, he emigrated to America in 1832 and thereafter spent most of his life in Dubuque, Iowa. Richard T. Ely, *The Labor Movement in America* (New York, [1886]), p. 220.

22. Schlüter, *Die Anfänge* . . . , p. 119. When the paper was first published it had about a thousand subscribers, according to the New York *Tribune* (January 31, 1850); when it failed, Weitling got a job as a clerk in the immigrant landing depot at Castle Garden. Clark, "A Neglected Socialist," *op. cit.,* p. 731.

23. Schlüter, *Die Anfänge* . . . , p. 85.

24. They included 234 tailors, 118 cabinetmakers, 95 shoemakers, 35 locksmiths, and 23 cigar makers. *Ibid.,* p. 119.

25. The blacksmiths, for example, established their own bakery. *Tribune,* May 31, 1850.

26. Commons, *op. cit.,* I, 567.

27. Across the East River in Williamsburg, Weitling's influence was reflected in the formation of a union of German workingmen without distinction of pursuit. *Tribune,* May 14, 1850.

28. Commons, *op. cit.,* I, 513, 566; Commons, *et al., Documentary History,* VII, 299–

300. Weitling also opposed the trade union movement, fearing it would result in productive associations, which would defeat his own plan for a bank of exchange. Commons, *History of Labour*, I, 577.

29. The delegates spoke in behalf of 700 cabinetmakers, 324 bakers (of whom 160 were American), 250 shoemakers, 120 upholsterers, 100 tailors, 92 sculptors, 63 turners, 40 furriers and hat- and capmakers, and 40 unspecified "mechanics." Schlüter, *Die Anfänge* . . . , p. 131. Regardless of membership, each trade was represented by three delegates. *Tribune*, May 17, 1850.

30. Schlüter, *Die Anfänge* . . . , p. 131; Commons, *History of Labour*, I, 567. The American consumers' co-operative was probably the New York Protective Union, which was organized in 1847. After three years it had about 400 members and operated the most successful co-operative store outside of New England. *Ibid.*, p. 572.

31. Commons, *History of Labour*, I, 567.

32. I.e., bank of exchange. *Staats-Zeitung*, March 16, 1850.

33. Commons, *History of Labour*, I, 515.

34. *Ibid.*, p. 516.

35. Cf. *ibid.*, pp. 568–569.

36. *Ibid.*, pp. 555–566, 568.

37. *Ibid.*, pp. 567–568.

38. *Republik der Arbeiter*, September 1851, cited in Commons, *History of Labour*, I, 568. There were also two German co-operatives in Buffalo, two in Pittsburgh, and one apiece in Philadelphia, Detroit, and Cincinnati. *Ibid.*

39. Commons, *History of Labour*, I, 569–571.

40. *Ibid.*, p. 589.

41. *Ibid.*, p. 617 n.; Karl Obermann, *Joseph Weydemeyer* . . . (New York, 1947), pp. 35–70.

42. *Ibid.*, p. 617; Schlüter, *Die Anfänge* . . . , p. 132.

43. Schlüter, *Die Anfänge* . . . , p. 136; Commons, *History of Labour*, I, 617–618. Members of the new *Bund* were Weydemeyer, Ahrends, Bluhm, Kellner, Meyerhoffer, and Zabel; the social reformers; the socialist Turner's Society; and *Vereine* of various trades, including the cigar makers, painters, printers, and shoemakers. *Protokoll-Buch des Centralvereins des Allgemeinen Arbeiter-Bundes in New York*, April 17, 1853–April 29, 1855. MSS in the American Labor Archive, New York City.

44. Schlüter, *Die Anfänge* . . . , pp. 138–139. Relations were maintained with socialist groups in New Haven, Buffalo, Cincinnati, and other cities. *Protokoll-Buch des Centralvereins* . . . , *passim.*

45. Schlüter, *Die Anfänge* . . . , pp. 140–141; *Protokoll-Buch des Centralvereins* . . . , *passim.*

46. Commons, *History of Labour*, I, 618 n.; Schlüter, *Die Anfänge* . . . , pp. 148–149. The first number appeared on March 5, 1853; after May 4 the paper was issued semiweekly until October 15, when it became a daily. Its last number appeared on April 26, 1854. *Ibid.*, p. 152.

47. Schlüter, *Die Anfänge* . . . , p. 149.

48. Cf. *supra*, n. 46.

49. Schlüter, *Die Anfänge* . . . , pp. 160–161.

50. *Ibid.*, pp. 160–162; *Protokolle des Communisten Clubs in New York*, October 1857, MSS in American Labor Archive, New York City.

51. Schlüter, *Die Anfänge* . . . , p. 175.

52. Hermann Schlüter, "Ein deutscher Arbeiter-Verein in New York," *Pionier* (1906) (An "Illustrirter Volks Kalender" published by the *New Yorker Volkszeitung*), pp. 55–68. The *Arbeiter-Verein* lasted until 1876. Among its members were F. A. Sorge, Friedrich Bolte, Conrad Carl August Hesse, S. Meyer, C. A. Petersen, A. Vollbrecht, Cluff, Schulte, and Weber. The society's *Protokoll-Buch*, covering the years 1865–1871, is in the possession of the American Labor Archive, New York City.

53. David J. Saposs, *Left Wing Unionism* (New York, 1926), pp. 9–10.

54. *New Yorker Volkszeitung,* 25th anniversary number, February 21, 1903, p. 51; Schlüter, *Die Anfänge . . .* , p. 176.

55. Schlüter, *Die Anfänge . . .* , p. 177.

56. *Ibid.,* p. 176.

57. *Ibid.,* p. 177; *New Yorker Volkszeitung, op. cit.,* p. 56.

58. The successful *Deutsche Typographia in New York,* founded in 1869, was preceded by three printers' *vereine:* in 1853–1854, 1859–1860, and 1863–1866, respectively. From the socialist viewpoint, they had failed largely because they lacked "Verkennung des Klassenstandpunktes." *New Yorker Volkszeitung, op. cit.,* p. 40.

59. Gompers, *Seventy Years of Life and Labor,* I, 47.

60. In some instances, they even refused offers of co-operation. The lack of English-speaking members of Weitling's *Arbeiterbund* handicapped its attempts in 1850 to influence the Industrial Congress at New York. F. A. Sorge, "Die Arbeiterbewegung in den Vereinigten Staaten," *Neue Zeit* (Stuttgart), IX, Part II, No. 34 (1890–1891), 235–236.

61. *Ibid.,* p. 235.

Chapter XI

1. Cf. the MSS letters to Thomas Lawrence, an English tailor who settled in New York City. This collection (in the New York Public Library) does not include any of Lawrence's letters, but the replies of his mother and friends in England make it possible to infer what he wrote.

2. *Ibid.;* "John Stokes's American Diary," *National Review,* CX, No. 659, p. 81. For poems, cf. *Albion,* September 17, October 29, 1831; *Allgemeine Zeitung,* April 25, 1840; *Staats-Zeitung,* July 8, 15, 1843. The *Irish American* printed poetry and ballads of Ireland and began a column in Gaelic on July 25, 1857; cf. the poetic effusions of "Shamrock," *Irish News,* April 3, 1858.

3. One German stationer included for Catholics views of the pilgrimage city of Rome. *Criminal-Zeitung,* June 3, 1859. For exhibitions in museums, cf., e.g., *Staats-Zeitung,* August 25, 1841; *Courrier des États-Unis,* May 11, 1843. The *Irish News* announced on March 20, 1858 that a new paper, the *Irish Pictorial Miscellany,* specializing in reprints from the old *Dublin Penny Journal* and in illustrations of Irish scenes, was fast extending its circulation.

4. *Irish American,* August 10, 1850; *Staats-Zeitung,* daily ed.: April 21, 1848, December 27, 1859; weekly ed.: July 13, 1853, July 16, August 1, 1859.

5. *Staats-Zeitung,* daily ed.: July 16, August 1, 9, 1859; *Irish American,* February 28, 1857; *Irish News,* June 20, 1857; *Freeman's Journal,* January 7, 1843; Lieber, *Stranger in America,* I, 236. Henry A. Brann, *Most Reverend John Hughes* (New York, 1892), p. 89, notes the disapproval of these societies by the Catholic hierarchy.

6. *Albion,* January 9, 1847. Cf. *Plebeian,* August 8, 1842; *Freeman's Journal,* July 23, 1842, January 2, 1847; *Irish American,* August 7, 1858.

7. *Aid to Ireland. Report of the Central Relief Committee of the City of New York . . .* (New York, 1848), pp. 20, 28, 34, 37, 40, 41, 44, 65.

8. *Irish American,* February 11, 1860, citing the Boston *Pilot's* figures, which included funds sent from all over America. In 1858 alone, the Irish in America remitted $2,360,000. *Ibid.* As early as 1835 the English authorities concluded that the Irish were much more disposed to help their people in the Old Country than the English or the Scotch. Johnson, *History of Emigration from the United Kingdom . . .* , p. 70.

9. *Scottish Journal of Intelligence and Literature,* January 29, February 5, 1842; *Tribune,* February 10, 1842.

10. *Courrier des États-Unis,* September 22, October 13, 1830, January 8, 1841, June 26, 28, July 30, 1856; *Franco-Américain,* November 23, 1846.

11. *Courrier des États-Unis,* May 16, September 26, 1859.

12. *Courrier des États-Unis,* June 20, 27, 1838; *Staats-Zeitung,* August 3, 1842; *Albion,* October 2, 1852, a black-bordered number on the occasion of Wellington's death;

twenty-one years before, the democratic *Old Countryman* (November 24, 1831) had printed a black-bordered number on the defeat of the Reform Bill of 1831.

13. *Scottish Journal of Intelligence and Literature,* January 25, 29, 1842; *Albion,* January 31, 1857, January 30, 1858.

14. Cf., e.g., *Albion,* May 18, 1839; *Citizen,* July 8, 1854.

15. *Staats-Zeitung,* November 19, 1859.

16. *Deutsche Schnellpost,* September 27, October 18, 1843; *Plebeian.* November 16, 1843. Collections also were made in other cities. Cf., e.g., *Deutsche Schnellpost,* November 1, 11, 1843.

17. Howard R. Marraro, "Eleuterio Felice Foresti," *Columbia University Quarterly,* XXV, No. 1 (March, 1933), 43; Howard R. Marraro, "Italians in New York during the First Half of the Nineteenth Century," *New York History,* XXVI, No. 3 (July, 1945), 285.

18. *Staats-Zeitung,* triweekly ed.: September 9, 1842; weekly ed.: June 1, 1850, November 19, 26, 1853; *Courrier des États-Unis,* November 29, 1854; *Républicain,* March 20, 1854.

19. *Staats-Zeitung,* April 15, 22, 1848, August 18, 1849, February 23, 1850; *Asmonean,* July 19, 26, 1850. The Germans lost much of their initial enthusiasm, however, when the revolution collapsed and the refugees bickered among themselves. As hopes for a united republican Germany faded, the New York fund-raising committee admitted the failure of the Germans to co-operate on a single plan of money collection. *Staats-Zeitung,* March 13, 1852; cf. Carl Wittke, *Against the Current; The Life of Karl Heinzen . . .* (Chicago [1945]), pp. 262–263.

20. Cf., e.g., *Courrier des États-Unis,* September 18, December 1, 1830, August 3, 1831, March 21, 23, 1848, August 28, 30, 1849, December 9, 1851, November 29, 1854; *Républicain,* March 20, September 1, 1854; *Staats-Zeitung,* March 25, 1848. Preparations for the reception of Garibaldi in 1850 were caustically described by the hostile Sardinian minister at Washington in a letter to the Minister of Foreign Affairs at Turin, August 10, 1850, translated from the French and quoted by Marraro, "Italians in New York . . . ," *loc. cit.,* p. 290.

21. Cf. *Citizen,* June 24, 1854; *Irish American,* September 3, 1859; McGee, *History of the Irish Settlers in North America,* (6th ed.), p. 133. The *Freeman's Journal,* a conservative Catholic newspaper, opposed the continental revolutionists but did not represent dominant Irish opinion at New York. Cf. the issues of April 1, 1848, July 7, September 1, 1849, December 21, 1850, May 3, 1851, July 29, 1854.

22. The Association of the Friends of Ireland in the City of New York was founded in 1828 and counted over a thousand members in the first six months of its existence. Cf. *Truth Teller,* August 9, 1828, January 10, 24, February 28, 1829, June 19, September 11, 1830. For an earlier movement, cf. *Globe and Emerald,* October 22, 1825. For the movements in general, cf. McGee, *op. cit.,* pp. 130–134.

23. *Weekly Register and Catholic Diary,* October 5, 1833; *Freeman's Journal,* August 8, 1840, June 17, September 23, 1843; *Plebeian,* June 10, 1843; McGee, *op. cit.,* pp. 132–133.

24. *Freeman's Journal,* September 23, November 11, 1843, and succeeding issues; McGee, *op. cit.,* p. 133.

25. *Freeman's Journal,* January 6, 20, March 9, 23, 1844, December 19, 1846, January 30, 1847; McGee, *op. cit.,* pp. 133–134. Cf. Handlin, *Boston's Immigrants . . . ,* p. 158.

26. McGee, *op. cit.,* p. 134.

27. Sporadic agitation continued at New York, but the opposition of the church weakened its force. *Irish American,* February 14, 1852; *Freeman's Journal,* July 15, 29, 1854; *Citizen,* June 24, July 1, December 30, 1854, April 28, 1855, February 9, 1856.

28. Then as now, the saloon was the poor man's club. *Courrier des États-Unis,* July 13, 1841. Cf. E. C. Moore, "The Social Value of the Saloon," *American Journal of Sociology,* III, No. 1 (July, 1897), pp. 1–12.

29. *Subterranean,* May 31, 1845; *Irish American,* October 14, 1849; *Citizen,* January 14, 1854.

30. Cf. Howitt, *Rural and Domestic Life of Germany* . . . , pp. 32, 34, 39, 90.

31. Haswell, *Reminiscences of New York by an Octogenarian* . . . , p. 360.

32. *Ibid.;* Browne, *Great Metropolis; A Mirror of New York* . . . , pp. 165–166. For other German *Lokale, Kosthäuser,* etc., cf. advertisements in almost any issue of the *Staats-Zeitung.*

33. *Old Countryman,* September 29, 1831, January 1, 1834; *Emigrant and Old Countryman,* December 9, 1835, October 19, 1836; *Courrier des États-Unis,* November 17, 1840, June 18, 1851, and almost any other issue; *European News,* September 11, 1847; *Eco d'Italia,* January 7, 1865.

34. Cf., e.g., *Courrier des États-Unis,* May 18, 1839 (advertisement), June 16, 1843, September 16, 1859; *Staats-Zeitung,* May 25, 1850; *Criminal-Zeitung,* June 29, 1860; *Meyer's Monats-Hefte,* September 1854, p. 397.

35. *Truth Teller,* April 8, 1826, January 26, March 29, 1828. The tenth annual ball of the Hibernian Benevolent and Burial Society was held at Castle Garden in 1849 and was attended by over two thousand Irish Americans. *Irish American,* December 2, 1849.

36. *Irish American,* December 6, 1851, March 20, December 18, 1852, April 1, 1854; *Staats-Zeitung,* January 26, 1842, April 28, 1858; Schlüter, *Die Anfänge* . . . , p. 128; Sorge, *"Die Arbeiterbewegung in den Vereinigten Staaten," Neue Zeit,* IX, Part I, No. 16 (1890–1891), 500.

37. *Daily Tribune,* May 8, June 10, 1850. The Association exacted a $2.00 Initiation fee.

38. Cf., e.g., The Christian Doctrine Benefit and Benevolent Society, attached to the Church of the Nativity. *Irish American,* November 6, 1852. Grinstein, *Rise of the Jewish Community* . . . , p. 107.

39. Grinstein, *op. cit.,* pp. 107–109. In the late forties the independent societies bought their own cemeteries, owing, probably, to the clamor of the unsynagogued Jews. *Ibid.*

40. Cf., e.g., *Man,* September 13, 1834; *Staats-Zeitung,* October 8, 1842, September 23, 1843, January 4, 1847; *Asmonean,* July 28, 1854; *Albion,* March 28, 1855.

41. *Scottish Journal of Intelligence and Literature,* May 29, December 18, 1841.

42. For example, the *Nederlandsche Societeit de Vriendschap (Staats-Zeitung,* September 24, October 14, 1859), the *Societa di Unione e Fratellanza Italiana (Eco d'Italia,* January 21, 1865), and the Hispanic *La Esperanza (Crónica,* April 23, 1864). For other societies, cf. p. 32.

43. Ross, *Scot in America,* p. 436; *Staats-Zeitung,* February 10, 1841, daily ed.: April 15, 1856; *Courrier des États-Unis,* June 24, 1857; Augustin P. Maugé, *Directory Français* . . . , p. 99; *Eco d'Italia,* April 29, 1855. The German Masonic organizations, less exclusive than in Europe, were open to barbers, tailors, cigar makers, and other humble folk, yet leadership was in the hands of a few men. Hopp, *Federzeichnungen aus dem Amerikanischen Leben,* p. 36.

44. *Courrier des États-Unis,* October 14, 1848, June 7, 1849, December 16, 1851; *Staats-Zeitung,* October 28, 1840, May 13, 1848; daily ed.: February 7, 1853, May 6, 1858; John P. von Grueningen, *Swiss in the United States* . . . (Madison, Wis., 1940), p. 106. Welsh Druids are mentioned in *Anglo American,* February 14, 1846.

45. Grinstein, *op. cit.,* pp. 109–110.

46. *Truth Teller,* October 5, 1833, August 2, 1834; *Anglo American,* January 3, 20, 1844. A "Jackson Fishing Party" was held by Irishmen in 1834 to the tunes of a "celebrated Irish piper." *Truth Teller,* August 2, 1834. For an "Anglo-American Shooting Club," cf. *Anglo American,* June 22, 1844.

47. *Staats-Zeitung,* March 18, 1840; *Minutes of the St. Andrew's Curling Club; Irish News,* December 12, 1857, January 2, 1858.

48. *Anglo American,* May 20, 1843, September 28, 1844; *Albion,* August 29, 1840,

September 11, 1853. Most of the members of the St. George Club also belonged to the St. George's Society. The New York Cricket Club was composed largely of Americans.

49. For predominantly Irish companies, cf. *Annual Report* of the Chief of the Fire Department, February 18, 1858, Board of Aldermen, *Documents*, XXV, No. 6 (1858), 43, 52, 53, 56, 69, 116, 129, 145, 171; for predominantly German companies, cf. *ibid.*, pp. 100, 103; for other nationalities, cf. *ibid.*, pp. 138, 166. From the names here given it is impossible to distinguish the English companies, if any; nevertheless many of the fire laddies were born in England. *Daily Tribune*, January 28, 1857.

50. M. D. Learned, "The German-American Turner Lyric," *Publications of the Society for the History of the Germans in Maryland*, X (1896), 122–123.

51. Wittke, *We Who Built America*, p. 146.

52. *Irish News*, April 12, 1856. Cf. Wittke, *op. cit.*, p. 145.

53. *Staats-Zeitung*, daily edition: (advertisements) April 24, May 4, June 7, 1858, August 1, 1859; *Citizen*, February 18, 1854; *Irish American*, February 25, 1860. The German socialists also formed a military company in the fifties, *Staats-Zeitung*, daily ed. (advertisement), September 25, 1858. For other German companies, cf. almost any issue of the *Staats-Zeitung*, daily ed., in the late fifties.

54. *Irish News*, April 12, 1856.

55. *Citizen*, August 15, 1857.

56. *Irish American*, January 6, April 21, August 10, 17, 1850; *Citizen*, August 15, 1857.

57. *Irish News*, May 17, 1856. Cf. John B. McMaster, *History of the People of the United States*, VIII, 75.

58. Cf. Nichols, *Forty Years of American Life* . . . , II, 79.

59. *Staats-Zeitung*, February 26, April 22, 1840.

60. *Deutsche Schnellpost*, December 16, 23, 1840, December 23, 1843; Körner, *Das deutsche Element in den Vereinigten Staaten von Nordamerika* . . . , pp. 108–109.

61. *Citizen*, February 25, 1854; McMaster, *op. cit.*, p. 75, which also mentions other German companies. Cf. *Staats-Zeitung*, January 18, 22, 1840; *Deutsche Schnellpost*, February 17, 1844.

62. *Courrier des États-Unis*, July 3, 1847, December 18, 1852, December 8, 1860.

63. *Anglo American*, August 31, 1844, November 22, 1845; *Courrier des États-Unis*, September 13, 1849; Liddel, *History of the New York Caledonian Club*, I, 25, 81–85, 175.

64. *Staats-Zeitung*, June 10, 1848; *Irish American*, August 26, 1849; *Courrier des États-Unis*, September 13, 1849.

65. *Courrier des États-Unis*, December 22, 1858, February 8, 1859.

66. *Asmonean*, November 12, 1850; *Jewish Messenger*, December 17, 1858; Grinstein, *op. cit.*, p. 200.

67. McMaster, *op. cit.*, p. 75.

68. Liddel, *op. cit.*, p. 19.

69. *Irish News*, April 11, 1857; *Staats-Zeitung*, daily ed.: February 14, 1856 (advertisement); *Anglo American*, January 10, 31, 1846; *Asmonean*, December 13, 1850; *Courrier des États-Unis*, August 27, 1850, February 21, 1852, February 27, 1854, July 24, 1856.

70. *Minutes of the Albion Club* (New York 1836–1839); *Albion*, August 13, October 29, December 3, 17, 1836.

71. Cf. Howitt, *op. cit.*, p. 90.

72. For advertisements of meetings of these *Vereine*, cf. almost any issue of the *Staats-Zeitung*, daily ed., 1858–1859.

73. *Criminal-Zeitung*, March 20, May 18, 1855; Gustav Ramsperger, *Geschichte des New-Yorker Deutschen Apotheker-Vereins* (New York, 1901), pp. 10–11, 14. Irish doctors met annually as the Irish American Physicians. *Irish American*, March 29, 1851. For chess clubs, cf. *Staats-Zeitung*, daily ed.: November 12, 1858, November 19, 1859.

74. *Staats-Zeitung*, January 1, 8, 15, April 29, September 23, 1840; Odell, *Annals of the New York Stage*, IV, 395. Cf. Leuchs, *Early German Theatre in New York, 1840–*

1872, pp. 68–74. No other nationality developed amateur theatricals as thoroughly as the Germans. It is noteworthy, however, that an amateur Irish group, the Murdoch Dramatic Association, held its third annual ball in 1850. *Irish American,* November 16, December 7, 1850.

75. *Albion,* March 15, 1851; *Phare de New-York,* June 26, 1852; Odell, *op. cit.,* V, 55, VI, 323. Cf. *Staats-Zeitung,* daily ed.: (advertisements) June 3, 1858, July 14, 1859, and a series of playbills of the dramatic society "Erheiterung," collected by Ludwig Engelhardt, and now in the possession of the New York Public Library.

76. *Albion,* March 15, 1851.

77. For early singing clubs, cf. *Staats-Zeitung,* March 1, 22, September 30, 1837; *Courrier des États-Unis,* April 25, 1838; *Deutsche Schnellpost,* October 19, 1844.

78. Hermann Mosenthal, *Geschichte des Vereins Deutscher Liederkranz in New York* (New York, 1897), pp. 6–7; Hopp, *op. cit.,* pp. 34–35.

79. Leuchs, *op. cit.,* p. 10. Mosenthal, *op. cit.,* p. 18, lists only fifteen clubs and fails to mention the *Yorkville Männerchor* and the *Lorelei,* a mixed chorus. *Staats-Zeitung,* daily ed. (advertisements) May 13, December 20, 1858. A Swiss singing society was formed the same year. *Staats-Zeitung,* daily ed., May 4, 1858; von Grueningen, *op. cit.,* p. 108.

80. Learned, *op. cit.,* p. 99.

81. Cf. *ibid.,* pp. 101–103; Henry Metzner, *Brief History of the American Turnerbund* (Pittsburgh, 1924), *passim;* Wittke, *op. cit.,* pp. 190, 221.

82. *Turn-Zeitung,* March 15, October 1, 1853; *Staats-Zeitung,* April 20, 1850, September 10, 1853; Wittke, *op. cit.,* p. 220. For occupations of the Turners, cf. Hugo Gollmer, *Namensliste der Pioniere des Nord-Amerik, Turnerbundes der Jahre 1848–1862* (St. Louis, 1885); cf. *Criminal-Zeitung,* September 18, 1857.

83. Cf., e.g., *Staats-Zeitung,* daily ed.: June 23, 24, 25, 1858 for a *Schützenfest,* and *ibid.,* weekly ed.: June 16, 1860 for a *Steubenfest* in memory of Baron von Steuben.

84. *Staats-Zeitung,* September 10, 1853. Cf. *Criminal-Zeitung,* August 26, 1859; Wittke, *op. cit.,* p. 220.

85. *Staats-Zeitung,* April 17, June 26, 1852.

86. *Staats-Zeitung,* daily ed.: June 28, 29, 1858; Leuchs, *op. cit.,* p. 10 n.

87. *Scottish Patriot,* September 5, 12, 1840; *Albion,* October 1, 1836; Liddel, *op. cit.,* pp. 19, 46, 55, 178.

88. *Anglo American,* February 14, March 7, 1846.

89. Cf., e.g., *Irish American,* March 24, 1850, March 27, 1852, March 15, 1856.

90. *Citizen,* February 11, 1854, January 27, 1855; *Irish American,* July 1, 1854; *Daily Tribune,* April 22, 1850; *Times,* June 23, 1854. Cf. *Scottish Journal of Intelligence and Literature,* February 6, November 6, 1841; *Subterranean,* May 2, 1846. In Massachusetts, the Know Nothing legislature forced immigrant militia companies to disband. Cf. Handlin, *op. cit.,* p. 210.

91. For group emigration schemes, cf. *Courrier des États-Unis,* January 30, 1849, July 23, 1851, and advertisements, January 23, 1848 ff. One French company boasted a capital of $12,000, of which $6,000 was furnished by twenty active members. *Courrier des États-Unis,* January 25, 1849. For instances of land speculators trying to stimulate the immigration of European farmers, cf., e.g., *Irish American,* September 4, 1852, October 10, 1857; *Citizen,* April 8, 1854; and the letters of Eduard Pelz in the Daly Papers [New York Public Library]. The Swiss immigrant, Lorenzo Delmonico, lost $500,000 of his restaurant profits through disastrous investments in oil stocks. *Dictionary of American Biography,* V, 226–227. According to the *Eco d'Italia* (December 30, 1865), the Italians, unlike the Irish and the Germans, showed an aversion to speculation. Of course, most Italians in New York City were still too poor to indulge in large-scale investment.

92. "Report of the Special Legislative Committee on Building Associations in the City of New-York," New York State, *Assembly Documents,* III, No. 46 (1856), 1–7.

93. *Courrier des États-Unis,* September 12, 14, October 15, 23, 1850; *Irish American,* April 24, 1852.

94. *Irish American,* April 24, 1852.

95. "Report of the Special Legislative Committee . . . ," *op. cit.,* p. 12. *Criminal-Zeitung,* November 18, 1853, July 7, 1854. Owing to their relative wealth and numbers and their experiences with *Vereine* of all sorts, the Germans were especially active participants in land and building associations. For some of these, cf. *Staats-Zeitung,* daily ed. (advertisements): January 19, May 9, 10, 13, 14, 19, 28, June 9, 13, August 18, 1853; February 20, March 3, 1856; *Criminal-Zeitung,* July 7, 1854. Of more than local importance was the development in the latter fifties of a German community near Egg Harbor River in New Jersey, about fifteen miles northwest of Atlantic City. Under the motto, "Eigener Heerd ist Goldes Werth!" the Egg Harbor project slowly gained strength. During the sixties it had agents in New York, Philadelphia, Pittsburgh, Newark, Washington, Baltimore, Buffalo, Cleveland, Chicago, Providence, and Pottsville, Pa. By 1863 the Egg Harbor group owned some 33,000 acres of land and claimed three thousand settlers. *Criminal-Zeitung,* advertisements, e.g., June 12, 1857, March 20, 1863, and news item July 17, 1863; cf. also the issues of May 29, August 7, 1857, March 11, 1864.

96. "Report of the Special Legislative Committee . . . ," *op. cit.,* pp. 5–7; *Criminal-Zeitung,* May 29, June 12, 1857.

97. *Criminal-Zeitung,* November 18, 1853, July 25, 1856; "Report of the Special Legislative Committee . . . ," *op. cit., passim.*

98. *Criminal-Zeitung,* July 14, 1854.

99. In the thirties Frances Lieber (*Stranger in America,* I, 91) noted that immigrants saved their money in stockings or little bags. For the Emigrant Industrial Savings Bank, cf. Thomas F. Meehan, "New York's First Irish Emigrant Society," United States Catholic Historical Society, *Historical Records and Studies,* VI, Part II (December, 1912), 211; *Irish American,* December 14, 1850. Many of the bank's trustees were either officers or members of the Society's executive committee.

100. *Irish American,* February 28, 1857; *Freeman's Journal,* March 8, 1856. Nearly all the depositors were natives of Ireland, although slightly more than two hundred were Germans, according to the bank's fifth annual report.

101. *Criminal-Zeitung,* March 5, 1858; *Staats-Zeitung,* August 11, 1855, May 12, 1860; daily ed.: November 1, 1859 (advertisement). The trustees of the German bank were leading business and professional men, including the banker August Belmont, the lawyer Friedrich Kapp, the publisher Oswald Ottendorfer, and several merchants who were members of the German Society. The Society itself was instrumental in the establishment of the bank. Cronau, *Denkschrift zum 150, Jahrestag der Deutschen Gesellschaft,* p. 92; *Staats-Zeitung,* daily ed.: November 1, 1859 (advertisement).

102. *Staats-Zeitung,* daily ed.: October 2, 1859. Cigar makers, carpenters, bakers, butchers, clerks, barbers, piano workers, servants, and house painters also were well represented. *Ibid.* On May 5, 1860 the *Sparbank* had 3,517 depositors, *Staats-Zeitung,* May 5, 1860.

103. *Report on Emigration by a Special Committee of the Chamber of Commerce of the State of New York* . . . (New York, 1865), Appendix, p. 17. The older Emigrant Industrial Savings Bank held most of the funds, but on July 1, 1860 the deposits in the *Sparbank* reached $1,134,575. Cronau, *Denkschrift* . . . , p. 92. Both banks prospered and are in existence today, the German institution having been renamed the Central Savings Bank.

104. *Staats-Zeitung,* December 15, 1858, advertisements: October 24, 1859, January 4, 1862. During the fifties German immigrants became aware of the desirability of insurance. The American branch of a London life insurance company had solicited business in 1846 from the Germans and French in New York, and in 1855 the *Staats-Zeitung* printed articles explaining and pointing out the importance of life insurance. *Staats-Zeitung,* January 3, 1846 (advertisement), August 25, September 1, 1855.

105. *New Yorker Handels-Zeitung,* July 22, 1865.

106. *Staats-Zeitung,* daily ed. (advertisements): April 12, 1853, October 24, 1859; George J. Manson, "The Foreign Element in New York City, the Germans," Supplement to *Harper's Weekly,* XXXII, No. 1650 (August 4, 1888), 582. Several non-Germans were on the board of directors of the *Germania* fire insurance company.

107. For French efforts, cf. *Courrier des États-Unis,* July 13, 17, 24, 1847, February 11, 15, 1848, October 4, 1854, February 27, May 5, 1856. For the early Irish schemes, cf. *Tribune,* June 22, 1850; *Irish American,* July 26, August 16, September 13, 1851, February 14, March 20, April 17, 24, 1852; *Irish News,* May 20, 1854, June 6, 1857. For the Galway and New York Steamship Company, which, under the guiding hand of John O. Lever, became the Atlantic Royal Mail Steamship Company, cf. *Irish American,* July 31, August 7, October 9, 16, 1858, April 21, 1860. The two German lines are mentioned in Leuchs, *op. cit.,* p. 6. It should be remembered that many of the entrepreneurs of these shipping lines were not immigrants, but the newcomers took an active part in the agitation for direct steamship services. The immigrant press publicized it with pride and enthusiasm.

Chapter XII

1. Maguire, *Irish in America,* p. 423; Brann, *Most Reverend John Hughes,* p. 88; *Staats-Zeitung,* January 19, 1850.

2. The standard work on anti-Catholicism prior to the Civil War, R. A. Billington's *Protestant Crusade, 1800–1860* (New York, 1938), pp. 21–23, gives undue attention to the antipopery sentiment of colonial times as a background of the nativist crusades of the nineteenth century. I am convinced that the chief popular strength of nativism lay in such social factors as dislike of foreigners in general, the obvious growth of pauperism and crime, the occasional political influence wielded by the church in city elections, and above all, the workingmen's fear of immigrant competition. Cf. Handlin, *Boston's Immigrants, 1790–1865,* pp. 186–187, n. 11.

3. *Evening Tattler,* August 17, 1839; *Protestant Vindicator,* June 17, 1835.

4. Billington, *op. cit.,* pp. 35–36, 339.

5. *Ibid.,* p. 35; Claghorn, "The Foreign Immigrant in New York City," United States Industrial Commission, *Reports,* XV, 452. For police and watch returns, cf., e.g., *Evening Tattler,* July 25, August 5, 26, 1835; cf. the dispassionate article on the subject in the *Courrier des États-Unis,* March 14, 1860.

6. John A. Hassard, *Life of Most Rev. John Hughes, D.D.* (New York, 1866), p. 212.

7. Maguire, *op. cit.,* p. 423.

8. John G. Shea (ed.), *Catholic Churches of New York City* . . . (New York, 1878), pp. 85–88, 537–538, 587–588; Thomas F. Meehan, "Very Rev. Johann Stephen Raffeiner, V.G.," United States Catholic Historical Society, *Historical Records and Studies,* IX (June, 1916), 161–165; *Andenken an das "Goldene Jubiläum," oder Fünfzigjährige Anniversarium der Gründung der St. Nicolaus Kirche* . . . (New York, c. 1883), p. 80; *Allgemeine Zeitung,* January 9, 1836. According to Georg J. Dusold's *Goldenes Jubiläum der Kirche zum Allerheiligsten Erlöser* . . . (New York, c. 1894), p. 1, at least a thousand German Catholics lived in New York City in 1832. At approximately the same time, the city's Irish Catholic population probably was more than 30,000. Cf. *Weekly Register and Catholic Diary,* February 1, 1834, which gave estimates of 30,000 and 40,000.

9. *Weekly Register and Catholic Diary,* February 1, 1834; Maguire, *op. cit.,* p. 431.

10. *Andenken an das "Goldene Jubilaum"* . . . , pp. 80–81.

11. *Ibid.,* p. 83.

12. *Courrier des États-Unis,* October 12, 1841.

13. Shea, *op. cit.,* pp. 178–181.

14. *Courrier des États-Unis,* February 9, 1865. There were twenty-four Catholic churches in 1855 and thirty-two in 1860 and 1865. *Ibid.*

15. Hassard, *op. cit.*, p. 256.
16. *Staats-Zeitung*, October 7, 1854.
17. *Staats-Zeitung*, December 19, 1846, October 7, 1854.
18. Cf. Hale, *Letters on Irish Emigration*, p. 37.
19. Israel Goldstein, *Century of Judaism in New York* . . . (New York, 1930), pp. vii, 46.
20. *Ibid.*, p. viii; Grinstein, *Rise of the Jewish Community*, p. 512.
21. Grinstein, *op. cit.*, pp. 49–50.
22. *Ibid.*, p. 50.
23. Grinstein, *op. cit.*, pp. 11–13, 35; Max J. Kohler, "German-Jewish Migration to America," American Jewish Historical Society, *Publications*, No. 9, 1901, p. 103.
24. Even in such co-operative efforts the Jews were far from unanimous. When in 1840 the arbitrary imprisonment of Jews in Damascus aroused in New York one of many Jewish indignation meetings, Shearith Israel refused to join in a request to the President of the United States that the American consul at Alexandria work with consuls of other nations to effect the release of the prisoners and to ask the Pasha of Egypt to treat the Jews more liberally. The aloofness of Shearith Israel was dictated by the fear of being overwhelmed by the newer and larger Jewish groups in the city. In 1853 and 1854 New York Jews contributed to the relief of famine stricken Jews in Palestine, in 1860 to aid the homeless and starving Jews from Tangiers who had taken refuge in Gibraltar during the war between Spain and Morocco, and in 1863 to aid unfortunate Jews in the Polish rebellion. *Asmonean*, July 8, 1853, June 30, 1854; *Staats-Zeitung*, August 18, 1860; *Corriere Israelitico* (Trieste), 1863, No. 5, p. 201; Grinstein, *op. cit.*, pp. 435–436, 438, 446–447.
25. Cf. Grinstein, *op. cit.*, pp. 430–433.
26. *Anglo American*, May 4, 1843 (advertisement), May 31, 1845; Moses Marcus, *Address to the Members of the "United Church of England and Ireland* . . . " (New York, 1846), p. 27. Declaring that the Irish were devoted and zealous churchgoers, Marcus decried the indifference of English immigrants who forsook the church for the tavern on Sundays. *Ibid.*, pp. 16–17. Such indifference, by no means confined to the English, may be explained by the relative absence in New York of community pressure for social conformity among Protestant immigrants, and the desire for simple recreation at the end of the long working week, perhaps under the influence of the Germans, whose observance of the Sabbath did not preclude merriment at beer gardens or picnics. Cf. George J. Manson, "The Foreign Element in New York City; The Germans," *Harper's Weekly*, XXXII, No. 1650 (August 4, 1888), 583.
27. *Scottish Journal of Intelligence and Literature*, February 6, 13, 27, 1841.
28. Hardie, *Description of the City of New York*, p. 164; *Longworth's . . . City Directory*, 1835–1836, p. 471, 1839–1840, p. 738.
29. Hardie, *op. cit.*, p. 177.
30. *Courrier des États-Unis*, December 15, 1848, February 6, 1849. A French directory listed the French churches as St. Vincent de Paul and St. François Xavier, both Catholic, and two Protestant churches, the Église du St. Esprit and the Église Evangelique Française. Maugé, *Directory Français* . . . , p. 100.
31. George U. Wenner, *Lutherans of New York: their Story and their Problems* (New York, 1918), p. 41. These figures do not include the first Swedish Lutheran congregation, which was organized in 1865. *Ibid.*, p. 37; Gustav Andreen, "The Early Missionary Work of the Augustana Synod in New York City, 1865–1866," Augustana Historical Society, *Publications*, No. 2, 1932, pp. 1–11.
32. Körner, *Das deutsche Element in den Vereinigten Staaten von Nordamerika, 1818–1848*, p. 109; Historical Records Survey, *Inventory of Church Archives in New York City. The Lutherans* (New York, 1940), p. 75.
33. *Staats-Zeitung*, May 24, 31, 1837, June 10, 1840.
34. *Staats-Zeitung*, May 4, 31, 1837; cf. Wenner, *op. cit.*, pp. 31–34; Hansen, *Atlantic Migration*, p. 138.

35. *Allgemeine Zeitung,* October 12, 1839.

36. Cf. advertisements, *Staats-Zeitung,* February 19, June 24, August 5, 1840; Albert Post, *Popular Freethought in America* (New York, 1943), pp. 72–75; Faust, *German Element in the United States* . . . , II, 428.

37. *Staats-Zeitung,* daily ed., advertisements, September 6, 26, 1853.

38. Board of Aldermen, *Documents,* IV, No. 40 (1839), 440. As early as 1833 the Frenchman Abdy wrote: "In New York . . . there is reason to believe that from 50,000 to 80,000 children are destitute of all instruction, besides the flood of adult foreigners." (Abdy, *Journal of a Residence and Tour in the United States of North America,* II, 333.) This estimate was far too high but was prophetic of the trend during the next three decades.

39. Children's Aid Society, *First Annual Report,* 1854, pp. 5–6. *Ninth Annual Report,* 1862, p. 4; Board of Education, *Annual Report,* 1856, p. 10; Brace, *Dangerous Classes of New York* . . . , pp. 90–93, 147–148, 356, 418–419; *Staats-Zeitung,* October 19, 1850; *London v. New York,* p. 22.

40. "Sabbath schools" were attended by an additional 2,500 pupils. Brace, *op. cit.,* p. 92.

41. An average of 3,000 children attended school; 2,631 were devoid of education, of whom 1,340 were born in the United States, 822 in Ireland, 338 in Germany, 93 in England, 11 in Scotland, and the remainder in Norway, France, the Netherlands, Italy, Wales, and Poland. *Daily Times,* November 10, 1856; *Staats-Zeitung,* daily ed., May 9, 1856; A.I.C.P., *Seventeenth Annual Report,* 1860, p. 78, Appendix B; Board of Education, *Annual Report,* 1856, pp. 14–15.

42. Sanger, *History of Prostitution* . . . , p. 472; *Irish American,* February 7, 1857; A.I.C.P., *Seventeenth Annual Report,* 1860, p. 78; Children's Aid Society, *Tenth Annual Report,* 1863, p. 43. Cf. Board of Education, *Annual Report,* 1856, p. 18.

43. Sanger, *op. cit.,* pp. 471–472, citing statistics of the federal census of 1850 and the report of the New York City Board of Education for 1856, from which he concluded that the proportion of school children between the ages of five and fifteen declined from 75.9 per cent in 1850 to 66 per cent in 1856. In the year 1858 the average attendance at the public schools was 51,430, yet 139,441 children were registered. A.I.C.P., *Seventeenth Annual Report,* 1860, p. 78. Cf. Board of Education, *Annual Reports,* 1850, p. 78, 1856, p. 10.

44. Hassard, *op. cit.,* p. 226; Brann, *op. cit.,* pp. 69–70; *Freeman's Journal,* July 4, 11, 1840, and almost any of the succeeding numbers; *Irish American,* January 29, 1853, May 22, 29, 1858.

45. Hassard, *op. cit.,* p. 227. The priests taught the boys, but the girls were under the supervision of the Sisters of Charity. *Ibid.* In 1826 both St. Peter's and St. Patrick's maintained schools. Protestant churches, including the German Lutherans, also conducted "charity schools." Hardie, *op. cit.,* p. 237. Cf. *Deutsche Schnellpost,* advertisement, May 8, 1844.

46. Hassard, *op. cit.,* p. 227. Some Catholic children attended the public schools, but many grew up without any formal education. *Ibid.;* Brann, *op. cit.,* p. 70. In the Fourth, Sixth, Twelfth, and Fourteenth wards, eleven public schools, whose pupils were almost entirely Catholic, omitted the reading of the Bible. Board of Education, *Report of the Committee on the Annual Apportionment* . . . *Relative to the Use of the Bible in the Public Schools* . . . (New York, 1844), p. 7. Cf. the description of Sixth Ward public schools in the *Irish American,* March 31, 1850.

47. Bishop Hughes stated that no less than two hundred teachers instructed twelve to fifteen thousand pupils in the Catholic institutions of the city. *Citizen,* December 13, 1856.

48. *Courrier des États-Unis,* January 18, 1845; *Staats-Zeitung,* October 7, 1854.

49. Many churches insisted upon strict religious orthodoxy, but the German Lutheran *Matthäus* Academy was conducted upon broader principles and in 1851 was the only German church school to resemble the city public schools. *Staats-Zeitung,* April 19, 1851.

For other sectarian schools, cf., e.g., *Staats-Zeitung*, March 22, 1837, and advertisements: September 27, 1837, December 18, 1839; *Asmonean*, March 1, 15, 1850. For a free "nonsectarian" German Sunday school, cf. *Staats-Zeitung*, August 28, 1858. For a German freethinkers' school in 1845, cf. *Deutsche Schnellpost*, advertisement, April 5, 1845, July 26, 1845. For the education in Europe of the children of wealthy immigrants or foreign-born residents in New York, cf., e.g., Morrison, *History of the St. Andrew's Society* . . . , p. 153, *Caspar Meier and his Successors* . . . , pp. 32, 37; Hopp, *Federzeichnungen aus dem Amerikanischen Leben*, p. 42. Cf. advertisements of European schools, e.g., *Courrier des États-Unis*, January 15, 1831; *Staats-Zeitung*, September 17, 1859.

50. The Jews likewise supported public education, yet continued to send their children to synagogue schools. *Asmonean*, March 22, 1850; cf. the issues of March 1, 15, 1850. Like the Catholics, however, some Jews objected to the textbooks in the public schools. Jewish criticism was directed toward the habitual emphasis upon the New Testament rather than any implicit derogation of Judaism. Board of Education, *Report of the Select Committee of the Board of Education, . . . in relation to the Sectarian Character of Certain Books in Use in the Schools . . .* (New York, 1843), *passim*.

51. *Staats-Zeitung*, November 2, 1850, February 1, April 19, 1851; *Criminal-Zeitung*, January 28, 1859. In 1837 the German communities in several cities, including New York, sent delegates to a convention in Pittsburgh for the purpose of fostering German schools and preserving the German language in America. However, the movement lacked popular support. *Staats-Zeitung*, September 20, October 4, 25, November 8, 1837.

52. *Staats-Zeitung*, January 22, May 20, 1840; L. D. Scisco, *Political Nativism in New York State* (New York, 1901), pp. 32 ff. Cf. p. 169.

53. According to the *Staats-Zeitung* (February 1, 1851), the masses of the German population, until then, had left educational matters to "custom, accident, and priests." Thus the indifference of the Germans was the greatest obstacle to the success of the teachers' association. *Ibid.*, April 19, 1851; cf. *ibid.*, daily ed., August 26, 1859.

54. *Courrier des États-Unis*, January 4, 1837.

55. A small *Deutsche Freischule* existed, however, from 1850 to 1855. *Staats-Zeitung*, May 5, 1855; Leuchs, *Early German Theatre in New York, 1840–1872*, p. 7.

56. *Staats-Zeitung*, daily ed., December 17, 1859; *Criminal-Zeitung*, January 13, 1860.

57. *Criminal-Zeitung*, February 17, 1860.

58. The school for German girls offered evening classes in sewing and singing and, on Saturday evenings, games and social amusements. Wealthy German merchants supported the project and subscribed about $1,000, and the Messrs. Steinway donated a piano. Children's Aid Society, *Seventh Annual Report*, 1860, p. 22. The Italian school was established in 1855–1857, but not until 1863 was the Italian community able to lift appreciably the burden from the Children's Aid Society. Among the leading Italian supporters of the school were Professor Vincenzo Botta, the ship owner E. P. Fabbri, and a number of Italian merchants. Brace, *op. cit.*, p. 209; Children's Aid Society, *Ninth Annual Report*, 1862, p. 16; *Eco d'Italia*, August 12, 1865.

59. Advertisements, *Albion*, April 28, 1827; *Crónica*, May 31, 1854. Cf. *Irish American*, September 18, 1852.

60. Advertisements, *Courrier des États-Unis*, August 24, 1831, May 30, June 2, 1832, August 1, September 5, 1843, August 20, 1858, August 26, October 9, 1865. The Institution Française, also known as the French Catholic Institute, enrolled American, German, and Spanish students in 1865. *Ibid.*, advertisement, October 9, 1865; *Irish News*, February 7, 1858.

61. *Staats-Zeitung*, March 17, 1841, August 31, 1850, April 19, 1851; daily ed., April 21, 1858, August 26, 1859; cf. Leuchs, *op. cit.*, pp. 6–7.

62. Hopp, *op. cit.*, p. 33. In 1875 the number of German private schools in the city had increased at least threefold.

63. For private schools, cf., e.g., *Irish American*, advertisements: June 5, August 28, 1852; *Asmonean*, advertisements: October 24, 1851, January 30, 1857; *Scottish Patriot*, March 7, 21, April 18, 1840.

64. Cf., e.g., advertisements, *Truth Teller*, February 3, 1827; *Citizen*, October 7, 1854. At one school, most of the students were "Irish laborers, mechanics, and female servants," and while some classes met the needs of architects and master masons, evening courses were "peculiarly adapted for those of a limited education." *Irish American*, October 2, 1852, October 22, 1853.

65. *Anglo American*, April 11, 1846, April 17, 1847; *Staats-Zeitung*, daily ed., June 3, 1853.

66. Committee on Evening Schools, *Fourth Annual Report*, in Board of Education, *Documents*, 1850, No. 8, pp. 2–4; Board of Education, *Annual Reports*, 1851, pp. 2–3, 1852, pp. 8–9, 1853, Appendix, pp. 29–30. Cf. *Irish American*, October 2, 1858. Fire companies and the *Turnvereine* drew away students and contributed to the irregular attendance of evening schools. Cf. Board of Education, *Annual Report*, 1853, Appendix, pp. 14–15.

67. *Staats-Zeitung*, daily ed., December 17, 1859; *Criminal-Zeitung*, January 13, 1860; *Eco d'Italia*, January 14, February 3, May 20, December 30, 1865.

68. *Truth Teller*, May 10, 1834; *Evening Tattler*, March 19, 1841; *Irish American*, December 17, 1853; *Irish News*, May 10, 17, 1856.

69. *Irish American*, July 10, 1858, September 8, 1860; *Irish News*, September 1, 1860.

70. *Deutsche Schnellpost*, January 15, 1845; *Staats-Zeitung*, daily ed., advertisements: April 7, 1856, May 14, 15, 1858. A letter published in the *Staats-Zeitung*, November 28, 1846, pointed to the absorption of the Germans in the business of making a living and the small amount of free time of workingmen as the reasons for the late establishment of literary societies. This was undoubtedly true.

71. *Asmonean*, December 23, 1853, January 9, 19, 1855, May 16, 1856; *Jewish Messenger*, November 4, 1859; Grinstein, *op. cit.*, pp. 195–196.

72. *Courrier des États-Unis*, March 4, April 4, 1864; *Messenger Franco-Américain*, March 22, 1865.

73. Cf. Grinstein, *op. cit.*, p. 196. This work refers only to Jewish societies, but there is no reason to assume that the Jews were different from other groups in this respect, unless it were in the direction of greater intellectual interests.

74. Cf., e.g., advertisements: *Weekly Register and Catholic Diary*, October 5, 1833; *Citizen*, December 2, 1854; *European News*, September 11, 1847; *Staats-Zeitung*, daily ed., April 21, 1858.

75. Cf. *Criminal-Zeitung*, advertisement, November 5, 1852, October 28, 1859; *Courrier des États-Unis*, advertisement, December 23, 1840; *Messager Franco-Américain*, February 7, 1862. Even the tiny Scandinavian population patronized a reading room in 1847. *Skandinavia*, April 15, 1847. Sometimes the Church fostered libraries, such as that of St. James Church in 1852. *Irish American*, March 20, 1852.

76. *Freeman's Journal*, March 26, 1842, January 28, 1843; *Irish News*, May 3, September 20, 1856.

77. *Irish American*, August 28, 1858; letter of Michael Hennessy, *ibid.*, September 4, 1858.

78. *Asmonean*, May 11, 1855; Grinstein, *op. cit.*, p. 203.

79. Cf., e.g., advertisements: *Albion*, September 6, 1851; *Irish News*, December 26, 1857; *Staats-Zeitung*, daily ed.: October 22, 29, 1859. For the French lending library, cf. *Courrier des États-Unis*, March 14, 1864.

80. Cf. advertisements of De Behr, *Courrier des États-Unis*, November 14, 1829, July 20, 27, 1836; cf. those of Berard and Mondon, *ibid.*, March 15, 1828, December 5, 1835. Cf. Thomas F. Meehan, "John Doyle, Publisher," United States Catholic Historical Society, *Historical Records and Studies*, X (January, 1917), 172; Ross, *Scot in America*, pp. 248–249, 251–252; Körner, *op. cit.*, p. 106.

81. *Courrier des États-Unis*, advertisement, January 20, 1830. Körner, *op. cit.*, p. 106, stated that the sale of German books was limited by their high prices and that educated Germans in New York who could read English bought the cheaper English books. In 1837 a few twenty-five cent editions of German works were advertised by Schulz and Bleidorn and by the editor of the *Staats-Zeitung*, but these were exceptional cases. Only when booksellers in America began to print popular German works did the booksellers in Germany issue cheap editions for export. *Staats-Zeitung*, January 4, May 17, 1837; Körner, *op. cit.*, p. 106.

82. Büchele, *op. cit.*, p. 283; *Amerika, Wie est Ist* . . . (Hamburg, 1854), pp. 99, 101; *Criminal-Zeitung*, February 25, March 4, 1853; *Irishman and Foreigners' Advocate*, advertisements, July 15, 1835; *Courrier des États-Unis*, December 30, 1848, October 1, 1853, December 1, 1855, February 5, 1864; *Eco d'Italia*, January 9, 1862.

83. Advertisements: *Courrier des États-Unis*, December 1, 1855; *Criminal-Zeitung*, January 25, 1856. Some of these books, selling for twenty-five cents, were entitled *Mysteries of Venus or Lessons of Love; Julia or Where is the Woman that Wouldn't; Secret Habits of the Female Sex* (with colored illustrations, fifty cents); and *Adventures of a French Bedstead*. For fifty cents one might buy *Venus's Album or Rosebuds of Love*, and for a dollar, the *Married Woman's Practical Medical Guide. Criminal-Zeitung*, January 1, 1856; cf. the issue of October 3, 1856.

84. James R. Bayley, *Brief Sketch of the Early History of the Catholic Church on the Island of New York* (2d ed., New York, 1870), Appendix, pp. 217–218. Doyle began publishing Catholic works about 1823. *Ibid.* Other Catholic or Irish booksellers, like Robert Coddington, Owen Phelan, Patrick Kavanaugh, and J. Kennedy, occasionally published religious works. *Ibid.*, p. 218.

85. *Ibid.*, p. 219; *Deutsche Schnellpost*, advertisements: January 28, April 26, 1843.

86. Radde's advertisement, *Staats-Zeitung*, April 7, 1841.

87. Cf., e.g., advertisements: *Allgemeine Zeitung*, December 2, 1835, May 14, 1836; *Deutsche Schnellpost*, January 4, 1843; *Staats-Zeitung*, September 9, 1848, July 7, 1849, September 7, 1850; *Meyer's Monats-Hefte*, June 1853, "Introduction to the American Public."

88. *Amerika, Wie es Ist*, pp. 100–101.

89. Körner, *op. cit.*, p. 106; *Staats-Zeitung*, March 11, 1848.

90. Körner, *op. cit.*, p. 106. Among the leading German booksellers were Eichthal and Bernhard, publishers of the *Deutsche Schnellpost* and agents of the Stuttgart firm of J. G. Cotta. *Deutsche Schnellpost*, advertisement, January 4, 1843. Cf. *Criminal-Zeitung*, March 4, 1853, which lists this company and other German book publishers and dealers and which traces the growth of the German book trade at New York.

91. *Staats-Zeitung*, November 28, 1846; cf. *Amerika, Wie es Ist*, p. 100. In 1843 the *Deutsche Schnellpost* (January 14) advertised works of Gutzkow, Rückert, Grün, Herwegh, Dingelstadt, von Sallet, and Schäfer.

92. *Citizen*, July 1, 1854; *Irish American*, April 28, 1855.

93. *Citizen*, July 1, 1854. For these and other Irish works, cf. advertisements: *Citizen*, January 1, 1855 and *Irish American*, November 20, 1858.

94. In 1856 fully two thirds of the purchasers of Irish books were Americans. *Citizen*, July 26, 1856.

95. *Courrier des États-Unis*, December 9, 26, 1848, May 22, 1849, January 31, 1850; *Albion*, January 12, 19, 1850; *Amerika, Wie est Ist*, p. 79.

96. When the backers withdrew, the *Albion* (January 12, 1850) hoped that they had "broken up an exclusive spirit in Art of which signs have recently been apparent. In all that ministers to intellectual improvement and harmless pleasure we are out and out free traders."

97. *Staats-Zeitung*, daily ed., advertisement, August 6, 1853. Admission to the gallery was at the customary rate of twenty-five cents for adults, twelve and a half cents for children.

98. *Albion*, January 19, 1850, May 24, 1852; *Criminal-Zeitung*, October 17, 1856

(advertisement), October 14, 1859, February 3, 1860, January 18, 1861; *Staats-Zeitung,* January 23, 1856; Leuchs, *op. cit.,* p. 10.

99. *Handels-Zeitung,* April 12, 1859; *Criminal-Zeitung,* April 3, 20, September 28, 1860, January 18, February 15, 1861.

100. *Criminal-Zeitung,* February 15, 1861. Of a more practical nature was a projected art school in the winter of 1853–1854. Apparently the scheme was dropped, for the German press failed to mention it again.

101. The International Art Union accomplished for European art what the American Art Union did for native art. For the critical attitude of Europeans toward American painting, architecture, and music, cf. (Th. Kfn.), "Ueber Einige Zweige der Kunst in Amerika," *Atlantische Studien von Deutschen in Amerika* (Göttingen), I (1853), 95–109; Theodor Raufmann, "Die Kunst in Amerika, mit besonderer Beziehung auf Malerei," *ibid.,* VIII (1875), 209–224. The *Anglo American* (September 5, 1845) commented severely upon the poor ártistic taste: "What is the reason that educated and refined foreigners perceive, in the midst of generous and profuse hospitality at the table, substantial and elegant furniture and plate, *bijoutrie* [*sic*], and ornamental *bagatelles,* that the rooms have their walls crowded with contemptible pictures chiefly vulgar and coarse copies from Europe, expressly 'for the American Market,' and utterly in contrast with all else in the apartments?"

102. For the French ballet at New York, cf. Odell, III, 24, 266, 323, 354, 399, 401, 585 ff, 701; *Courrier des États-Unis,* May 25, 1832. For the French opera company, cf. *ibid.,* August 7, 1833; Odell, *op. cit.,* p. 401. For the Italian opera, cf. Odell, *op. cit.,* pp. 637, 642 ff, 690 ff; *Courrier des États-Unis,* October 3, 10, 1832, November 30, 1833.

103. For Fanny Elssler, cf. *Staats-Zeitung,* September 2, 1840; *Courrier des États-Unis,* March 14, 1840; Körner, *op. cit.,* p. 110.

104. *Staats-Zeitung,* January 1, 8, 15, February 19, March 25, April 1, 22, 29, May 20, September 23, 1840, August 4, 11, 25, October 13, 20, 27, November 3, 27, 1841, May 30, June 10, 1843. Cf. contemporary advertisements in the *Staats-Zeitung* and the *Deutsche Schnellpost;* Leuchs, *op. cit.,* pp. 17–47; Odell, *op. cit.,* IV, 581, 663.

105. *Amerika, Wie es Ist,* pp. 96–97; cf. Leuchs, *op. cit.,* pp. 48–67. For the marionette company, cf. Odell, *op. cit.,* VI, 254.

106. *Amerika, Wie es Ist,* p. 97.

107. Leuchs, *op. cit.,* pp. 75–124; *Criminal-Zeitung,* June 20, 1856. For a report of the premier performance cf. *Meyer's Monats-Hefte,* October 1854, pp. 463–465. Other less pretentious German theaters appeared in the fifties; some were adjuncts of beer gardens, like the group which performed at the *Deutscher Volksgarten* in the Bowery, where women and children were admitted free, but men paid ten cents, which entitled each man to a glass of beer. Cf. *Staats-Zeitung,* daily ed., advertisements, April 21, 1858; cf. Leuchs, *op. cit.,* pp. 68–74.

108. *Courrier des États-Unis,* October 14, November 29, December 13, 1851.

109. *Courrier des États-Unis,* May 8, 1852, January 11, 12, 13, 14, 19, 21, 1853; March 16, June 17, 1854; May 22, June 7, 19, July 7, 12, August 20, 22, 23, 1855; July 12, 14, August 2, December 27, 1856; March 7, 11, 1865; *Phare de New-York,* April 3, 17, 1852.

110. *Courrier des États-Unis,* May 13, 26, June 16, 22, 1858.

111. *Courrier des États-Unis,* July 17, 20, 1858.

112. *Courrier des États-Unis,* March 8, 9, 1859; cf. *ibid.,* advertisement, November 20, 1858.

113. *Courrier des États-Unis,* December 12, 13, 17, 21, 1859; January 6, 9, 10, 16, March 15, June 5, 1860.

114. The friendly relation which existed between the French and German theaters is treated by Carl E. Marquardt, "An Entente Cordiale in New York's Civil War Days," *Essays in Honor of A. Howry Espenshade* (New York, 1937), pp. 72–87.

115. Cf. the many theatrical notices in the *Albion;* cf., e.g., *Anglo American,* September 20, 1843, or almost any other number; *Scottish Patriot,* April 4, 1840. Members

of the Caledonian Club went as a group to the theater and were on intimate terms with Dion Boucicault, Lester and James Wallack, and other actors. Liddel, *History of the New York Caledonian Club*, I, 48, 60, 91. The Jews included ardent drama enthusiasts, the poorer Jews of the Chatham Street district attending the German theater. Griesinger, *Lebende Bilder* . . . , p. 147.

116. Booth, *History of the City of New York*, II, 749–751; cf. *Albion*, May 12, 1849; *Irish American*, September 30, 1849.

117. Odell, *op. cit.*, III, 353.

118. *Irish American*, October 28, 1849, March 22, 1851, January 24, 1852; Odell, *op. cit.*, VI, 3, 12, 116, 197–198, 313.

119. *Irish American*, October 28, 1849. Cf. Odell, *op. cit.*, VI, 36, 211.

120. *Irish American*, October 28, 1849, September 20, 1851; Odell, *op. cit.*, IV, 608–609. By 1854 the Broadway and National theaters were advertising in the *Irish American* (February 11, 1854 ff).

121. *Irish American*, September 6, 1851.

122. *Irish American*, April 11, 1857; Kenneth R. Rossman, "The Irish in American Drama in the Mid-Nineteenth Century," *New York History*, XXI, No. 1 (January, 1940), 46–47. "To Samuel Lover is due the credit of having been the first to openly express his indignation at the English stage representation of an Irishman for over two hundred years," wrote Thomas Addis Emmet. "He was shown in print, as in our day, with a gorilla shaped face, as needing a bath, and whiskey soaked, a brimless hat and a pipe with too short a stem for use, and on the stage as a boor and buffoon in manners, together with a supposed inexhaustible supply of senseless jokes and songs. This 'Get up' was accepted the world over as the typical Irishman." Thomas A. Emmet, *Incidents of My Life* (New York, 1911), p. 131.

Chapter XIII

1. *Truth Teller*, February 2, 1833; but cf. *European*, December 17, 1836, which stated that not more than two thousand of the twenty thousand Irishmen in New York City supported their own papers.

2. Cf. pp. 158–160.

3. The earliest Irish papers in the city were the *Shamrock* (1810) and the *Western Star and Harp of Erin*. Cf. Lawrence Kehoe (ed.), *Complete Works of the Most Rev. John Hughes, D.D., Archbishop of New York* . . . (New York, 1866), II, 686; Scisco, *Political Nativism in New York State*, p. 19; and *Western Star* . . . , May 16, 1812–May 1, 1813. For later attempts, cf. *Irishman*, June 19, 1824; *Globe and Emerald*, December 25, 1824 ff; *Emerald*, June 19, July 31, 1824; *European*, April 16, May 23, September 24, 1836; *Irishman and Foreigner's Advocate*, July 15, 20, 1835. For the *Irishman* (1832), cf. *Albion*, September 22, 1832. Cf. John D. Crimmins, *Irish-American Historical Miscellany* (New York, 1905), p. 215. For the *Irish Volunteer*, cf. *Young America*, October 4, 1845.

4. *Irish American*, July 27, 1850, which stated that in a little over a year four new papers had failed to survive.

5. Handlin, *Boston's Immigrants* . . . , p. 180. McGee moved the *American Celt* to Buffalo and later to New York, probably in 1853. In 1855 the paper's circulation was reported at the exaggerated figure of 19,000. MSS schedules of the *New York State Census of 1855*, "Second Ward, Newspapers and Periodicals."

6. *Citizen*, January 7, 1854 ff. The Irish American (July 8, 1854) overestimated the *Citizen's* circulation at 45,000.

7. *Citizen*, December 30, 1854, July 14, 1855; MSS, schedules of the *New York State Census of 1855*, "Second Ward, Newspapers and Periodicals."

8. Cf. *Irish News*, April 12, 1856 ff.

9. *Citizen*, May 30, 1857; *Irish American*, May 30, 1857. Lynch came to America at an early age and lived at Philadelphia and New York, but he returned to Ireland to

agitate for Repeal. When the movement collapsed, he sailed for New York in 1847 and contributed to several newspapers before launching the *Irish American.*

10. Cf., e.g., *Irish American,* September 30, December 23, 1849, July 26, 1851.

11. For *Irish American's* circulation figures cf. issues of: October 9, 1852, June 11, August 20, 1853; April 22, 1854, June 30, 1855, March 12, November 26, 1859, January 14, February 4, April 7, 1860, April 6, August 24, 1861. Most of these figures were sworn to by the printer and probably were accurate. It was estimated that five persons read each copy of the paper. The *New York State Census of 1855* (MSS schedules: "Second Ward, Newspapers and Periodicals") listed the *Irish American's* circulation as 19,000.

12. Cf., e.g., *Truth Teller,* November 3, 22, 1832; *Irish American,* September 28, October 26, 1850; *Citizen,* October 28, 1854; *Irish News,* September 6, 1856. For the Irish vote, cf. p. 166.

13. Cf., e.g., *Citizen,* March 18, December 16, 1854, June 28, 1856; *Irish American,* September 2, 30, 1849, December 13, 1851, October 24, November 7, 1857, *Irish News,* April 3, 1858.

14. For the defense against nativism, cf., e.g., *Truth Teller,* February 6, 13, 1836; *Irish American,* March 4, 1854, April 6, 1856; *Citizen,* August 26, September 9, 1854. For militia companies' justification, cf., e.g., *Truth Teller,* August 7, 1830; *Irish American,* April 28, May 5, 1850. For the loyalty of Irish-Americans, cf., e.g., *Truth Teller,* July 26, 1828, December 29, 1832, May 18, 1833, July 1, 1835; *Irish American,* May 28, 1850, January 10, 1857; *Citizen,* July 8, 1854; *Freeman's Journal,* July 4, 1840.

15. Cf., e.g., *Truth Teller,* September 5, 1835; *Irish American,* September 23, 1854. The *Irish American* (January 31, 1857) was for the "wholesome administration of the laws, for the harmonious cohesion of the masses, for the supremacy of order, for a ready, well-regulated obedience to the principle of discipline, for the public weal and the happiness of ALL."

16. *Irish American,* May 1, 1852. For the attitude toward marriage and womanhood, cf., e.g., *Irish American,* May 5, 1850, July 7, 1855; *Citizen,* February 4, 11, 1854, December 6, 1856; *Irish News,* May 10, June 28, 1856.

17. *Freeman's Journal,* December 19, 1857, expressing a widespread Catholic view. Cf. *Irish News,* May 10, 1856.

18. Cf., e.g., *Citizen,* February 4, 1854.

19. *Truth Teller,* November 20, 1830.

20. *Irish American,* May 1, 1852. "The part taken by Irish-Americans against Abolition is not *for* Slavery, but *against* the dissolution of the Union." *Ibid.,* October 29, 1853. For opposition to abolitionism, cf. *ibid.,* e.g., March 17, June 2, 1850, January 1, May 17, 1851; *Citizen,* March 18, 1854; *Irish News,* June 28, August 23, 1856.

21. *Irish American,* October 29, 1853.

22. *Citizen,* March 4, 1854; *Irish American,* January 31, 1857.

23. *Weekly Register and Catholic Diary,* July 29, 1834.

24. I have no direct evidence of the fear of possible competition from colored workers, but this is a reasonable assumption. For friction between the Irish and the colored population, cf. pp. 104, 105.

25. The file of the *Staats-Zeitung* in the New York Public Library begins with the issue of January 1, 1837. The circulation figure is given in the MSS schedules of the *New York State Census of 1855,* "Fourth Ward, Newspapers and Periodicals." Cf. *Staats-Zeitung,* July 19, 1856, which claimed a circulation of 15,300 for the daily and 11,000 for the weekly edition.

26. The *Staats-Zeitung* was begun as a joint stock venture, but in 1837 Neumann became proprietor; he was succeeded by Uhl in 1845. The latter died in 1852, and his wife managed the paper until 1859, when her second husband, Oswald Ottendorfer assumed control of the paper. Cf. *Epitome of the New Yorker Staats-Zeitungs Sixty-Five Years of Progress* (New York[?], 1899), *passim;* Körner, *Das deutsche Element in den Vereinigten Staaten von Nordamerika, 1818-1848,* p. 105.

27. I have discovered no evidence that the *Staats-Zeitung* was bought by the Democratic politicians. The paper thrived upon its own merits, especially as a medium of communication for the German merchants, who supported it with their advertising. Cf. the forthcoming work by Ferdinand Schultz on the history of the *Staats-Zeitung*.

28. The *Abendzeitung*, which circulated almost exclusively in inns and taverns, had a daily circulation of 2,300 in 1856, according to the *Staats-Zeitung* (July 19, 1856). Wilhelm Schlüter, editor of the *Demokrat*, also edited the *Beobachter*, a Sunday paper with a claimed circulation of 6,000 in 1855, or about the same as that of the *Demokrat*. (MSS schedules of the *New York State Census of 1855*, "Fourth Ward, Newspapers and Periodicals.") For political viewpoints, cf. the weekly ed. of the *Demokrat* August 3, September 7, 1861; *Courrier des États-Unis*, September 20, 1859; *Handels-Zeitung*, daily ed., February 4, 1858; *Staats-Zeitung*, February 23, July 19, 1856, August 4, 1860.

29. *Deutsche Schnellpost*, January 4, 1843 ff. Cf. Carl Wittke, *Against the Current; the Life of Karl Heinzen* . . . (Chicago [1945]), pp. 84–85; Körner, *op. cit.*, p. 105. In 1851 the *Deutsche Schnellpost* had a circulation of 1,150, according to the *Staats-Zeitung*, August 23, 1851.

30. Cf. *Criminal-Zeitung*, March 20, 1852 ff.

31. According to the *New York State Census of 1855* (MSS schedules, "Fourth Ward, Newspapers and Periodicals"), the *Criminal-Zeitung* had a circulation of 20,000, which seems far too high a figure. Nevertheless this paper became the *Staats-Zeitung's* strongest rival. In 1856 the *Staats-Zeitung* credited the *Criminal-Zeitung* with a circulation of 6,000, a figure which the latter rejected as too low, without giving its correct circulation. *Staats-Zeitung*, July 19, 1856; *Criminal-Zeitung*, July 18, 1856.

32. The *Handels-Zeitung* was founded in 1851. (*Staats-Zeitung*, November 15, 1851.) Cf. the issues of April 10, May 30, 1855 for its absorption of the *Geschaefts-Bericht*.

33. *Staats-Zeitung*, daily ed., December 21, 1859; *Handels-Zeitung*, August 6, 1859. For the *Bank Noten Reporter*, cf. *Staats-Zeitung*, daily ed., March 1, April 28, 1856; *Handels-Zeitung*, August 31, 1857. The *Commercial Gazette* was originally a German paper, the *Handelsblatt*, which first appeared in English in 1854. *Staats-Zeitung*, September 23, 30, 1854. Germans, however, were not the only publishers of such business papers. Cf. p. 157, and *Courrier des États-Unis*, April 18, 1855.

34. *Staats-Zeitung*, August 4, 1855 ff.

35. Körner, *op. cit.*, p. 105; *Staats-Zeitung*, October 21, 1840; July 19, 1851; daily ed.: September 11, 1858; Hermann Schlüter, *Die Anfänge* . . . , pp. 26–27, 119, 148–149; *Amerika, Wie es Ist*, p. 57; *Criminal-Zeitung*, January 6, 1854; Wittke, *op. cit.*, pp. 55, 88–90, 95–99.

36. Körner, *op. cit.*, p. 105; Leuchs, *Early German Theatre in New York, 1840–1872*, p. 277; Post, *Popular Freethought in America*, pp. 72–74; Wittke, *op. cit.*, p. 124.

37. *Turn-Zeitung. Organ das Socialistischen Turnerbundes*, November 15, 1851–November 1, 1853; *Turn Blatt für die Vereine*, October 1856 ff.

38. Wittke, *op. cit.*, p. 133; *Courrier des États-Unis*, April 18, 1855.

39. Advertisements: *Criminal-Zeitung*, September 30, October 28, 1853, September 30, 1859; *Staats-Zeitung*, January 9, October 6, 1858, December 6, 1862; daily ed., October 6, 1858.

40. *Deutsche Monats-Hefte*, June 1853 ff. Franz Sigel edited a monthly *Revue* in 1856 and 1857. (Advertisement, *Criminal-Zeitung*, September 5, 1856; *Turn Blatt für die Vereine*, November, 1857.) In the mid-sixties another German family-type periodical, the *Deutschamerikanische Gartenlaube*, flourished in New York City. Leuchs, *op. cit.*, p. 278; advertisement, *Staats-Zeitung*, April 12, 1862.

41. The *Theater Journal* was said to contain a historical sketch of the German-American stage. Leuchs, *op. cit.*, p. 277. I have found no other reference to the *Theater Journal* and assume that it succumbed early. A decade later, another magazine dealt with art, drama, and other cultural subjects. Leuchs, *op. cit.*, p. 278.

42. *Staats-Zeitung*, April 8, 1858, advertisements: April 22, 1858, August 27, 1859; daily ed., December 17, 1859; *Handels-Zeitung*, April 7, 1858.

43. *Albion*, June 22, 1822 ff. In 1855 the *Albion* had a weekly circulation of 6,000. MSS schedules of the *New York State Census of 1855*, "Third Ward, Newspapers and Periodicals."

44. The *Emigrant* asserted that its original motive was to offset the influence of the *Old Countryman* and counterbalance its "unprovoked abuse" of the *Albion*. The proprietor of both the *Albion* and the *Emigrant* was John S. Bartlett, who by initiating the latter, tried to make a genuine appeal to British immigrants. *Emigrant* July 3, 10, 1833. In 1855 another British paper, the *European*, began its life of at least two years. *European*, November 15, 1856–May 2, 1857.

45. A complete file of the *Anglo American* (April 29, 1843–November 13, 1847) is in the New York Public Library.

46. Cf., e.g., *Scottish Patriot*, July 11, October 24, 1840; *Scottish Journal of Intelligence and Literature*, September 25, December 18, 1841. This paper probably perished shortly after July 16, 1842. Handlin (*op. cit.*, p. 177) refers to a short-lived *Scottish American* in New York in 1857 which may be the *Scottish American Journal* mentioned by Ross, *Scot in America*, p. 397, and in city directories during the early sixties.

47. *Tribune*, July 14, 1855; "New York City Register," p. 31, in *Trow's New York City Directory . . . for the year ending May 1, 1862*.

48. The short-lived *Skandinavia*, started in 1847, employed Danish and Swedish in its columns and allotted about equal space to Swedish, Norwegian, and Danish affairs. Many of its subscribers lived in the West, however, and its lack of concern over the local affairs of the West, its pan-Scandinavianism, and perhaps its failure to take a political stand probably accounted for its early demise. Blegen, *Norwegian Migration to America*, II, 288. For other ephemeral Scandinavian papers, cf. *Criminal-Zeitung*, April 10, 1852.

49. Cf. Blegen, *op. cit.*, p. 401; O. Fritiof Ander, "Swedish-American Newspapers and the Republican Party, 1855–1875," Augustana Historical Society, *Publications*, No. 2, 1932, p. 76. The German newspaper corporation was undoubtedly the *Staats-Zeitung*, the only strong German Democratic paper in the city during the sixties.

50. *Courrier des États-Unis*, March 1, 1828, November 14, 1829, November 12, 1839, April 24, June 10, 1851.

51. MSS schedules of the *New York State Census of 1855*, "Fifth Ward, Newspapers and Periodicals."

52. *Franco-Américain*, March 28, 1846 ff. Some of the other short-lived French papers were the *Papillon* in 1829 (*Redactor*, August 29, 1829; *Albion*, August 22, 1829), *l'Indicateur* in 1839–1840 (*Courrier des États-Unis*, March 7, 1840; Louis H. Fox, "New York City Newspapers, 1820–1850, a Bibliography," *Papers of the Bibliographical Society of America*, XXI, Parts I–II, 1927 [Chicago, c. 1928], 56), the *Reflet de Paris* in 1844 (*Deutsche Schnellpost*, March 23, 1844), and the *Moniteur Américain* in 1851 (*Eco d'Italia*, July 5, 1851). *L'Estafette*, a French language paper owned and edited by an Englishman, H. D. Robinson, supported the Canadian rebellion of 1837–1838 and vigorously attacked "despotism" in Canada. (*Estafette*, February 13, 16, 20, 23, March 30, April 6, 8, June 8, 1838).

53. *Phare de New-York*, May 10, 1851 ff; *Courrier des États-Unis*, March 12, 1853.

54. *Républicain*, May 7, 1851 ff.

55. *Progrès*, January 2, 1855 ff. By June 1855 the *Progrès* had 2,000 subscribers. MSS schedules of the *New York State Census of 1855*, "Fifth Ward, Newspapers and Periodicals."

56. *Messager Franco-Américain*, February 7, 1862 ff.

57. The *Redactor*, published three times a month in 1827, probably was the earliest Spanish language paper in New York; it was concerned largely with literature, Latin American news, and commerce. By 1831 it had become a weekly; since it was published "for a Spanish Society," it carried very little news of the United States. *Redactor*, January 8–December 31, 1831. For the *Mercurio de Nueva-York* and the *Mensagero Semanal*, cf. advertisement, *Courrier des États-Unis* (August 24, 1849) and in 1865 a masonic paper, the *Espejo Macenico* (*ibid.*, October 30, 1865).

58. For the *Verdad's* viewpoint, cf., e.g., the issues of April 27, 1848, May 18, 1850. Miguel T. Tolon, editor of the *Verdad* in June 1850, was secretary of the Cuban junta at New York. (*Staats-Zeitung,* June 1, 1850.) The New York *Sun* advertised in the *Verdad,* April 27, 1850.

59. *Citizen,* June 17, 1854; MSS schedules of the *New York State Census of 1855,* "Fifth Ward, Newspapers and Periodicals."

60. For the earlier commercial papers, cf. O. L. Holley (ed.), *New York State Register* (Albany, 1843), p. 147, which mentioned a *Noticioso de Ambos Mundos* as a weekly newspaper. Cf. *Courrier des États-Unis,* August 4, 1859, which announced a new paper, the *Noticioso,* to be published six times a month to correspond with the departure of steamers for the Antilles and the isthmus. The *Continental* was established in 1861.

61. *Crónica,* January 27, 1849 (Vol. I, No. 28 ff). Cf. the issues of March 6, 1850, January 11, June 7, 17, 1854, March 3, June 21, 1856, December 9, 1859 for typical expressions of its viewpoints.

62. For the *Crónica's* mercantile appeal, cf. especially the issues of January 27, February 15, April 7, June 25, July 11, 1849, March 23, April 9, July 18, 1859. During the fifties almost every issue carried much Cuban news.

63. Letter of Rocco Martuscelli to the Neapolitan Minister of Foreign Affairs, February 10, 1850, quoted by Howard R. Marraro, "Italians in New York . . . ," *New York History,* XXVI, No. 3 (July, 1945), 294. For the *Europeo Americano,* cf. *ibid.,* p. 293. Printed in English and Italian, this paper was also known as the *European American.*

64. Marraro, "Italians in New York . . . ," *op. cit.,* p. 296; *Staats-Zeitung,* July 20, 1850. The refugee priest, Filopanti, edited and published an Italian paper at about the same time, but I can not state whether he succeeded Torricelli (or Torrecelli) or whether his paper was another revolutionary journal. Cf. *Staats-Zeitung,* August 23, 1851.

65. *Proscritto,* August 7, 1851 ff; Marraro, "Italians in New York," *op. cit.,* pp. 296–297; *Courrier des États-Unis,* January 27, 1852.

66. *Eco d'Italia,* 1851–1852, 1862 ff. For local news and reports of Italian activities, cf., e.g., the issues of February 8, June 28, 1862.

67. The *Eco* was supported by the wealthier Italians in the United States among whom it attained a circulation of 2,000 in 1855. MSS schedules of the *New York State Census of 1855,* "Sixth Ward, Newspapers and Periodicals." For the *Eco's* politics, cf. the issues of October 25, November 1, 1851, and April 22, 1865. In 1851 Secchi de Casali asked President Fillmore for a Custom House job, averring that he had "always zealously advocated the Whig and Union principles." (Marraro, "Italians in New York . . . ," *op. cit.,* pp. 297–298.) This must be discounted somewhat because of the editor's natural desire to place himself in a favorable light and because of the *Eco's* emphasis upon European rather than American news.

68. For the *Truth Teller,* cf. pp. 150–151. *Weekly Register and Catholic Diary,* October 5, 1833 ff; Cf. United States Catholic Historical Society, *Historical Records and Studies,* XXVIII, 237, XXX, 140.

69. *Freeman's Journal,* July 4, 1840 ff. For the merger of the *Register* and the *Freeman's Journal,* cf. *ibid.,* January 2, 1841.

70. *Freeman's Journal,* July 11, 1846; MSS schedules of the *New York State Census of 1855,* "Fourth Ward, Newspapers and Periodicals."

71. *Freeman's Journal,* December 19, 1846, January 30, 1847, July 7, September 1, 1849, December 21, 1850. For the paper's support of the Repeal movement, cf., e.g., the issues of July 24, August 7, 14, 28, September 25, 1841, June 17, 24, 1843.

72. *Freeman's Journal,* July 12, October 4, 1845.

73. *Freeman's Journal,* July 7, September 1, 1849, May 25, June 1, 1850, April 19, May 3, August 2, September 13, October 25, December 13, 1851.

74. *Freeman's Journal,* May 3, 1851. Cf. the issues of September 13, December 12, 1851. A typical *Freeman's Journal* comment follows: "A herd of German and French

Socialists, including some of the most degraded scape-gallows of those countries, flocked to Hoboken last Monday for a Socialist glorification." *Ibid.*, September 14, 1850.

75. *Freeman's Journal,* October 25, November 11, 1851.

76. *Freeman's Journal,* September 21, 1850.

77. *Freeman's Journal,* October 25, 1851. The paper revealed its reverence for authority by apologizing for the Austrian government which "had for its object to render the *whole* of the people of its Empire happy and contented." *Ibid.*

78. *Freeman's Journal,* July 15, 1854.

79. For Fourierism, cf. *Freeman's Journal,* May 6, 1843; for the diatribe against Weitling, *ibid.*, March 8, 1851. This communication was signed by seven German Catholics, who supported a German Catholic priest in Detroit who had warned his flock against the nefarious doctrines of the German workingmen's associations. For abolitionism, cf. *ibid.*, February 9, 1856; cf. C. E. Allen, "The Slavery Question in Catholic Newspapers, 1850–1865," United States Catholic Historical Society, *Historical Records and Studies,* XXVI (1936), 99–169.

80. *Freeman's Journal,* July 22, 1843. Not only did the Irish hate the abolitionists; the abolitionists hated Ireland and Catholicity: "They are ready to plunge the South into ruin, and convulse the nation, for the sake of the negro slave, and yet they can spare no word, no wish, but their wicked ill-will for struggling Ireland." *Ibid.*

81. The *Freeman's Journal* referred to its German readers in the issue of February 20, 1841.

82. *Freeman's Journal,* November 10, December 22, 1849; *Staats-Zeitung,* March 23, June 1, July 6, 1850, January 24, 1852. The *Sion* may have been a continuation of the *Bote,* for both were edited by one Vögele.

83. *Freeman's Journal,* December 27, 1851; *Staats-Zeitung,* July 19, 1856. Maximilian Oertel, a capable journalist, was a former Lutheran minister. Körner, *op. cit.,* p. 133; Charles G. Herbermann, "John James Maximilian Oertel," United States Catholic Historical Society, *Historical Records and Studies,* IV (1906), 139–144.

84. *Staats-Zeitung,* March 23, April 6, June 23, 1850, January 24, 1852; cf. *Freeman's Journal,* March 8, 1851.

85. MSS schedules of the *New York State Census of 1855,* "Second and Third wards, Newspapers and Periodicals." Cf. *Der Deutsche Pionier,* III, No. 6 (August 7, 1871), 165.

86. Cf. Grinstein, *Rise of the Jewish Community . . . ,* pp. 214–215. The first Jewish periodical published in the United States was a monthly, *The Jew,* published in English during the years 1823–1825 in an attempt to combat Christian proselyting among the Jews. *Ibid.*, p. 214; Bernard Postal, "The Early American Jewish Press," *Reflex,* II, No. 4 (April, 1928), 69, 75; Albert M. Friedenberg, "American Jewish Journalism to the Close of the Civil War," American Jewish Historical Society, *Publications,* No. 26, 1918, pp. 270–273.

87. *Asmonean,* October 26, 1849 ff. Cf. Grinstein, *op. cit.,* pp. 215–216.

88. Cf. *Asmonean,* October 18, November 29, 1850, February 7, 1851, June 4, 1852, February 11, 18, August 19, 1853, March 10, 1854, November 6, 13, 1857.

89. The *Asmonean's* German language supplement began with Volume IV, No. 10, June 27, 1851.

90. *Jewish Messenger,* January 2, 1857 ff. Cf. Grinstein, *op. cit.,* p. 72.

91. Postal, "The Early American Jewish Press," *op. cit.,* p. 72.

92. On the question of abolitionism, for example, the *Asmonean* (July 24, 1851, July 25, August 8, 15, 1856) adhered to the Democratic Party and opposed the abolition of slavery. The *Jewish Messenger,* on the other hand, opposed slavery and supported the North during the Civil War. Postal, "The Early American Jewish Press," *op. cit.,* p. 72; cf. Max J. Kohler, "Jews and the Anti-Slavery Movement," part II, American Jewish Historical Society, *Publications,* No. 9, 1901, pp. 48–49, 51–52.

93. Of all the sizable national groups in the city, only the Dutch and the Swiss failed to support their own journals; they read German and French papers.

94. *Irish American,* January 11, 1851; *Staats-Zeitung,* January 21, 1854; *Criminal-*

Zeitung, November 23, December 7, 1860, January 3, 1862. Cf. *Handels-Zeitung,* daily ed., January 4, 1858. Until the sixties, most of the German literature contests proved barren of results. (*Criminal-Zeitung,* November 23, 1860.) However, when Reinhold Solger's "Anton in Amerika" won a $300 prize offered by the *Criminal-Zeitung* late in 1860, that paper announced jubilantly that many Germans had taken part in the contest. *Criminal-Zeitung,* January 3, 1862.

Chapter XIV

1. For Tammany's early opposition to the Irish, cf. M. R. Werner, *Tammany Hall* (New York, 1928), p. 26. Before 1840 New York apparently was the only city in the United States in which the Irish had political power. Cf. Adams, *Ireland and Irish Emigration* . . . , p. 378; Handlin, *Boston's Immigrants* . . . , p. 198.

2. Dixon R. Fox, *Decline of the Aristocracy in the Politics of New York* (New York, 1919), p. 374; Gustavus Myers, *History of Tammany Hall* (New York, 1901), pp. 152–153; Alvin F. Harlow, *Old Bowery Days* (New York, 1931), pp. 299 ff. For advertisements of the naturalization bureau, cf., e.g., *Staats-Zeitung,* April 8, 1843; *Irish American,* October 16, 1852. For an early account of fraudulent voting, cf. Abdy, *Journal of a Residence and Tour in the United States of North America* . . . , II, 2–3. To a lesser degree other political parties adopted the same tactics: "Instances have been known during hot election contests in the State or municipality of New York, when the whole male immigration, landed in the morning from a Cork or Liverpool vessel, has voted ere the afternoon for one 'ticket' or the other," wrote the traveler, Charles Mackay. *Life and Liberty in America* . . . , I, 178. In the middle thirties one third of the 18,000 Democratic voters were said to be of foreign birth. Fox, *op. cit.,* p. 374; Myers, *op. cit.,* pp. 87, 119, 139–140, 151–154.

3. *Testimony Relating to the Great Election Frauds of 1838* . . . (New York, 1840), pp. 1, 5, 8, 9, 30; James B. Glentworth, *Statement of the Frauds on the Elective Franchise in the City of New York, in the Fall of the Year 1838 and Spring of 1839* (New York, 1841), *passim;* MSS record of the Fifth Ward Whig Committee, October 16, 1840; *Congressional Globe,* 28th Congress, 4th Session, XIV, Appendix, 118; John I. Davenport, *Election and Naturalization Frauds in New York City, 1860–1870* (2d ed.; New York, 1894), *passim;* Fox, *op. cit.,* pp. 417–418; *Times,* October 31, 1856.

4. "Report of the Commissioners of the Alms House in relation to Male Paupers voting . . . ," Board of Aldermen, *Documents,* XI, No. 51 (February 10, 1845), 506. For other charges of fraud hurled at both parties, cf., e.g., *Daily Plebeian,* October 26, 1842; *Staats-Zeitung,* October 19, November 9, 1850; *Allgemeine Zeitung,* October 26, November 9, 1839.

5. Fox, *op. cit.,* p. 374; Myers, *op. cit.,* pp. 152–153. Cf. e.g., *Truth Teller,* March 31, April 7, 1832; *Working Man's Advocate,* April 12, 1834; *Staats-Zeitung,* November 8, 1837, April 1, 8, 1840, March 11, 1854; *Plebeian,* April 8, 1843, October 31, 1844. In the fifties Republican politicians made a bid for the German vote by using popular German orators to address German assemblies. *Meyer's Monats-Hefte,* September 1856, p. 238.

6. Myers, *op. cit.,* pp. 154–155. The use of gangs in New York City politics is said to have originated with Mike Walsh, Irish-born radical Democrat, who sought to destroy Tammany control of the local Democratic organization by forcibly removing the enemy from ward meetings. The method was so effective that it was widely copied, and the organized gang became an accepted weapon of political warfare. *Dictionary of American Biography,* XIX, 390–391. Myers, *op. cit.,* pp. 154–155; Asbury, *Gangs of New York,* pp. xiv, 28, 37–38; *Tribune,* April 12, 14, 1842.

7. Werner, *op. cit.,* pp. 63–64; Harlow, *op. cit.,* pp. 299 ff. Despite Rynders' cultivation of the Irish, he espoused the Native American cause briefly in the fifties. Asbury, *op. cit.,* p. 43. For Morrissey, cf. Jack Kofoed, *Brandy for Heroes* . . . (New York, 1938) and Asbury, *op. cit.,* pp. 87–100.

8. Werner, *op. cit.,* pp. 62–63.

9. Edward F. Roberts, *Ireland in America* (New York, 1931) p. 127; James F. McLaughlin, *Life and Times of John Kelly* (New York, 1885), pp. 24–25; [Burn], *Three Years Among the Working-Classes* . . . , p. 15. At Thomas Dunlap's "Pewter Mug" in Frankfort Street, next door to Tammany Hall, "names were made and unmade, the laurel crown was placed upon or snatched from the brows of aspiring statesmen, and not a nomination for governor, congressman, state legislature, or city or county office could be made unless the sanction of the 'Pewter Mug' was first obtained." Augustine E. Costello, *Our Firemen* . . . , pp. 536–537.

10. Myers, *op. cit.*, p. 212.

11. Computed from data in Board of Aldermen, *Documents,* XXII, No. 43 (November 12, 1855), 2.

12. *Ibid.*

13. *Ibid.* The *Staats-Zeitung* (March 24, 1855) reported inaccurately the same set of figures. A special committee of the Board of Aldermen, which was hostile to Police Chief Matsell, claimed that at least 600 foreign-born policemen were on the force. Board of Aldermen, *Documents,* XXII, No. 20 (April 23, 1855), 22.

14. Cf. p. 22.

15. *Staats-Zeitung,* March 24, 1855. These figures, adapted from the *Staats-Zeitung's* tabulation, while not perfectly accurate, indicate that linguistic, social, and political reasons dictated the careful dispersal of the city police force. At the Grand Street station, an Irish traveler noticed the policemen, "all," he wrote, "from the Emerald Isle." Jeremiah O'Donovan, *Brief Account of the Author's Interview with his Countrymen, and of the Parts of the Emerald Isle whence they Emigrated* . . . (Pittsburgh, 1864), p. 93; Costello, *Our Police Protectors* . . . , pp. 527, 557, lists members of the police force up to May 1, 1885 and notes the dates of their appointment.

16. Fallon's particular friends on the Board of Aldermen were Cornelius Timpson and Abraham Hatfield, through whose influence Fallon was made warden of the Tombs prison. In 1848 Fallon was secretary of the Tammany Hall General Committee, but despite his powerful position, he joined the gold rush to California in the following year. Costello, *Our Firemen,* pp. 506–507; McLaughlin, *op. cit.,* p. 24. Thomas Dunlap, keeper of the "Pewter Mug," was also a former fireman. Dunlap became one of the Commissioners of Emigration, was a member of the Common Council in 1854, a deputy naval officer in the Pierce and Buchanan administrations, collector of city revenue for many years, commissioner of jurors, and delegate to national, state, and county Democratic conventions. He served on many Tammany committees and was an intimate friend of Horatio Seymour, Governor of New York. Costello, *Our Firemen,* pp. 536–537.

17. Denis T. Lynch, *"Boss" Tweed* (New York, 1927), pp. 57–66; Costello, *Our Firemen,* p. 458; McLaughlin, *op. cit.,* p. 25.

18. McLaughlin, *op. cit.,* p. 25; T. L. Stoddard, *Master of Manhattan; the Life of Richard Croker* (New York, 1931), p. 30.

19. Costello, *Our Firemen,* pp. 751–754, mentions these organizations but fails to stress the role of the Irish.

20. *Ibid.,* pp. 506–507, 609–612, 653, 660, 675, 686, 689, 697.

21. Fox, *op. cit.,* p. 374; Myers, *op. cit.,* pp. 152–153. Matthew Murray, an accomplished Irish politician, was for many years a contractor for the city government and in 1856 was elected to the Common Council. *Daily Times,* November 6, 1856.

22. Myers, *op. cit.,* pp. 153, 228; Fox, *op. cit.,* p. 374; *Truth Teller,* April 14, 1832; *Irish American,* October 26, 1850, November 6, 1852; *European,* December 6, 1856. Cf. *City Election Hand-book* . . . (New York, 1844), p. 14; *Brown Book, op. cit.,* pp. 75, 84, 90, 108, 161, 180, 216, 218, 219, 241, 289, 302, 303.

23. Cf. Handlin, *op. cit.,* pp. 198–199.

24. "The whole Irish vote is always cast *in bulk,*" declared the *Times* (November 7, 1856), which excepted the educated Irish, asserting that they would be the first to concede the truth of the statement. Roberts (*op. cit.,* pp. 126, 127) refers to "the innate ability of the Irish for political organization, an ability fostered through centuries of

absorption in political struggles" and to "the racial characteristics which make most Irishmen 'good mixers.'"

25. *Citizen*, November 12, 1856. Irish editors complained that the sons of Erin did not get their proportional share of offices, while native editors exclaimed that they received too many. *Citizen*, November 12, December 6, 1856. Cf. *European*, December 6, 1856.

26. *Staats-Zeitung*, April 12, 1837, January 17, 1843, November 4, 1848, September 17, 1853; *European*, December 6, 1856; *Daily Times*, November 7, 1856; Büchele, *Land und Volk der Vereinigten Staaten von Nord-Amerika* (Stuttgart, 1855), p. 284; Matthew P. Breen, *Thirty Years of New York Politics Up-to-date* (New York, 1899), p. 253. Cf. names in *City Election Hand-book, op. cit.*

27. *Staats-Zeitung*, October 20, 1841.

28. *Staats-Zeitung*, June 24, July 8, 29, 1843.

29. Howard R. Marraro, "Italians in New York . . . ," *New York History*, XXVI, No. 3 (July, 1945), 302, citing the *Evening Post*, December 14, 1839. In 1843 Del Vecchio tried to enlist the political aid of the prominent Democratic judge, Charles P. Daly, to whom he wrote: "As you . . . know my influence among the Adopted Citizens generaly [*sic*] your exertions would have great influence with the Governor." MSS letter, February 10, 1843, in the Daly Papers, New York Public Library. Del Vecchio's influence with the Italians counted for little at this period, however, for as late as 1865 most Italians in New York were little interested in local politics, and many failed to become American citizens. *Eco d'Italia*, December 30, 1865.

30. There were, of course, exceptions, such as the nomination for the state assembly of the popular German leader, Francis Lassak, who later betrayed his followers, and the enormously influential leader of the French, Auguste Davezac. *Staats-Zeitung*, November 8, 1837, March 25, April 17, 1840; *Courrier des États-Unis*, October 21, 1841.

31. *Times*, November 6, 1856, which noted, appropriately, that the other successful candidates were native-born and had experience in fire companies, liquor stores, and restaurants. Myers (*op. cit.*, p. 228) states that the election of 1858 was the first in which the city's Democratic voters of Irish birth or lineage insisted upon a full share of the best places on the party ticket.

32. Computed from data in the *New York State Census* of 1845 (unpaged) and the *New York State Census of 1855*, p. 8. Cf. Appendix, pp. 192, 223. The Fourth and Sixth wards contained the largest proportion of immigrants, but the First Ward was not far behind, 48.7 per cent of its population having been born abroad. The First Ward, however, was a source of Whig strength until the 1850's. This may be explained by the relatively greater wealth of its residents prior to the middle of the century and their connection in one way or another with the city's trade. After the mid-forties, the ward's immigrant population underwent a remarkable change: foreign-born merchants and clerks moved uptown and abandoned the district to the more recently arrived immigrants of lower social and economic status. In 1855, half of New York City's voters were naturalized citizens. (*New York State Census of 1855*, p. 8.) Comparable statistics of the composition of the voting population in 1845 are not available. Information on the extent of the immigrant vote is fragmentary, and no statement about voters in this period of the city's history can be completely accurate. In my analysis I have had to ignore what was evident to any contemporary: illegal voting.

33. For statistics of the vote in each ward in the mayoralty elections, cf. D. T. Valentine (ed.), *Manual of the Corporation of the City of New York*, 1854, pp. 486–516, which breaks down the votes in the years 1834, 1835, 1836, 1837, 1839, 1840, 1841, 1842, 1844, 1845, 1846, 1848, and 1849; *ibid.*, 1843–44, p. 301; *ibid.*, 1848, p. 354; *ibid.*, 1851, p. 344; *ibid.*, 1858, pp. 378–385; *ibid.*, 1860, p. 449; *ibid.*, 1862, p. 427; and *ibid.*, 1864, p. 454, for the mayoralty elections of 1843, 1847, 1850, 1857, 1859, 1861, and 1863, respectively. Breakdowns of the mayoralty vote in 1852 and 1854 are given in the *Daily Tribune*, November 6, 1852, *Weekly Tribune*, November 11, 1854, and *Times*, November 10, 1854. For a handy breakdown, by wards, of the vote for President of the United States from 1840 to the Civil War period, cf. Davenport, *op. cit.*, pp. 22–23.

34. *Ibid.* In 1837 the Locofocos split the Democratic vote. Aaron Clark, Whig candidate for Mayor, won both the Fourteenth and Fourth wards, but in the latter, the combined Democratic and Locofoco vote was larger than the Whig vote. *Valentine's Manual, op. cit.,* 1854, p. 491. For the Locofocos, cf. pp. 168–169. In the mayoralty election of 1854, Fernando Wood, the regular Democratic candidate, lost the Fourth Ward in a close four-way contest, but a change of a handful of votes probably would have won the ward for Wood. Allegations of fraud seemed to be confirmed by the delay in issuing the election returns. The breakdown of the vote, as given by the *Times* (November 10, 1854) must be considered only as an approximation of the actual vote. Slightly different returns are given in the *Weekly Tribune* (November 11, 1854). The Fourteenth Ward, 61.1 per cent of whose voters were naturalized citizens, solidly backed Fernando Wood. *Ibid.* The computation of the percentage is based upon data in the *New York State Census of 1855,* p. 8. For statistics of the vote for President, cf. Davenport, *op. cit.,* pp. 22–23.

35. Körner, *Das deutsche Element . . . ,* p. 107; Ernest Bruncken, "German Political Refugees in the United States during the Period from 1815–1860, "*Deutsch-Amerikanische Geschichtsblätter,* (Chicago, 1904), pp. 22–23.

36. *Ibid.*

37. *Ibid.* Francis J. Grund, a political turncoat who had addressed the apparently Whig-inspired meeting of 1834, declared two years later that the New York Germans had "great influence on the election of mayor and the other city officers, the number of those who are entitled to vote amounting now to three thousand five hundred. Under these circumstances, 'the *German vote,*' as it is termed becomes a matter of great solicitude with politicians . . . " Grund, *Americans in their Moral, Social, and Political Relations,* pp. 215–216. Grund may be excused for exaggerating the political strength of his own nationality; he admitted that the Germans in America had not formed political policies and were unconscious of their power. *Ibid.,* p. 216. The *Staats-Zeitung* (April 12, 1837) more conservatively, and probably more correctly, estimated the German vote in New York City at 2,000.

38. Computed from data in the *New York State Census of 1845* (unpaged) and the *New York State Census of 1855,* pp. 8, 110–118. Cf. Appendix, p. 192 ff. In the Eleventh Ward 56.7 per cent of the voters in 1855 were immigrants. *Ibid.* No information is available which gives the proportion of German-born voters, but some indication is afforded by the fact that in this ward the Germans were twice as numerous as the Irish.

39. In 1845 the Germans comprised 10.9 per cent of the population in each of the Tenth and Seventeenth wards and 9.3 per cent of the population of the Thirteenth Ward. In 1855 German immigrants comprised 30.3 per cent of the inhabitants of the Tenth, 27.3 per cent of those living in the Seventeenth, and 22.6 per cent of those in the Thirteenth wards. Cf. Appendix, p. 192 ff.

40. Cf. *Staats-Zeitung,* August 30, 1851, for an account of a German free-soil, pro-homestead, antimonopoly meeting addressed by Försch, Arnold, Richter, and Sonne. Cf. *ibid.,* September 13, 1851; *Tribune,* August 26, 1851. Although Kriege and Weitling joined the Democratic Party, Weydemeyer and the socialists, including many of the Turners, gave considerable attention to the slavery question. Schlüter, *Lincoln, Labor and Slavery,* pp. 74–75, 77; Metzner, *Brief History of the American Turnerbund,* p. 14; *Turn-Blatt für die Vereine des socialistischen Turnerbundes von Nordamerika,* February and March, 1857; *Deutsche Monats-Hefte,* September 1856, p. 238, November 1856, p. 395.

41. *Staats-Zeitung,* September 29, 1855; Andreas Dorpalen, "The German Element and the Issues of the Civil War," *Mississippi Valley Historical Review,* XXIX, No. 1 (June, 1942), 65–68, 72. In reply to a statement by the *Times* that the Irish and German votes went for Buchanan and that not one tenth of the German vote was Republican, "a German Republican" claimed that the majority of the Germans voted the Republican ticket. He gave an estimate of the *Abend Zeitung* (a Republican paper) that between

7,000 and 8,000, or three quarters of the German votes were Republican. In an editorial reply, the *Times* admitted underrating the German vote for Fremont and conceded that probably a third of the Germans living in the strong German wards voted Republican. *Times,* November 7, 1856. For the efforts of the Republican Party leaders to win the foreign vote, cf., e.g., *Tribune,* October 29, 1856; *Times,* October 31, 1856; Commons *et al., History of Labour* . . . , I, 619–620.

42. *Albion,* March 21, 1863.

43. *Daily Times,* November 7, 1856; *Albion,* September 30, 1843, July 16, 1853; *Courrier des États-Unis,* April 19, 1834, November 2, 1841 (a front page article on Catholicism as a political and social force in the United States); *Républicain,* February 4, May 1, 1854; Grund, *op. cit.,* pp. 65–66; Macrae, *Americans at Home* . . . , I, 67. Cf. the letter from a thoroughly aroused English resident, *Times,* November 18, 1854. In 1844 the French Democrats organized to meet the threat of nativism, and French and Swiss Republican clubs were formed to help elect Lincoln in 1860. *Plebeian,* October 31, 1844; *Courrier des États-Unis,* September 6, 1860; von Grueningen, *Swiss in the United States,* p. 109.

44. *Asmonean,* November 17, 1854, July 27, 1855; Max J. Kohler, "German-Jewish Migration to America," American Jewish Historical Society, *Publications,* No. 9, 1901, p. 102.

45. Dixon R. Fox, "The Negro Vote in Old New York," *Political Science Quarterly,* XXXII, No. 2 (June, 1917), 252–275; Fox, *Decline of the Aristocracy* . . . , pp. 269–270; *Colored American,* January 18, 1837.

46. *Rules for the Organization and Government of the Central Clay Committee of the City and County of New York* . . . (New York, 1844), p. 30; *Staats-Zeitung,* March 11, April 17, May 20, 1840, March 4, 1843 (advertisement); *Allgemeine Zeitung,* October 26, 1839, February 29, 1840 (advertisement). *Deutsche Schnellpost,* November 4, 1843 (advertisement).

47. *Evening Post,* April 17, 1834; *Courrier des États-Unis,* November 2, 1841; *Herald,* quoted by *Staats-Zeitung,* February 19, 1848; *Phare de New-York,* August 7, 1852. Upper-class Englishmen called themselves "British residents," read British papers, drank British ale in British beer halls, and rarely voted on the same side of an issue as the Irish. Nichols, *Forty Years of American Life,* II, 79.

48. *European,* November 12, 1836; MSS letter of A. Warner to Charles P. Daly, April 10, 1844, Daly Papers, New York Public Library. It is likely, of course, that immigrants were paid for electioneering. Cf. *Staats-Zeitung,* November 9, 1850.

49. *Asmonean,* April 27, 1855, August 15, 1856. Cf. *Freeman's Journal,* April 28, 1855.

50. Cf. Scisco, *Political Nativism in New York State,* pp. 20–21, 209. Referring to the outcry against adopted citizens, the president of the Cartmen's Society exclaimed: "And who raised this cry? Why, foreigners themselves—Englishmen, brutal Britishers, and North of Ireland weavers, butchers and ruffians. And against whom? The Irish Catholics, as also the native-born Catholics. . . . The most members of this Society are adopted citizens—or, as the English and Orange Irish nativists would designate us, foreigners." *Daily Times,* July 10, 1854.

51. Thorburn, *Fifty Years' Reminiscences* . . . , p. 222. Thorburn was naturalized while Washington was President.

52. Scisco, *op. cit.,* pp. 68, 208–209.

53. *Citizen,* September 16, 1854, commenting upon a riot in Newark. For a biased but interesting account of a riot resulting from Tammany's unwillingness to afford police protection to an annual celebration of Orangemen, cf. *Civil Rights; the Hibernian Riot and the "Insurrection of the Capitalists."* (New York, 1871).

54. *Working Man's Advocate,* March 13, 1830. The Englishman was Francis Pares, a representative of the Fourth Ward.

55. *Old Countryman,* November 10, December 1, 1831. This was a public meeting, without regard to nationality, but the *Old Countryman,* which reported it, was at the time the only newspaper in New York City which appealed to British workers.

56. The *Herold* was a short-lived paper which appeared in 1836. *Staats-Zeitung,* October 21, 1840. In his *Life of Most Rev. John Hughes,* p. 249, Hassard stated that prior to the 1840's the Locofoco Party counted upon the Irish vote. Since the label "Locofoco" became synonymous with "Democrat," at least to the Whigs, Hassard's statement may not be entirely accurate. Cf., e.g. *Courrier des États-Unis,* November 2, 1841; *Staats-Zeitung,* February 26, 1840. In his *History of the Loco-foco or Equal Rights Party* (New York, 1842, pp. 61, 78, 100, 106, 130, 146), Fitzwilliam Byrdsall gave many names of genuine Locofoco leaders but not their birthplaces. I have been unable to ascertain the nativities of many of these men. Most appear to have been natives.

57. *Staats-Zeitung,* November 8, 1837. Cf. *ibid.,* September 27, November 1, 1837.

58. *Staats-Zeitung,* November 15, 1837, February 5, 1840. I have no evidence of specific political activities of other national groups in this election.

59. Hassard, *op. cit.,* pp. 228 ff; Scisco, *op. cit.,* pp. 32 ff. The Germans, in particular the German Catholics, sought German teachers in the public schools. *Staats-Zeitung,* January 15, 22, 1840.

60. Hassard, *op. cit.,* pp. 247–248.

61. *Ibid.;* Scisco, *op. cit.,* pp. 35–36. The Whigs polled about 15,980 votes and the Democrats about 15,690. Scisco, *op. cit.,* p. 35, citing the *Tribune,* November 12, 1841. The leaders of the Democratic organization failed to support nativist sentiment in the next election, but in several wards the party split into native-born and Irish factions. Scisco, *op. cit.,* p. 36.

62. *Freeman's Journal,* April 9, 1842; Hassard, *op. cit.,* pp. 249–250. The new act established a city board of education composed of two commissioners, two inspectors, and five trustees in each ward. *Ibid.*

63. *Staats-Zeitung,* August 30, November 29, 1851, July 24, 1852; cf. Chapter X. *The Deutsch-amerikanisch-demokratischer Bund von New York* consisted of *Vereine* in the city wards, a general committee made up of delegates of the ward *Vereine,* and an executive committee. The party was opposed to despotism in Europe as well as to the manipulations of the New York Democrats. *Staats-Zeitung,* July 24, 1852.

64. *Volks-Tribun,* April 2, November 7, 1846, cited by Commons, *op. cit.,* I, 535.

65. Commons, *op. cit.,* I, 530, 560. The Germans were conspicuous at the Industrial Congress. Cf. Commons *et al., Documentary History . . . ,* VIII, 285–289, 300–303. Cf. *supra,* pp. 116, 117.

66. *Staats-Zeitung,* October 20, 1855. The Hard Shells and Soft Shells differed mainly in the matter of distribution of offices. Cf. Myers, *op. cit.,* p. 191. Werner (*op. cit.,* p. 73) states that the Softs got their name because they "believed in compromise when necessary" and the Hards because they "steadfastly refused to deviate from their uncompromising conservative principles."

67. Scisco, *op. cit.,* p. 206; Lynch, *op. cit.,* p. 110. Cf. [Abijah Ingraham], *Biography of Fernando Wood . . .* (New York, 1856 [?]), pp. 21–22. Nativist influences appeared in both Democratic factions, especially the Hard Shells. The secrecy of the Know Nothing order enabled Wood to retain his strong immigrant following. As early as 1850 the Irish and Germans looked upon Wood as a "friend of the working classes" and of the foreign born. The *Irish American* welcomed his utterances of sympathy for the Irish, his stand in favor of the abolition of the contract system in city public works, and his advocacy of better tenement house regulation. *Irish American,* October 26, 1850; cf. *ibid.,* October 28, 1854, October 24, 1857; *Staats-Zeitung,* November 2, 1850.

68. Scisco, *op. cit.,* pp. 209–210.

69. *Staats-Zeitung,* October 20, 27, 1855. In the interest of party unity, the *Staats-Zeitung* opposed a purely German ticket, as long as the Democrats nominated unobjectionable candidates. The German Democrats tried to accomplish this by setting up ward organizations to name delegates to a central committee charged with the duty of picking the best (i.e. nonnativist, nontemperance) nominees of the Hards and Softs. *Staats-Zeitung,* September 29, 1855.

70. Myers, *op. cit.,* pp. 179, 214, 221. Cf. *supra,* p. 22.

71. Myers, *op. cit.*, p. 224.

72. *Ibid.*, p. 228; Scisco, *op. cit.*, p. 223.

73. The new organization was known as the "Mozart Hall" Democracy. Cf. William C. Gover, *Tammany Hall Democracy of the City of New York* . . . (New York, 1875), p. 47. With solid Irish backing Wood was re-elected in 1859 but was eclipsed in the early sixties by John McKeon's faction of dissatisfied Democrats, which included a new Irish following. *Ibid.*, pp. 48–50; Myers, *op. cit.*, p. 230.

Chapter XV

1. Cf. pp. 153, 155, 159. German commercial and financial circles were, on the whole, bitterly opposed to the Republicans and to Lincoln, but in their desire to see the Union preserved they rallied to the northern cause. When hostilities broke out, August Belmont and other German Douglas Democrats took a leading part in the raising of German money for the Union cause. Dorpalen, "The German Element and the Issues of the Civil War," *loc. cit.*, pp. 65–66.

2. Metzner, *Brief History of the American Turnerbund,* pp. 14, 18, 20; advertisements in the *Irish American* (e.g., April 27, 1861).

3. *Criminal-Zeitung,* April 26, May 3, 1861; cf. *Irish American,* May 4, 1861; cf. pp. 128–129.

4. *Criminal-Zeitung,* May 3, 1861. The Garibaldi Guard, a unit of the 39th Regiment, New York State Volunteers, included Italian, Spanish, French, Swiss, and Belgian members. *Eco d'Italia,* July 26, 1862. For Italian volunteering, cf. Howard R. Marraro, "Lincoln's Italian Volunteers from New York," *New York History,* XXIV, No. 1 (January, 1943), 56–57.

5. *Criminal-Zeitung,* July 31, 1863.

6. *Courrier des États-Unis,* January 16, March 21, 1864. Letters of two Irish immigrants, who landed at Portland, Maine, described the inducements; they were met at the pier and were offered "Brandy, Whiskey, Pies, Pudding, cigars, or anything we wished for to enlist along with them." Letters accompanying Despatch No. 57, April 20, 1864. *Consular Despatches,* Dublin, Vol. VI, State Department Archives, Washington, D.C.

7. *Report on Emigration by a Special Committee of the Chamber of Commerce of the State of New York* . . . (New York, 1865), p. 23. Cf. *ibid.*, pp. 25–26.

8. Wittke, *Against the Current* . . . , p. 179.

9. Fred A. Shannon, *Organization and Administration of the Union Army* (Cleveland, 1928), II, 78; Wittke, *op. cit.*, p. 179.

10. Consular letter (unnumbered), July 31, 1862, in *Consular Despatches,* Dublin, Vol. III, State Department Archives, Washington, D.C. "I shall do all in my power to Encourage Irish Emigration," wrote the United States Consul at Dublin in response to State Department circulars urging such action. *Consular Despatches,* Dublin, Vol. III, No. 24, August 28, 1862. Cf. despatch No. 25, September 11, 1862, *loc. cit.*, Vol. III, and despatch Nos. 41, 51, 61, and 66, April 23, 1863, March 5, May 6, and June 4, respectively, *loc. cit.*, Vol. IV. Some European officials tried to discourage emigration to America by telling would-be emigrants that all they could hope for in the United States was induction into the Union army *Eco d'Italia,* February 11, 1865. Early enthusiasm for joining the colors on the part of both natives and most immigrants wore off after the first year or so of fighting.

11. *Freeman's Journal,* March 7, 21, July 18, 1863; *Courrier des États-Unis,* March 14, May 11, July 24, 1863; *Criminal-Zeitung,* July 24, 1863; *Staats-Zeitung,* daily ed., July 15, 1863; *Albion,* March 14, 21, July 18, 1863. "Every citizen, naturalized or foreign, is subject to the arbitrary caprice of a newly-appointed Provost-Marshal, and this Provost-Marshal, who is supreme over law, is nothing more than the Superintendent of Police." *Albion,* August 16, 1863.

12. *Irish American,* July 18, 1863; *Albion,* July 18, 1863; *Courrier des États-Unis,* July 14, 1863; Basil L. Lee, *Discontent in New York City, 1861–1865* (Washington, D.C.,

1943), pp. 90–92, 97–104, 124. This is by all odds the best and only complete account; cf. especially chapters iii–vii. Cf. Joel T. Headley, *Great Riots of New York, 1712–1873* . . . (New York, 1873), pp. 136, 139, 148, 149.

13. Letter from Archbishop Hughes to the New York *Herald* (July 15, 1863), quoted in Thomas F. Meehan, "Archbishop Hughes and the Draft Riots," United States Catholic Historical Society, *Historical Records and Studies,* I, Part II (January, 1900), 174.

14. *Ibid.* Cf. Lee, *op. cit.,* pp. 106–107.

15. *Freeman's Journal,* August 16, 18, 1862; *Courrier des États-Unis,* August 6, October 7, 1862, April 14, 1863; *Albion,* November 18, 1863. Cf. Madeleine H. Rice, *American Catholic Opinion in the Slavery Controversy* (New York, 1944), pp. 124, 154. Cf. Lee, *op. cit.,* Chapter iv.

16. *Staats-Zeitung,* April 18, 1863; *Criminal-Zeitung,* April 24, 1863; Dorpalen, "The German Element and the Issues of the Civil War," *loc. cit.,* p. 68. In New York City, at least, the evidence seems to disprove the assumption that, in the main, the German workingmen "sided with the opponents of slavery." Cf. Herman Schlüter, *Lincoln, Labor and Slavery,* p. 209.

17. Archbishop Hughes had written in 1861 to Secretary of War Cameron of insinuations "to the effect that the purpose of this war is the abolition of slavery in the South. If that idea should prevail among a certain class, it would make the business of recruiting slack indeed. The Catholics, so far as I know, whether of native or foreign birth, are willing to fight to the death for the support of the constitution, the Government, and the laws of the country. But if it should be understood that, with or without knowing it, they are to fight for the abolition of slavery, then, indeed, they will turn away in disgust from the discharge of what would otherwise be a patriotic duty." Hassard, *op. cit.,* p. 437.

18. *Albion,* July 18, 1863; *Messager Franco-Américain,* July 15, 1863. The latter was a Republican paper, which suspected Democratic politicians of promoting the draft riots. *Ibid.,* July 20, 21, 1863. For a graphic description of the riots, cf. Headley, *op. cit.,* pp. 136–289.

19. Emmet, *Incidents of My Life,* p. 184; *Freeman's Journal,* July 25, 1863; *Albion,* July 18, 1863; *Messager Franco-Américain,* July 15, 20, 1863.

20. A. I. C. P., *Twentieth Annual Report,* 1863, pp. 44–45. The confused character of the riots is indicated by the fact that a number of Irish, Germans, and even Chinese were among the victims. German proprietors of beer gardens, grocery and liquor stores, a tobacconist, and an apothecary suffered personal injury and losses of property at the hands of the rioters. (County of New York, Board of Supervisors, *Document No. 13,* December 27, 1867 [New York, 1868], I, 90–91, 101, 111, 193, 207, 465, 507, 550–552, 684–686, 694–696.) For Irish victims, cf. *ibid.,* pp. 222–224, 424–425; Lee, *op. cit.,* p. 105. For the attack on the Chinese by a crowd, persuaded that the Orientals were but a "modification" of the Negro, cf. *Herald,* July 16, 1863; *Anglo African,* July 25, 1863. According to the *Criminal-Zeitung* (July 31, 1863), a Negro was hanged by a gang of murderers who put a cigar in his mouth, stuffed his nostrils with matches, put a beer mug in his hand, and stuck a sign on his coat reading "Black Dutchman." For thievery committed by Germans during the uproar, cf. *Criminal-Zeitung,* July 31, 1863; *Courrier des États-Unis,* July 15, 1863.

21. For emigration from America, especially during years of hard times, cf. Thomas W. Page, "Some Economic Aspects of Immigration before 1870," Part II, *Journal of Political Economy,* XXI, No. 1 (January, 1913), 54; Eickhoff, *op. cit.,* Appendix, pp. 48, 58–59; Hale, *op. cit.,* p. 21; *London* v. *New York,* pp. 64–65; German Society of the City of New York, *Annual Report,* 1858, p. 10; *Population of the United States in 1860* . . . *Eighth Census* (Washington, D.C., 1864), p. xix; *Staats-Zeitung,* August 2, 1837; *Freeman's Journal,* April 29, 1843; *Irish American,* November 11, 1849, March 10, June 9, 1855; *European,* January 17, 1857.

22. Cf., e.g., Griesinger, *Lebende Bilder* . . . *aus Amerika* (Stuttgart, 1858), pp. 91–92; [James Boardman], *America and the Americans* . . . (London, 1833), pp. 35–

36; *London* v. *New York*, p. 67; Nichols, *op. cit.*, II, 73; *Albion*, March 20, 1847; *Staats-Zeitung*, October 24, 1859.

23. [Boardman] *America* . . . , pp. 16–19.

24. Mudie, *Immigrant's Pocket Companion*, pp. 69–70.

25. Cf., e.g., *Staats-Zeitung*, January 4, 25, 1837; *Deutsche Schnellpost*, April 12, 15, 20, 22, 1843.

26. Augustana Historical Society, *Publications*, VII (1937), 130.

27. *Staats-Zeitung*, January 29, 1840.

28. Cf., e.g., *Staats-Zeitung*, daily ed., September 1, 1853 ff, October 9, 11, 1858; *Deutsche Schnellpost*, January 10, 1844, October 11, 1845; *Courrier des États-Unis*, October 17, 1829, April 23, 1840, January 3, 1845; *Eco d'Italia*, November 18, 1865. In 1850 a legal interpreter advertised a course in English for French "workers and litigants," in 1854 the *Société de la République Universelle* (*Section La Montagne*) offered free English instruction to its French members and French lessons for its English-speaking members, and in 1851 the Mercantile Library held classes in English especially designed for the French and Germans. (*Courrier des États-Unis*, March 16, 1850, October 17, 1851; *Citizen*, October 28, 1854.)

29. MSS schedules of the *New York State Census of 1855*, "Tenth Ward, Third Election District"; cf. Griesinger, *op. cit.*, p. 91.

30. *Staats-Zeitung*, February 17, August 11, 1855, February 9, April 12, June 7, 1856; daily ed.: August 21, October 6, November 19, 1858; *Criminal-Zeitung*, November 16, 1855; cf. the issue of March 18, 1853, which contains an article on the use of non-German words, including "yes," "no," and "well."

31. *Staats-Zeitung*, December 13, 20, 1856; daily ed.: October 27, 1858. In 1874 a German writer noted the protests of German literary purists at New York over such phrases as *ein bissness meinden* (mind a business), *einen Schopp thun* (do a job), *mit Jemand setteln* (settle with someone), *einen Bargen gemacht* (made a bargain), *all über die Stadt* (all over the city), *er ist gemuvt* (he has moved), and *först rätes Bier* (first-rate beer). Among the New York Germans, *Erdgeschoss* became "Basement"; *Stockwerk* became "Fluhr" (floor); *Schlafzimmer*, "Bedruhm"; *Küche*, "Kitsch'n"; *Grundeigenthum*, "Riälestat" (real estate); *Besitztitel*, "Died" (deed); *Commis*, "Klerk"; *Lohn*, "Wädsches" (wages); and *Miethe*, "Rent." Joseph Pachmayr, *Leben und Treiben der Stadt New York* . . . (Hamburg, 1874), pp. 127–130. Cf. H. L. Mencken, *American Language* (4th ed.; New York, 1936), pp. 616–621; Robert E. Park, *Immigrant Press and Its Control* (New York, 1922), pp. 79–88.

32. *Courrier des États-Unis*, July 16, 1836, May 12, June 30, July 12, 1842, May 25, 1843, June 11, 1844 (advertisement), September 30, November 2, 1848, August 20, 1859.

33. For an entertaining discussion of non-English dialects in America, cf. Mencken, *op. cit.*, pp. 616–697. Mencken's copious examples are not limited to those which appeared in New York City; many of the words were adopted after the Civil War by peoples of the "new" immigration during and after the turn of the century. Among the inhabitants of Little Italy in 1932, for instance, American loan-words comprised perhaps one fourth of the spoken language. *Ibid.*, p. 643, citing Anthony M. Turano, "The Speech of Little Italy," *American Mercury*, July, 1932, p. 357. Italian politics in the metropolis were reflected, apparently, in the word "temeniollo" (Tammany Hall) meaning a large glass of beer. Mencken, *op. cit.*, p. 644. For immigrant contributions to the American language, cf. *ibid.*, pp. 155–162.

34. A.I.C.P., *Twenty-fourth Annual Report*, 1867, p. 42. "Though neither desirable nor practicable in former years," continued this report, segregation became a social necessity during the fifties and sixties until immigrant communities became so heterogeneous that they could not "coalesce with each other, much less with Americans." *Ibid.*, p. 43. For an earlier and somewhat more sympathetic view of the nature of the immigrant community, cf. Wyse, *America, Its Realities and Resources* . . . , III, 4–5.

35. This was notable in the case of the Germans, with their large professional ele-

ment. Cf., e.g., Löher, *Geschichte und Züstande der Deutschen* . . . , pp. 410–411; Büchele, *Land und Volk* . . . , pp. 280–281.

36. *London* v. *New York*, p. 81. Italics in the original. For further evidence of social and economic distinctions within the immigrant community, cf. *European*, March 25, 1837; *Courrier des États-Unis*, August 31, 1836, February 15, 1837, March 25, 1848, January 18, 1855; *Citizen*, September 30, 1854; *Albion*, September 3, 1853, April 11, 1857; *Staats-Zeitung*, September 16, 1840, April 29, 1848; *Criminal-Zeitung*, March 5, 1858; Struve, *Diesseits und Jenseits des Oceans*, p. 2.

37. *Albion*, April 18, 1857.

38. *Albion*, March 13, 1847; cf. the issue of March 20, 1847.

39. *Courrier des États-Unis*, March 30, 1854; cf. the issue of February 5, 1855.

40. *Handels-Zeitung*, daily ed., November 11, 1857.

41. *Scottish Journal of Intelligence and Literature*, February 13, 1841. "We have seen reform after reform—countries revolutionized—universal franchise enjoyed—and what has been the consequence? any improvement in the condition of the working classes? None: An extension if possible but no alleviation, and so it would be though every man, woman, and child, ox and ass, had a *vote*, but no improvement would arise. . . ." *Ibid.*

42. Cf. pp. 105, 122. Löher, *op. cit.*, pp. 409–410.

43. *Ibid.*, p. 409; Büchele, *op. cit.*, p. 320.

44. Nichols, *op. cit.*, II, 69–70. Some of the forty-eighters, however, were Catholics. William Bannard, *Discourse on the Moral Aspect and Destitution of the City of New York* (New York, 1851), p. 20.

45. *Staats-Zeitung*, June 7, 1851, January 3, March 20, 1852, May 13, 1854, August 4, 1855.

46. Hermann Lindemann, "Die Europaisch-Amerikanischen Ideen in der deutschen Einwanderung," *Meyer's Monats-Hefte*, May, 1855, pp. 383–389. This article was highly critical of the "greens," asserting that their "Phantasierepublik" would work only if men were demigods. Cf. "Yankeethum und Deutschthum," *Deutsche Monats-Hefte*, October, 1854, pp. 456–457; Büchele, *op. cit.*, pp. 280–281; Ernest Bruncken, "How Germans Become Americans," State Historical Society of Wisconsin, *Proceedings*, 1897 (reprint, Madison, Wis., 1898), p. 15; Wittke, *op. cit.*, pp. 124, 282; *Staats-Zeitung*, June 17, 1854; daily ed.: February 18, 1856.

47. *Staats-Zeitung*, March 6, August 13, 28, October 2, 1852, February 26, 1853.

48. *Staats-Zeitung*, February 14, 1852. For some of the radical German organizations opposed by the *Staats-Zeitung*, cf. the issues of February 14, August 28, 1852, February 26, 1853. By 1856 the noisy activities of the forty-eighters had quieted down. *Times*, December 31, 1856.

49. Howard R. Marraro, "Italians in New York . . . ," *loc. cit.*, pp. 289–290.

50. *Freeman's Journal*, October 21, 1854. For a calmer but still unfavorable appraisal of Gavazzi, cf. *Courrier des États-Unis*, March 25, 1853. The *Républicain* (June 16, 1853) opposed reactionary Catholicism but disapproved, however, of Gavazzi's "vulgar declarations." For Bedini, cf. Hassard, *op. cit.*, p. 361; Peter Guilday, "Gaetano Bedini," United States Catholic Historical Society, *Historical Records and Studies*, XXIII (1933), 87–107.

51. *Albion*, August 26, November 4, 1848.

52. For attitudes toward feminism, women's rights conventions, and "free love," cf., e.g., *Irish News*, December 6, 1856; *Albion*, February 24, 1849, August 16, 1851, October 16, 1852, September 10, 1853; *Staats-Zeitung*, December 7, 1850; *Courrier des États-Unis*, February 28, 1850, November 11, 1851, October 20, 1855. For opinions of abolitionism, cf., e.g., *Irish American*, January 18, 1851, May 1, 1852, October 29, 1853; *Citizen*, February 4, 11, 1854; *Freeman's Journal*, March 5, 1842, July 22, 1843; *Staats-Zeitung*, October 24, 1846, August 26, 1848, January 1, 1849, March 29, 1862; *Courrier des États-Unis*, August 23, 26, 1845, May 9, 1850; *Républicain*, May 18, 1853, June 30,

1854; Rice, *op. cit.*, Chapter V. Views of the temperance movement ranged from severe condemnation of Protestant fanaticism, "absurd puritanism and plain hypocrisy" (cf., e.g., *Freeman's Journal*, September 6, 1845; *Irish American*, November 4, 1854; *Staats-Zeitung*, August 11, 1841, February 3, June 23, 1849; *Albion*, September 10, 1853; *Courrier des États-Unis*, February 28, July 14, 1852, November 29, 1853; *Progrès*, April 5, 1855) to actual approval by a small minority, especially among the Scots, whose strict Presbyterianism was conducive to a gloomy Sabbatarianism. ([Burn], *Three Years Among the Working-Classes* . . . , p. 94.) Some Germans favored the temperance cause, and in 1845 a (presumably) German total abstinence society collaborated with the native temperance movement. (*Deutsche Schnellpost*, advertisement, June 7, 1845; cf. New York State, *Assembly Documents* [1861], V, No. 114, Minority Report, 6.) Members of a Scottish Temperance Society and at least two Welsh benevolent associations abstained from alcoholic indulgence, while the Catholic clergy tried to inculcate temperate habits among the Irish. (The Scottish society soon disappeared. Liddel, *History of the New York Caledonian Club*, I, 25; *Albion*, March 4, 11, 1843, March 6, 1847; Nichols, *op. cit.*, II, 71.) The Irish developed their own temperance movement, especially after the eloquent Father Mathew "gave it new impulse and direction, separated it from perverse elements, and drew to it the approving sanction of religion." *Freeman's Journal*, September 6, 1845. Cf. Patrick Rogers, *Father Theobald Mathew, Apostle of Temperance* (Dublin, [1943]; New York, 1945). Devoid of fanaticism, the Catholic movement was based upon the principle that religion, divine grace, the sacraments, and prayer were the only means of reclaiming the drunkard. The chapel was to be the only temperance hall and the priest the only orator. (*Freeman's Journal*, September 6, 1845.) As early as 1836 a Hibernian Temperance Society was formed, and during the fifties a number of total abstinence societies were founded. (*Allgemeine Zeitung*, June 25, 1836; *Irish American*, March 20, 1852, March 21, 1857; cf. *Freedman's Journal*, May 29, 1841, June 21, 1845.) On the issue of the observance of the Sabbath, the Scotch and some English were, perhaps, the only immigrants who were "Sunday tyrants." (*Courrier des États-Unis*, September 16, 1859; [Burn], *Three Years among the Working-Classes* . . . , pp. 48, 94.) When Gustav Schwab, an influential German merchant, took the position that German immigrants should conform to the American custom of stern observance of the Sabbath, he brought upon himself the wrath of the German community, which was most outspoken in its approval of Sunday merrymaking, concerts, and liquor sales. (*Caspar Meier and his Successors* . . . , p. 105; cf. *Staats-Zeitung*, March 25, 1848, March 16, 23, June 29, 1850; cf. the notice of a German society for protection against laws limiting Sunday liquor sales, *Staats-Zeitung*, daily ed., July 14, 1859.)

53. *Irish American*, October 27, 1855.

54. *Progrès*, February 27, 1855.

55. *Criminal-Zeitung*, April 4, 1856. Cf. *Irish American*, January 24, 1857.

56. *Allgemeine Zeitung des Judenthums* (Berlin), 1879, p. 499, cited in Marcus, *op. cit.*, Vol. I, p. 146; Grinstein, *op. cit.*, pp. 259, 288 ff. For cases of "anti nuptial fornication" brought before the Presbyterian court, cf. *Records of the Session of the Reformed Presbyterian Church, New York* (MSS covering irregularly the years 1819–1856), II, 19, 21–22, 31.

57. *Freeman's Journal*, August 13, 1859; cf. the issue of July 4, 1857. The *Républicain* (August 25, 1853) opposed obligatory public education and state measures to aid the poor.

58. McGee, *History of the Irish Settlers* . . . , p. 236.

59. Cf. speech of John McGrath, *Irish American*, May 8, 1852.

60. Brace, *Dangerous Classes of New York* . . . , pp. 41–42. As early as the 1830's more than half of the children in the House of Refuge were either foreign born or the offspring of foreigners. Society for the Reformation of Juvenile Delinquents, *Fifteenth Annual Report*, 1840, p. 9. Cf. R. E. Park and H. A. Miller, *Old World Traits Transplanted* (New York, 1921), pp. 61 ff.

61. [Burn], *Three Years among the Working-Classes* . . . , pp. 29, 69–70, 86; Löher, *op. cit.*, pp. 384–386; Hopp, *Federzeichnungen*, p. 54; *Criminal-Zeitung*, July 31, 1857; Marcus, *op. cit.*, I, 41. Cf. Marcus L. Hansen, *Problem of the Third Generation Immigrant* (Rock Island, Ill., 1908), pp. 6–7.

62. Speech of Francis O'Reilly, *Irish American*, May 15, 1852.

63. Cf. marriage announcements, e.g., *Staats-Zeitung*, August 9, September 20, 1837, January 15, 1840; *Allgemeine Zeitung*, March 14, May 16, July 11, 1840; *Deutsche Schnellpost*, February 18, 1843.

64. McGee, *op. cit.*, p. 237; cf. Maguire, *op. cit.*, p. 426, who states that the children of such unions usually were Catholics. Among the cases of intermarriage of nationalities, I have noted Irish-German, Irish-French, Irish-Chinese, German-French, French-English, and numerous instances of immigrants marrying native Americans. MSS schedules of the *New York State Census of 1855*, "Eleventh Ward"; Löher, *op. cit.*, p. 393; *Caspar Meier* . . . , pp. 31, 32; *Staats-Zeitung*, August 12, 1840; *Courrier des États-Unis*, September 22, 1840, June 6, July 7, 1844; MSS *Parish Register* of the Church of St. George the Martyr, *passim;* Beck, *op. cit.*, pp. 9, 11, 250; Adam G. de Gurowski, *America and Europe* (New York, 1857), p. 284. Intermarriage was closely related to the preponderance of marriageable males over marriageable females and to rises in economic status. For an analysis of these factors in the twentieth century, cf. Julius Drachsler, *Intermarriage in New York City* . . . (New York, 1921), pp. 31, 42–51, 66–68. Statistical information about intermarriage in New York City in the pre-Civil War period unfortunately is lacking. If we may apply Drachsler's conclusions to these earlier immigrants, intermarriage occurred more frequently among the middle or intermediate classes than among the rich or educated, on the one hand, and the poor, on the other. (*Ibid.*, p. 62.) The highest ratio of intermarriage occurred among northern and western Europeans, followed by the Irish, the Italians, Jews, and Negroes, respectively. Negroes were at the bottom of the list because of the distinction of color. (*Ibid.*, pp. 43–52, 67.) Among the Jews, arguments against intermarriage were rarely biological but based upon the desire to retain the integrity of Jewish home life and the social solidarity of the Jewish people. (*Ibid.*, p. 48, note 21.) In general, the immigrants from Europe preferred to marry among themselves. The American-born children of foreign parentage likewise preferred to marry among themselves, but since they usually had less in common with their parents' generation than they did with native Americans, there was a greater proportion of intermarriages in the second generation. (*Ibid.*, pp. 34–36.)

65. It is impossible to determine precisely what proportion of immigrants rose in the social scale. I base my judgment upon a comparison of occupations of immigrant parents and their children in two typical immigrant wards, the Sixth and Tenth, in the year 1855. Cf. Appendix, pp. 220–221. For immigrant land owners in these wards, cf. Appendix, p. 222.

66. I was unable to discover any direct evidence of political subsidies to the foreign press, despite the frequency of the contemporary charges that newspapers were "bought."

67. *New York State Census of 1825*, New York County (unpaged).

68. Kennedy (ed.), *Population of the United States in 1860* . . . , p. xxxii. The city's population dropped during the Civil War. In 1855 some 313,000 immigrants comprised 77 per cent of Manhattan's 721,000 inhabitants. The First, Third, Fourth, Sixth, Tenth, and Fourteenth wards had more foreign-born than native inhabitants; in the Second Ward the natives and the foreign born were almost equally divided, while the Seventeenth Ward showed but a slight preponderance of natives. *New York State Census of 1855*, pp. 130–131.

69. For contemporary opinions on the assimilability of these national groups, cf., e.g., Grund, *op. cit.*, p. 61; Lieber, *op. cit.*, I, 39–44; Gurowski, *op. cit.*, p. 261; Hopp, *op. cit.*, pp. 54–55; *Staats-Zeitung*, October 24, 1859.

BIBLIOGRAPHY

Census Returns

Manuscript schedules of the New York State Census of 1855.

Printed summaries of New York State censuses, 1825, 1835, 1845, 1855, 1865.

Seventh Census of the United States, 1850, printed summaries; manuscript schedules of the Fourth, Sixth, and Tenth wards of New York City.

Eighth Census of the United States, 1860, printed summaries.

Public Documents, New York City

Alms-House Commissioner. Annual Reports, 1846, 1847, 1848.

Alms House Governors. Annual Reports, 1849–1858.

Board of Aldermen. Documents, 1834–1865.

Board of Assistant Aldermen. Documents, 1831–1865.

Board of Education. Annual Reports, 1848–1865.

City Inspector. Annual Reports, 1835, 1839–1844, 1856–1860.

Revised Ordinances of the Mayor, Aldermen and Commonalty of the City of New York, 1856.

Valentine, D. T. (compiler). Manual of the Corporation of the City of New York, 1843–1865.

Documents of special interest

Annual Report of the City Inspector, of the City of New York, for the Year Ending December 31, 1856.

Memorial and Remonstrance of the Trustees of the Public School Society against the Application of the Catholics Relative to the School Fund. Board of Aldermen. Documents, Vol. VII, No. 20, October 19, 1840.

[New York City, Registry Committee] Register of Electors of the Tenth Ward of the City of New-York. 1841.

Petition of the Catholics of the City of New York, relative to the Distribution of the School Fund. Board of Aldermen. Documents, Vol. VII, No. 19, September 21, 1840.

Report of the Commissioners of the Alms House in Relation to Male Paupers Voting. . . . Board of Aldermen. Documents, Vol. XI, No. 51, February 10, 1845.

Report of the Committee on the Annual Apportionment, on the Communications of the County Superintendent, Relative to the Use of the Bible in the Public Schools of the City of New York. 1844.

Report of the District Attorney, with Statistics of Crime in This City for

Twelve Years Last Past. Board of Aldermen. Documents, Vol. VIII, No. 57, January 17, 1842.

Report of the Proceeding of the Sanatory Committee of the Board of Health, in Relation to the Cholera, as It Prevailed in New York in 1849. 1849.

Report of the Select Committee of the Board of Education, to Which Was Referred a Communication from the Trustees of the Fourth Ward, in Relation to the Sectarian Character of Certain Books in Use in the Schools of That Ward. 1843.

Sanger, W. W., History of Prostitution: Its Extent, Causes, and Effects throughout the World (Being an Official Report to the Board of Alms-House Governors of the City of New York). 1858.

Semiannual Report of the Chief of Police, for the Six Months Ending June 30, 1854.

Public Documents, New York State

Assembly. Documents, 1830–1860.

Senate. Documents, 1830–1860.

Annual Reports of the Commissioners of Emigration of the State of New York, from the Organization of the Commission, May 5, 1847 to 1860, Inclusive. 1861.

Documents of special interest

Abstracts of Annual Reports of Superintendents of the Poor, 1831–1844.

Annual Reports of the Secretary of State Concerning Criminal Statistics, 1847–1860. Cf. especially the reports for 1850 and 1860.

Annual Reports of the Secretary of State Relative to Poor Statistics, 1846–1860. Cf. especially the report for 1850.

Metropolitan Board of Health. Second Annual Report, 1867. Assembly. Documents, 1868, Vol. IX, No. 122.

Report . . . of the Committee on Medical Societies and Colleges on . . . Cholera. Senate. Documents, 1850, Vol. III, No. 92.

Report of the Majority of the Committee Appointed To Investigate Certain Charges against the Commissioners of Emigration. Assembly. Documents, 1859, Vol. II, No. 53.

Report of the Minority of the Committee Appointed To Investigate Certain Charges against the Commissioners of Emigration. Assembly. Documents, 1859, Vol. II, No. 52.

Report of the Select Committee To Examine into the Condition, Business Accounts, and Management of the Trusts under the Charge of the Commissioners of Emigration, etc. Assembly. Documents, 1852, Vol. II, No. 34.

Report of the Select Committee Appointed To Examine into the Condition of Tenant Houses in New-York and Brooklyn, Albany, 1857. Also in Assembly. Documents, 1857, Vol. III, No. 205.

Report of the Select Committee Appointed To Investigate Frauds upon Emigrant Passengers Arriving in This State. Assembly. Documents, 1847, Vol. VIII, No. 250.

Public Documents, United States

[Aldrich, N. W.], Wholesale Prices, Wages, and Transportation. 52d Congress, 2d Session, Senate Report No. 1394. Washington, D.C., 1893.

Foreign Paupers: Message from the President of the United States Transmitting Information Required . . . in Relation to the Introduction of Foreign Paupers into the United States. 25th Congress, 2d Session, House Document No. 370. Washington, D.C., 1838.

On the Sickness and Mortality on Board Emigrant Ships. 33d Congress, 1st Session, Senate Committee Report No. 386. Washington, D.C., 1854.

Passenger lists of ships arriving at the port of New York in 1825 and in 1835. These original lists are in the Treasury Department Archives, National Archives, Washington, D.C. They are too fragmentary and fragile to be of statistical use.

Population of the United States in 1860: Compiled from the Original Returns of the Eighth Census. Washington, D.C., 1864.

Report of the Committee on Foreign Affairs of the House of Representatives on "Foreign Criminals and Paupers," August 16, 1856. 34th Congress, 1st Session, House Document No. 359. Washington, D.C., 1856.

Report from the Secretary of the Treasury, Relative to the Deportation of Paupers from Great Britain . . . , 24th Congress, 2d Session, Senate Document No. 5. Washington, D.C., 1836.

State Department, Bureau of Statistics. European Emigration; Studies in Europe of Emigration Moving out of Europe, Especially That Flowing to the United States. Washington, D.C., 1890.

State Department, reports and correspondence of United States Consuls serving in the following cities:

Belfast, 1830–1864	Genoa, 1830–1864
Bremen, 1825–1865	Hamburg, 1829–1864
Cork, 1831–1864	Havana, 1829–1860
Dublin, 1829–1864	Le Havre, 1829–1866
Frankfurt on the Main, 1829–1866	Liverpool, 1829–1865
Galway, 1834–1864	Naples, 1829–1864.

United States Immigration Commission. Reports. Washington, D.C., 1911, Vol. III.

United States Industrial Commission. Reports. Washington, D.C., 1901, Vol. XV.

Reports of Private Organizations

Chamber of Commerce of the State of New-York. Annual Reports, 1858–1865.

Report on Emigration by a Special Committee of the Chamber of Commerce of the State of New-York, January 5th, 1865. New York, 1865.

Citizens' Association of New York. Report of the Council of Hygiene and Public Health. New York, 1865. Excellent material on slums.

German Society of the City of New York (Deutsche Gesellschaft der Stadt New-York). Annual Reports, 1846–1865. These reports, printed in German, are packed with detailed information on aid to newly arrived German immigrants and include valuable statistics.

Magdalen Society. First Annual Report of the Executive Committee. . . . Philadelphia, 1831. Data on prostitution.

New York Association for Improving the Condition of the Poor. Annual Reports, 1845–1865. Absolutely essential for any study of economic and social conditions in New York City during this period.

New York Association for Improving the Condition of the Poor. First Report of a Committee on the Sanitary Condition of the Laboring Classes in the City of New-York. New York, 1853.

Society for the Reformation of Juvenile Delinquents in the City of New York. Annual Reports, 1825–1865.

Directories, City Guidebooks, and Miscellaneous Printed Documents

Aid to Ireland; Report of the Central Relief Committee of the City of New York. New York, 1848.

City Election Hand-Book: Containing the Returns of Votes in Each of the Election Districts and Wards . . . in Nov. 1843: Votes for Mayor from 1834 to 1843: List of Office Holders . . . Naturalization Law, and Other Political Information. New York, 1844.

Guidebooks to New York City. The New York Public Library and the New York Historical Society have good collections.

Holley, O. L. (ed.). New-York State Register, 1843, 1845–1846.

Longworth's American Almanac, New-York Register, and City Directory, 1825–1826, 1832–1833, 1840–1841, 1842–1843.

Maugé, Augustin P. Directory français et guide des affaires en Amérique contenant les noms et demeures des résidants français à New-York et aux environs. . . . New York, 1864.

Register of the St. Andrew's Society of the State of New York. Three pamphlets, n.p., 1922–1923.

Rode's New-York City Directory, 1853–1854.

Testimony Relating to the Great Election Frauds of 1838, Taken in the Recorder's Court, New York, in October, 1840. New York, 1840.

Trow's New York City Directory, 1860–1865.

Valentine, D. T. Compilation of the Laws of the State of New York, relating particularly to the City of New York. New York, 1862.

Williams, E. (ed.). New-York Annual Register. 10 vols., published irregularly. New York, 1830–1845.

Church Records, Manuscript Material, and Scrapbooks

Charles Patrick Daly Papers. New York Public Library.

Church of St. George the Martyr. Parish Register. 1859–1863.

[Erheiterung] . . . Seinem N.Y. Turnverein zur Errinerung an die Mitglieder des Dramatischen Section . . . (a series of playbills and programmes collected by Ludwig Engelhardt). New York Public Library.

Extracts from Printed Sources . . . Relating to the social history of New York City, 6 vols. of typed transcript given to the New York Public Library in 1935 by I. N. Phelps Stokes.

Gold, A. B. History of Manufacturing in New York City, 1825–1840. Unpublished Master's thesis (1932) in Columbia University Library.

Letters to Thomas Lawrence, an English tailor who settled in New York City. New York Public Library.

Liddel, Charles W. History of the New York Caledonian Club. 5 vols. of typed transcript (1935) in the possession of the club.

Minutes of the Albion Club. 1836–1839. New York Historical Society.

Minutes of the St. Andrew's Curling Club. 1873–1930. New York Historical Society.

New York Union Society of Journeymen House Carpenters. Constitution and By-Laws. 1833. A list of members during the years 1833–1836 is included. New York Public Library.

Records of the Session of the Reformed Presbyterian Church, New York. 1819–1856.

St. Matthew's Lutheran Church. Marriage Records. 1833–1836.

Sturtevant, John J. Recollections of a Resident of New York City from 1835 to 1905. . . . Typed transcript in New York Public Library.

Turnvereine. A scrapbook of pamphlets, letters, and publications of the Turners. Includes the Satzungen des socialistisches Turner-Bundes in Nord-Amerika. New York Public Library.

Newspapers: a Sampling of the American Press

Depositories are abbreviated as follows:

AAS	American Antiquarian Society, Worcester, Mass.
AIHS	American Irish Historical Society, New York City
BPL	Boston Public Library
CUL	Columbia University Library
HCL	Harvard College Library
LC	Library of Congress
NEDL	New England Deposit Library, Boston
NYHS	New York Historical Society
NYPL	New York Public Library
NYSL	New York Society Library

Anglo-African, 1861–1865 (HCL: on deposit in NEDL).

Champion of American Labor, 1847. A nativist labor paper. (The only known file is in the library of the New York Historical Society).

Daily Plebeian, 1842–1845 (NYSL).
Gazette and Times, 1846 (NYHS).
Herald, 1848, 1853 (NYPL).
Man, 1834–1835 (NYHS).
National Police Gazette, 1845–1847 (NYPL).
New York Farmer, 1833–1834. A monthly (CUL).
Protestant Vindicator, 1834–1838 (NYPL).
Subterranean, 1845–1847 (NYPL, NYHS).
Times, 1854, 1856 (NYPL).
Tribune, 1841–1843, 1848–1857 (NYPL).
Union, 1836 (NYPL).
Working Man's Advocate, 1830–1836, 1844–1847 (NYPL).
Young America, 1845–1847 (NYPL).

Newspapers: the Catholic, Immigrant, and Foreign Language Press
Depositories are abbreviated according to the key in the preceding section; (*) indicates the more useful sources.

Adopted Citizen, April 4, 1834 (NYHS).
*Albion; or, British Colonial and Foreign Gazette, 1827–1863 (NYPL).
Allgemeine Zeitung, 1835–1836 (NYHS), 1839–1840 (BPL: on deposit in NEDL).
*Anglo American, 1843–1847 (NYPL).
*Asmonean, 1849–1858 (NYPL).
*Citizen, 1854–1857 (NYPL, NYHS).
Continental, 1862–1863 (HCL: on deposit in NEDL).
*Courrier des États-Unis, 1828–1865 (NYPL).
*Criminal-Zeitung, 1852–1863. Title varies: also known as the *Belletristisches Journal* (NYPL).
*Crónica, 1849–1864 (LC).
Wochentlicher New-Yorker *Demokrat*, 1861–1863 (HCL: on deposit in NEDL).
Deutsche Monats-Hefte, 1853–1856. A periodical, also known as *Meyer's Monats-Hefte* (NYPL).
*Deutsche Schnellpost, 1843–1845 (NYHS), 1845–1848 (HCL).
*Eco d'Italia, 1851–1852 (BPL: on deposit in NEDL), 1862, 1865 (NYPL).
Emerald; or, Political Literary and Commercial Recorder, June 19, July 31, 1824 (AAS).
*Emigrant, 1833–1835 (LC).
*Emigrant and Old Countryman, 1835 . . . 1837; scattered numbers, 1838–1840 (LC).
Estafette, 1838 (LC).
European, 1836–1837 (NYPL).
European, 1856–1857 (NYPL). No connection with the earlier paper of the same name.
European News, September 11, 1847 (AAS).

Franco-Américain, 1846–1847 (LC).

**Freeman's Journal*, 1840–1860, 1862–1864. (The most complete file is in the possession of the Dominican College of the Immaculate Conception, Washington, D.C. A fairly complete file is in the library of the Catholic University of America. The New York Public Library has volumes for 1862–1864).

Friedrich Gerhard's Deutsch-Amerikanische Gartenlaube, 1865–1866. A biweekly, later a weekly, periodical (NYPL).

Globe and Emerald, 1824 . . . 1826 (AAS).

*New-Yorker *Handels-Zeitung*, 1855, 1857–1859, 1865 (NYPL).

Indicateur, January 9, 1840. (LC).

*Irish American, 1849–1865 (NYPL).

*Irish News, 1856–1858, 1860 (AIHS).

Irish Vindicator, May 7, 1859 (AAS).

Irishman, June 19, 1824 (AAS).

Irishman and Foreigners' Advocate, July 15, 20, 1835 (AAS).

*Jewish Messenger, 1857–1860 (NYPL).

Mensagero Semanal de Nueva York, 1828–1831 (NYPL).

Mercurio de Nueva York, June 25, 1831 (LC).

Messager Franco-Américain, 1862–1865 (LC).

Old Countryman and English, Irish, Scotch, Welsh, and Colonial Mirror, 1831–1832, January 1, 1834, July 13, 1842, September 13, 1843 (AAS).

Phare de New-York, 1851–1852 (BPL: on deposit in NEDL).

Progrès, 1855 (HCL: on deposit in NEDL).

Redactor, January 21, 1828, 1831 (LC).

[New York] *Weekly Register and Catholic Diary*, 1833–1834 (NYPL).

*Républicain, 1853–1854 (HCL: on deposit in NEDL).

**Scottish Journal of Intelligence and Literature*, 1841–1842 (NYHS).

*Scottish Patriot, 1840 (NYHS).

Shamrock for the Country, October 6, 1823 (NYHS).

Skandinavia, January 15, April 15, 1847 (AAS).

*New-Yorker *Staats-Zeitung*, 1837, 1839–1843, 1846, 1848–1856, 1858–1865; daily ed.: 1853, 1856, 1858, 1859; Sunday ed.: 1859; triweekly ed.: 1842–1843 (NYPL).

*Truth Teller, 1825–1836 (NYPL, AIHS).

Turn-Blatt für die Vereine des socialistischen Turnerbundes von Nordamerika, 1856–1858 (NYPL).

**Turn-Zeitung; Organ des socialistischen Turnerbundes*, 1851–1853 (NYPL).

Verdad, scattered numbers, 1848, May 18, 1850 (LC).

New-Yorker *Volkszeitung*, February 21, 1903. Twenty-fifth anniversary number of sixty-seven pages, containing useful historical material on the German labor movement in New York (American Labor Archive).

Western Star and Harp of Erin, 1812–1813 (NYHS).

Immigrant Guidebooks

Scores of these little volumes were examined. Among the most useful were the following:

Amerika, Wie es Ist; Ein Buch für Kunde der neuen Welt (Serie III der Volkschriften des deutsch-amerikanischen Vereins). Hamburg, 1854.

Bauer, F. A. Taschenbüchlein für Auswanderer und Reisende nach den Vereinigten Staaten von Nordamerika. . . . Augsburg, 1854.

Behr, Ottomar von. Guter Rath für Auswanderer nach den Vereinigten Staaten von Nordamerika. Leipzig, 1847.

Bogen, F. W. Der Deutsche in Amerika oder Rath und Belehrung für deutsche Einwanderer in den Vereinigten Staaten von Amerika, zugleich ein Lesebuch für Anfänger. . . . 4th ed., rev. New York, 1856.

Buchanan, A. C. Emigration Practically Considered; with Detailed Directions to Emigrants . . . to British North America. . . . London, 1828.

Collins, S. H. Emigrant's Guide to and Description of the United States of America. 4th ed. Hull, 1830.

Colton, Calvin. Manual for Emigrants to America. London, 1832.

Dyke, Thomas. Advice to Emigrants. London, 1832.

Emigrant's Hand-Book and Guide to the United States; or England and America Contrasted. London, n.d. [after April, 1848].

Emigrant's Handbook; or, A Directory and Guide for Persons Emigrating to the United States of America. New York, 1848.

Emigrant's True Guide: Comprising Advice and Instruction in Every Stage of the Voyage to America. . . . New York, 1844.

Mudie, Robert. Emigrant's Pocket Companion. London, 1832.

[Nettle, George], Practical Guide for Emigrants to North America, including the United States . . . by a Seven Years' Resident of North America. London, 1850.

Struve, Gustav. Wegweiser für Auswanderer. Bamberg, 1866.

Thomason, D. R. Hints to Emigrants; or to Those Who May Contemplate Emigrating to the United States of America, and California. Rev. ed. London, 1849.

Ueber Auswanderung; von einem Kaufmanne in Bremen. Bremen, 1842.

Wander, K. F. W. Auswanderungs-Katechismus; Ein Rathgeber für Auswanderer, besonders für Diejenigen, welche nach Nordamerika auswandern wollen . . . Glogau, 1852.

Winke über Auswanderung besonders nach Nord-Amerika. Zwickau, 1849.

Wohlgemeinter Rath der Vorsteher der deutschen Gesellschaft in New-York, an Deutsche, die nach den Vereinigten Staaten von N. Amerika auszuwandern beabsichtigen. New York, 1833.

Travelers' Accounts

Abdy, E. S. Journal of a Residence and Tour in the United States of North America, from April, 1833, to October, 1834. 3 vols. London, 1835.

Beaufoy, Mark. Tour through Parts of the United States and Canada. London, 1828.

[Boardman, James.] America and the Americans; by a Citizen of the World. London, 1833.

Brauns, Ernst L. Skizzen von Amerika. Halberstadt, 1830.

Bromme, Traugott. Nordamerika's Bewohner, Schönheiten und Naturschätze. . . . Stuttgart, 1839.

Büchele, C. Land und Volk der Vereinigten Staaten von Nord-Amerika. Stuttgart, 1855.

[Burn, James D.] Three Years Among the Working-Classes in the United States during the War. London, 1865.

Busch, Moritz. Wanderungen zwischen Hudson und Mississippi 1851 und 1852. 2 vols. Stuttgart, 1854.

Büttner, J. G. Briefe aus und über Nordamerika oder Beiträge zu einer richtigen Kenntnis der Vereinigten Staaten und ihre Bewohner. 2 vols. Dresden and Leipzig, 1847.

Dicey, Edward. Six Months in the Federal States. 2 vols. London, 1863.

Duden, Gottfried. Bericht über eine Reise nach den westlichen Staaten Nordamerika's. Elberfeld, 1829.

Dudgeon, Thomas. Nine Years Residence and a Nine Months Tour. . . . (In Sidney Smith, Settlers New Home, Edinburgh, 1841.)

Ferguson, William. America by River and Rail; or, Notes by the Way on the New World and Its People. London, 1856.

Finch, John. Travels in the United States of America and Canada. London, 1833.

Frei, Johann. Drei Monate in New-York, oder: Die Grosse Metropole der neuen Welt. Zürich, 1869.

Griesinger, Theodor. Freiheit und Sclaverei unter dem Sternenbanner oder Land und Leute in Amerika. Stuttgart, 1862.

—— Lebende Bilder aus Amerika. Stuttgart, 1858.

Gudehus, Jonas H. Meine Auswanderung nach Amerika im Jahre 1822, und Meine Rückkehr in die Heimath im Jahre 1825. Hildesheim, 1829.

Gurowski, Adam G. de. America and Europe. New York, 1857.

Hecke, J. Val. Reise durch die Vereinigten Staaten von Nord-Amerika. Berlin, 1820.

Löher, Franz. Geschichte und Zustände der Deutschen in Amerika. Cincinnati, 1847.

Mackay, Alexander. Western World; or, Travels in the United States in 1846–47. 4th ed., 3 vols. London, 1850.

Mackay, Charles. Life and Liberty in America: or, Sketches of a Tour in the United States and Canada in 1857–8. 2 vols. London, 1859.

Macrae, David. Americans at Home: Pen-and-Ink Sketches of American Men, Manners and Institutions. 2 vols. Edinburgh, 1870.

Marjoribanks, Alexander. Travels in South and North America. London, 1853.

Mitchell, D. W. Ten Years in the United States: Being an Englishman's Views of Men and Things in the North and South. London, 1862.

O'Donovan, Jeremiah. Brief Account of the Author's Interview with His Countrymen, and of the Parts of the Emerald Isle whence They Emigrated, together with a Direct Reference to Their Present Location in the Land of Their Adoption, during His Travels through Various States of the Union in 1854 and 1855. Pittsburgh, 1864.

Pulszky, Francis and Theresa. White, Red, and Black; Sketches of American Society in the United States during the Visit of Their Guests. New York, 1853.

Shirreff, Patrick. Tour through North America; together with a Comprehensive View of the Canadas and the United States. As Adapted for Agricultural Emigration. Edinburgh, 1835.

Simonin, L. Monde Américain; Souvenirs de mes voyages aux États-Unis. Paris, 1876.

Stuart, James. Three Years in North America. 2d ed., 2 vols. Edinburgh, 1833.

Techla, Georg, Drei Jahre in New-York. Zwickau, 1862.

Vetter, Christoph. Zwei Jahre in New-York; Schilderung einer Seereise von Havre nach New-York und Characteristik des New-Yorker politischen und socialen Lebens. Hof, 1849.

White, John. Sketches from America. London, 1870.

Wyse, Francis. America, Its Realities and Resources: Comprising Important Details Connected with the Present . . . State of the Country, Its Laws and Customs. . . . 3 vols. London, 1846.

Other Writings of Contemporaries

[Armstrong, William.] Aristocracy of New York, Who They Are and What They Were; Being a Social and Business History. . . . New York, 1848.

Asmodeus in New-York. New York, 1868.

Atlantische Studien von Deutschen in Amerika. 8 vols. Göttingen, 1853–1857.

Bannard, William. Discourse on the Moral Aspect and Destitution of the City of New York. New York, 1851.

Beach, Moses Y. (compiler). Wealth and Biography of the Wealthy Citizens of New York City. . . . 6th and 13th ed. New York, 1845, 1855.

Becker, August. Geschichte des Religiösen und Atheistischen Frühsozialismus; erstausgabe des von August Becker 1847 verfassten . . . Geheimberichtes an Metternich. . . . (Vol. VI of Christentum und Sozialismus Quellen und Darstellungen. Kiel, 1932.)

Belden, E. P. New-York Past, Present, and Future. . . . New York, 1849.

Bogen, F. W. Annual Report . . . of His Labors among the German Emigrants in New-York and Neighborhood. . . . New York, 1854.

Browne, Junius H. Great Metropolis: a Mirror of New-York. . . . Hartford, 1869.

Byrdsall, Fitzwilliam. History of the Loco-Foco or Equal Rights Party, Its Movements, Conventions and Proceedings. . . . New York, 1842.

Child, Lydia Maria. Letters from New-York. 1st Series. New York, 1843.

Civil Rights; the Hibernian Riot and the "Insurrection of the Capitalists." A History of Important Events in New York, in the Midsummer of 1871. New York, 1871.

[Curry, Daniel.] New-York: a Historical Sketch of the Rise and Progress of the Metropolitan City of America. New York, 1853.

Engels, Friedrich. Condition of the Working-Class in England in 1844. Trans. by Florence K. Wischnewetzky. London, 1892.

[Five Points Mission.] Old Brewery, and the New Mission House at the Five Points. By Ladies of the Mission. New York, 1854.

Fleischmann, C. L. Erwerbzweige, Fabrikwesen und Handel der Vereinigten Staaten von Nordamerika. . . . Stuttgart, 1850.

Flint, C. S., and associates. Eighty Years' Progress in the United States. . . . 2 vols. Hartford Conn., 1868.

[Foster, George G.] New York in Slices: by an Experienced Carver, Being the Original Slices Published in the N. Y. Tribune. New York, 1849.

Foster, Vere. Work and Wages. 6th ed., London [1856].

Freedley, Edwin T. Leading Pursuits and Leading Men; a Treatise on the Principal Trades and Manufactures of the United States. . . . Philadelphia, c. 1854.

Gallenga, A. Episodes of My Second Life. 2 vols. London, 1884.

[Gardiner, O. C.] "Foreign Immigration, Its Natural and Extraordinary Causes," *American Whig Review*, Vol. VI, November, December, 1847.

Glentworth, James B. Statement of the Frauds on the Elective Franchise in the City of New York, in . . . 1838 and . . . 1839. New York, 1841.

Green, Jonothan H. Report on Gambling in New York. New York, 1851.

Griscom, John H. Sanitary Condition of the Laboring Population of New York. New York, 1845.

Grund, Francis J. Americans, in their Moral, Social, and Political Relations. Boston, 1837.

Gunn, Thomas B. Physiology of New York Boarding Houses. New York, 1857.

Hale, Edward E. Letters on Irish Emigration. Boston, 1852.

Hardie, James. Description of the City of New York. New York, 1827.

Hibernicus (pseud.). "What Brings So Many Irish to America!" A Pamphlet . . . One Part of Which Explains the Many Causes of Irish Emigration; the Other the Consistency or Inconsistency of "Native Americanism" As It Is. New York, 1845.

Hone, Philip. Diary. Ed. by Allan Nevins. New York, 1927.

Howitt, William. Rural and Domestic Life in Germany . . . Collected in a General Tour, and during a Residence . . . 1840, 41 and 42. Philadelphia, 1843.

Hughes, John. Complete Works. Ed. by Lawrence Kehoe. 2 vols. New York, 1864.

Kingsbury, Harmon. Immigrants Good Samaritan. New York, c. 1848.

Lieber, Francis. Stranger in America: Comprising Sketches of the Manners, Society, and National Peculiarities of the United States, in a Series of Letters. . . . 2 vols. London, 1835.

London v. New York; by an English Workman. London, 1859.

[Lyon, Isaac S.] Recollections of an ex-Cartman. Newark, 1872.

Marcus, Moses. Address to the Members of the "United Church of England and Ireland," and of the Protestant Episcopal Church in the United States of America, on the Subject of Emigration. . . . New York, 1846.

Nicholson, Peter. Mechanic's Companion. . . . Philadelphia, 1863.

Pachmayr, Joseph. Leben und Treiben der Stadt New York, mit hinweis auf die Einwanderung und das deutsche Element. Hamburg, 1874.

Peep into Catharine Street, or the Mysteries of Shopping; By a Late Retailer. New York, 1846.

Pelz, Eduard. Deutschen in den Vereinigten Staaten von Nordamerika; Eine Beleuchtung. Gotha, 1870.

—— Transatlantische Federzeichnungen Rudolstadt, 1854.

Rice, F. A. (ed.). "John Stokes's American Diary," *National Review,* Vol. CX, No. 659, January, 1938.

Scrope, G. Poulett (ed.). Extracts of Letters from Poor Persons Who Emigrated Last Year to Canada and the United States. . . . London, 1832.

Smith, William. Emigrant's Narrative; or, A Voice from the Steerage; Being a Brief Account of the Sufferings of the Emigrants on the Ship "India" on Her Voyage from Liverpool to New-York in . . . 1847–8 . . . with a Statement of the Cruelties Practiced upon the Emigrants in the Staten Island Hospital. New York, 1850.

Struve, Gustav. Diesseits und Jenseits des Oceans. Coburg, 1863.

Stryker, Peter. Lower Depths of the Great American Metropolis. New York, 1866.

Thorburn, Grant. Fifty Years' Reminiscences of New-York; or, Flowers from the Garden of Laurie Todd. . . . New York, c. 1845.

—— Forty Years' Residence in America: or, The Doctrine of a Particular Providence Exemplified in the Life of Grant Thorburn, Seedsman, New York. Boston, 1834.

—— Life and Writings. . . . New York, 1852.

[Whitman, Walt.] New York Dissected by Walt Whitman; a Sheaf of Recently Discovered Newspaper Articles by the Author of Leaves of Grass. ed. by Emory Holloway and Ralph Adimari. New York, 1936.

Willis, Nathaniel P. Prose Works. Philadelphia, 1855.

Young Germany; an Account of the Rise, Progress, and Present Position of German Communism; with a Memoir of Wilhelm Weitling, Its Founder: —and a Report of the Proceedings at the Banquet Given by the English Socialists . . . London, September 22, 1844. London, c. 1844.

Secondary Works: Books

Abbott, Edith. Historical Aspects of the Immigration Problem; Select Documents. Chicago, c. 1926.

—— Immigration; Select Documents and Case Records. Chicago, c. 1924.

Adams, T., Lewis, H. M., and McCrosky, T. T. Population, Land Values and Government. . . . (Vol. II of the Regional Survey of New York and Its Environs, copyrighted by the Committee on Regional Plan of New York and Its Environs, New York, 1929.)

Adams, William F. Ireland and Irish Emigration to the New World from 1815 to the Famine. New Haven, 1932.

Albion, Robert G. Rise of New York Port. . . . New York, 1939.

Andenken an das "Goldene Jubiläum," oder Fünfzigjährige Anniversarium der Gründung der St. Nicolaus Kirche. . . . New York, c. 1883.

Arnold, John P., and Penman, Frank. History of the Brewing Industry and Brewing Science in America. Chicago, 1933.

Asbury, Herbert. Gangs of New York. New York, 1939.

Bagenal, Philip H. American Irish and Their Influence on Irish Politics. Boston, 1882.

Baumgartner, Appolinaris W. Catholic Journalism: A Study of Its Development in the United States, 1789–1930. New York, 1931.

Bayley, James R. Brief Sketch of the Early History of the Catholic Church on the Island of New York. 2d ed. New York, 1870.

Beck, Louis J. New York's Chinatown; an Historical Presentation of Its People and Places. New York, c. 1898.

Becker, M. J. Germans of 1849 in America. Mt. Vernon, Ohio, 1887.

Bidwell, Percy W., and Falconer, John I. History of Agriculture in the Northern United States 1620–1860. Washington, D.C., 1925.

Billington, Ray A. Protestant Crusade, 1800–1860; a Study of the Origins of American Nativism. New York, 1938.

Bishop, J. L. History of American Manufactures from 1608 to 1860. . . . 3d ed., 3 vols. Philadelphia, 1868.

Blegen, Theodore C. Norwegian Migration to America. 2 vols. Northfield, Minnesota, 1931–1940.

Booth, Mary L. History of the City of New York. . . . Limited ed., 2 vols. New York, 1867.

Bosse, Georg von. Deutsche Element in den Vereinigten Staaten. Stuttgart, 1908.

Brace, Charles L. Dangerous Classes of New York and Twenty Years' Work Among Them. New York, 1872.

Brandt, Lilian. Growth and Development of AICP and COS . . . Report to the Committee on the Institute of Welfare Research, Community Service Society of New York, 1942 (multigraphed).

Brann, Henry A. Most Reverend John Hughes. New York, 1892.

Breen, Matthew P. Thirty Years of New York Politics Up-to-Date New York, 1899.

Bromwell, William J. History of Immigration to the United States; Exhibiting the Number, Sex, Age, Occupation, and Country of Birth, of Passengers Arriving in the United States by Sea from Foreign Countries . . . 1819 to . . . 1855. . . . New York, 1856.

Brown Book; a Biographical Record of Public Officials of the City of New York for 1898–9. New York, 1899.

Campbell, Helen E. Darkness and Daylight; or, Lights and Shadows of New York Life. Hartford, Conn., 1892.

Čapek, Thomas. Čechs (Bohemians) in America. . . . Boston, 1920.

Carpenter, Niles. Immigrants and Their Children, 1920; a Study Based on Census Statistics Relative to the Foreign Born and the Native White of Foreign or Mixed Parentage. Washington, D.C., 1927.

—— Sociology of City Life. New York, 1931.

Carter, Peter. Peter Carter, 1825–1900. New York, 1901.

Childs, Frances C. French Refugee Life in the United States, 1790–1800. Baltimore, 1940.

Clapham, John H. Economic Development of France and Germany, 1815–1914. Cambridge, England, 1921.

—— Economic History of Modern Britain. . . . 3 vols. Cambridge, England, 1926–1938.

Clark, Victor S. History of Manufactures in the United States. 3 vols. New York, 1929.

Cochran, Annie C. Christian Publisher: Life and Work of Robert Carter. New York, c. 1891.

Cole, Arthur H. American Wool Manufacture. 2 vols. Cambridge, Mass., 1926.

Commons, John R. Races and Immigrants in America. New York, 1907.

—— and associates. Documentary History of American Industrial Society. 10 vols. Cleveland, 1910–1911.

—— History of Labour in the United States. 4 vols. New York, 1918–1935.

Costello, Augustine E., Our Firemen; a History of the New York Fire Departments; Volunteer and Paid. New York, 1887.

—— Our Police Protectors; History of the New York Police. . . . New York, 1885.

Cox, E. H. M. History of Gardening in Scotland. London, 1935.

Crapsey, Edward. Nether Side of New York. New York, 1872.

Cronau, Rudolf. Denkschrift zum 150. Jahrestag der Deutschen Gesellschaft der Stadt New York, 1784–1934. New York, 1934.

—— Drei Jahrhunderte deutschen Lebens in Amerika. Berlin, 1909.

Davenport, John I. Election and Naturalization Frauds in New York City, 1860–1870. 2d ed. New York, 1894.

De Forest, R. W., and Veiller, L. (eds.). Tenement House Problem. 2 vols. New York, 1903.

Deutsche Pionier (monthly periodical, 1869–1887).

Dodd, A. H. Industrial Revolution in North Wales. Cardiff, 1933.

Dorfman, Joseph. Economic Mind in American Civilization, 1606–1865. 2 vols. New York. 1946.

Drachsler, Julius. Intermarriage in New York City; a Statistical Study of the Amalgamation of European Peoples. New York, 1921.

Dusold, Georg J. Goldenes Jubiläum der Kirche zum Allerheiligsten Erlöser. . . . New York, c. 1894.

Dyer, Walter A. Early American Craftsmen. New York, 1915.

Eickhoff, Anton. In der Neuen Heimath; Geschichtliche Mittheilungen über die deutschen Einwanderer in allen Theilen der Union. New York, 1884.

Ely, Richard T. Labor Movement in America. New York, c. 1886.

Emmet, Thomas A. Incidents of My Life. New York, 1911.

Epitome of the New-Yorker Staats-Zeitungs Sixty-Five Years of Progress. New York[?], 1899.

Faust, A. B. German Element in the United States. 2 vols. Boston, 1909.

Fite, Emerson D. Social and Industrial Conditions in the North during the Civil War. New York, 1910.

Flick, A. C. (ed.). History of the State of New York. 10 vols. New York, 1933–1937.

Foerster, Robert F. Italian Emigration of Our Times. Cambridge, Mass., 1919.

Fox, Dixon R. Decline of the Aristocracy in the Politics of New York. New York, 1919.

Gerard, James W. Impress of Nationalities on the City of New York. New York, 1883.

—— London and New York, Their Crime and Police. New York, 1853.

Gjerset, Knut. Norwegian Sailors in American Waters. Northfield, Minn., 1933.

Goldstein, Israel. Century of Judaism in New York; B'nai Jeshurun, 1825–1925. . . . New York, 1930.

Gollmer, Hugo (compiler). Namensliste der Pioniere des Nord-Amerik. Turnerbundes der Jahre 1848–1862. St. Louis, 1885.

Gompers, Samuel. Seventy Years of Life and Labor. 2 vols. New York, c. 1925.

Gover, William C. Tammany Hall Democracy of the City of New York. . . . New York, 1875.

Grinstein, Hyman B. Rise of the Jewish Community of New York, 1654–1860. Philadelphia, 1945.

Grueningen, J. P. von. Swiss in the United States. . . . Madison, Wis., 1940.

Halévy, Élie. History of the English people. . . . 2 vols. New York, 1924–1926.

Hammond, Jabez D. History of Political Parties in the State of New-York. . . . 4th ed., 2 vols. Cooperstown, N.Y., 1846.

Hammond, John L., and Barbara. Village Labourer, 1760–1832. . . . 4th ed. London, 1936.

Handlin, Oscar. Boston's Immigrants 1790–1865; a Study in Acculturation. Cambridge, Mass., 1941.

Hansen, Marcus L. Atlantic Migration 1607–1860; a History of the Continuing Settlement of the United States. Cambridge, Mass., 1940.

—— Immigrant in American History. Cambridge, Mass., 1940.

—— Mingling of the Canadian and American Peoples. New Haven, 1940.

Harlow, Alvin F. Old Bowery Days; the Chronicles of a Famous Street. New York, 1931.

Hassard, John A. Life of Most Rev. John Hughes, D.D. New York, 1866.

Haswell, Charles H. Reminiscences of New York by an Octogenarian (1816 to 1860). New York, c. 1896.

Haynes, George E. Negro at Work in New York City. New York, 1912.

Headley, Joel T. Great Riots of New York, 1712 to 1873; Including a Full and Complete Account of the Four Days' Draft Riot of 1863. New York, 1873.

Hokanson, Nels. Swedish Immigrants in Lincoln's Time. New York, c. 1942.

Holden, V. F. Early Years of Isaac Thomas Hecker (1819–1844). Washington, D.C., 1939.

Hollander, J. H., and Barnett, G. E. (eds.). Studies in American Trade Unionism. New York, 1912.

Hopp, Ernst O. Federzeichnungen aus dem Amerikanischen Leben. Berlin, c. 1878.

Hourwich, Isaac A. Immigration and Labor; the Economic Aspects of European Immigration to the United States. New York, 1912.

[Ingraham, Abijah.] Biography of Fernando Wood; a History of the Forgeries, Perjuries, and Other Crimes of Our "Model" Mayor. New York, c. 1856.

Jacoby, George P. Catholic Child Care in Nineteenth Century New York. Washington, D.C., 1941.

Janson, Florence E. Background of Swedish Immigration, 1840–1930. Chicago, 1931.

Johnson, Stanley C. History of Emigration from the United Kingdom to North America, 1763–1912. London, 1913.

Jones, Howard M. America and French Culture 1750–1848. Chapel Hill, 1927.

Kapp, Friedrich. Aus und Über Amerika. 2 vols. Berlin, 1876.

—— European Emigration to the United States. New York, 1869.

—— Immigration and the Commissioners of Emigration of the State of New York. New York, 1870.

Kofoed, Jack. Brandy for Heroes; a Biography of the Honorable John Morrissey. New York, 1938.

Körner, Gustav. Deutsche Element in den Vereinigten Staaten von Nordamerika, 1818–1848. Cincinnati, 1880.

Lane, Francis E. American Charities and the Child of the Immigrant; a Study of Typical Child Caring Institutions in New York and Massachusetts between the Years 1845 and 1880. . . . Washington, D.C. 1932.

Lee, Basil L. Discontent in New York City, 1861–1865. Washington, D.C., 1944.

Lemke, Theodore. Geschichte des Deutschthums von New York von 1848 bis auf die Gegenwart. New York, 1891.

Lenel, Edith. Friedrich Kapp 1824–1884; Ein Lebensbild aus den Deutschen und den Nordamerikanischen Einheitskämpfen. Leipzig, 1935.

Leuchs, Fritz A. H. Early German Theatre in New York 1840–1872. New York, 1928.

Lossing, Benson J. History of New York City. New York, c. 1884.

McCabe, James D. Secrets of the Great City. . . . Philadelphia, 1868.

Maguire, John F. Irish in America. 4th ed. New York, c. 1887.

McGee, Thomas D'Arcy. History of the Irish Settlers in North America. 6th ed. Boston, 1855.

McKay, Richard C. South Street; a Maritime History of New York. New York, c. 1934.

McLaughlin, James F. Life and Times of John Kelly, Tribune of the People. New York, 1885.

McNeill, George E. (ed.). Labor Movement: the Problem of Today. Boston, 1887.

Magnan, D. M. A. Histoire de la Race Française aux États-Unis. Paris, 1912.

Marcus, Jacob R. (compiler). Index to Americana in Foreign-Jewish Periodicals (1806–1938). 3 vols. of typed transcript. Cincinnati, 1939. (In New York Public Library.)

Masquerier, Lewis. Sociology: or, The Reconstruction of Society, Government, and Property. New York, 1877.

Metzner, Henry. Brief History of the American Turnerbund. Rev. ed. Trans. by Theodore Stempfel, Jr. Pittsburgh, 1924.

Meyborg, Bernhard. Geschichte des Plattdütschen Volksfest-Verein von New York un Umgegend. New York, 1892.

Miller, Herbert A. Races, Nations and Classes. . . . Philadelphia, c. 1924.

Morrison George A., Jr. History of Saint Andrew's Society of the State of New York, 1756–1906. New York, 1906.

Mosenthal, Hermann. Geschichte des Vereins Deutscher Liederkranz in New York. New York, 1897.

Myers, Gustavus. History of Tammany Hall. New York, 1901.

National Bureau of Economic Research. International Migrations. 2 vols. New York, 1929–1931.

Nichols, Thomas L. Forty Years of American Life, 1821–1861. New York, 1937.

Norcross, Frank W. History of the New York Swamp. New York, 1901.

Noyes, John H. History of American Socialisms. Philadelphia, 1870.

Obermann, Karl, Joseph Weydemeyer, Pioneer of American Socialism. New York, 1947.

Odell, George C. D. Annals of the New York Stage. 14 vols. 1927–1945.

[Oelrichs & Co.] Caspar Meier and his Successors. . . . New York, 1898.

Park, Robert E. Immigrant Press and Its Control. New York, 1922.

—— and Miller, Herbert A. Old World Traits Transplanted. New York, 1921.

Peirce, Bradford K. Half Century with Juvenile Delinquents; or, the New York House of Refuge and its Times. New York, 1869.

Pollard, H. B. C. Secret Societies of Ireland; Their Rise and Progress. London, 1922.

Pope, Jesse E. Clothing Industry in New York. Columbia, Mo., 1905.

Porter, Kenneth W. John Jacob Astor, Business Man. 2 vols. Cambridge, Mass., 1931.

Post, Albert. Popular Freethought in America, 1825–1850. New York, 1943.

Pound, Arthur. Golden Earth. New York, 1935.

Pratt, Edward E. Industrial Causes of Congestion of Population in New York City. New York, 1911.

Prume, Jules J. de. Canadiens-Français à New York; historique de la colonie canadienne-française et de la Société Saint-Jean-Baptiste de Bienfaisance de New York. Montreal, c. 1921.

Ramsperger, Gustav. Geschichte des New-Yorker Deutschen Apotheker-Vereins. New York, 1901.

Rhys, John, and Brynmor-Jones, David. Welsh People. London, 1909.

Rice, Madeleine H. American Catholic Opinion in the Slavery Controversy. New York, 1944.

Ritter, Frédéric L. Music in America. New York, 1883.

Roberts, Edward F. Ireland in America. New York, 1931.

Rogers, Patrick. Father Theobald Mathew, Apostle of Temperance. Dublin, c. 1943.

Ross, Peter. Scot in America. New York, 1896.

Ruprecht, Ludwig. Geschichte der Entstehung und Entwickelung des New Yorker Deutschen Apotheker-Vereins. New York, 1876.

[St. George's Society.] History of St. George's Society of New York from 1770 to 1913. New York, 1913.

Saposs, David J. Left Wing Unionism; a Study of Radical Policies and Tactics. New York, 1926.

[Schaefer Brewing Company.] Our One Hundredth Year, 1842–1942. New York [?], 1942.

Schiavo, Giovanni. Italians in America before the Civil War. New York, 1934.

Schlesinger, Arthur M., Jr. Age of Jackson. Boston, 1945.

Schlüter, Herman [Hermann]. Lincoln, Labor and Slavery. New York, 1913. [The author has Americanized his given name.]

Schlüter, Hermann. Anfänge der deutschen Arbeiterbewegung in Amerika. Stuttgart, 1907.

—— Brewing Industry and the Brewery Workers' Movement in America. Cincinnati, 1910.

Schmoller, Gustav. Zur Geschichte der deutschen Kleingewerbe im 19. Jahrhundert. Halle, 1870.

Schneider, David M. History of Public Welfare in New York State, 1609–1866. Chicago, 1938.

Scisco, Louis D. Political Nativism in New York State. New York, 1901.

Scoville, J. A. [Walter Barrett, pseud.] Old Merchants of New York City. 5 vols. New York, 1885.

Shannon, Fred A. Organization and Administration of the Union Army, 1861–1865. 2 vols. Cleveland, 1928.

Shaughnessy, Gerald M. Has the Immigrant Kept the Faith? New York, 1925.

Shea, John G. (ed.). Catholic Churches of New York City, with Sketches of Their History and Lives of the Present Pastors. . . . New York, 1878.

—— History of the Catholic Church in the United States. 4 vols. New York, 1892.

Skelton, Isabel M. Life of Thomas D'Arcy McGee. Gardenvale, Canada, 1925.

Smith, W. B., and Cole, A. H. Fluctuations in American Business, 1790–1860. Cambridge, Mass., 1935.

Smith, William C. Americans in the Making. . . . New York, 1939.

[Spengler, Otto, ed.] Deutsche Element der Stadt New York. New York, 1913.

Spillane, Daniel. History of the American Pianoforte; Its Technical Development, and the Trade. New York, 1890.

Stelzle, Charles. Son of the Bowery. New York, c. 1926.

Stephenson, George M. History of American Immigration, 1820–1864. Boston, c. 1926.

—— Religious Aspects of Swedish Immigration; a Study of Immigrant Churches. Minneapolis, 1932.

Stewart, David. Sketches of the Character, Manners, and Present State of the Highlanders of Scotland. . . . 2d ed., 2 vols. Edinburgh, 1822. (Also a later ed., with slightly altered title, Inverness, 1885.)

Stokes, Isaac N. P. Iconography of Manhattan Island, 1498–1909. 6 vols. New York, 1915–1928.

Stürenberg, Caspar. Kleindeutschland; Bilder aus dem New Yorker Alltagsleben. New York, 1886.

Suhr, Heinrich P. Hundert Jahre Deutsche Evangelisch-Lutherische St. Pauls Kirche in der Stadt New York. New York, 1941.

Sweeney, Helen M. Golden Milestone, 1846–1896; Fifty Years of Loving Labor among the Poor and Suffering by the Sisters of Mercy of New York City. New York, 1896.

Taylor, Henry. New York As It Was Sixty Years Ago. Brooklyn, 1894.

Tracy, George A. History of the Typographical Union. Indianapolis, 1913.

Tryon, Rolla M. Household Manufactures in the United States, 1640–1860. . . . Chicago, 1917.

Vogt, Paul L. Sugar Refining Industry in the United States. Philadelphia, 1908.

Waller, R., Beddall, E. F., and Racker, H. A. Sketch of the Origin, Progress, and Work of the St. George's Society of New York, A.D. 1786 to 1886. . . . New York, 1887.

Ware, Norman. Industrial Worker, 1840–1860. Boston, 1924.

Wenner, George U. Lutherans of New York; Their Story and Their Problems. New York, 1918.

Werner, M. R. Tammany Hall. New York, 1928.

Wilson, James G. (ed.). Memorial History of the City of New-York. . . . 4 vols. New York, 1892–1893.

Wittke, Carl. Against the Current; the Life of Karl Heinzen (1809–80). Chicago, c. 1945.

—— We Who Built America; the Saga of the Immigrant. New York, 1939.

Articles in Periodicals and Learned Journals

Abbott, Edith. "Wages of Unskilled Labor in the United States, 1850–1900," *Journal of Political Economy*, Vol. XIII, June, 1905.

Adams, Charlotte. "Italian Life in New York," *Harper's Magazine*, Vol. LXII, April, 1881.

Allen, Cuthbert E. "The Slavery Question in Catholic Newspapers, 1850–1865," United States Catholic Historical Society, *Historical Records and Studies*, Vol. XXVI, 1936.

American Council of Learned Societies. "Report . . . on Linguistic and National Stocks of the United States," American Historical Association, *Annual Report*, 1931.

Bean, William G. "An Aspect of Know-Nothingism—the Immigrant and Slavery," *South Atlantic Quarterly*, Vol. XXIII, No. 4, October, 1924.

Binsse, Henry. "The Church of Saint Vincent de Paul (The French Church) New York," United States Catholic Historical Society, *Historical Records and Studies*, Vol. XII, June, 1918.

Bruncken, Ernest. "German Political Refugees in the United States during the Period from 1815–1860," *Deutsch-amerikanische Geschichts-blätter*, 1904.

—— "Germans in America," American Historical Association, *Annual Report*, 1898.

—— "How Germans Become Americans," State Historical Society of Wisconsin, *Proceedings*, 1897 (reprinted, Madison, 1898).

Clark, Frederick C. "A Neglected Socialist," *Annals of the American Academy of Political and Social Science*, Vol. V, March, 1895.

Cowan, Helen I. "British Emigration to British North America, 1783–1837," University of Toronto, *Studies; History and Economics*, Vol. IV, No. 2, 1928.

Carman, Harry J., and Luthin, Reinhard. "Some Aspects of the Know-Nothing Movement Reconsidered," *South Atlantic Quarterly*, Vol. XXXIX, No. 2, April, 1940.

Commons, John R. "American Shoemakers 1648–1895. A Sketch of Industrial Evolution," *Quarterly Journal of Economics*, Vol. XXIV, No. 1, November, 1909.

Dorpalen, Andreas. "The German Element and the Issues of the Civil War," *Mississippi Valley Historical Review*, Vol. XXIX, No. 1, June, 1942.

[Dubois.] "Bishop Dubois on New York in 1836," United States Catholic Historical Society, *Historical Records and Studies*, Vol. X, January, 1917.

Eisenstein, J. D. "The History of the First Russian-American Jewish Congregation," American Jewish Historical Society, *Publications*, No. 9, 1901.

"Erinnerungen und Erlebnisse eines Achtundvierzigers," *Pionier*, Vol. II, No. 1, October 1, 1899.

Foik, Paul J. "Anti-Catholic Parties in American Politics, 1776–1860," American Catholic Historical Society, *Records*, Vol. XXXVI, No. 1, March, 1925.

Fox, Louis H. "New York City Newspapers, 1820–1850, a Bibliography," *Papers of the Bibliographical Society of America*, Vol. XXI, Parts I–II, 1927.

Fox, Dixon R. "The Negro Vote in Old New York," *Political Science Quarterly*, Vol. XXXII, No. 2, June, 1917.

Friedenberg, Albert M. "The Jews and the American Sunday Laws," American Jewish Historical Society, *Publications*, No. 11, 1903.

Guilday, Peter. "Gaetano Bedini," United States Catholic Historical Society, *Historical Records and Studies*, Vol. XXIII, 1933.

Hansen, Marcus L. "The Problem of the Third Generation Immigrant," Augustana Historical Society, *Publications*, 1908.

—— "The Revolutions of 1848 and German Emigration," *Journal of Economic and Business History*, Vol. II, No. 4, August, 1930.

Herbermann, Charles G. "John James Maximilian Oertel," United States Catholic Historical Society, *Historical Records and Studies*, Vol. IV, October, 1906.

Hourwich, I. A. "Immigration and Crime," *American Journal of Sociology*, Vol. XVII, January, 1912.

Jamme, L. T. "Historical Sketch of the Society of St. Vincent de Paul in the United States," United States Catholic Historical Society, *Historical Records and Studies*, Vol. V, April, 1909.

Kelly, Mary G. "Catholic Immigrant Colonization Projects in the United States," United States Catholic Historical Society, *Monograph*, XVII, 1939.

Kisch, Guido (ed.). "A Voyage to America Ninety Years Ago. Diary of a Bohemian Jew on His Voyage from Hamburg to New York, 1847," American Jewish Historical Society, *Publications*, No. 35, 1939.

Kohler, Max J. "The Board of Delegates of American Israelites, 1859–1878," American Jewish Historical Society, *Publications*, No. 29, 1925.

—— "The German-Jewish Migration to America," American Jewish Historical Society, *Publications*, No. 9, 1901.

—— "The Jews and the American Anti-Slavery Movement," American Jewish Historical Society, *Publications*, No. 5, 1897, and No. 9, 1901.

Learned, M. D. "The German-American Turner Lyric," *Publications of the Society for the History of the Germans in Maryland*, Vol. X, 1896.

Manson, George J. "The Foreign Element in New York City, the Germans," Supplement to *Harper's Weekly*, Vol. XXXII, August 4, 1888.

Marquardt, Carl E. "An Entente Cordiale in New York's Civil War Days," *Essays in Honor of A. Howry Espenshade*. New York, 1937.

Marraro, Howard R. "Eleuterio Felice Foresti," *Columbia University Quarterly*, Vol. XXV, No. 1, March, 1933.

—— "Italians in New York during the First Half of the Nineteenth Century," *New York History*, Vol. XXVI, No. 3, July, 1945.

—— "Lincoln's Italian Volunteers from New York," *New York History*, Vol. XXIV, No. 1, January, 1943.

Maurer, Heinrich H. "Earlier German Nationalism in America," *American Journal of Sociology*, Vol. XXII, No. 4, January, 1917.

—— "The Problems of a National Church Before 1860," *American Journal of Sociology*, Vol. XXX, No. 5, March, 1925.

Meehan, Thomas F. "Archbishop Hughes and the Draft Riots," United States Historical Society, *Historical Records and Studies*, Vol. I, January, 1900.

—— "Very Rev. Johann Stephen Raffeiner, V. G.," United States Catholic Historical Society, *Historical Records and Studies*, Vol. IX, June, 1916.

Moncada, F. "Incidents in Garibaldi's Life in America," *Atlantica*, October, 1932.

—— "The Little Italy of 1850," *Atlantica*, January, 1933.

Moore, E. C. "The Social Value of the Saloon," *American Journal of Sociology*, Vol. III, No. 1, July, 1897.

Morehouse, Frances. "The Irish Migration of the Forties," *American Historical Review*, Vol. XXIII, April, 1928.

O'Grady, John. "Irish Colonization in the United States," *Studies* (Dublin), Vol. XIX, No. 75, September, 1930.

"Oldest New York's Past and Present Racial and Religious Conditions," *Federation*, Vol. III, No. 4, December, 1904. (This was a special number of the quarterly issued by the Federation of Churches and Christian Organizations in New York City.)

Page, Thomas W. "The Distribution of Immigrants in the United States Before 1870," *Journal of Political Economy*, Vol. XX, No. 7, July, 1912.

—— "Some Aspects of Immigration Before 1870," *Journal of Political Economy*, Vol. XX, No. 10, December, 1912, and Vol. XXI, No. 1, January, 1913.

Park, Robert E. "Human Migration and the Marginal Man," *American Journal of Sociology,* Vol. XXXIII, No. 6, May, 1928.

Pekari, Matthew A. "The German Catholics in the United States of America," American Catholic Historical Society, *Records,* Vol. XXXVI, No. 4, December, 1925.

Phillips, Naphtali. "Sketch of the Spanish and Portuguese Congregation Shearith Israel written about 1855 . . . ," American Jewish Historical Society, *Publications,* No. 21, 1913.

Postal, B. "The Early American Jewish Press," *Reflex,* Vol. II, April, 1928.

Purcell, Richard J. "The Irish Emigrant Society of New York," *Studies* (Dublin), Vol. XXVII, No. 108, December, 1938.

—— and Poole, John F. "Political Nativism in Brooklyn," American Irish Historical Society, *Journal,* Vol. XXXII, 1941.

Roemer, Theodore. "The Leopoldine Foundation and the Church in the United States (1829–1839)," United States Catholic Historical Society, *Monograph,* Vol. XIII, 1933.

Rossman, Kenneth R. "The Irish in American Drama in the Mid-Nineteenth Century," *New York History,* Vol. XXI, No. 1, January, 1940.

Saposs, David J. "The Role of the Immigrant in the Labor Movement," *Amalgamated Illustrated Almanac,* 1924.

Sorge, F. A. "Die Arbeiterbewegung in den Vereinigten Staaten," *Neue Zeit* (Stuttgart), Vol. IX, Nos. 16, 17, 24, 33, 34, 39, and 40 (1890–1891), and Vol. X, Nos. 3, 4, 6, 7, 13, 33, 34, 35, 37, 41, 42 (1891–1892).

Stander, Golda G. "The Jesuit Institutions in the City of New York (1683–1860)," United States Catholic Historical Society, *Historical Records and Studies,* Vol. XXIV, 1934.

Steiner, E. A. "The German Immigrant," *American Outlook,* Vol. LXXIII, 1903.

Stephenson, George M. (ed). "Letters relating to Gustav Unonius and the Early Swedish Settlers in Wisconsin," Augustana Historical Society, *Publications,* Vol. VII, 1937.

Trimble, William. "The Social Philosophy of the Loco Foco Democracy," *American Journal of Sociology,* Vol. XXVI, No. 6, May, 1921.

Wirth, Louis. "The Ghetto," *American Journal of Sociology,* Vol. XXXIII, No. 1, July, 1927.

INDEX

Abendzeitung, 154

Abolitionism, 130-131, 153, 178, 279; German workers and, 291; Irish oppose, 153, 279; other opposition to, 157

Accidents, 52

Actors, 98

Agriculture: European, 2, 3-7; revolution in, 3-6; *see also* Farmers

Albany, 14, 27, 34, 130, 162

Albion, 130, 155, 177, 178

Allgemeine Zeitung, 154

Almshouse, 25, 29, 56, 162

American and Foreign Emigrant Society, 65

Anglo American, 156

Anticlericalism, 123, 135, 139, 158, 168, 177, 178

Architects, 97

Army, *see* Military organizations

Arnold, Franz, disciple of Weitling, 116

Art, 146, 276, 277

Artists, 97

Asiatics, 125, 225; *see also* Chinese

Asmonean, 160

Assimilation, 99, 111, 150, 160-161, 172-184, 295; and clannishness, 176, 181, 292; and family, 179-180; and immigrants' disunity, 176-178; intermarriage exceptional, 180; language factor, 175-176; newspapers and, 150, 160-161; organized labor and, 99, 111; politics and, 176; relation to children and schools, 174, 176, 180; slow process, 174, 181-184

Associated Working Men's Committee, 83

Association for Improving the Condition of the Poor, 19, 35, 36, 56, 103; and Mott Street baths, 51, 238

Association of the Friends of Ireland, 266

Astor, John Jacob, 15, 20, 94, 229, 257

Astor Place riot, *see* Riots

Astoria, 70

Attitudes, social: 152-160, 172-174, 177-181; British, 155-156; Catholic, 158-160 (*see also* Catholic Church, Catho-

lics); French, 156; German, 153-155; Irish, 152-153; Jewish, 160; Spanish language press, 157; *see also* Abolitionism, Nativism, Temperance, etc., and various nationalities

Authors, 98

Baden, 4, 7, 9, 77, 122

Bakers and confectioners, 73, 88, 108, 109; 255

Baltimore, 14, 38, 112, 131, 232, 251, 261; Germans in, 112, 131, 251, 261

Bankers, 94

Baptists, 8, 139

Barbers, 104, 244

Battery Park, 31

Bavaria, 4, 77, 122

Bedini, Gaetano, Papal nuncio, 178

Beggars, *see* Paupers

Belgium, 2, 5, 9; Belgians in New York, 236

Benevolent societies, 29, 32-35, 64-65, 107, 126-127, 129, 141, 231, 232, 243

Bierwirth, Leopold, German merchant, 29

Blacksmiths, 82, 109

Boardinghouses, 28-29, 37, 39, 233, 235

Boating, 127

Boatmen, 71

Bohemians, *see* Czechs

Bonding system, 26, 29-30, 230

Books, 144, 145-146, 276

Bookbinders and -folders, 82

Booksellers, 144-146, 275, 276

Bootblacks, 67

Boston, 14, 15, 34, 77, 86, 113, 232, 244, 246, 251; clothing industry, 77; German land reformers, 113; immigrant aid society, 34; immigrant port, 232; Italian organ grinders, 86; piano industry, 251; servants and laborers, 244, 246

Bowery, *see* Streets

Bremen, 12, 133

Brewers, 90-91, 256

British Protective Emigrant Society, 35

Broadway, *see* Streets

Brooklyn, 20, 40, 43, 88, 103, 107, 118, 130, 235; Germans, 43, 130; Irish, 40; Negroes, 235

Building and loan associations, 132, 270

Building trades, 73-75, 103, 109, 248, 251, 262; advancement in, 75; British in, 74; carpenters by nationality, 74, 248; contractors, 75, 248; French carpenters, 262; Germans in, 73-75, 251; Irish in, 73-75

Burn, James D., on Negroes, 104

Butchers, 87, 254

Cabinet making, 73, 80-81, 102-103, 108, 120, 251; earnings in, 80; French styles, 80, 251; Germans in, 73, 80-81, 251; Irish in, 23, 80

Canada, emigration to, 34, 61, 70, 148, 232, 246

Canadian immigrants, 58, 66, 74, 76, 83, 236, 245, 246, 252; building trades workers, 74; clothing workers, 76, 245; criminality among, 58; maritime trades, 83; in metallurgical trades, 252; population, 236; servants, 66

Canal Street, see Streets

Carpenters, see Building trades

Carpet shakers, 67

Carrigan, Andrew, Irish leader, 29

Cartmen, 106

Castle Garden, 31-32, 36, 172, 231, 242; immigrant landing dock, 31-32, 231

Catholic Church, 135-137; and anticlericalism, 135, 178; attitudes toward, 135, 168; charities, 35-36; churches in city, 136-137; as a cohesive force, 135; conservatism, 158-160, 178, 282-283; and family relations, 179-180; French in, 136; Germans in, 136-137, 141, 159, 383; growth of, 137; and immigrants, 135-137; Irish clergy dominate, 137; Irish in, 135-137, 141; Italians in, 136; newspapers, 151, 158-160; opposes public education, 140, 158, 179; as a political force, 169; schools, 140-141, 169; temperance movement, 249; see also Catholics; Hughes, John; Irish

Catholics, 124, 135-137, 140, 178-180, 271, 291; and Church, 135-137; and Civil War, 291; conservatism, 158-160, 178, 283; Emancipation movement, 124; and family relations, 179; German, 271; Irish, 135-137, 141; library movement, 144; mutual aid, 126; oppose public education, 140, 169, 179; population, 135, 271; prejudice against, 36, 66, 68, 135, 168, 271; repeal movement, 124; temperance movement, 294; see also Catholic Church

Central Park, 40

Champion of American Labor, 102, 107

Charitable societies, see Benevolent societies, Philanthropy

Chatham Street, see Streets

Chemists, 97

Children: delinquent, 59, 241-242; disease among, 53; employment of, 65, 66, 77, 86, 140; family relations of, 179-180; mortality among, 53; peddlers and organ grinders, 86; schooling of, 140-142; vagrants, 140; see Education, Family

Children's Aid Society, 142, 274

Chicago, 112, 113

Chimney sweeps, 67

Chinese, 45

Churches, 8-9, 136-140, 272; Anglo-American, 138; Catholic, 136-137; educational role, 140-141; financial problems, 136; French, 136, 139, 272; German Protestants, 139; Jewish synagogues, 137-138; Mormons, 8-9, 139; Protestants less cohesive, 138; Scotch, 138; social function, 139-140; Swedish Lutherans, 272; see also Catholic Church, Catholics, Protestant denominations, Religion

Cigar makers, see Tobacconists

Cincinnati, 34, 112, 113, 155, 264

Citizen, 150, 151, 153

Civil War, 172-174, 290, 291; attitude of Archbishop Hughes and Catholics, 291; attitude of German businessmen, 290; attitude of German workers, 291; draft riots, 173-174, 291; immigrant military units, 172, 290; immigrants and conscription, 173; immigrants support Union, 172; recruiting of immigrants, 172, 290

Class distinctions, immigrant, 155-156, 176-177, 293

Clergy, 97, 137

Clerks, 96, 258

Clothing industry, 17-18, 68-69, 75-78, 86, 92, 93, 109, 229, 245, 249, 254; contractors, 18; division of labor, 77, 249; dominance of Irish and Germans, 76-77; earnings, 68, 77-78, 249; European

home spinning, 247; factory system, 17-18; family system, 77, 229; Germans in, 18, 68, 76-77, 249; immigrant employers, 68, 76-77, 245; immigrants in, 75-78, Irish in, 18, 68, 249, 254; Jews in, 18, 68, 77, 86, 92, 245, 254; nationalities of workers, 18, 68, 76, 245; secondhand dealers, 86, 254; women in, 17-18
Coachmen, etc., 67, 71
Commissioners of Emigration, 29-32, 65, 231, 243-244; acquire Castle Garden, 31; criticized, 30-31; employment agency, 65, 243-244
Commons, John R., on labor unions, 99
Communist club, 119
Confectioners, see Bakers
Congregationalists, 138
Connaught, 122
Connecticut, 15, 29
Conscription Act, 173
Conservatism, 19, 152, 155, 158-160, 178-179, 282, 283
Conventions, 104, 105, 123-124, 131, 138, 179
Cooks, 66, 67, 88, 104; see also Servants
Co-operatives, 116-117, 264
Cork, 12, 122
Corlear's Hook, 38, 82
Courrier des États-Unis, 156, 176, 177
Cricket, 127, 268
Crime, 57-59, 240, 241; gangs, 57; juvenile, 59; police inefficiency, 240
Criminal-Zeitung, 154
Crónica, 157
Cubans, 88-89, 123, 157; see also Latin Americans
Czechs, 45

Dance halls, 58
Delmonico family, restaurateurs, 88-89
Del Vecchio, Charles, politician, 166, 286
Democratic party, 162-171
Demokrat, 154
Denmark, 4, 8
Dentists, 97
Discrimination, see Prejudice, Nativism
Diseases, 13-14, 22-23, 52-55, 238, 239; see also Insanity
Dispersion, see Population
Doelger, Joseph, brewer, 90
Domestic servants, see Servants
Down, 122
Draft Riots, see Riots

Dressmakers, 68-69, 104, 244, 245, 249; see also Clothing Industry
Drunkenness, 57
Duane Street, see Streets
Dutch Hill, 40, 234
Dutch immigrants, 45, 74, 76, 80, 245; building trades workers, 74; cabinetmakers, 80; clothing workers, 76, 245

Eco d'Italia, 157-158
Education, 140-143, 169, 179, 273-275, 289; see also Schools
Elections, see Politics
Emancipation Proclamation, 173
Emigrant Assistance Society, 34
Emigration, 1-14; agents, 12-13, 228; assisted, 6-7; frauds during, 12-13, 27-28, 106, 231; motives, 1-11, 227, 249; New York to Canada, 34, 61, 70, 232; New York to Europe, 174; ports of embarkation, 12, 227-228; voyage, 13-14
Employment, 61-98, 102-111, 233, 243-246; agencies, 64-65, 243
Engineers, 97, 247
England, 2, 3
English immigrants, 3, 43-44, 97, 98, 184, 235; actors, 98; building trades workers, 74-75; cabinetmakers, 80-81; clothing workers, 68, 76; criminality among, 58; disease among, 54; engineers, 247; farm hands, 70; in labor unions, 99, 100; laborers, 69-70; lawyers, 97; photographers, 97; printers, 81-82; professionals, 98; river transport workers, 71; servants, 66; shoemakers, 78; skilled workers, 72, 81, 82, 252; stable keepers, 71; textile agents, 94; upper West Side settlement, 44, 235
Engravers, 97
Epidemics, see Diseases
Episcopalians, 138, 139
Erie Canal, 1, 14, 228
Evans, George H., land reformer, 100-101, 260, 263
Eviction, 50

Factories, 17-18; see also Clothing industry
Family, 179-180; see also Children
Farmers and farm hands, 70-71, 244, 246-247; demand for in West, 244; in New York area, 70, 246, 247

Feminism, 152, 155, 178, 179, 293; Mathilde Wendt, German editor, 155; *see also* Attitudes

Firemen and fire companies, 106, 127, 164-165, 268; nationalities, 268; political importance of, 164; rivalry of, 106; source of prestige, 127, 164-165

Fishing, 127

Five Points, 39, 45, 57, 86, 136

Flatbush, 70

Food, 63, 87-88

Food dealers, 63-64, 84, 86-89, 96, 255; cafés and taverns, 88-91; kosher, 88; relation to liquor dealers, 90-91, 254, 255-256; *see also* Bakers, Butchers, Grocers, Restaurants

Foresti, Felice, Italian leader, 123

Forty-eighters, 9, 119-120, 167, 177-178, 266; bickering among, 266; in city politics, 167; and German labor struggles, 119-120; "grays" and "greens," 177-178, 293; *see also* Refugees

Foster, Vere, aids Irish emigration, 7

Foundries, 43, 82

France, 2, 4-5

Fraternal societies, 125-127, 267; *see also* Benevolent societies

Frauds, 12-13, 27-28, 105-106, 231, 260, 261

Freeman's Journal, 32, 151, 158-160, 178, 266; conservatism of, 158-160; dominated by Archbishop Hughes, 158; aids Irish Emigrant Society, 35

Freethinkers, 139, 143

French immigrants, 44-45, 184; bakers and confectioners, 88; building trades workers, 74, 109; cabinetmakers, 80; cafés, 88-89; clothing workers, 68, 76; criminality among, 58; disease among, 239; gardeners, 70; in labor unions, 108; laborers, 69; literary clubs, 143; militia, 129; schools, 141, 142, 274; servants, 66; settle in New York, 44-45; shoemakers, 78; workers in skilled trades, 72, 81, 82, 252

Friends of Civil and Religious Liberty, 124

Fulton Street, *see* Streets

Gabriel, "Angel," anti-Catholic agitator, 152

Galway, 12, 133

Gambling, 58

Gavazzi, Alessandro, Anti-Catholic agitator, 178

German Emigrant Society, 33, 232

German immigrants, 1, 2-3, 4, 7-8, 9-10, 41-43, 63, 112-121, 123, 132; artists, 97; bakers, 88; building trades workers, 73-75, 251; business district, 42-43; cabinetmakers, 73, 80-81, 251; carters, teamsters, and hostlers, 71; clash with Irish, 106-107; clerks, 96; clothing workers, 68, 76-77, 229, 249; criminality, 58; dispersion from New York, 61; education among, 141, 142, 143; family migrations, 63; farmers and gardeners, 70; groceries and food dealers, 87, 88; health and medical care among, 54, 55-56; itinerants, 84; journalism of, 153-155; labor organization, 108-110, 161-176; laborers, 69; literary and reading clubs, 143; maritime occupations, 71, 82; militia, 128-129; motives for emigration, 1, 2-3, 4, 7-8, 9-10; musicians, 97; pauperism among, 56; peddlers, 84; piano makers, 80-81; politics, 165-167, 169, 170, 287, 288, 289; printers, 81; recreation, 129-131; servants, 66; settle in New York, 41-43, 167, 287; shoemakers, 78; skilled workers, 72, 81, 82, 252; socialism among, 118-120; sugar refiners, 250-251; theaters, 147; tobacconists, 91

German labor movements, 112-121; agrarianism, 113; class consciousness of, 99, 109, 110, 119-121; co-operatives, 116-117; German unions parallel native unions, 99, 108-110, 111, 121; Lassalleans, 120; Marxian socialism, 118-120; New York as center of, 112; Weitling, 112, 113, 114-116; Weydemeyer, 118-119, 120

German Society, 29, 32, 33, 54, 56, 64-65, 107, 129, 243, 270

Germany, 1, 2-3, 4, 7-8, 9-10

Glasgow, 12

Glaziers, 74, 85

Gompers, Samuel, labor leader, 51, 120

Greenock, 12

Greenwich Street, *see* Streets

Greenwich Village, 20, 41, 44, 163, 235

Grocers, 87, 254

Gymnastics, 127, 130-131

Hairdressers, *see* Barbers

Hamburg, 12
Handels-Zeitung, 154, 177
Hanover Square, 20, 38
Haugeans, 8
Havre, 12
Head tax, 27
Health, *see* Diseases, Hospitals, Medical care
Hoboken, 20, 43, 127, 130, 131
Homesickness, 122
Hospitals, 25, 26-27, 231; Bellevue, 26, 29, 53, 54; Blackwell's Island, 54, 58; German, 56; insane asylums, 54-55; Jews', 56; Marine, 26-27
Hostlers, 71
Hotels, 89-90, 125, 255
House of Refuge, 59, 241, 294
Houston Street, *see* Streets
Hughes, John, Bishop and Archbishop, 34, 36, 136, 137, 141, 151, 158, 169, 173, 291; on aid of Church to Irish immigrant, 136; on Catholic attitude toward Civil War, 291; on conscription, 173; on parochial school attendance, 141; on public school question, 169; versus Irish republican journalists, 151
Hungarian exiles, 123

Illinois, 33, 60
Immigrant aid societies, 1, 32-35, 64-65; functions, 33-34, 64-65; *see also* German Society, Irish Emigrant Society, Benevolent societies
Immigrant communities, 37-47, 63-64; employment opportunities, 37-38, 42-43, 63-64; function of, 46; typically conservative, 178-179
Immigration, 1-14, 61, 262; affected by American conditions, 11; decline after 1854, 262; motives for, 1-11, 227, 249; remittances aid, 61, 63; stimulated by interested parties, 1-2, 10; *see also* Emigration and various nationalities
Importers, 87-88, 93-94, 96; *see also* Merchants
Industrial Congress of 1850, 116, 117, 170, 289
Industrial revolution: in America, 17-20; in Europe, 2-3
Insanity, 54-55
Insurance, 133, 270
Intermarriage, 180, 295
Iowa, 61

Ireland, 5-7
Irish American, 30-31, 62, 63, 67, 73, 91, 150, 151-152, 153, 179
Irish Emigrant Society, 29, 34-35, 65, 243
Irish immigrants, 1, 6-7, 39-40, 56-58, 62-63, 66-71; and abolitionism, 153; and American reformers, 152-153; building trades workers, 73-75; cabinetmakers, 73, 80; carters, coachmen, etc., 71, 106; clash with Germans, 106-107; clash with Negroes, 105, 153, 173; clerks, 96; clothing workers, 68, 76-77, 249; communities, 39-40; criminality among, 57-58; disease and lack of medical care, 52-56; emigration changes character, 6, 226; famine and emigration of, 6-7; food dealers, 84, 87, 88; insanity among, 54, 239; journalism of, 150-153; laborers, 69-70, 244; lawyers, 97; library movement, 144; literary and debating clubs, 143; migrate as individuals, 63; militia, 127-128; motives for emigration, 1, 5-7; pauperism among, 56; peddlers, 84; prefer urban life, 62-63; prejudice against, 229, 244 (*see also* Nativism); Repeal movement, 124; "riots," 105-107, 260, 261; secret societies, 105, 265; servants, 66-68, 244; settle in New York, 39-40, 43, 234; shoemakers, 78-79; theater affected by, 148-149; various trades employ, 81, 82
Irish Poor Law of 1838, 6
Irish Repeal movement, 124, 266
Irish Volunteers, 128
Italian immigrants, 45, 69, 74, 76, 85-86, 88, 95, 97, 123, 125, 129, 241, 274; artists, 97; bootblacks, 85; building trades workers, 74; clothing workers, 76; criminality among, 241; itinerants (peddlers, organ grinders, etc.), 85-86, 226; laborers, 69; militia, 129; musicians, 97; padroni, 86, 226; schools for, 142, 143, 274; settle in New York, 45; wine merchants, 88
Italy, 5, 9

Jansonites, 8
Jersey City, 20, 43
Jewish Messenger, 160
Jews, 1, 8, 45-46, 249, 272; bakers, 88; clothing workers, 68, 77, 86, 92; concern for Jews abroad, 138, 272; criminality among, 58, 240-241; group conscious-

Jews (*cont.*)
ness, 138; journalism of, 160; library and literary activities, 143; medical care, 56; militia, 129; motives for emigration, 1, 8, 249; mutual aid, 126, 127; no "Jewish vote," 167; pawnbrokers, 86; peddlers, 84-85, 253; Polish, 46, 76, 77, 78, 84-85, 225, 249; Russian, 46, 76, 77, 85; servants rare, 245; settle in New York, 45-46; synagogue's role, 126, 137-138

Jones' Wood, picnic grounds, 131

Journalism, *see* Newspapers and periodicals

Jung-Amerika, 113

Junk shops, 86

Kapp, Friedrich, German intellectual, 29, 270

Katholische Kirchen-Zeitung, 159-160

Kleindeutschland, 41-43, 63

Knickerbocker element, 15, 41

Know Nothing party, 150, 161, 168, 170

Kossuth, Louis, Hungarian revolutionist, 158, 159, 178

Kriege, Hermann, German reformer, 113, 170, 263, 287

Labor: apprentice question, 103, 260; Brooklyn dock strike, 107; charges of immigrant low standards, 101, 102-104; charges of immigrant radicalism, 100, 101; clashes among immigrants, 102, 106-107; early movements, 18-19; effect of Civil War, 111; effect of panics, 102, 110-111; Germans form own unions, 99, 108-110, 111 (*see also* German labor movement); immigrant co-operation with native, 107-110; immigrant strikebreakers, 107; Irish dominate unskilled, 108; loss of status, 100-101; natives and German co-operatives, 117; nativism of, 101-104; tailors' strike, 109-110; unemployment, 102, 111; *see also* Labor unions, various occupations, etc.

Labor contractors, 1-2, 10, 23, 64, 105-106, 260, 261

Labor unions, 99-176; apprenticeship and immigrants, 103; assimilation of immigrants, 99, 111; bakers, 109, 110, 255; British immigrants in, 99, 100, 259; building trades workers, 109; carpenters, 116, 259, 262; cigar makers, 120, 262; conspiracy trial of tailors, 101; co-

operation of native and immigrant, 107-110; economic nativism, 101-104; French carpenters, 109, 262; German unions, 108-110, 111, 116, 120, 251, 262, 265; Germans class conscious, 99, 109, 110, 119-121; immigrant, 108; immigrants in native, 100, 108; Laborers' Union Benevolent Association, 126, 262; language difficulties, 108, 262, 265; mid-century demands and strikes, 108-110; tailors, 109-110; turners, 110; upholsterers, 108; *see also* German labor movement

Laborers, 38, 67, 69-70, 104, 244, 246; by nationality, 69-70, 246; compared with Boston's, 246; demand for in West, 244; farm hands, 70; longshoremen, 108, 246; majority Irish, 69; Negro, 67

Language, 175-176, 292; and business, 86

Latin Americans, 23, 45, 66, 89-90, 123, 156-157

Laundresses, 66, 67; *see also* Servants

Lawyers, 97, 259

Library movements, 143-144, 275

Liquor dealers, 90-91, 254, 255

Literary, reading, and debating clubs, 143, 275

Liverpool, 12, 54

Living costs, 56, 83, 108-109, 110-111, 120, 253, 260

Locofocos, 101, 168-169, 287, 289; German newspaper, 154, 169

London, 12

Long Island, 25, 70, 125, 127, 131

Longshoremen, 38, 69, 108, 109

Lutherans, 8, 70, 138, 139

Lynch, Patrick, Irish editor, 151, 278-279

Macneven, W. J., and Irish Emigrant Society, 34

McGee, Thomas D'A., Irish editor, 151, 179-180, 278

McKeon, John, and Irish Emigrant Society, 34-35

Marine Hospital, 26-27

Manufacturers, 88, 91-93, 256, 257; advancement opportunity, 93; obstacles to becoming, 91

Maritime trades, 82-83, 252, 253

Marriage, *see* Family, Intermarriage

Marx, Karl, 112, 118, 119

Masons, 73, 74, 75

Massachusetts, 16

Mathew, Father Theobald, temperance advocate, 294

Mazzini, Giuseppe, Italian republican, 123, 157, 158, 178

Meagher, T. F., Irish editor, 124, 151, 159

Medical care, 55-56; see also Hospitals

Merchants, 93-96; aloofness, 257; and bankers, 94; nationalities, 95; services to immigrants, 96; speculate in real estate, 94, 257

Messager Franco-Américain, 156

Metallurgical trades, 82, 252

Methodists, 8, 139

Michigan, 61

Military organizations, 122, 127-129, 172, 290; basically social, 127; German, 128-129, 268; Irish, 128; Jewish, 129; Massachusetts disbands, 269; native, spurn immigrants, 128; other immigrant, 128-129; target and chowder clubs, 128, 131, 165

Military service, opposition to, 9-10, 172-173

Milwaukee, 112, 113, 119

Minnesota, 2

Minturn, Robert, emigration commissioner, 16

Missouri, 61

Mitchel, John, Irish editor, 124, 151

Mobility, see Population

Mormons, 8-9, 139, 152

Mortality, 53

Mott Street, see Streets

Music, 130, 131, 146-147

Musicians, 97

National pride, 123-124, 130-131; celebrations, 123, 131; Germans and Irish express, 73; political refugees, 123, 124; Turnvereine, 130-131

National Republican party, see Whig party

Native American party, 168

Nativism, 101-104, 135-136, 271; and immigrant labor, 101-104, 271; and Irish Catholics, 135-136, 244; immigrant nativists, 168; opposed by immigrant press, 150, 152, 158, 161; Protestant Irish, 168; relation to pauperism and crime, 135-136; social basis of, 135, 271

Naturalization, 162, 170

Nebraska, 2

Needle trades, see Clothing industry

Negroes, 40-41, 67, 104-105, 173, 230, 235; barbers, 104, 244; class consciousness, 104; competition and clashes with Irish, 71, 104, 105; convention of 1850, 104; draft riot victims, 173; dressmakers, 244; laborers, 67, 104, 105; lack of opportunity, 104; population decline, 230, 235; segregation, 40-41, 104; servants, 67, 104, 105; strikebreakers, 105, 261; tuberculosis among, 238; waiters ask wage increase, 104; Whig loyalties, 167; whites refuse to work with, 104

Netherlands, 5, 8, 9

Neumann, G. A., German publisher and editor, 153

New Braunfels, Texas, 114

New England, 14, 15, 78, 100

New Englanders, 15-16

New Jersey, 14, 25

New Orleans, 34, 114

New York City, 12-24; business moves northward, 19-20; commercial center, 14-15; cosmopolitan and polyglot, 23-24, 46-47, 232; Erie Canal a boon, 14; fires, 20; gaslight, 22; illegal landings in, 29; immigrant arrives in, 14, 25-36, 232, 242; industries, 17-18, 249, 250; manufacturers, 17; merchant aristocracy, 15-16; police, 22, 240; poor relief, 25; population growth, 20, 39, 61-62; prison conditions, 57-58; public health, 22-23, 25, 26-27; railroads aid growth, 15; real estate values, 15, 39, 70; trade, 38; "watch," 22

New York State immigration laws, 25-26, 29-30

Newark, 113

Newspapers and periodicals, 150-161, 278-284, 295; and assimilation, 150, 160-161; attacks upon immigrant press, 160; Catholic, 151, 158-160, 282-283; circulation: Catholic, 158, 159-160, German, 153, 279, 280, Irish, 151-152, 278, 279, other, 156, 160; English and Scotch, 155-156, 281; French, 156, 281; German, 153-155, 160, 279-280, 283; Irish, 150-152, 278-279; Italian, 157-158, 282; Jewish, 160, 283; obstacles or reader poverty and ignorance, 150; oppose nativism, 150, 152, 158, 161; Spanish language, 156-157, 281-282; typical contents, 150; Welsh, 156; see also Attitudes

Norway, 3, 8

Nurses, 66, 67

O'Connell, Daniel, Irish statesman, 124, 151, 159

O'Connor, Thomas, and Irish Emigrant Society, 34

Ohio, 61

Old Brewery, 39

Old Countryman, 155-156

Old Lutherans, 8

Opera, *see* Music

Orangemen, *see* Protestant Irish

Organ grinders, 85-86

Orientals, *see* Asiatics, Chinese

Ottendorfer, Oswald, German publisher, 84, 270, 279

Owen, Robert D., reformer, 100

Painters, *see* Building trades

Palatinate, 122

Patriotism, *see* National pride

Paupers and pauperism, 25-26, 35-36, 56, 232; majority foreign-born, 56; overtax city institutions, 25-26, 231; vote in elections, 162

Pawnbrokers, 86

Pearl Street, *see* Streets

Peddlers, 84-86, 253

Pennsylvania, 61

People's Washing and Bathing Establishment, 51

Perth Amboy, 29

Philadelphia, 38; Germans in, 112, 113, 116, 131, 251, 264; immigrant aid society, 34; immigrant port, 232; Italian organ grinders, 86; political floaters, 162; workingmen's party, 100

Philanthropy, 16, 32-36, 51, 56, 65, 243

Photographers, 97

Physicians, 55-56, 97, 130

Piano makers, 80-81, 120, 251-252

Pintard, John, merchant, 19

Pittsburgh, 116, 264; German convention in, 274

Plasterers, *see* Building trades

Plattdeutschen, 87, 177

Poland, and natives of, 1, 9, 74, 76, 77, 78, 84, 85, 95, 97, 123, 225, 245, 249, 253

Policemen, foreign-born, 163-164, 285

Politics, 162-171, 284-290; Carroll Hall ticket, 169; contracts awarded, 165; fire companies' relation to, 164; "foreign vote," 166-170, 295-298; French in, 167, 286, 288; gangs, 284; Germans: Democrats, 166-167, 287, 288, freesoilers and Republicans, 167, independent ticket, 170, 289, land reformers, 113, 170, 287, politicians, 165-167, Whigs, 167; Hard and Soft Shell Democrats, 170, 289; immigrants and corruption, 162-163, 284; immigrants in early workers' party, 168; Irish: hold minor offices, 165, "Irish vote," 166, 285; politicians, 165; Italians uninterested in, 158, 286; Lassak, German leader, 129, 167, 169, 286; Locofocos, 101, 168-169, 287, 289; nativism supported by some immigrants, 168, 288; "Negro vote," 167; no "English" or "Jewish vote," 167; policemen's relation to, 163, 285; public school question and Bishop Hughes, 169; Republicans woo Germans, 167, 287-288; saloons, liquor stores' relation to, 163, 285; *see also* Tammany Hall and various political parties

Population, 20, 61-62, 184, 225; Asiatic, 225; Catholic, 135, 271; decline during Civil War, 295; density, 49, 237; dispersion of immigrants, 61, 242, 244, 246; German, before 1848, 43; migration northward, 49; Negro, 230, 235; proportion of foreign-born grows, 39, 61-62, 184; various nationalities in 1855, 45, 61-62, 225; *see also* English immigrants, French immigrants, etc.

Portuguese, 45, 125, 129, 236

Poughkeepsie, 15, 103

Prejudice against: Catholics, 36, 66, 68, 135, 168, 271; immigrants, 135-136, 173; Irish, 66-67, 135-136, 244; Jews, 138; Negroes, 40-41, 104-105, 173; Protestants, 180; the poor, 19, 173, 176-177; *see also* Nativism

Presbyterians, 138; *see also* Protestant Irish

Printing trades, 81-82, 120, 265

Professional people, 96-98, 146-149; proportion of each nationality, 98; proportionally few, 96; refugees, 97; scant encouragement to in New York, 96

Proselyting, 36, 140, 283

Prostitution, 58-59, 241

Protestant Irish, 6, 62, 95, 105, 168

Protestants, 138-139; *see also* various denominations

Provincialism, 105, 122, 177, 180

Prussia, 77, 139

Public school controversy, 140, 158, 169, 273, 274

Publishers, *see* Booksellers

Quakers, 7, 8, 140

Railroads, 15, 63, 75, 94, 106
Recreation, 125-131, 143-144, 146-148;
fire companies, 127, 164-165; Germans:
dramatic and singing societies, 129-131,
269, music festivals, 131, *Schützenfeste*,
131, *Vereine* in occupations, 112, 130;
"groceries," restaurants, and taverns,
88-91, 125; groups a source of prestige,
127; Irish and Welsh celebrate patron
saints, 131; professional groups, 130,
268; Scots hold annual games, 131; social clubs, 129; sporting and athletic
clubs, 127; theater, 146-149
Reformed Church, 8, 138, 139
Refugees, political, 9, 97, 112-121, 123;
bickering among Germans, 266; forty-
eighters, 9, 119-120, 260; grays versus
greens, 177-178; journalism of: German, 154-155, Irish, 151, 159, Italian,
157-158; New York politics, 167; opposed by Catholic Church, 178; stimulate book trade, 145-146
Regional loyalties, *see* Provincialism
Religion, 135-140; divisive force among
Protestants, 138, 139; group conscious-
ness, 135, 138; indifference to, 138, 177;
see also Churches, Catholics, Jews, and
various Protestant denominations
Remittances, 61, 63, 96, 122-124, 265
Rents, 49-50, 89
Républicain, 156
Republican party, 162, 166, 167, 170,
171
Restaurants, 88-90
Revolutionists, *see* Refugees
Rhineland, 4, 7, 87, 95
Rhode Island, 16, 29
Riots, 105-107, 152, 260, 261; abolition,
153; Astor Place, 22, 148; draft, 173-
174, 291
Rochester, 34
Runners, 27-28, 231
Russia, immigrants from 45, 46, 74, 76, 77,
85, 95

St. Louis, 34, 112, 113, 116
St. Vincent de Paul Society, 36
Saloon keepers and saloons, 90, 91, 124-
125, 163, 165; *see also* Liquor dealers
Savings banks, 132-133, 270
Scandinavian immigrants, 45, 236; build-
ing trades workers, 74; cabinetmakers,

80; clothing workers, 76; laborers, 69;
maritime trades, 71, 72, 82-83, 253;
motives for emigration, 3-4, 8; piano
makers, 81; reading room, 275; settle
in New York, 45, 236; transportation
workers, 71
Schaefer brothers, brewers, 90
Schnellpost, 154
Schools, 140-143, 169, 273-275; Catholic,
140-141, 273, 274; Children's Aid Society, 142, 274; evening, 142-143, 275;
French, 141, 142, 274; German, 141,
142, 273, 274; immigrants' free, 141,
143; industrial and commercial, 142-
143, 275; Irish, 142, 275; Jewish, 142,
274; private, 141-143; public, 140, 141,
142-143, 273, 274, 275; Public School
Society, 140, 169; sectarian, 140-141,
273, 274; *see also* Education
Scientists, 97, 259
Scotland, 2, 3
Scottish immigrants, 3, 44, 92, 235-236;
annual games, 131; bakers, 88; building
trades workers, 74, 75; cabinetmakers,
80; clothing workers, 68, 76; criminality among, 58; disease among, 54; engineers, 247; farm hands, 70; gardeners,
70; laborers, 69; metallurgical workers,
252; militia, 129; motives for emigration, 3; piano makers, 80, 81; printing
trades workers, 81, 82; servants, 66; settle in New York, 44, 235-236; shoemakers, 78; textile agents, 94; textile
manufacturers, 92, 93
Scottish Patriot (*Journal of Intelligence
and Literature*), 156
Sculptors, 97
Secchi de Casali, G. F., Italian editor, 157,
282
Secondhand dealers, 86, 254
Secret societies, 105, 265
Self-defense clubs, 240
Servants, 65-68; few Jewish, 245; Irish,
66-68; Negro, 67, 104; proportions
among nationalities, 66
Sewage, 51-52
Seward, Governor William H., 141, 169
Shamrock Society, 33
Shanty towns, 40, 43, 234
Shipping houses, 14, 15-16, 69, 133, 271
Shipwrights, *see* Maritime trades
Shipyards, 43, 72, 75, 82-83
Shoemaking, 78-79, 109, 120, 250, 260;
Irish contractors, 79; nationalities of

Shoemaking (*cont.*)
  workers, 78; wages paid by contractors, 79
Shopkeepers, 38, 41-43, 86-88, 91
Sigel, Franz, German refugee, 9
Silesia, 77
Singing societies, 130, 131, 269
Skidmore, Thomas, 100
Skilled workers, 72; *see also* various occupations
Slums, 20, 48-60; cellar dwellers, 49; crime in, 57-58; density of population, 20, 49; disease in, 52-56, 238; fire hazards, 52; Five Points, 39; industrial accidents, 52; juvenile delinquency, 59; mortality, 53, 238; prostitution, 58-59; unsanitary, 50-52; *see also* Crime, Disease, Tenements, etc.
Smith, James McC., Negro spokesman, 104
Smiths, 73, 82
Socialism, Marxian, 118-120; Catholic opposition to, 159; *see also* Weydemeyer, Joseph
Society for the Encouragement of Faithful Domestic Servants, 65
Society for the Promotion of Knowledge and Industry, 65
Society for the Reformation of Juvenile Delinquents, 241
Sorge, F. A. socialist, 119
Spanish, 45, 90, 95, 96, 98, 236
Speculation by immigrants, 131-132, 269, 270; *see also* Building and loan associations
Sports, *see* Recreation
Staats-Zeitung, 73, 119, 137, 153-154, 165, 167, 178
Stablekeepers, 71
Staten Island, 118, 125
Stephan, Martin, religious mystic, 7-8
Streets: Anthony, 57; Attorney, 42, 46; Avenue C, 43; Barclay, 44; Baxter, 45, 46; Bayard, 46; Beekman, 38, 42; Bowery, 41, 42, 43, 46, 57, 86, 125, 147; Broad, 20, 38; Broadway, 20, 38, 46, 88, 147, 148; Broome, 44, 46; Canal, 42, 46, 49, 80; Catherine, 86; Cedar, 38; Centre, 46, 89; Chambers, 93; Chapel, 44; Charlton, 46; Chatham, 46, 77, 86, 89; Cherry, 40, 45, 57; Chrystie, 42; Clinton, 46, 52; Delancey, 45, 136; Dey, 89; Division, 45, 46; Duane, 57, 88, 89; East Broadway, 42; Eighth Avenue, 44; Eightieth, 40; Eldridge, 42; Eleventh, 43; Elm, 46; Elizabeth, 41, 42, 89; Essex, 45; Ferry, 38; Fifth Avenue, 44, 45; First Avenue, 40; Fletcher, 38; Forsyth, 42; Fortieth, 40, 41, 45, 75; Fourteenth, 44, 46, 75; Fourth Avenue, 46; Franklin, 46; Front, 20, 38; Fulton, 44, 89, 93, 139; Gold, 45; Grand, 46, 86, 89, 120; Greene, 41, 44, 46; Greenwich, 28, 37, 39, 46, 86; Hague, 52; Hanover Square, 20, 38; Henry, 46; Houston, 42, 44, 45, 46, 80; Hubert, 30, 37; Lafayette, 42; Laight, 46; Laurens, 44; Leonard, 41; Liberty, 38; Lispenard, 44; Ludlow, 46; Market, 46; Mercer, 41; Mill, 46; Monroe, 40; Mott, 46, 51; Mulberry, 41, 44, 138; Murray, 44; Nassau, 93; Park Place, 129; Park Street, 45; Pearl, 20, 38, 42, 46; Pike, 49; Pine, 38; Pitt, 46, 136; Reade, 44; Ridge, 46; Rivington, 42, 45, 46; Second Avenue, 43; Seventh Avenue, 44, 46; Sheriff, 51; Sixth Avenue, 40; South, 38, 52; Spring, 44; Stanton, 46; Sullivan, 41, 235; Tenth, 45; Third Avenue, 43; Thirty-third, 46; Thomas, 41, 44, 57; Twentieth, 46; Twenty-second, 44, 45; Twenty-sixth, 41; Walker, 44, 139; Wall, 15, 20; Warren, 44; Water, 20, 38, 40, 46, 57; West Broadway, 41, 57; White, 44, 46; Whitehall, 45-46; William, 20, 38, 42; Wooster, 44, 46
Sweden, 3, 8
Swiss immigrants, 45, 66, 68, 69; bakers, 88; building trades workers, 74; clothing workers, 76, 77, 245; servants, 66; settle in New York, 45; shoemakers, 78; skilled workers, 72, 81; watchcase makers, 81
Switzerland, 8, 9
Sylvis, W. H., labor leader, 120
Synagogues, 46, 126, 137-138

Tailors, *see* Clothing industry
Tammany Hall: awards minor offices to Irish, 165; bids for German vote, 166, 170; captures Industrial Congress, 170; controlled by Fernando Wood, 170; cultivates immigrants, 162-163, 284; Empire Club, 163; immigrant jobholders, 165-166, 285; land reformers won over, 113, 170; naturalization bureau,

162; saloon keepers and, 163, 285; *see also* Politics
Tapscott's Poor-House and Hospital, 26
Teachers, 96, 98, 175, 259
Temperance: attitudes toward, 161, 294; liquor interests fight, 90; movements, 294
Tenements, 28, 30, 66-83, 300
Theater, 129-130, 146-149, 277; amateur, 269; British actors, 148; Fanny Elssler, 147; French ballet, 146; French opera and vaudeville, 146; French theater, 147; German theater, 147; Irish influences, 148-149; Italian opera, 146-147; protests against stage Irishman, 148-149, 278; theater parties, 148, 278
Thorburn, Grant, seedsman, 64
Tobacconists, 91, 120, 256, 260, 262
Transportation workers, 71
Truth Teller, 150-151, 152
Turnvereine, 130-131; and abolition, 131; in labor movements, 120; promote Civil War enlistments, 172; publish journals, 155; socialist, 120
Tweed, W. M., "Boss," 164

Ulster, 6, 62
Unemployment, *see* Employment
Union, 101
Union Emigrant Society, 34, 232
Unskilled; *see* Laborers
Upholsterers, 108, 109, 120; *see also* Cabinetmakers

Wages, 67, 68, 70, 71, 77-78, 79, 80, 81, 82, 83, 87, 91, 96, 102, 104-105, 109
Waiters, 66, 67, 104-105
Wales, 2
Walsh, Mike, politician, editor, 30, 103
Wards of New York City: First, 39, 42; Second, 39, 40, 42, 78; Third, 39, 42, 44; Fourth, 20, 40, 42, 43-44, 45, 57, 166; Fifth, 41, 42, 44, 45; Sixth, 39, 41, 42, 45, 53, 57, 166; Seventh, 40, 42, 45, 49, 82; Eighth, 41, 42, 45, 78; Ninth, 42, 44; Tenth, 42, 44, 49, 167; Eleventh, 42, 43, 82, 167; Twelfth, 42; Thirteenth, 42, 167; Fourteenth, 42, 44, 166; Fifteenth, 42, 45; Sixteenth, 42, 45; Seventeenth,

42, 43, 45, 167; Eighteenth, 42, 45, 140; others, 42
Washington Square, 41, 45
Water Street, *see* Streets
Weavers, 62, 81, 252
Weed, Thurlow, and immigration, 29
Weekly Register and Catholic Diary, 158
Weitling, Wilhelm, 113-116, 263, 264; *Arbeiterbund*, 115; *Bund der Gerechten*, 112, 113, 114; bank of exchange, 114-115, 116; *Befreiungsbund*, 114; clerk at Castle Garden, 263; "Communia," 115, 263; co-operatives, 115-116; creates central organization of German workers, 116, 264; Democrat, 287; Fourier's influence upon, 114, 263; opposes trade unionism, 264; *Republik der Arbeiter*, 115, 116, 263
Welsh immigrants, 2, 44; building trades workers, 74; clothing workers, 76; Congregationalists, 138; laborers, 69; motives for emigration, 2; servants, 66; settle in New York, 44
Weydemeyer, Joseph, Marxian socialist, 118-120; antislavery views, 287; *Arbeiterbund*, 118, 120, 264; introduces Marxism to American labor, 118; *Die Reform*, 119, 264
Wheelwrights, 109, 110
Whig party, 162, 167, 169, 171
Whitewashers, 67, 85
Williamsburg, 20, 43, 118, 130, 147, 155, 263
Wisconsin, 61, 115
Women, *see* Clothing industry, Family, Servants, etc.
Women's rights, 152, 155, 178, 179
Wood, Fernando, politician: captures Tammany Hall, 170; corruption of mayoralty, 170; creates independent faction, 170; end of political career, 290; large immigrant following, 170, 287, 289; police question, 22, 163, 170; secretly a Know Nothing, 170, 289
Working Men's party, 18, 168
Wright, Frances, 19, 100, 152
Württemberg, 4, 8

Young Ireland, 124, 172
Young Italy, 123, 157